ISLAMIZATION FROM BELOW

BRIAN J. PETERSON

Islamization from Below

THE MAKING OF MUSLIM COMMUNITIES IN
RURAL FRENCH SUDAN, 1880–1960

Yale UNIVERSITY PRESS

NEW HAVEN AND LONDON

Published with assistance from the Kingsley Trust Association Publication Fund established by the Scroll and Key Society of Yale College.

Yale University Press books may be purchased in quantity for educational, business, or promotional use. For information, please e-mail sales.press@yale.edu (U.S. office) or sales@yaleup.co.uk (U.K. office).

Set in Scala type by IDS Infotech, Ltd., Chandigarh, India.
Printed in the United States of America.

Library of Congress Cataloging-in-Publication Data

Peterson, Brian James.
  Islamization from below : the making of Muslim communities in rural French Sudan, 1880–1960 / Brian J. Peterson.
    p. cm.
  Includes bibliographical references and index.
  ISBN 978-0-300-15270-8 (pbk. : alk. paper)
    1. Islam—Mali—Bougouni Region (Sikasso)—History. 2.   Bougouni Region (Sikasso, Mali)—History. 3.   France—Colonies—Africa—Religion.   I. Title.
  BP64.M29P47 2011
  297.096623—dc22

                                                                                    2010035697

A catalogue record for this book is available from the British Library.

This paper meets the requirements of ANSI/NISO Z39.48–1992 (Permanence of Paper).

10 9 8 7 6 5 4 3 2 1

CONTENTS

CHAPTER OUTLINE

This book moves chronologically from the late nineteenth century to independence in 1960. In terms of formal periodization, I divide the book into the following epochs: wars of Samori (1882–93), postconquest and early colonialism (1893–1905), era of slave emancipation (1905–14), interwar years (1919–40), and postwar, which I use exclusively as a shorthand reference to the period after the Second World War. The book emphasizes the ways in which historical transformations were characterized by different social temporalities and varying rates of change. As a result, although there were important discontinuities and eventful turning points, my focus is on long-run trends and multigenerational social processes that spanned periods and are difficult to compartmentalize in epochs.

The book's arguments proceed in the following manner. Chapter 1 sketches the religious and political landscape of the nineteenth century, while locating southern French Sudan, and in particular the district of Buguni, within the context of the internal slave trade, African state building, and the spread of Islam. Once the religious habitus has been properly situated, the chapter focuses on the late nineteenth century, when the region became a battleground in wars of enslavement. From 1882 to 1893, Samori Touré, the leader of a Muslim state, occupied the region for economic and political advantage, while using jihad to justify enslavement and to create unity across his culturally variegated internal empire. In the aftermath of French conquest and Samori's defeat, tens of thousands of refugees streamed back into the region. Chapter 2 looks at the experiences of refugee returnees, exploring the various social, environmental, and religious dimensions of the reintegration process. It seeks to frame these changes within the political and economic contexts of early colonial rule. On the religious front, although the district of Buguni was considered fetishist at this time, the administration kept an eye on Muslim traders and notables. I establish the French administration's rather haphazard Muslim policy but also emphasize how the mass dispersal of people resulted in widespread social mixing. In the postconquest era there was a resurgence of bamanaya, which, benefiting from the French peace, was recast in more translocal forms.

Chapter 3 explores the relationship between slave emancipation and the spread of Islam. Following the abolition decree of 1905, hundreds of thousands of slaves left their masters in a mass exodus and returned to their homelands across the French Sudan. One of the largest destinations of returning slaves was the district of Buguni. Owing to the size of this social group, freed slaves, some of whom had embraced Islam while in slavery, were important agents in the transfer of Muslim practices to rural areas. After examining the exodus and shifts in the political economy, I discuss administrative developments, the chieftaincy, and French policy vis-à-vis Muslims. I end by reconstructing the formation of early Muslim communities and exploring changes in rural religious practices.

Chapters 4 and 5 serve to establish underlying material and political conditions from the 1920s to the 1950s. Some of the most far-reaching social transformations had their origins in the interwar period, as colonial rule forced permanent shifts in subsistence practices and rural social relations. Chapter 4 tells the story of how Africans dealt with the everyday demands of colonialism. It begins with an overview of changes and continuities in colonial governance. Then, it assesses the impact of forced labor, violence, and compulsory cotton production on rural communities. It ends by examining labor migration and gender relations. Chapter 5 delves deeper into the subject of social change. It starts by looking at the war effort on the African home front during the Second World War and proceeds with a discussion of labor migration and emerging intergenerational tensions and conflicts. It strives to link these developments to transformations in marriage practices and agriculture.

After establishing changes in nonreligious domains of social life, I return to religious transformations. Chapter 6 looks at the broader cultural contexts of migration and the role of social networks. Building on arguments in chapter 5, I show how this era of greater mobility and individualism was characterized by the appropriation of new cultural styles, ideas, and forms of material culture that served as important generational markers of difference. At the same time, as many of the commercial networks were in Muslim hands, taking on an external Muslim identity was often necessary in finding work. Later, upon returning to their villages with prayer, migrant workers added their numbers to the growing Muslim communities. This chapter extends the analysis of local social pressures, discussing the role of public ceremonies and the colonial census. I end by exploring the Islamization of the colonial chieftaincy.

Chapter 7 discusses the processes through which Islamic identities and practices were elaborated in local communities. It charts the emergence of Muslim communities, as local leaders held public prayer, set up Qur'anic schools, and supervised the building of mosques. Although Arabic literacy was still rather restricted in southern French Sudan, holy men translated passages from the Qur'an and *hadith* into local dialects of Bamanankan, resulting in forms of indigenized Islamic thought and practice known as *kankònòla*. This chapter draws considerably on the biographies of local imams and holy men, whose experiences in rural Qur'anic schools illuminate wider social contexts of religious change. I show how the religious habitus was being transformed in the postwar era, and how local holy men grew in popularity as rural peoples incorporated alternative healing, divination, and rainmaking practices into local repertoires. Concomitantly, public pressures to abandon indigenous practices mounted, even leading to religious violence. In time, as indigenous religious institutions and leaders disappeared from public view, Muslim figures filled the void, cultivating ties with renowned Sufi shaykhs of the Qadiriyya order. What emerged was a very heterodox Islamic sphere, as strains of Qadiriyya and unaffiliated Sufism intermingled with non-Muslim practices. The chapter ends by exploring the influence of Muslim reform movements in Buguni.

NOTE ON ORTHOGRAPHY

I make frequent reference to various French, Bamanankan, Arabic, and Wolof words and names derived from oral histories and archival documents.

For the sake of simplicity and clarity I have opted for English translations, except in cases where the original term is commonly understood, such as *imam*, or where there is no easy translation, as with *bamanaya*. In many cases, I have elected to use Anglicized spellings to facilitate pronunciation. For example, the French "ou" is replaced by "u," as in the place-names Sudan, Wasulu, and Buguni. But in reference to patronyms and in the use of terms like *marabout* that have found their way into the Anglophone scholarly lexicon, I have kept the French versions. The reader should be aware that Bamanankan plurals have the letter "w" at the end. Non-English terms are italicized only in their first citation. All translations quoted in the text and footnotes are my own, unless I have indicated otherwise.

ACKNOWLEDGMENTS

The making of this book has taken place against the backdrop of disparate localities in Mali, France, and the United States. It was researched in rural villages of southern Mali, and in the archives of Kuluba, Mali, and Aix-en-Provence, France; and it was written primarily in New York City. It has also been the product of networks of support, intellectual influence, personal encouragement, and collaboration. Through my peregrinations and the book's permutations, I have accumulated a number of debts.

First, I owe gratitude to my informants, whose history I have set out to write. Their oral testimonies provided the bulk of the evidence upon which this book is based, and their stories and opinions profoundly altered the trajectory of my research. I wish to thank them for their willingness to share their memories, and for their *jatigiya*, or hospitality. In southern Mali, my deepest gratitude goes to my interpreter and friend, Yacouba Danyoko, from the village of Tenemakana. I extend special appreciation to the archivists in Kuluba, Mali, including Alia Almouctar Baby, Ali Ongoiba, and Timothée Saye. Their camaraderie made for an easy transition from being a fumbling *étranger* poking around in crumbling dossiers to an active *chercheur*. In much shorter trips to Aix-en-Provence and Dakar, archivists graciously and efficiently facilitated my requests.

My debts in the intellectual field will become clear in the notes. However, over the years, I have benefited from several mentors. At Yale

University, I thank my Ph.D. dissertation advisor, Robert Harms, a constant source of support and advice. Thanks also to John Merriman and Michael Mahoney for their encouragement. Abbas Amanat, Lamin Sanneh, John Demos, and James Scott left their imprint on my thinking. Earlier, I benefited from the guidance of David Anthony, Terry Burke, James Clifford, and Tyler Stovall. Finally, a special acknowledgment to Richard Roberts, who generously shared his time and steered me toward francophone Africa.

This book has been written with the financial support of a number of institutions: Yale University Graduate School and History Department, J. William Fulbright Fellowship Program, Yale Center for International and Area Studies, Foreign Language and Area Studies Program (FLAS), Union College Humanities Development Fund, and Howard R. Lamar Center for the Study of Frontiers and Borders. During the writing phase, support came from the Harry Frank Guggenheim Fellowship Program, Yale University, and Union College, in the form of a Junior Faculty Sabbatical.

In Bamako, a special thanks to Mamadou Diawara at *Point-Sud*. Sekou Camara and Adama Koné did the transcriptions of recorded interviews. For assistance in establishing research infrastructure, I want to acknowledge Gaoussou Mariko, Issa Traoré, and Robin Yeager at the American Cultural Center and U.S. Embassy in Bamako. I also thank the staff of Save the Children, Mali, especially Lynn Lederer, Fodé Missa Traore, Bakary Sangare, Adama Koné, and Yusuf Coulibaly. Also, my gratitude to Tlegné Coulibaly of Helvetas in Yanfolila, and the Peace Corps volunteers in southern Mali. Finally, thanks to Brandon County, Stephanie Diakité, Modi Kassogué, Scott Lacy, Greg Mann, and Mamadou Niang for companionship and good cheer in Mali.

The manuscript, or portions of it, benefited from the constructive criticism of Robert Harms, Martin Klein, Julie Livingston, Mike Mahoney, Melis Ece, Ben Talton, Greg Mann, Andy Feffer, Ken Aslakson, Mike McGovern, and Shobana Shankar. At Yale University Press, my thanks to Chris Rogers, Laura Davulis, Margaret Otzel, and two anonymous reviewers, who provided incisive feedback and suggestions for revision. I also thank Lawrence Kenney for his guidance and skillful editing and John Norton for his work on the maps.

Arguments and evidence I originally presented in two articles, "History, Memory and the Legacy of Samori in Southern Mali, c. 1882–1898," *Journal of African History* 49 (2008), and "Slave Emancipation, Trans-local Social Processes and the Spread of Islam in French Colonial Buguni (Southern Mali), 1893–1914," *Journal of African History* 45 (2004), have been substantially reworked and rewritten for portions of chapters 1 and 3. Themes from my article "Quantifying Conversion: A Note on the Colonial Census and Religious Change in Postwar Southern Mali," *History in Africa* 29 (2002), have been elaborated upon in the section entitled "Making Muslims: Conversion and the Colonial Census" in chapter 6.

Finally, close to home, I thank my father, my mother, Larry, and Barb, as well as Vince and Anne. Special thanks also to Thomas Farber for his much-needed perspective and advice on writing. And most of all I am grateful to my wife, Andrea Camuto, who supported this project in innumerable ways, including a twelve-month stint in Mali. I have been blessed by her patience, intelligence, and sense of adventure.

ANM:	Archives Nationales, Koulouba, Mali
ANS:	Archives Nationales, Dakar, Senegal
AOF:	L'Afrique Occidentale Française
CAOM:	Centre des Archives d'Outre-Mer, Aix-en-Provence, France
CdC:	Commandant de Cercle
CEA:	Cahiers d'Études Africaines
CHEAM:	Centre des Hautes Études d'Administration Musulmane
CSSH:	Comparative Studies in Society and History
FR:	Fiche de Renseignements
GG:	Governor-General
HSN:	Haut-Sénégal-Niger
IJAHS:	International Journal of African Historical Studies
JAH:	Journal of African History
LG:	Lieutenant-Governor
PSP:	Parti Progressiste Soundanais
RA:	Rapport Agricole
RP:	Rapport Politique
RE:	Rapport Economique
SF:	Soudan Français
US-RDA:	Union Soudanais-Rassemblement Démocratique Africain

After the Second World War, a strident Muslim preacher, Bakari Koné, raided *bamana* religious sites around his village of Diaka in rural French Sudan. In a lurid demonstration of Islam's supremacy, he then publicly burned sacred objects and masks. While most rural holy men took a more quietist approach to proselytization, Koné's unexpectedly iconoclastic acts represented an open challenge to the village elders. Not since the wars of Samori of the late nineteenth century had anyone desecrated local sites so overtly. It was sheer sacrilege.[1]

According to oral traditions, in response the head of the indigenous *kòmò* power society quickly dispatched his most loyal henchmen to reassert religious control in the village. As a host of villagers looked on, the men chopped down the preacher's fruit trees in a symbolic affront. It was a simple warning shot. But Bakari redoubled his efforts and persevered in leading public prayer, his followers proudly chanting the shahada, or the Muslim profession of faith. "He was not afraid of anything," said his sister. "He would fight until his opinion prevailed."[2] There were reprisals. First, the traditionalists used sorcery, but this failed. Then they recruited an assassin from a neighboring village to eliminate the preacher by using *koroté*, or poison. This too failed. None of the old ways seemed to be working. In the meantime, Bakari's power continued to grow, as he withstood the most powerful magic the kòmò could muster. In the end, the ranks of young Muslims came to the preacher's aid in a public show of force the elders could not ignore.

Such local events were religious turning points in the community, marking the "coming of Islam" in village hagiographies. However, even as these stories often emphasize the acts of heroic individuals, preachers, and saints, they also hint at deeper, translocal social processes. Elsewhere, across rural French Sudan, the religious landscape was changing in the postwar era as Muslims established themselves firmly in the majority after years of hiding their religious practices. Village mosques were being built, Qur'anic education was spreading, Sufi holy men were growing in popularity, and forms of colonial governmentality were reconfiguring the political bases of religious belonging. On rare occasion, religious conflicts erupted, resulting in attacks on sacred sites and intercommunal violence. In these circumstances, figures such as preacher Koné from Diaka seemed to confirm what colonial officials had long feared: that a Pan-Islamist fifth column of virulent agitators with ties to Salafi reform movements in Cairo would forcefully convert the masses and lead a broad-based holy war (*jihad*) against the French empire in Africa. However, most rural holy men had no ties to Arab reformists, had never even heard of the Muslim Brotherhood. They focused their energies on providing religious services to peasants, such as rainmaking ceremonies, divination, healing, and on leading community religious rituals. Rather than troublemakers from out of town, they were homegrown products of grassroots and multigenerational processes of religious change.

Years before Bakari Koné's father had been a migrant worker in Guinea, where he learned Islamic prayer. "My father went to work in Guinea, to find money and return, and that is how he came back with prayer," said Mariame Koné. "Later he took his first son and sent him to Qur'anic school in Segu."[3] As in many localities, these first-generation Muslims invested in their futures by acquiring forms of Islamic knowledge and sending their sons away to Qur'anic school.[4] But what Diaka and other village histories also illustrate is that migrant workers traveling back and forth between their villages in the hinterland and destinations in Ivory Coast, Senegal, and Guinea were embracing Islam and joining nascent Muslim communities in their rural homelands. They were not pioneers. Rather, they followed in the footsteps of freed slaves, colonial soldiers, and other mobile social groups who, a generation before, had similarly introduced prayer into their villages.

These social and religious changes deepened with each new generation, eventually leading to the emergence of village imams and holy men who were instrumental in the making of Muslim communities. In this way, Islamization was a gradual process that unfolded in an uneven manner across the region. The transformation of the religious habitus occurred over many decades as individuals and communities adopted new ritual practices and slowly drifted in the direction of Islam.[5] Eventually, when Muslims became more dominant and claimed positions of power, minority-held traditionalist views and practices lost their influence and retreated from public view. *Bamanaya*, or indigenous religious practices, became something shameful; and sacred sites, rituals, and institutions, such as the kòmò and *jò* societies, were abandoned. Rather than dramatic and openly confrontational wars of maneuver in the form of iconoclasm and street battles, in most localities events such as the building of a mosque or the holding of public prayer served as definitive turning points after more subtle positional wars had been won.[6] These local processes were further shaped by shifts in power relations. As rural areas became more thoroughly administered state-spaces after the Second World War, the relationship between religious identity and state power changed.[7] In a kind of looping effect within the context of the colonial census, villagers sorted themselves into discrete religious categories and made public declarations of faith, thus opening the door to future possibilities of personhood while objectifying religious change within the community.[8]

In this book, I tell the story of how one important but neglected region in France's vast colonial empire became Muslim over an eighty-year period. As a story that was reproduced in many rural localities across the world, it was one of the grand narratives of the twentieth century and part of larger transregional processes through which Islam emerged as the religion of the majority.[9] But more than just a religious history, this book situates Islamization processes within different temporalities and social contexts, such as the aftermath of slavery, changing patterns of mobility, and agricultural transformations. Focusing primarily on the colonial era, I examine the impact and unintended consequences of French rule in the rural district of Buguni in southern French Sudan, while exploring the ambiguous relationship between empire and religious

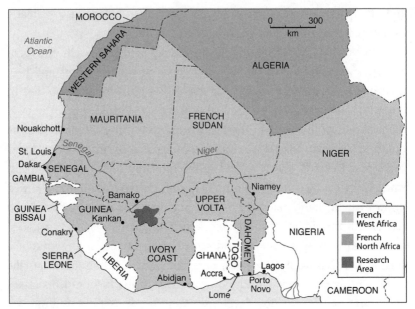

Map 1. French West Africa and Research Area.

difference. Moving beyond colonial discourse and policy, this book uses rural microhistorical and regional units of analysis to assess processes of grassroots religious change.

In its imperial forms and expressions of power, French colonialism did not represent a monolithic crusade against Islam. As early as the Napoleonic conquest of Egypt in 1798, the French empire-state fashioned itself as something of a "Muslim power."[10] In West Africa and the Maghreb, the colonial state cultivated useful alliances with Muslim leaders and built its structures and methods of governance on certain indigenous logics and institutions. In some cases, it even subsidized pilgrimage to Mecca and the construction of Qur'anic schools and mosques.[11] However, as we shall see, in the district of Buguni and other regions deemed "fetishist," the administration often fought hard to prevent or at least slow the expansion of Islam. Although the colonial state pursued more or less pragmatic policies aimed at preventing rebellion and maintaining order, it routinely bolstered the authority and power of fetishist chiefs, while monitoring and arresting Muslim notables.[12] It also pursued a policy of containment, preventing the extension of Arabic literacy and foreign Arab influence and even demolishing unauthorized mosques and

Qur'anic schools, all in the interest of protecting colonial subjects from the social breakdown that would result from mass conversion.[13]

In certain ways, such state actions reflected the radical secularism of the French Third Republic, particularly after the separation of church and state in 1905, which unleashed disputes even among colonial administrators and Christian missionaries.[14] However, the fight against the spread of Islam followed rather different political contours and fluctuating sets of imperial interests through phases of conquest, consolidation, retreat, restoration, and decolonization. It also reflected profound discursive continuities. As the French saw it, Pan-Islamism, with its links to reformist Islam and anticolonial nationalism, represented an imminent threat to the very existence of the empire-state. But even as the colonial state simultaneously sought to modernize and preserve African societies, it initiated shifts in the political economy and deployed new forms of political rationality and governance that fundamentally reshaped social relations. The state may have succeeded, partially at least, in forcing Africans to pay taxes, produce cash crops, and provide forced labor. But it failed as a cultural project of control. In its heavily diluted "civilizing mission," rather than making peasants into Frenchmen or preserving Africans as fetishists, it inadvertently produced Muslim subjects.[15]

In the precolonial era, the cultural gradient reflected different configurations. Ideas, practices, and information traveled from cores to peripheries in correlation with state expansion, trade, warfare, and the topographical friction of distance. As in the case of East Africa, where Islam was confined to Indian Ocean coastal trade towns for many centuries before making inroads into the hinterland, Muslims in West Africa were concentrated along commercial arteries stretching from the Saharan fringe to the Atlantic coast.[16] A major difference was the existence of large Islamic states in the interior of West Africa. But outside of Muslim state-spaces and networks, most agrarian people remained adherent to traditional religions. Not until the nineteenth and twentieth centuries did Islam make much progress in these out-of-the-way rural areas, particularly among decentralized societies.

One of the unexplored conundrums of the colonial era in Africa is that it ushered in a more rapid expansion of Islam than during the previous one thousand years.[17] Scholars have long commented on this process, while also examining Islamic institutions, Muslim notables, and changing forms of authority under colonialism. Still, very little is known about the expansion of Islam among ordinary people during the colonial era.[18] What accounted for such processes of religious change? Why did Islamization occur at a much greater rate under French colonial rule? What sorts of people converted, and why and how? How did the meaning of being Muslim change over time as different generations and different social groups embraced practices and beliefs associated with Islam? How was the expansion of Islam tied to changes in rural life introduced by colonialism? What does the case of southern French Sudan reveal about the broader relationships between French empire and religious difference?

In seeking to answer these questions, this book provides a new perspective on Islamization, which I use as a covering term to describe religious transformations occurring in specific historical, social, and cultural contexts leading to the emergence of Muslim majorities. In contrast to the extant literature on Islam in West Africa, which focuses mainly on Muslim elites, precolonial states, trade, jihad movements, and the large Sufi brotherhoods, I examine the grass-roots spread of Islam among rural peoples. Although Islamization has certainly been linked to precolonial state expansion, Muslim chiefs and kings were rarely able to forcibly convert people in decentralized societies. Thus, a central premise of my book is that there are limitations to models that restrict the agency of religious change to elites and states and that embrace jihad-centric explanations.[19] In the case of southern French Sudan, as I argue, the expansion of Islam owed its success to the many thousands of slaves, migrant workers, former soldiers, farmers, and rural preachers who gradually and usually peacefully adopted the new religion. Focusing on the colonial district of Buguni, I demonstrate how such social actors were important agents in the transmission of Islamic religious culture in its diverse forms and practices to previously non-Muslim rural regions.[20] Rather than embracing class-based explanations, however, this book assesses the various modes of entry of Muslim prayer into communities across the entire social field. I explore the dialectical manner in which processes of Islamization reflected shifting social bases of religious power and authority, and how in turn these transformations undergirded the efforts of chiefs and holy men to shape emergent forms of public religious expression and belonging.

CONVERSION RECONSIDERED: ON METHOD AND THEORY

Conceptualizing processes of Islamization as conversion, in the sense of individuals or whole communities moving unambiguously across clear religious boundaries after carefully weighing doctrinal differences, simplifies a rather multistranded, long-term cultural process. As Jonathon Glassman has remarked, "It would be more useful to recognize that the impact of Islam manifested itself in a wide spectrum of behaviors, ranging from conventionally defined conversion at one end to passive curiosity at the other."[21] I will address the limitations of certain analytic categories and modify existing explanatory frameworks to fit African social realities. To begin, I turn to the rich body of literature on Christianity in colonial Africa, which has provided some of the most sophisticated studies of conversion.[22] In this vein, Jean and John Comaroff pose two important questions that serve as conceptual starting points for this discussion: how well does *conversion* embrace the "highly variable, usually gradual, often implicit, and demonstrably 'syncretic' manner in which social identities, cultural styles, and ritual practices" were transformed through the encounter with world religions? and does the concept capture "the complex dialectic of invasion and riposte, of challenge and resistance" so characteristic of such historical transformations? In essence, the Comaroffs question the very utility of the foundational Pauline model of conversion and demonstrate how *conversion* tends to conflate individual religious experience and wider cultural transformations. The word also reifies the notion that people rationally chose among belief systems without consideration of the social contexts in which these supposed choices were made.[23] Similarly, J. D. Y. Peel has argued that it is difficult to use the concept without extending certain "theological or phenomenological assumptions of a Euro-Christian and Protestant background to historical and cultural settings where they do not apply." Peel also states that given the "interiority of the experience of conversion," the concept is not particularly valuable in exploring "large-scale processes of religious change where we have little or no evidence about the inner states of the individuals concerned."[24] For these reasons, and given the paucity of contemporaneous sources on "inner states" of consciousness, I am moving away from conversion and adopting a more gradualist approach based on practice rather than cosmology. Echoing Peel, I think it makes little sense to extend "theological or phenomenological assumptions" of the Islamic normative tradition to settings where Muslim rituals and practices were only loosely integrated into the religious habitus, and usually in an incremental and piecemeal manner. Although there were likely changes in religious imagination, as Muslims embraced supralocal forms of identification through expanding networks and greater mobility and imagined belonging to a more universal Muslim *umma*, "doing prayer" did not necessarily constitute a complete overhaul of one's mental and moral framework.

I realize that this perspective contrasts with Robin Horton's influential model of a two-tier cosmological framework. Horton emphasizes the ways in which conversion to world religions entailed a cognitive adjustment to what he described as an "increase in social scale."[25] In other words, as individuals and communities were incorporated into larger social orders, there was an inevitable dissolution of local microcosmic boundaries that served to push people to embrace more universalistic religious orientations. Conversion, then, constituted a movement from the microcosm of the small community, with its more or less bounded world of lesser spirits, to the macrocosm of larger, or higher, gods. Certainly, the "social scale" was expanding, and people were being exposed to new ideas, knowledge, and information. However, as scholars have pointed out, Horton's rather "mentalistic" theory, with its focus on "preexisting thought patterns" and internal influences, tends to neglect the sorts of external political and structural factors that determined the shape of this larger social order in the first place.[26] Indeed, Peel has argued that Horton's theory "does not treat colonialism as a necessary condition of conversion [and] discounts the common view that colonial power was the main factor inducing conversion."[27] For these reasons and others one needs to look elsewhere for explanatory or conceptual devices.

There is little sustained focus on the subject of conversion to Islam in the historiography of West Africa.[28] Historians have examined the expansion of Islam in studies of precolonial states and trade, and scholars have advanced models with sequences of typical stages. Yet such models, for example, those proposed by Spencer Trimingham and Humphrey Fisher, tend to be too linear and teleological to embrace the diversity of forms and complex shifts of cultural processes. Furthermore, the underlying social logics and political conditions that shaped religious change under colonialism were very different.[29]

In one of the more noteworthy efforts to propose an interpretive framework for understanding processes of Islamization in French West Africa, the anthropologists Robert Launay and Benjamin Soares argue that colonial rule, by establishing greater peace and security, led to the formation of what they call an "Islamic sphere," or a Muslim space conceptually separate from particular social affiliations such as ethnicity, kin, and slave status. The appearance of this Islamic sphere was linked to changes in the political economy and to the "removal of restrictions" on the movement of people and commodities.[30] While the framework of Launay and Soares is a provocative and useful one, there is room for revision. First, with their emphasis on the personalization of religious authority, which came with the erosion of old ethnic religious identities, their analysis of the spatial expansion of Islam depends on a rather general notion of diffuse mobility driving religious change. My book elaborates on their thesis, but it pluralizes the paths to Islam through its focus on mobile social groups like slaves, migrant workers, soldiers, and rural holy men. Certainly, as the French projected their power outward from colonial capitals through so-called distance-demolishing technologies such as roads, railroads, bridges, telegraph, and telephone, the friction of distance governing the spread of social and cultural influences was considerably reduced.[31] But given the relative weakness of the colonial state and the uneven penetration of roads into rural hinterland areas, there were enormous differences between localities in terms of economic integration and the corresponding regional cultural gradients.[32] Still, the pace and regularity of mobility quickened as commercial activity and social transactions increased, so that even where markets failed to expand, migrant workers took the initiative by going on foot in the absence of roads.[33] At the same time, while there was a "freer circulation of goods and people," forms of coercion were also common and must be taken into consideration.[34] Second, I explore the dynamics of religious change in the countryside, a subject that falls outside the purview of Launay's and Soares's framework, while developing a rural microhistorical perspective. This approach helps to demonstrate the heterogeneity of translocal processes of religious change across regions and within villages and families. A final modification is the incorporation of non-Muslim religious practices, which are largely excluded from the conceptualization of an Islamic sphere.[35]

Sufi brotherhoods like the Muridiyya, Tijaniyya, Qadiriyya, and Hamawiyya have been at the center of research on Islam in Africa.[36] These Sufi orders have played important roles in driving religious change. But with their greater historical visibility, characterized by identifiable leaders and institutional structures, and relatively richer documentary sources, they have largely obscured more inchoate forms of rural Islam.[37] A distinctive urban bias in the historiography has led scholars to tacitly reinforce the notion that Islam trickled down to peasant communities. This is not surprising. Islam has been primarily an urban religion that spread through trade networks, although I would not want to unduly dichotomize urban and rural life-worlds.[38] The apparent marginalization of rural areas and of grass-roots processes of religious change from regional Islamic history has come at a cost. In the twentieth century the expansion of Islam has been most active in precisely these regions.

With respect to the colonial period, historians like David Robinson, Louis Brenner, Christopher Harrison, and Jean-Louis Triaud have deepened scholars' understanding of France's policies toward Islam and shed light on the many forms of accommodation in French relationships with Muslim leaders and institutions. Yet in following the discursive contours of French policy and ethnographic knowledge they have inadvertently reproduced certain colonial views and categories.[39] Most important, the continuing attention to Sufi leaders, hierarchies, and formal institutions has resulted in an unintended scholarly blind spot. Indeed, just as colonial officials and ethnographers were unable to see decentralized forms of rural Islam, owing to the lack of recognizable Muslim institutional features, contemporary historians have tended to neglect rural areas, where Sufism was often unaffiliated and loosely organized.[40] This bias has begun to change. For example, more recent works by James Searing and Cheikh Anta Babou on colonial Senegal have revisited the expansion of the Muridiyya and situated these developments within the contexts of widespread social change and slave emancipation. Both of these studies, though, and most others posit large Sufi brotherhoods as their main units of analysis and end their coverage before the First World War.[41] My book builds on this rich body of research by grounding the analysis in rural religious life. It also shifts the geographical focus to the French Sudan, which has been much less studied than Senegal and Nigeria, and extends the temporal boundaries to include the entire colonial period. And it makes the question of Islamization, which has been treated only peripherally, its main subject.[42]

Beyond Africa, the subject of conversion to Islam and the growth of individual Muslim communities has been unsatisfactorily studied. Most works examine societies that were already Muslim and thus reveal very little about how they came into being. Conversion to Islam in the "old Islamic lands" of the Near East, according to one leading scholar, remains "one of the most poorly examined fields in Islamic studies."[43] Scholars working on Islamization processes in Central and South Asia have similarly noted the paucity of works on conversion.[44] One of the rare exceptions is the remarkable study on Bengal by Richard Eaton, which links the movement of agrarian frontiers to religious change and conceptualizes Islamization as a process which proceeded "so gradually as to be nearly imperceptible." Indeed, of the many conversion models, Eaton's approach is perhaps the most useful, as it allows room for both local cultural dynamics and long-term change. In Eaton's account, which emphasizes cosmological shifts, processes of Islamization span five centuries and reflect medieval and early modern political and social conditions, whereas I suggest that while such processes were certainly gradual, the pace of change could be considerably greater under colonialism with its widespread mobility and twentieth-century forms of governmentality. Furthermore, I draw attention to the ways in which presumed stages of Islamization, such as inclusion, identification, and displacement, often overlapped spatially and temporally. Although change was a constant, there was no strict evolutionary progression of typical forms, even within small communities.[45]

In order to enrich readers' understanding of conversion and to move away from linear models, I have drawn on certain theoretical tools. First of all, as I have suggested, conversion often amounted to a gradual drifting, to adopt a term from the recent philosophy of rational choice. As Edna Ullmann-Margalit has explained, at one end of the spectrum there could be abrupt discontinuities, as people opted to change their future selves through "life-transforming" and "core-affecting" decisions. And in some instances there was a powerful negation of one's previous life, as in the case of preachers burning sacred objects. There might also be technical or nominal conversions, perhaps in the interest of economic opportunity. But in assessing long-term religious change, it makes more sense to view such processes as drifting rather than opting. Ullmann-Margalit describes the drifting person as someone who "carries on with the business of his or her life, making incremental, stepwise decisions," and for whom "only in retrospect" can it be seen "how a particular series of such incremental steps—or in particular one step among them—had been all-important in transforming the future shape of their life."[46] In this book, I will be emphasizing how individuals and communities embraced different practices and identities in a piecemeal fashion without necessarily having a systematic understanding of the different cultural logics that new religious practices represented. People did not convert blindly; rather, they constantly strove for a sense of religious belonging and social affiliation in changing circumstances.

As a conceptual counterweight to the subjectivism of personal conversion narratives and the excesses of rational decision theory, I have also had recourse to the idea of habitus developed by the French sociologist Pierre Bourdieu.[47] Although Bourdieu has used a variety of formulations to describe this concept, I will work with a composite definition. Habitus is a system of durable, transposable, and embodied dispositions and practices which integrate past experiences and function as the generative basis of practices and representations.[48] Certainly, the analytic utility of habitus is situationally specific; it depends on particular social contexts and historical circumstances. But, as Craig Calhoun has observed, habitus is most useful in undifferentiated societies, in which normative rules are less explicit and social relations are characterized by direct, interpersonal ties rather than by impersonal institutions. It is therefore a more processual conception of culture, one which emphasizes repertoires of strategies rather than cultural rules and practice rather than discourse.[49]

To further clarify, habitus is durable in that it is overwhelmingly the product of early socialization; the unconscious internalization and embodiment of external structures during childhood plays a profoundly formative role. As Bourdieu explains, "The child imitates not 'models' but other people's actions . . . children are particularly attentive to the gestures and postures which, in their eyes, express everything that goes to make an accomplished adult, a way of walking, a tilt of the head, facial expressions, ways of sitting and of using implements, always associated with a tone of voice, a style of speech . . . schemes are able to pass from practice to practice without going through discourse or consciousness."[50] An individual or collective habitus is also transposable in that people carry sets of practices and dispositions with them into different contexts and new settings.[51] As James Clifford has suggested in his theorization of transnational cultural processes, habitus is uniquely suited for studying migrants, diasporas, and traveling cultures.[52] The concept can be useful even in contexts characterized by experiences of dislocation and rupture. Thus, rather than being fragmented by history, the habitus of the locality feeds on and incorporates experiences of displacement and war. Along these lines, Rosalind Shaw has employed habitus in drawing attention to the ways in which cultural practices, memory, ritual, and bodily techniques have been reproduced and transformed since the era of the slave trade in Sierra Leone. Shaw emphasizes how habitus does not constitute "a closed cycle of repetitive change" by showing how it continually integrates historical events and processes.[53]

In my book, habitus is a tool for conceptually linking micro and macro levels of analysis and for examining the tensions between local cultural institutions and even the most disruptive processes, such as war, refugee flight, enslavement, colonial conquest, and so forth. I use habitus to highlight continuity in times of change and to conceptualize Islamization as gradual processes of localization of Islam. Even as people began praying and embracing Muslim forms of religious life, the generative cultural grammar, as it were, remained rooted in bamanaya. For the concept to be most useful, one needs to incorporate more agency and structural pliability in the face of rapid social change. Furthermore, by placing greater emphasis on the emergence of new social and religious imaginaries and on the roles of social networks and transfers of knowledge and information, it will be possible to situate changes in the religious habitus within wider translocal cultural contexts.

Building on the aforementioned works and concepts, this book emphasizes how Islamization was a gradual, dialectical process, one characterized by forms of cultural translation and identity negotiations within wider social fields.[54] I will show how changing sets of practices and the trajectories of meaning tied to them underpinned the dialogical processes through which Islam engaged, complemented, and gradually supplanted indigenous religious institutions and practices. I attempt to illustrate how religious transformations were the historical products of accumulated strands of minor social adjustments, changing practices, and political shifts, all worked out in community and translocal settings.

A SENSE OF PLACE

My book is based largely on fieldwork I conducted in rural villages and roadside trade towns in the former colonial district of Buguni. This district covered thirty-four thousand square kilometers, or roughly the equivalent of Connecticut and Massachusetts combined; its smallest administrative unit was the canton. Over the span of sixty-seven years of French rule, the cantons fluctuated in size and number as a result of amalgamation, redistricting, and political reforms. In 1912 there were 52 cantons. On the eve of independence in 1960, the number had shrunk to 36. Overall, the district comprised 837 villages with a population of 247,189 in 1957. Within this context, my most intensive fieldwork site was the former canton of Fulala, which had a land area of one thousand square kilometers. Fulala had a population density of just four people per square kilometer, so its 5,175 inhabitants were spread very thinly over the land.[55] This former canton provided much of the microhistorical data I use in this book.

Methodologically, the microhistory approach has allowed me to probe many of the complexities of communities, social networks, and individual lives. It has also served to retrieve forms of human agency and complexity normally hidden within categories and processes.[56] As the French historian Jacques Revel explains, "[The] most elementary experience, that of the small group, even the individual, is the most clarifying—because it is the most complex and because it is inscribed in the largest number of different contexts. . . . [Each] historical actor participates, directly or indirectly, in processes . . . of variable dimensions and levels, from the most local to the most global."[57] Yet to properly contextualize the microhistory, and in order to avoid seeing general patterns through a more or less bounded and myopic lens, it has been imperative to employ other observational scales.[58] In addition to Fulala, I draw on fieldwork conducted in the former cantons of Céndugu, Basidibé, Gwancédugu, and Niené. Among these comparative cases, Céndugu and Basidibé were two of the most populous cantons in the district, and both are situated along major colonial roads. Basidibé was located in Wasulu, near the district's western border with Guinea, and was exposed to labor migration, trade, and Islamization long before other cantons that appear in this book. In contrast, Niené was more remote, located at the district's frontier along the border with Ivory Coast. Its lack of all-weather roads and bridges meant that Niené was isolated during the rainy season and as a result slow to embrace both migration and Islam. It was also the only ethnically Senufo canton in the district. Finally, Fulala was rather ordinary, located in the middle of southern Mali. It was not incredibly remote, but given the poor condition of dirt roads and its location sixty kilometers off the main road it was not easily accessible and therefore infrequently visited by colonial officials. It was average in land area but reportedly one of the poorest in natural and human resources. Along with Céndugu and Gwancédugu, it was one of the regions that suffered the worst predation and enslavement in the late nineteenth-century wars.

In terms of the physical landscape, the region is part of a vast pene-plain and savanna-woodland transition zone that stretches from eastern Guinea to central Mali. Although flat, this red-soil plain is interspersed with lightly undulating hills and valleys as well as numerous rivers and streams.[59] In 1894, one colonial official described the area as "in general a flat land, lightly wooded, and crossed by numerous watercourses. . . . There are quite a number of isolated hills, but not seeming to have any general direction."[60] In short, it is the ordinary savanna, with dusty harmattan winds in the dry season and verdant fields and trees after the rains come.

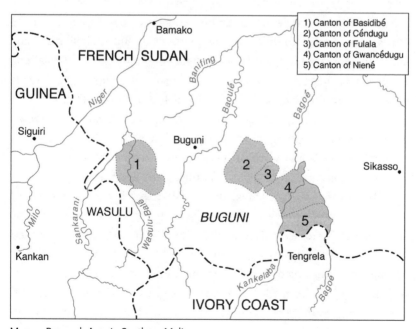

Map 2. Research Area in Southern Mali.

While this vast savanna plain unifies the region, south-north rivers, including the Baoulé, Sankarani, Wasulu-Balé, Bagoé, and Kankelaba, divide it. As natural boundaries, these parallel rivers have served as important cultural and linguistic boundaries, resulting in east-west cultural gradations and diversity.[61] Human geography and settlement patterns also responded to variations in local topography, ecology, and soil type. Generally speaking, because of the lack of organic material these soils tend to be low in fertility and rather sensitive to erosion. In fact, much of the wider region is covered by a thin, gravelly, dry soil called *fuga*, which is characteristically unsuitable for farming.[62] As we shall see, added to these natural structures, the region has been prone to agricultural disruption by devastating droughts, disease, and other environmental events. This has produced small-scale decentralized societies inured to uncertainty.

A NOTE ON SOURCES, MEMORY, AND ORALITY

At first glance, the former district of Buguni would seem unsuited for writing local Islamic histories. There are no internal Arabic manuscripts, as the vast majority of village imams under colonialism were nonliterate. Despite the growing scriptural authority of the Qur'an, literacy was restricted to magical and ritual contexts. These days, some religious figures can read in Arabic, and they possess copies of the Qur'an and certain foundational religious texts. But their libraries are small and contain no contemporaneous accounts from the colonial era. Furthermore, deemed an animist or fetishist zone, Buguni was largely excluded from the colonial ethnography of Islam. In fact, Paul Marty, in his four-volume study of Islam in the French Sudan, *Études sur l'Islam et les Tribus du Soudan*, ignored the region altogether.[63] The only in-depth colonial ethnographic work on religion in Buguni, dating from 1954, focuses on non-Muslim religious institutions and practices.[64]

There are French archival documents, which are indispensable in getting a bird's-eye view of the colonial landscape. I have drawn on such materials from archives in Bamako, Dakar, and Aix-en-Provence. Fortunately, the annual and monthly political reports produced by various *commandants* of the district of Buguni are nearly complete for the entire period from 1893 to 1959. These include detailed statements from census tours at the canton level, inspection tours, and modest ethnographic missions. Agricultural reports and economic reports have also been instrumental in my piecing together of the region's agrarian history. For reconstructing chieftaincy histories and local political changes, I have drawn on personnel records. In order to situate the case of Buguni within wider political contexts and to establish a more empirewide perspective, I have used circulars and special reports on a range of topics produced at higher levels in the colonial government. There are no missionary diaries or letters from the region and no memoirs of Muslim converts from the colonial period. There is one memoir by a former French commandant, Maurice Méker, but it largely reproduces material from the archives and contains only scant detail on African social life.[65] There are a few surviving letters written by literate African functionaries, but most archival documents were written by Frenchmen.

Although these written sources are crucial in establishing chronologies, different temporalities, and discursive formations, colonial reporting was always characterized by certain "epistemic habits" that served to distort the processes and events being described.[66] In the district of Buguni and the wider French Sudan, this was particularly the case with respect to Islam, which constantly stirred fears of Pan-Islamic jihad in the colonial imagination. Furthermore, as I have noted, with their focus on identifiable Sufi leaders, brotherhoods, and hierarchies, officials routinely dismissed more inchoate forms of rural Islam. And their faith in the concept of *Islam Noir*, a sort of essentialized "black Islam" that was more superficial, docile, and governable, led them to ignore local, grass-roots processes and politics of religious change.[67] This does not mean that colonial officials could not also be astute observers; it was in their interest to keep accurate records, to prevent rebellion, and to govern efficiently. But they could not escape the political interests of the colonial state and even their own mental habits. For this reason their policies and understandings of African societies were often flawed. Moreover, even as the state's intelligence tentacles reached further into rural areas, the census tours and palavers that produced such information were conducted very infrequently. This means that even the most detailed reports provide only snapshots of social change. Still, these brief glimpses, separated by intervals of a decade or more, form important historical baselines from which to measure transformations. Furthermore, as Luise White has observed, archival documents can be used to contextualize and explain the words of informants, while affording crucial starting points for venturing into oral historical research.[68]

I tack between archival and oral sources, using one set of data to coax more out of the other, generating insights and identifying areas of tension, disagreement, and overlap. For example, working in the archives in Bamako, I read in a colonial census report from 1951 on the canton of Fulala that Tenemakana had a "real mosque" and an authorized Qur'anic school. I also discovered that a man named Kojugu Suntura from the village of N'Golobala had been a central figure in the spread of Islam in Fulala.[69] Around the same time, I read in another census report from 1912 that there were "around fifty Muslims" in the canton. They belonged to the Qadiriyya and practiced its rituals, but they did not have a Qur'anic school and maintained no organizational links to a particular Sufi *muqaddam*, or official deputy, authorized to initiate people into the order.[70] In short, a span of almost forty years separated the first mention of Muslims in the small canton and the emergence of the mosque and Qur'anic school of Tenemakana. Armed with this knowledge that Islam had been around much longer than normative declarations would suggest, I sought out the village imam of Tenemakana, whose testimony was the first to suggest that freed slaves, among whom Kojugu Suntura was one of the most important, had returned to their homelands "with prayer" during the era of slave emancipation.[71]

Most of my informants were elderly Muslim men and women born in the 1920s and 1930s, and so their experiences and memories were generationally specific.[72] Interviews dealt with a wide range of nonreligious topics, including farming, slavery, marriage, colonialism, the chieftaincy, village foundation narratives, and so forth. And this allowed me to situate religious change within multiple social contexts. The fact that most informants were at least nominally Muslims meant that in exploring the dialectical relationship between old and new, testimonies could be rather value laden and even teleological. For Muslim elders, Islamization was something to be celebrated. It represented Islam's superiority and the triumph of God's will as well as the movement of their community away from the era of *jahiliyya*, or ignorance. Along the perceived continuum from barbarism to civilization, with all of its dichotomous values, Muslim elders saw the public emergence and dominance of Islam and the related shunting aside of bamanaya as a sign of distinct progress. For many, the question of how Islam was introduced into their village or how people became Muslim was rather uncomplicated and required no explanation beyond, "It was Allah who did that" or "It was Allah who brought us prayer." Hence in my early fieldwork I often encountered cursory responses to such inquiries. In popular understandings, the supposed arrival of Islam was a fairly straightforward result of the "descent of the Qur'an" and its inevitable spread. It was predestined, as elders commonly stated. Anything else in this world was just the minor detail of people struggling on the straight path. There was also a tendency to reduce Islamization processes to the proselytization efforts of particular rural Sufi saints and preachers, even in cases in which the particular saint in question, such as Muhammad Fanta-Mady Sharif of Kankan, never actually set foot in a given locality. Thus, there were strong hagiographical dimensions to local oral traditions which elevated the role of Sufi saints over that of traders, chiefs, migrants, and so forth. Furthermore, for informants, "the coming of Islam" was read retrospectively: they thought about Islam today and then tried to remember when things started looking like they do now. They referred to local turning points, when Islam became the religion of the majority. For example, an informant would cite the moment when, suddenly, it was socially acceptable to pray publicly or when the village mosque was built or when the first village imam was designated. Therefore, the beginnings of Islamic prayer in a village were obscured by normative declarations. And since most of the villages were not nominally Muslim until after the Second World War, the religious changes anterior to this time were often invisible. Eventually, however, and through repeated interviews, informants offered clues that there was something more to the village just-so stories. Through conversations with former migrant workers and the descendants of slaves as well as religious specialists, I learned that people had started praying long before mosques were built and public Muslim rituals were performed.

Many elderly informants were reluctant to admit engaging in non-Muslim practices, given the generalized silence and shame (màlòya) attached to such subjects. But I interviewed bamana traditionalists, such as blacksmiths and hunters, and running through their testimonies are rueful counterdiscourses of discontent. On occasion, elders gave voice to concerns over the consequences of religious change. They stated that in neglecting their old ways they had betrayed local spirits and lost their connection to the vital forces that enable fertility and rain. The result was a fragmented religious landscape. One elder, Amadou Sidibé, said, "The abandonment of our 'old ways' led to the breakup and fragmentation of this region. The people no longer feared. When Islam came, everyone abandoned the 'old ways' of our fathers and of our grandfathers. Now we know neither our front nor our back. We have become wanderers."[73] Namakoro Bamba went even further, stating that Muslim leaders in the community had led people astray. He argued passionately, "The decline of bamanaya was the work of the *mori* [Muslim holy man]. But they have not put people on the right path. When you yourself are not correct, you cannot tell others to be correct. . . . Now the beliefs have become numerous, and we are neither in the house nor in the bush, that is the situation."[74] Even nominally Muslim elders expressed regret about religious changes. Reflecting local understandings and perceptions of environmental change, they stated that recent drought conditions had resulted from the abandonment of old ways. Hawa Diallo, an elderly Muslim woman in Tenemakana, sorrowfully said, "Before, there was no shortage of rain, not at all. When the drought raged, raged, raged in Tenemakana, the elders went to visit the patriarch ancestor [*cémò*]. They decided to go perform a libation ceremony to the ancestor . . . then the rains fell. So what has caused this shortage of rain? All of our 'old ways' have been abandoned."[75] Her husband, Broulaye Doumbia, added, "Everything that you worship, will worship you in return. There was a stream here, when we worshiped it, the people would fish and the rain fell. Each time that there was a shortage of water, the people went to do the libation ceremonies and the rain would fall. . . . Presently, we worship only Allah in the world. But in the past, we did not think of Allah, we only did offerings to the power objects, to the spirits. These practices were our religion. Now we have abandoned them."[76]

As these divergent views of Islamization suggest, the oral accounts used in this book do not represent an authentic and unified African voice. There were always intravillage, intercommunal, and lineage-based differences and conflicting accounts, particularly with respect to oral traditions, upon which the first three chapters of this book are based. Oral traditions, as such, are mainly personal or family traditions and in some cases village accounts in wider circulation. They are categorically from the past "beyond the present generation" rather than life histories.[77] Oral traditions have evolved over time and been influenced by new forms of national and transnational media as well as by migration, urbanization, and changing settlement patterns.[78] Furthermore, oral traditions are commonly shot through with competing visions of the past. Village elders debate history, retooling and contesting village foundation narratives, seeking to marshal oral historical evidence and genealogical data in establishing their status as "first comers" or the legitimate holders of particular titles or status.[79] In such circumstances, the local reconstruction of history is often aimed at supporting distinct claims or at maintaining and justifying, or criticizing, the current state of affairs rather than at achieving a balanced assessment of the past. As James Scott has stated, "Every villager is entitled, indeed required, to become something of a historian—a historian with an axe to grind."[80]

Although there can be considerable overlap between the various types of accounts, besides oral traditions there are oral histories of people who are still alive and who lived through the events and experiences they have described.[81] These first-person narratives, which figure prominently in the final four chapters of the book, can be quite elliptical and take the form of stories and memories that are far from infallible. As research on "autobiographical memory" has shown, people are constantly revising their pasts, especially in light of shifts in their individual interests and the search for new meaning over the life cycle. There is a tendency to construct "generic memories" that conflate "actual episodes" in the constitution of composite accounts. According to John Kotre, such phrases as *used to* or *would* are often telltale signs of generic memories.[82]

In writing this book and selecting and framing oral testimonies, I have sought to privilege accounts that contain specific reconstructions of life episodes. Checking testimonies against each other and against colonial documents, I have tried to establish what, in my best judgment, was the general form and direction of historical change. I have integrated "generic memories" and other normative statements as examples of how certain processes have been remembered in popular understandings, as all testimonies reflect the inherent subjectivity of their speakers.[83] Their memories and stories constitute "a means of comprehending how Africans saw their lives, their worlds, their histories." They can even be seen as representing local historiographies, combining bits of argument, evidence, and a kind of normative vision of things. Along these lines, oral histories provide an important corrective to archive-driven narratives by "complementing silences" and opening up new subjects of inquiry.[84]

I have framed oral testimonies as local understandings but have primarily weighed and interpreted the accounts for what they might say about actual lived historical experiences and processes.

To describe the social contexts in which oral narratives were recorded, I want to briefly discuss my primary interpreter, Yacouba Danyoko. Born in 1952, Yacouba Danyoko is considered a *cékoroba*, or elder, and something of an organic intellectual. One could call him a polymath by profession; he is an expert carpenter, farmer, hunter, healer, musician, storyteller, mechanic, and electrician. His father, Mamadujan Danyoko, was the first imam in the village of Tenemakana but died prematurely in 1959, leaving Yacouba to be raised by his uncle. During his youth in the 1960s, Yacouba played guitar and sang in a touring band and then left for Ivory Coast, where he worked in the cocoa and coffee trade for many years, learning French along the way. These days he works as a mechanic, but his real passion is traveling around and recording local oral histories on his tape recorder. For no other reason than to, in his words, "gain knowledge," he enjoys "sitting at the feet of his elders" listening to their stories.[85]

Not surprisingly, given his interest in history and knowledge, Yacouba proved to be an invaluable intermediary. Through him and his extensive network of kin and friends, he and I were able to visit numerous villages and households without going through official or government channels. But his greatest asset was as an interviewer. He knew the local history and as an elder could ask questions that younger interpreters would be afraid to broach. He understood the correct protocols, which, in most cases, meant gift giving and spending considerable amounts of time on benedictions and praises. This meant allowing elders to recount village foundation narratives before proceeding to questions on colonialism and other prearranged topics. We often returned several times for repeat interviews to clarify points and deepen the conversation. On a couple of occasions we did group interviews. But generally we conducted interviews privately in elders' homes. We never did surveys, but we generally recorded the interviews and gave copies of the tapes to the informants as gifts.

Inevitably, depending on social location, even the best interpreters have inherent biases and limitations. For Yacouba, female domains of knowledge were very distinct from those of men, and only women were authorized to discuss certain subjects. So, at first, Yacouba was resistant to the idea of interviewing women. Eventually, he relented, but our work with female informants was never quite as intensive as I would have hoped. We did conduct a dozen interviews with women, mostly in Tenemakana or neighboring villages. Yet even in these sanctioned settings, where Yacouba had family and close friends, the range of questions was limited. Finally, there was another limitation: Yacouba was understandably resistant to random sampling or visiting villages outside his network of kin and friends. He preferred to work in familiar villages and speak with elders he already knew. I do not know how the research would have been different had I insisted on casting the net wider, but I do know that our worst interviews took place in villages where Yacouba had no contacts. In such cases, everything was channeled through the village chief, a situation that often attracted crowds of curious villagers, although it might mean that, as visitors, we were treated to honorary drum and dance presentations, or what people called folklore. Mali, especially in the south, is characterized by rich cultures of orality, deep stores of hospitality, and favorable political circumstances for fieldwork.[86] Nevertheless, these hit-and-run interviews, conducted in the absence of contacts or deeper social investment, produced the most opaque testimonies. Thus, quality interviews and access to secrets, as common sense would suggest, depended on trust and some sort of social connection.[87]

CHAPTER 1

The Wars of Samori

RELIGION, POWER, AND PREDATION ON THE EVE OF COLONIAL CONQUEST

"There is a stream in this region named Jaban. Do you know this stream? Jaban? It is located between Soloba and Guélélénkoro. Samori killed, killed and killed the people of Basidibé along the banks of this stream. Even today, the waters of this stream are red."[1] Suleyman Sidibé, an elder in the village of Solona, was repeating a common motif in local oral traditions on Samori Touré, the founder of an internal West African empire. He continued, "There was such massacre and destruction that the refugees who fled came here saying, 'It is terrible along the banks of Jaban. The rest of the people who are still alive, if you do not come together to survive, the war is coming, and the war chief will massacre all of Wasulu.' It was for that reason that we later formed a coalition and rose up against Samori." The stream of Jaban is one of numerous "sites of memory" scattered across the historical landscape of southern Mali and marking important battlefields, massacre sites, and old fortifications.[2]

The wars of Samori were imperial in nature, characterized by the seizure of territorial control and widespread predation. As a major historical rupture, they also carved a destructive path across the social and religious landscape.[3] One of the most important consequences of the wars was the enslavement of many thousands of people and the forced displacement of refugees. But the vanquished populations were far from passive victims. They not only resorted to small-scale enslavement and kidnapping themselves, but also vigorously resisted. Indeed, the Samorian wars produced internal resistance, which played an important role in wearing down Samori's war machine on the eve of colonial conquest. He might have held out longer against the French had he won the support of his imperial subjects, who eventually took up arms to end his rule. In the end, the Samorian occupation would cast a long shadow over the region, violently marking the end of the precolonial social and political order and determining the shape of colonialism in the future district of Buguni.

Samori's main aim was to dominate the region for economic and political advantage over his neighbors, while responding to the encroachments of the French conquest armies. Beyond these interests, the Samorian state also relied upon forms of symbolic power and violence to fulfill certain political functions. Owing to Samori's lack of traditional legitimacy, Islam came to represent a powerful translocal basis of authority as well as an ideology of enslavement and a tool for unifying the empire. Far from being a monolithic holy warrior and much less committed to scholarly pursuits than other Muslim state-builders and reformers like Uthman dan Fodio, Seku Amadu, and al-Hajj Umar Tal, Samori nevertheless took a decisively religious turn. During the so-called theocratic episode, from 1884 to 1888, he implemented a policy of forced conversion to Islam, dispatching soldiers to destroy bamana religious sites and objects, enforcing *shari'a* law,

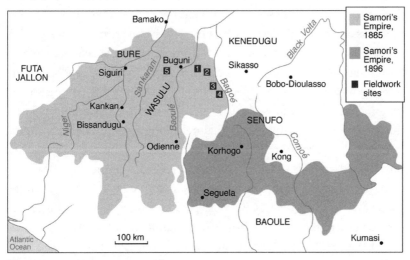

Map 3. Samori's Empire in West Africa.

and delegating Qur'anic teachers to establish schools. As it happened, the embrace of theocracy coincided with the Samorian incursions into southern Mali. Thus, many of the worst acts of religious violence occurred in this region.[4] More broadly, across West Africa Samori left a highly ambiguous legacy. His holy war was uneven over space, short in duration, and something of an anomaly in the roughly thirty-year span of the Samorian state.

This chapter seeks to document the effects of Samori's wars in the district of Buguni, which have been remembered locally as jihads. The result, whatever Samori's motivations may have been, was that Islam became associated with violence and enslavement, making it a relatively unattractive faith in the early colonial era. At the same time, the wars of Samori caused the displacement of tens of thousands of refugees and slaves from the region. This mass dispersal of people would have far-reaching social and cultural consequences. In short, while Islamization from above won few lasting converts, many of the region's first Muslims were slaves captured during the wars of Samori.

BAMANAYA AND THE RELIGIOUS HABITUS

Like most ethnonyms, *bamana*, or *Bambara*, was a term used by outsiders to designate non-Muslim and largely agrarian peoples living in a wide swath of territory in central and southern Mali. To Muslim merchants and scholars, the bamana was an uncivilized barbarian, pagan, and slave. Bamanaya, which I will use as shorthand for a wide range of non-Muslim religious and political practices, was not a self-contained religious system. Rather, it constituted an eclectic set of practices and beliefs. As scholars have long noted, in predominantly nonliterate societies, in which there were no founding texts, religious practices have tended to be much more pragmatic and open to change. The myths and mental frameworks for thinking about natural and supernatural processes represented a kind of intellectual *bricolage*. Given this undocumented quality, one can establish only the most general contours of precolonial religious life.[5]

The Bamanankan-speaking people of southern Mali belong to the larger Mande world, with its vast diaspora stemming from the thirteenth-century expansion of the Malian empire. Ethnographic studies have illustrated the great heterogeneity of practices associated with bamanaya, documenting the ways in which particular institutions, power objects, and rituals have been localized in time and space. However, there were many shared cultural characteristics and social forms as well as translocal networks of territorial cults and political patronage. Mande societies were traditionally divided into three main groups, sometimes called castes. First, the nobles (*hòrònw*) were at the top of the social hierarchy. Then, there were the people of caste (*nyamakalaw*), including such occupational subgroups as blacksmiths, woodworkers, leatherworkers, musicians, and storytellers. Finally, there were slaves (*jònw*). These three basic social categories were then subdivided, each smaller group having gradients of privilege and varying positions of power in the social hierarchy. Among slaves, the most important distinction was between first-generation slaves, or jònw, who had usually been captured in battle or purchased, and those born in the house (*wolosow*), who generally saw an improvement in their status as they were integrated into the household. In subsequent generations, such as the *kenkenkegeye*, household slaves became virtually indistinguishable from members of the family.[6]

Ordinarily, the noble families produced the village chiefs. And such lineages were credited with having founded their villages; they were the first comers, who had accommodated strangers, granting settlement, hunting, fishing, or grazing rights in exchange for symbolic tribute. Within villages, the gravesites of these founding patriarchs became the centers of cults of political ancestors. Typically, in foundation narratives such ancestors were usually hunters who, through magical encounters with forest spirits and animals, had settled new lands following supernatural mediation. But not all villages were founded in virgin territory, as many revered political ancestors had displaced previous inhabitants and assumed autochthonous identities.[7] Among people of caste, the most important subgroup was the blacksmith, or *numu*. Blacksmiths were considered leaders in the key social and agrarian rites of passage of the community, but they were also feared because of their mastery of the occult sciences. As a result, there were restrictions on intermarriage between blacksmiths and others, and blacksmiths often lived in separate quarters or hamlets. Male blacksmiths were in charge of initiation and circumcision rites as well as numerous power associations. The wives of blacksmiths were potters, who also served as midwives and ritual specialists in female-oriented rites of passage.[8]

At the core of bamanaya, as in many West African cosmologies, there was a dichotomy between the cultivated and the wild, between civilization and nature. And the purpose of civilization was to tame or domesticate the wild. Cultivated areas, towns, and roads were the safer domains of human activity, whereas the forest, by contrast, was considered a place of danger and evil. But it was also a place of power. Only those who had considerable esoteric knowledge and large stores of *nyama*, or the powerful energy of action animating all of life, could go into the bush. Nyamakalaw (literally, the "handlers of nyama") were the best equipped to work with this occult power, although such noncaste people as hunters and healers could also harness nyama to great effect. Hunters were often venerated as village founders, possessors of magic and occult knowledge. In the annals of local histories, they were credited with slaying dangerous bush animals and providing food during times of famine. In contrast to Western and Muslim views of African religions as fetishism or idolatry, the bamana believed in a Supreme Being as well as ancestral and local earth spirits living in streams, forests, rocks, and such. All of these deities were accessed through ritual experts. Given the impediments to population growth, such as recurring drought, devastating diseases, slavery, warfare, and high infant mortality rates, a central concern of bamanaya was fertility. Concomitantly, people believed that all personal misfortunes such as infant mortality, illness, crop failure, and premature death were caused by the malevolent acts of people and spirits. The culprits were often assumed to be sorcerers, who transformed themselves into cats, snakes, and other night animals to invade people's dream worlds, where they "ate souls" and generally engaged in nefarious, misanthropic activities.[9]

There were important hierarchies of ritual specialists in village life with no clear separation between political and religious power. As a rule, most temporal political offices, such as the village chief, were achieved through seniority, but there were also the heads of the power associations and various religious priests, known as *jòtigiw* or *somaw*, who performed sacrifices and interceded between individuals and spiritual forces. Their power was normally tied to particular power objects, known as *jòw*. In the wider social field, through participation in power associations and initiation societies, engaging in the ritual practices associated with the different sacred sites and power objects, and going through the normal rites of passage, villagers became local citizens. Naming ceremonies, circumcision, scarification, and ritual acquisition of esoteric forms of knowledge were all ways in which the village locality was inscribed into the minds and onto the bodies of villagers. Conversely, through the demarcation of fields, the clearing of village and intervillage paths, the building of huts, the burying of the dead, the designation of sacred sites, and the ritual domestication of the land, villagers etched themselves into the locality spatially.[10]

In the bamana religious landscape, most villages had their sacred trees, normally a kapok tree, which was viewed as a kind of ladder or antenna used by the divine spirit to descend to earth and by the ancestors to climb into the heavens. Sacrifices at the foot of the village tree served to nourish the souls of ancestors, who, in return, were purveyors of fertility. The religious landscape was also spotted with sacred pools and large stones, usually located to the south or west of the village, and serving as the home of a crocodile. There were sacred woods where secret initiation rites were performed. And most villages also had a sacred village python. Temporally, the flow of religious life was governed by seasonality, astrology, and the agricultural calendar. As in the larger Afro-Eurasian ecumene, seven-year cycles were common in the organization of initiation rites.[11] In short, until the colonial era, the religious habitus was rooted in bamanaya and shaped by the particular ecologies and social relations of the locality.

THE EXPANSION OF ISLAM IN THE WESTERN SUDAN

Following the conquest of Egypt, Arab armies pushed westward into the Maghreb, where the new faith would find itself transplanted.[12] Soon, by the eighth century, Muslim merchants extended their commercial networks across the desert, tapping into the lucrative sub-Saharan gold trade. Early evidence drawn from Arab accounts of the *Bilad al-Sudan* (Land of the Blacks), as it was called, suggest that intercultural encounters within the context of trade were often characterized by peaceful coexistence between Muslims and practitioners of indigenous religions. An oft-cited account from 1068 by Abu 'Ubayd al-Bakri, an Arab scholar based in Andalusia, sheds light on such dynamics. Al-Bakri reported how kingdoms in the Sahel often had two separate towns, representing the symbiotic relations between Muslim traders and local chieftaincies. One of these towns was in the kingdom of Ghana, roughly 375 kilometers north of Buguni in southeastern Mauritania.[13] According to al-Bakri, it had an outward-looking market town "inhabited by Muslims," including "salaried imams and muezzins, as well as jurists and scholars." It even had twelve mosques. The king's town, although possessing a mosque for visitors, had "domed buildings and groves and thickets," frequented by "sorcerers" and those "in charge of the religious cult." These non-Muslim sacred sites were hidden in the woods and housed "the tombs of their kings." The town's religion was described as "paganism and the worship of idols."[14]

Eventually, the alleged pagan chiefs and kings embraced Islam, facilitating their transactions with Muslim traders and reflecting their role as mediators between their rural constituencies and the far-flung trade networks of the Muslim world. Beyond trade, however, early religious transformations were also based in the spiritual needs of farming communities. Thus, al-Bakri described an environmental calamity in one Sahelian kingdom, Malal. As he tells it, the region had been hit by recurring droughts, which spurred the people to sacrifice nearly all of their cattle. Desperate to bring rain, the king enlisted the help of a Muslim cleric who had taken up residence in town and who, after converting the king, performed a successful rainmaking prayer. Al-Bakri wrote, "They prayed for part of the night, the Muslim reciting invocations and the king saying 'Amen.' The dawn had just started to break when God caused abundant rain to descend upon them. So the king ordered the idols to be broken and expelled the sorcerers from his country. He and his descendants after him as well as his nobles were sincerely attached to Islam, while the common people of his kingdom remained polytheists."[15]

By the thirteenth century, the kings of the Malian empire, whose capital lay along the Niger River at Niani, had become nominally Muslim. One king in particular, Mansa Musa, who ruled from 1312 to 1337, made the pilgrimage to Mecca and devoted himself to building mosques.[16] When the Moroccan traveler Ibn Battuta visited ancient Mali in the fourteenth century, he spoke highly of how the people meticulously observed prayer and turned out in large numbers for Friday prayer. He also lauded the local scholarly efforts to learn "the sublime Qur'an by heart" as well as the "prevalence of peace." As a pious Islamic judge, or *qadi*, however, Battuta was quick to point out moral affronts, such as female nudity, casual relations between the sexes, musical performance, and forms of local expressive culture.[17] Eventually, nominal Muslim chiefs like Sunjata of Mali and Sonni Ali, the magician-king of Songhay, gave way to more pious kings who invested in Islamic institutions and became far less tolerant of pre-Islamic retentions. But Islam could hardly be called the state religion, at least until the reign of Askiya Muhammad in Songhay in the fifteenth and sixteenth centuries. There were exceptions to the tradition of quietism, such as the zealous militancy of the king of Takrur and the Almoravid jihad of the eleventh century. These were anomalies, however, before the jihad movements and formation of Muslim states in the eighteenth and nineteenth centuries, when Islam first spread into rural areas.[18]

For most of Islamic history in West Africa, the new faith spread incrementally along trade routes, in much less dramatic ways, as African traders saw the advantages in conversion. As elsewhere in the early Islamic world, particularly in coastal South Asia and East Africa and around the Malay Archipelago, what Marshall Hodgson called the "bandwagon principle" of religious change linked to commercial expansion was in full effect.[19] In the western Sudan, Jula and Soninke merchants were the dominant commercial groups. Spanning the Middle Niger River, Jula traders eventually expanded their operations further south into the forest zones, transporting gold from the mines in Buré and Akan to northern markets. Linked to trade, Muslim clerics took up residence within merchant communities, providing religious services for traders and neighboring non-Muslims. In this way, though an imported and minority faith, Islamic religious culture began seeping into indigenous practices. But even as the eclectic and pragmatic religious practices of West Africa allowed for external influences, most agrarian peoples did not take up Muslim prayer. And as a minority, rarely were the Jula in the position to impose their religious will on the countryside. As such scholars as Ivor Wilks, Lamin Sanneh, and Robert Launay have shown, the prevailing current of thought among the Jula was influenced by the sixteenth-century cleric Al-Hajj Salim Suwari, who argued that Muslims should focus their energies on observing their own piety rather than pursuing proselytization efforts. As long as Muslims were able to practice their religion in safety, Suwari maintained, they could accept living under non-Muslim jurisdiction. Subscribing to this Suwarian tradition that emphasized tolerance and peaceful coexistence, most Muslims did not feel compelled to try converting their neighbors.[20]

In Africa and elsewhere, the Sufi orders often operated as missionary organizations and as such served as more effective agents of proselytization on the frontiers of the Muslim world than the caliph's armies. Historically, long before the foundation of the Sufi orders, pious Muslims in the Near East had begun exploring certain mystical practices, such as the repetitive recitation of Qur'anic verses and the chanting of God's many names. Derived from the Arabic *tasawwuf,* for the early mystics who wore wool (*suf*) as a form of asceticism in the hot weather, Sufis sought closeness to God. Like mystics of other world religions, they cultivated an indifference to wealth and renounced worldly pleasures; they spent long periods in isolation, fasting and praying, and engaging in other devotional exercises. The transformation of these wandering mystics and the traditions of sainthood they represented into routinized and institutionalized forms occurred from the ninth century to the eleventh, as Sufis founded centers of worship and study.[21] Of the many Sufi orders, Muslims in the district of Buguni would overwhelmingly embrace the Qadiriyya.

As one of the most widespread and loosely structured brotherhoods, there was no single Qadiri way. The Qadiriyya originated with the figure 'Abd al-Qadir al-Jilani (d. 1166), an orthodox Hanbali preacher born in Gilan, along the Caspian Sea in northern Persia. Although he gained a wide reputation, he was not considered a Sufi and left no body of rules and techniques. At a time when the mysticism of elites was being replaced by popular devotionalism, Qadiri rituals were mostly devoid of the excesses of the spiritual dances used to induce ecstasy. In fact, the Qadiri litany, or *dhikr,* was composed of basic passages from the Qur'an. It was perhaps owing to this simplicity that the Qadiriyya was able to find such a geographically dispersed following. Furthermore, Qadiri mystics often transgressed religious boundaries and drew on pre-Islamic practices, which facilitated the order's adaptation to local settings.[22]

The Qadiriyya spread into West Africa via Morocco sometime during the fifteenth century. In the Sahara, the Sanhaja Berbers were the first to embrace the order, disseminating it through desert transhumance and trade. Further south the Kunta clan extended the Qadiriyya via preaching tours and commerce. Aside from formal studies in Islamic law, followers undertook spiritual retreats alone in the desert, fasting, praying, and undergoing material deprivations in order to achieve annihilation of the self and absorption in God. Subsequently, the Kunta clan split into two groups, the eastern Kunta sending caravans southward, trading and proselytizing among the Tuareg along the Niger Bend. Later, after languishing for two centuries, there was a revival of the Qadiriyya in the eighteenth century led by Sidi al-Mukhtar al-Kunti. Unlike some of his disciples, however, Sidi al-Mukhtar opposed jihad as a way of spreading Islam. Still, he represented the culmination of the Kunta role in propagating the Qadiriyya and served as a crucial inspiration for the nineteenth-century jihad movements.[23]

THE POLITICAL AND RELIGIOUS LANDSCAPE IN THE
NINETEENTH CENTURY

After the fatal denouement of the expedition to Timbuktu by the Scottish explorer Gordon Laing, René Caillié would not only reach the fabled city and live to tell about it but even cross the Sahara. More of a Richard Burton than a Henry Stanley in his approach, he traveled light, blended in with the surroundings, and lived in close contact with Africans. Born in the shadow of the French Revolution, and not far from Nantes, France's key port in the slave trade, he grew up in poverty, his only escape being travel books. But Caillié adopted an alternative and more exotic life story: he fashioned himself as an Egyptian Arab who had been seized by the French at the time of Napoleon's invasion and raised in France. Since then, he had been in the service of infidels, working in commercial enterprises in Senegal, but had decided to reunite with his family in Egypt and devote himself to Islam. To back up his story, he lived and studied Arabic in Mauritania before finally heading inland on his journey, dressing the part and praying fervently.[24]

The Frenchman struck out from coastal Guinea in April 1827 and soon found himself in the Futa Jallon highlands, where a revolution had brought about the creation of an Islamic state in the mid-eighteenth century. Building on previous failed revolutions—under the Berber Shaykh Nasir al-Din in Futa Toro and Malik Sy in Bundu in the late seventeenth century in the Senegal River valley—the theocratic state in Futa Jallon drew its sustenance from the Atlantic slave trade. It thus made extensive use of slave labor in agriculture, which freed up the ruling class to concentrate their efforts on Muslim statecraft, proselytization, and Islamic education. In particular, the Futa Jallon revolution inspired future generations of Islamic scholars and aspirant state builders, while producing a rich Pulaar literature written in Arabic script.[25]

Much later, Samori's military campaigns would put him in contact with the *torodbe* scholars of Futa Toro and the leaders of the Umarian state. But he was most impressed by the successes of Futa Jallon. Yves Person suggests that Samori was tempted to follow this example, particularly as he became convinced that a theocratic regime was the only way of unifying his community and confronting the European threat. However, not everyone found inspiration in the jihad of Futa Jallon. The theocratic regime also triggered a mass exodus of disenchanted pastoralists who headed eastward, where they eventually settled in Wasulu. There, they encountered the descendants of other Fulbé clans who, centuries before, had fled persecution under the Songhay empire.[26]

From the foothills of Futa Jallon, Caillié continued eastward to Kankan, another important Muslim center, which, as we shall see, would figure prominently in the religious history of colonial Buguni. In Kankan, the traveler first learned about Wasulu, known to be teeming with pagans and "infested with thieves," and learned about the wars between Segu and Jenné, which were forcing traders directly eastward via Sambatiguila and Tengrela before angling north to Jenné. This was the old route that pilgrims took to Mecca. Harboring concerns about safety, Caillié, in the rainy season of 1827, crossed the Sankarani River into Wasulu. Although he provided few details about political changes in the region, he did note that the population was "divided into many small states, and governed by independent chiefs, who often make war with each other in order to procure slaves." He also described villages with large, mud-walled fortifications built to protect people from slave raiders, a common defensive strategy in the region. Thus, while centralized, militarized states certainly depended heavily on predation for their reproduction, decentralized societies not only resisted incursions, but also engaged in the slave trade themselves.[27]

In Wasulu, the Frenchman's fears of brigands and marauders were dispelled, as his first written description suggests: "The inhabitants came in crowds to see me; they looked at me with curiosity. . . . They are pagans. . . . They are naturally very cheerful, and enjoy themselves under the large bombax trees, where I saw the youth assembled. They had a kind of music like I had never yet seen. It was composed of twenty musicians, of which many had a wood instrument, carved and covered with a piece of sheepskin. . . . Two small blacks, well dressed, with feathers on their heads, jumped in cadence, and accompanied the music while hitting two pieces of metal together. . . . Since my departure from the coast, I have seen nothing like this that gave me so much pleasure." Later, in the

Senufo *kafo*, or small state, of Niené. Caillié would again observe groups of musicians, spurring him to contrast the joyous and festive ambiance of pagans with the more reserved Muslims: "These people are always in celebration. They are of a cheerfulness that makes a striking contrast with the sad and monotone air of the Muslim fanatics."[28]

Aside from dancing, Caillié described salutations and the interiors of households, revealing traces of religious identification in local material culture. One Wasulunké chief, wealthy in gold and slaves, had his home decorated with bows, quivers of arrows, spears, horse saddles, metal vases, a teapot of apparently Portuguese extraction, and a leather plate. The chief was not Muslim, and there were no outward signs of Islam or the presence of Muslim traders in his court. By contrast, in nearby trade towns like Sambatiguila and Tengrela men wore turbans, performed ablutions and prayer, dressed in clean white robes, attended mosques, and recited the Qur'an. But these Muslim settlements were few and far between, strung out along trade routes, Muslim islands in a "sea of paganism." Outside Muslim trade towns there were surrounding belts of slave villages, and the vast "Bambara" countryside, where men worked in the fields and went around wearing cotton loincloths, glass bead earrings, and fetish amulets made of ram horns and sheep tails.[29]

While religious differences were ideologically reinforced in changing political circumstances, there was space for mutual borrowing and exchange of cultural practices, as bits and pieces of Muslim practices were absorbed into bamanaya over the centuries through trade. Even certain indigenous practices, such as forms of divination, had Islamic roots. In Wasulu, Caillié described young men shaving their heads and wearing cotton clothing, which, according to Jean-Loup Amselle, demonstrated "great respect for the Prophet and his religion."[30] Still, there is no evidence to suggest that rural areas came anywhere near being Muslim, in the sense of people either identifying as Muslims or performing prayer. And inhabitants may have even rejected Islam in the nineteenth century. Caillié observed, "Far from welcoming Muslims and their amulets with kindness, they reject them, in order to occupy themselves only with the religion of their country." Equally important, while people may have appropriated elements of Muslim material culture, their rituals and rites of passage continued to be based in bamanaya. Near the Bagoé River, Caillié encountered a ceremony associated with the *lo* initiation society: "Among all the

Bambara, there are men who stay in the woods, they lodge in huts made of tree branches, and have with them young children that they instruct in the secrets of their ceremonies. All night they leave the bush and go accompanied by the initiated children, running around the village. . . . At their approach, each person closes himself in his hut to avoid their encounter that they fear. There are many men . . . who do not fear these *lous*. I learned that these men were initiated, and that it was an institution."[31]

Despite the cultural cross-fertilization and cosmopolitanism of this part of the West African hinterland, the field of religious practice was shot through with power differences. Religious identity was often mobilized as a justification of enslavement or as a basis of resistance to slave traders or conquest states. In most rural areas that were far removed from trade routes, people refrained from venturing out beyond the locality, out of fear of enslavement. As Caillié reported, "The inhabitants of Wasulu do little commerce and do not travel, because their idolatry would expose them to the worst slavery."[32] It would seem that by the nineteenth century, within the contexts of the slave trade and the era of jihads, religious differences had hardened.

As scholars have noted, most trading communities were Muslim, and many slaves ended up working in Muslim households or slave villages. Once in slavery, they usually farmed, performed domestic labor, produced cotton textiles, mined for salt and gold, or served as porters or soldiers, their labor often underwriting the religious and scholarly activities of Muslim clerics. The wider relationship between Islam and slavery was complicated by the fact that the Qur'an and hadith implicitly recognized the institution of slavery and authorized the enslavement of idolaters but also recommended the liberation of slaves as a pious act. Furthermore, it was a fundamental principle of Islamic law that Muslims could not be enslaved and that pagans should be given religious instruction and manumitted once in captivity, although conversion to Islam by slaves did not necessarily lead to their liberation. Still, there were large discrepancies between normative rules and actual practices, or, as Humphrey Fisher comments, "The strict application of all these rules, or any of them, proved impracticable" in West Africa. Most slave owners, it would seem, provided little Qur'anic instruction for their slaves, and few masters willingly manumitted their slaves for religious purposes. However, there were cases in which slaves were adopted as Qur'anic students and were incorporated into the Muslim community. Some slaves even developed as scholars in their own right and founded important religious lineages.[33]

Depending on the size of slaveholdings, slaves could be integrated into the household culture. In such circumstances, particularly in cases where they were children, slaves embraced Islam. Whether encouraged or deterred, they converted for various reasons.[34] The French ethnographer and administrator Paul Marty later noted that slaves converted through close contact with their Muslim masters; that despite being subalterns within the host environment, slaves participated in the household culture.[35] According to Marty, young slaves would "imitate, several times each day, what they saw around them in performing their prayer."[36] Marty characterized the Muslim practices of slaves as one of mimicry, imitation, and superficial exteriority, but he noted that even when masters discouraged slaves from converting to Islam in order to maintain boundaries of authority and to avoid manumission, slaves appropriated Muslim ideas and practices on their own. This process was far from universal, however, as conversion depended on the nature of the relationship between slave and master within the household; assimilation into the hegemonic household culture was proportionate to the degree and frequency of communications between masters and slaves.

RELIGION, ETHNICITY, AND THE POLITICAL ORDER IN A ZONE OF REFUGE: THE CASE OF FULALA

The region of southern Mali was historically something of an ethnic mosaic characterized by porous ethnic boundaries and considerable fluidity and movement between identity categories. While ethnic markers could refer to religious and occupational differences, shifts in ethnic identity or the rejection or adoption of different ethnonyms or clan names generally constituted changes in political affiliation. This ethnic pluralism reflected the highly variegated political landscape of the region, where local chiefs sought to acquire dependents through slave raiding, and a premium was placed on the incorporation of strangers.[37]

The wider region was something of a zone of refugee that had absorbed waves of population over the centuries. Strangers were accommodated, and cultural diversity was tolerated. Fittingly, Jean-Loup Amselle has described Wasulu as "a community of expelled groups" and noted the region's absorptive qualities. He states that Wasulu and the broader region constituted "a zone of low political pressure, where an entire series of groups came seeking refuge. They took their place as dominators or dominated, either by creating chiefdoms or by becoming dependants of powerful lineages."[38] In certain ways, southern Mali constituted what James Scott has recently called a "shatter zone," populated by refugees, pastoralists, hunters, and shifting cultivators who fled "state-spaces" and whose principal goal was the evasion of state control and enslavement.[39]

One current in this larger ingathering of refugees was comprised of Fulbé herders, who formed a far-flung archipelago of communities, concentrated primarily in Wasulu but also scattered between the Baoulé and Bagoé rivers. After many generations of assimilation into the ways and language of the indigenous population, these settlers were almost entirely absorbed culturally. In 1827, Caillié observed that Wasulu was "inhabited by Fula idolaters, pastoralists and cultivators" who did not speak any of the Pulaar language.[40] And roughly half a century later Joseph Gallieni, one of the architects of the French conquest of the western Sudan, similarly noted, "They still assert that they are of Fulbé origin, but they have only retained a few vague characteristics. One could even say that they are much closer to Bambaras, whose language they speak, and whose customs they keep."[41] In any case, these Fulbe groups, with their military skills and herds, were instrumental in the foundation of many small states, one of which was Fulala.

Around the time Caillié was angling north toward Jenné, numerous Fulbe clans were setting out in the opposite direction, seeking refuge from the Masina state. Some of the families headed to Wasulu, where they imposed their will on autochthonous populations, while others made strategic alliances with local clans. Their emigration came in the wake of Seku Amadu Bari's jihad and founding of an Islamic state at Hamdullahi in the interior delta of Middle Niger. In time, the state became highly centralized and sought to sedentarize the Fulbe, forcing nomadic herders to settle in circumscribed zones and to follow tightly organized routes during their seasonal transhumance. These impositions as well as the rigorous enforcement of Islamic law threatened the Fulbé way of life.[42] Therefore, in the second decade of the nineteenth century, as a state-evading strategy, pastoralists drove their herds southward, seeking greater freedom and open land.

According to oral traditions, one emigrant clan left their village of Mudaba, near Masina, after "quarreling with the chiefs of Masina," and migrated to Céndugu, where they founded a small kafo, which they named Fulala, or "place of the Fula."[43] Upon arriving in Céndugu, the Suntura strangers from Mudaba went to see the local king (fàama), Nco Jakité, to inquire about pasturing their herds in nearby lands. Although originally a Muslim, the king had come to embrace bamanaya and now worshiped a powerful oracle, the kòmò of Tenemakana. One informant recounted a local story: "The fàama consulted Tenemakana kòmò, which predicted what was going to happen in his territory, and what sacrifices had to be done to face such problems. They made sacrifices to prevent future calamities. . . . The fàama said: 'I am looking to enlarge my territory. If I have more people in my kingdom, nobody can attack us.' So he allowed the strangers to settle with them. He said: 'You can go settle down there, next to the hamlet for my slaves [jònbuguda], in Massala.'"[44] But in time the immigrants, led by Tumani Suntura, took Massala by force and waged war with Nco, before a tributary arrangement was established. As another informant said, "Massala remained the 'slave' of Tigiya, to which the chief of Massala, Tumani, gave the chest and thigh of his game."[45] Thus Massala was a vassal to Tigiya rather than a slave village in the proper sense. Eventually, as the cattle began to multiply, Tumani's brothers, Watanin and Maliki Suntura, broke away from the clan and headed eastward to settle new lands. The lineage subdivided and branched out as the three brothers went their separate ways.[46]

Before the Fulbe invasions, various bamana clans had inhabited the territory that comprised the kafo of Fulala. In reference to this period, village foundation narratives are imbued with magical tales and myths and stories of hunters. They tell that local lineages fled Kaba, near Kangaba, when the Malian empire went into decline, and groups were spun off in search of political security and fertile land. In particular, the Danyoko clan traveled for many years, settling and resettling, before finally reaching their current home in Tenemakana. In one story, a talking red monkey saved the lineage after it led the people to a waterhole during severe drought. The monkey became the clan's totem (tana). Nevertheless, while genealogies do not reach that far back, the founder of Tenemakana, Bazumana, is still revered today. His gravesite, known as tonjugu, is the site of ancestor worship and village sacrifices. Whatever historical veracity there might be in such local traditions, one thing that emerges from multiple accounts is that Tenemakana possessed the most powerful kòmò in this region.[47]

All rulers, whether indigenous or alien, sought to build their legitimacy by currying favor with indigenous religious authorities. One man recounted, "At this time, there was no kòmò in Tigiya or Massala. So it was the oracle of Tenemakana that they worshiped. And on occasion, the kòmò of Tenemakana was transported to the court of Nco, where it would read the future for him. When it came to predict the future, the kòmò said that Nco must sacrifice a bull with white and black spots. . . . The person, and his descendants, who would eat the head of this bull would come to govern this country. And all the meat would be distributed across the country. In the localities where this meat was consumed, these places would be the extent of the sovereign's territory." As the story goes, Tumani married the king's daughter, Nyene, and produced one son, Jenba. Later, Nyene stole the head of the bull and smuggled it to Massala, where Jenba consumed it. Years later, Jenba rose to power, and under his command the kafo of Fulala took shape. He waged war against the people of Céndugu, taking possession of prized territories, fishing spots and grazing land. Then he sent his five sons to occupy new villages, as the inhabitants were forced into tributary arrangements. As the case of Fulala suggests, religious power was inextricably tied to political power.[48]

As we have seen, one of the most prominent characteristics of the human and cultural geography of the region was the settlement of immigrant pastoralists, who were incorporated into local political structures through alliances but also through outright conquest. Such local wars, however, would pale by comparison to what lay on the horizon. After centuries as a zone of refuge from state control, in the late nineteenth century an expansive African empire eventually captured the region, resulting in widespread enslavement. The late nineteenth century would be a dark era for the peoples of southern Mali, as paroxysms of violence swept across the land.

HISTORIES OF THE VANQUISHED: ENSLAVEMENT AND DISPLACEMENT ON THE IMPERIAL PERIPHERY, C. 1880S

The case of the Samorian state and its imperial wars of conquest draws attention to the existence of African empires which were absorbing new peoples and territories on the eve of European conquest. From the standpoint of particular rural localities, the nineteenth century was a period of successive waves of conquest, both European and African. In fact, even before the Samorian invasion in 1882, local wars of enslavement and widespread kidnapping had turned Wasulu into "the principal purveyor" of slaves in the western Sudan. Gallieni reported on the internal wars and predation in Wasulu: "This population would be more numerous were it not for the permanent state of war that, in diverting [labor] from the peaceful task of agriculture, occasions appalling famines, causing death everywhere. These internal wars have already had the result of multiplying the pillaging of slaves, and one could say that Wasulu has become the principal purveyor of the slave markets in this region. . . . Slavery has become unfortunate in this country, something so natural that it does not scare anyone: everyone realizes that he could become a slave one day. . . . The chiefs sell their subjects, the heads of family, in times of dearth, bring their children to the market, brothers take their own sisters to sell. This social and political disorder has the main consequence of leading to the depopulation of the country."[49] Such internecine warfare was one of the reasons Wasulu would fall so quickly to Samorian forces. It explains how Samori was able to successfully divide and conquer rival chiefs in bringing disparate chiefdoms to submission. In short, as a result of these internal wars, the region had been softened up, and, as Person described, "offering itself for the taking to whoever wanted to conquer it."[50]

Aside from local slave raiders and warlords engaged in the internal slave trade, there were other state builders in southern Mali during the late nineteenth century. One of the most important was Tiéba Traore, the king of Kenedugu, and his successor Babemba, based in Sikasso.[51] Later, the eventual wars between Samori and the kings of Sikasso would bring about widespread pillaging and enslavement in the buffer zone separating the two states. Wedged in the politically fragmented margins between these competing states, decentralized societies were constantly raided. In 1887, the French military explorer Louis Binger observed this zone: "On all the frontiers of Samori, villages are annexed or treated as enemy territory. . . . Neutrality does not exist. . . . If they've been conquered by Samori the inhabitants are sold or pillaged. . . . This deplorable state of things creates [a situation in which] leaving from one country, one always crosses a zone, varying between forty and fifty kilometers, in which the inhabitants do not know of whom they are the subjects. This zone is always subject to pillage, either by the bandits in the area or by the inhabitants of neighboring villages. One could compare this frontier zone to the *marches* of ancient Europe."[52] As the pillaging and skirmishes developed into outright war, the region was left depopulated and in ruins. By the time of French conquest, most people had fled as refugees or been enslaved.

As I have indicated, while the accounts of Binger and Gallieni are quite useful, much of my historical reconstruction is based on oral traditions. However, reflecting the breadth of Samori's conquests and their overlap with those of his rivals, there are many generic Samori accounts in circulation. There is a tendency to conflate historical processes, using *Samori* as shorthand; informants might speak of Samori enslaving people, whereas Samori himself never actually set foot in many of the villages subjugated by his troops. I have chosen not to reproduce the widespread "Samori the bloodthirsty" clichés, such as "burning people like peanuts" and "cutting open pregnant women," which reveal little about local histories.[53] Alongside these more generic accounts, there are particular village and family oral traditions that often contain rich local detail.[54] Certainly, they too occupy the gray area between oral histories and traditions. Even the most local stories are inflected with legendary references and motifs that animate and color accounts. However, they are useful in recasting the standard narrative by inserting elements of human agency based on the perspectives of vanquished peoples in southern Mali.

According to Person, Samori was born in the Konya region of Guinea in 1830 and grew up in a community that was well outside the normative tradition of Islam. Although a trader, his father remained an unrepentant animist, forcing young Samori to leave home to acquire his religious education. Until late in life, Samori knew only the rudiments of the faith and remained largely illiterate. In any case, while working in the kola caravan trade, his mother was seized in a raid in 1853, which spurred Samori to offer up his soldiering services as a replacement to secure her freedom. Then, after years of fighting as a slave soldier, he fled to form his own warrior band. Eventually, in 1873, drawing support from Jula traders, he founded a new state, with its capital at Bissandugu, Guinea. At first, he allied himself with the Muslim establishment in Kankan, while expanding his state's frontiers. But by the late 1870s, the modest Bissandugu state was evolving into an empire as new territories across the savanna and forest fringe were slowly being incorporated. This process of imperial expansion brought with it widespread enslavement and also a component of jihad.[55] Although the Samorian state eventually embraced theocracy, early in his state-building efforts, Samori took a more pragmatic approach, allying with both animists and Muslims, ultimately with the aim of protecting trade. As Person has shown, although most of Samori's followers were Muslims, they fought more out of economic than religious interest. However, once Kankan had been taken and the power of the Kaba clan was effectively marginalized, Samori had no other Muslim rivals with which to contend and still wide fields of animist territories yet to conquer. Soon he embraced jihad as an ideology of enslavement.[56]

By the 1880s, the Samorian state was depending heavily on the internal slave trade for its procurement of horses, as cavalry forces were a crucial part of the enslavement mechanism. Further contributing to Samori's military effectiveness were technological changes in the manufacture of firearms during the late nineteenth century, which led to a regional arms race. As Europe modernized militarily, and repeating rifles replaced breechloaders, the African coastal market became flooded with secondhand firearms. Samori was able to tap into this weapons trade in Sierra Leone, making his army one of the best equipped with modern rifles in West Africa.[57] Indeed, from his initial contacts with the French in 1882 he had become aware of the importance of military modernization, while also making a strategic decision to expand to the east. Over the next sixteen years, Samori would be simultaneously fighting wars of conquest against his fellow Africans, including a major siege of Sikasso, and waging a defensive guerrilla war against the French.

It was around the time Samori first encountered the French that his conquest of Wasulu began. East of the Sankarani River, direct occupation would last roughly eleven years, from 1882 to 1893. The invasion started among the kafow of Basidibé, Jallon-Fula, and Gwanan, just as the French were expanding from the Upper Senegal River to the Niger River. At first, Samori exploited internal divisions, playing one group off another. However, the kafo of Basidibé resisted the Samorian incursions and, as a result, was conquered militarily and left in ruins. Many people were enslaved or massacred but most fled after their failed resistance, taking refuge under the former chief of Siekorole, San Musa Sidibé, in Kati, located near Bamako. Many refugees from Basidibé also asked for protection from the war chief (*kélétigi*) Moriba Balan in Gualala or other chiefs such as Wòyò in Jadafara or Debiningué in Solona. Refugees were forced "to entrust themselves to a war chief, who would be their protector, otherwise the people would be taken away as slaves."[58] But even as refugees fleeing through the forests, people were often enslaved. Hari Sidibé recounted her family story:

> My own mother and my husband's mother lived through the
> wars of Samori. According to them, the wars of Samori came to
> lay siege to the village. At this time a large mud wall surrounded
> the village. But it was the rainy season, so when Samori's troops
> arrived, half of the people were out in the fields, while the other
> half were in the village. The people fled into the hills above
> the village. From the tops of the hills, they threw large stones
> down on Samori's troops. These rocks hit the soldiers on their
> heads. . . . The people dumped boiling maize water down onto
> the *sofaw* [Samorian troops]. But, when the population had run
> out of weapons and they had nothing to eat, they decided it was
> time to flee the village. The people fled at night. When Samori
> came the next day and began firing on the village, there was no
> more resistance. He found the village was empty. The only people
> who remained were the handicapped, the sick, the old people and
> the late-sleepers who had missed the signal to flee.

Inserting human agency into local Samorian history, Hari Sidibé recalled the fate of her ancestors, who were captured in flight and forced to farm in Samori's "collective fields" (*Almami fòròw*) before managing to escape. Her account conveys a sense of the collective mental map of the locality, emphasizing particular markers in the landscape: the symbolic importance of "crossing the Balé" into Gualala—hence ending "their slavery"—and arriving at the Niger River, where her ancestors were reunited with their family and other refugees. She continued,

> Samori's troops captured all the slaves they could and then they
> went in pursuit of the refugees. All of those who were captured
> were marched side by side until they arrived at the war camp.
> The men were sent out to the collective fields to cultivate, and the
> women were kept in the village to do domestic work, looking for
> wood. N'ténén and Samba passed the rainy season farming. And
> then they decided to flee when the maize was mature and the

fonio [a small short-cycle millet] was ready. They escaped under
a full moon and they passed by Yanfolila here. . . . [Samba] said,
'There is the Kapok tree on the route of Harijan.' He led them
across the stream all the way to the Balé River. Then they crossed
the Balé and arrived at Gualala, and that is when their slavery was
ended. They found their family on the banks of the Niger, and
they settled behind the Niger, where all the fugitive slaves and
refugees had formed their village.[59]

After successfully subjugating Wasulu in the west, Samori continued
eastward on his path, crossing the Baoulé. Then, during the dry season
of 1884, his forces began their invasion of Fulala and Céndugu.[60] Despite
the fierce resistance of an intervillage coalition of fighters drawn from
around the region, the people of Céndugu were forced to capitulate. Many
had heard news that Samori was coming and fled before facing combat.
After a lengthy trek, the refugees found safe haven in the village of Maàlé,
across the Kankeleba River, where displaced peoples from diverse villages
in the region had gathered. They would spend nine years in exile before
returning to their homes.[61]

Having occupied Céndugu, Samori's forces turned their attention to
Fulala, starting with Sekana. Although there is very little documentary
evidence from Fulala at this time, Binger did report in 1887 that "Sekana
was destroyed, some of its inhabitants fleeing to settle in Niamala, but
most of the people of Niamala were sold as slaves."[62] Oral accounts also
suggest that the inhabitants who fled northern Fulala were part of the
stream that alerted the villages of southern Fulala of the impending war,
thus saving many lives. One elder said, "The chief of Sekana sent a messenger to Tenemakana warning the people that a warrior chief was soon
arriving among them." As a result, the people of Tenemakana fled without
ever witnessing the attack on their village. However, Samori's cavalry forces
swept through the forests and waited at key river crossings for potential
booty, enslaving refugees as they fled. Even those who made it safely into
exile in Maàlé were often forced to pawn themselves to survive.[63]

As oral and documentary sources indicate, most villages were plun-
dered and left in ruins. But a few managed to hold out, at least temporarily, for example, critical Senufo villages located across the Kankeleba
River, which had been a major ecocultural frontier dividing peoples whose

languages and bodily scarifications bore distinct differences.[64] One village, Moro, whose people were regarded as the landlords in the region, was not even attacked. An informant explained, "Samori came through the region, but he never came to our village. . . . None of his wars destroyed our village. It was protected by our spirits."[65] Similarly, in the village of Woblé, villagers today tell of having been shielded by protective spirits. One man explained, "When Samori came to Woblé, his troops surrounded the village. But he was not able to penetrate the village because there was a powerful spirit, named Jisòda. The spirits gave protective powder to the people of Woblé, and Samori couldn't penetrate here."[66] Although fear of Senufo occult powers may have played some role, Binger also reported that villages in this region often had large mud fortifications which kept the Samorian forces at bay.[67]

As Samori pushed further east, he came into direct conflict with the armies of Kenedugu in 1884. According to Person, the main factor that attracted both states to the region was that the Bagoé River frontier seemed to be suddenly closing, and neither party wanted to see the other assume hegemony over the rather fertile and populous zone. At first, Tieba Traoré, the king of Sikasso, sent his brother, Siaka, at the end of the rainy season of 1884 to patrol the trade routes along the river, preventing Jula traders from selling horses to Samori's troops. He also began drumming up support among the villages to revolt against Samori.[68] The eventual conflict between the two states would begin with small skirmishes along this frontier, provoked by Samori's raids across the river into Ganadugu. Siaka would then retaliate, provoking local revolts to break out. In short order, the area became a battleground caught between the two warring states. The villages located in the no-man's-land were pillaged for people and food. Then, following Samori's initial invasion of Niené. Siaka conquered the region. Faced with famine, many people simply surrendered. One informant emphasized the fact that they "voluntarily" submitted to slavery:

> After Samori, it was then Siaka who was the war chief. He laid
> siege to Nangalasso here and they did all that without being able
> to conquer the village. But according to our elders, the troops
> were unable to take Woblé, it was not destroyed by war. It was
> at the end of the rainy season, the soldiers from Sikasso came

into our fields and took our crops and returned to Sikasso with
our harvest. How could we fight this famine? Our elders were
concerned, so they took the measures necessary to survive
following the famine. The solution was to sell our people
voluntarily to the kings of Sikasso to avoid future wars and permit
our villagers to survive. . . . They gathered our elders and brought
them to Sikasso, and from there they went to fight Samori. The
people left on their own, they didn't have anything to eat so they
sold themselves voluntarily. . . . That way they would survive and
save the future of our bloodline.[69]

Not everyone fled or submitted to slavery. In the villages that accepted
Samorian rule, peasants continued to work in the fields and served as
slave porters. But even under occupation villagers were threatened by the
occasional raids of the war chiefs who engaged in the slave trade for their
own profit.[70] Binger observed one such war chief in the kafo of Niené.
Every two or three days, he would head out at night with his soldiers
and wait until morning, when the women and children left the village to
look for wood or to dig up yams. Binger commented that the chief never
returned to his camp without at least "four or five of these unfortunate
ones, mothers without children, or children without mother."[71] In villages
that were destroyed, those who were too weak for the long journey into
exile hid in the forests and man-made caves waiting for the fighting to
pass. Despite the hardships, by the dry season of 1885 people were
planning to revolt.

RESISTING RESISTANCE: HOLY WAR AND ITS DISCONTENTS, 1884–93

In 1884 the Samorian state took a distinctly theocratic turn, Samori adopting the title *Almami* (the imam). This move seems to have been inspired
by the leaders of the Islamic state in Futa Jallon, whose influence had
continued to grow. Now, Samori fashioned himself as the prayer leader of
the Muslim community and the *amir al-mu'minîn* (the commander of the
faithful). Initially, lacking scholarly pedigree and Arabic literacy, he struggled to command respect among the clerical class. But soon he undertook
Qur'anic studies with Sidiki Sharif Haidara, the head of the Qadiriyya
in Kankan and the father of Muhammad Fanta-Mady Sharif. Beyond his
personal endeavors, at the end of Ramadan in 1884 Samori assembled

his family members and associates and promulgated his plans to spread Islam among his imperial subjects. But, as Person has described, when he announced that shari'a law would be applied, some members of his own family protested. As a symbolic challenge, even his father, Laafiya, defiantly made sacrifices to the earth spirit in Sanankoro. Furious at this affront to his authority, Samori had his father arrested. But the family drama did not end until Samori had two of his daughters stoned for perceived immoral behavior to set an example.[72]

Samori would use Islam and forms of religious violence as tools in state formation aimed at creating cohesion and order across a vast, culturally diverse empire. In some of the territories conquered, he built mosques, set up Qur'anic schools, and enforced shari'a law. To carry out his religious policies, Samori enlisted religious officials and tasked them with policing the public religious culture of their localities and recruiting the sons of chiefs for Qur'anic education. In the large slave market of Tenetu, Binger encountered one of these religious officers, al-Hajj Mamadu Lamine, who was dressed in a turban and scarf and sat on a Turkish carpet with two copies of the Qur'an next to him. He was Soninke, and he had traveled widely across Africa and the Middle East. Because al-Hajj had spent time among "civilized peoples in Egypt during his three pilgrimages to Mecca," he had taken on a certain "veneer of education." However, he was unfamiliar with the Ta'rikh es-Sudan and had never heard of Ibn Khaldun.[73]

The institutions and impact of Samori's new religious policy varied considerably across the empire. In Wasulu, Islamization was pursued mainly through the establishment of Qur'anic schools and an order for compulsory attendance by the sons of chiefs.[74] There is scant evidence of the local enforcement of shari'a law across Samori's empire or in the provinces of Wasulu. However, when Binger passed through the region in 1887, he did report on the mutilation of thieves, according to shar'ia, in one marketplace. After the thieves' hands had been amputated by sword, they were displayed on stakes as public reminders.[75] Further to the west, in the region between the Baoulé and Bagoé rivers, Islam was also imposed through "particularly brutal and inquisitorial methods" under the direction of Tari-Mori, one of Samori's more zealous war chiefs.[76] When he visited this region, Binger emphasized the brutality of the Samorian occupation, which used religious violence for domination. He wrote, "To augment his prestige among the people he conquers,

Samori employs terror above all. . . . [But] the only strict observance of the Qur'an is the prohibition of drinking millet beer [dòlò] under the threat of death."[77] In local understandings, conversion "at the point of the sword" accompanied conquest. In the kafo of Céndugu, one man said, "Samori waged his wars as jihad. If you did not pray, he killed you. If you already prayed, he left your village alone."[78] In fact, most informants indicated that this holy war, with its widespread religious persecution of non-Muslims, was the main reason Samori failed to gain support among the people in his wars against the French. As Samori began forcing people to convert to Islam and to abandon their religious practices—outlawing the kòmò society and consumption of millet beer and sending soldiers to destroy village sacred sites, power objects, and masks—villagers became more determined to revolt. At first, they responded with bamana sorcery, but eventually they took up arms. Even as warfare between Samori and the French escalated in 1885, people in the region fought their own wars of resistance against the Almami.[79]

Within days of the initial revolt the Samorian troops in Siondugu and Fulala had been massacred. In nearby Céndugu, it was the chief of Kolondieba, Ba Nopéné Kone, who led the rebellion. One informant recalled the heroic acts of key individuals who are still praised to this day: "My grandfather revolted during the wars of Samori. You know, there were some brave men here, eh! There was one man named Nopéné. He was the village chief. When the wars of Samori returned to Kolondieba, people loaded a rifle and handed it to him and he would fire, to the left and to the right, without stopping. He decimated a regiment like this . . . Nopéné lived right here. Then there was another man named Ba Sonya. He was from the Sonyalaka clan. He ran behind the enemy at such great speed that they couldn't stop him. He was one of our grandfathers. I saw him alive. He wasn't a chief, but he was a brave man here in Kolondieba."[80]

In Céndugu and elsewhere women contributed to the wars of resistance against Samori in diverse ways. Aside from helping to procure food by gathering wild fruits and plants, women served as warriors.[81] Broulaye Kone recalled, "At this time, on the field of battle, some women fought more than their husbands, because they did not want to have themselves and their children taken away as slaves." Even those women who stayed at home did their part to help their husbands, performing rituals and wearing special power objects. Furthermore, men wore amulets made by their wives, which protected them against the enemy. As we have seen, the construction of mud fortifications was common in the region, enabling villagers, especially those who lived in the open plains, to resist slave raiders. The numerous dispersed settlements and small villages in the savanna region were often amalgamated into larger and better-protected villages equipped with mud walls. Since most men were practiced hunters, with either bow and arrow or firearms, the hunters would perch atop the walls and shoot at intruders as they approached. If the village had acquired firearms, one man would sit in position to fire as other people loaded the guns. Fields were cultivated closer to the villages, and men always carried their weapons and worked in large, collective groups. Lookouts were posted in the treetops to warn of intruders by blowing a horn or beating a drum.[82] As Namakoro Bamba explained, "The men who cultivated took their weapons into the fields with them when they farmed together. If you were not armed, Samori's troops would come and attack and lead you away in slavery. All of the farmers went into the fields armed together. Therefore, some people would have to stand guard, sitting high up in the treetops in order to watch out over the fields for any bandits or warriors. If there were many attackers coming, the farmers would be forced to flee, but if there were only two or three, they would confront them."[83]

There were honor (dànbé) and manliness (céya) in fighting in defense of one's village, and, by contrast, being defeated militarily and sold into slavery brought shame.[84] Many informants emphasized that submission was rarely the direct result of battle; it was because of starvation. Musa Sumoaro explained: "If you say that Samori captured many slaves here, it was because of famine. It was out of hunger, not because of Samori's bravery. . . . At this time, everyone cultivated together and kept their harvest in the field. When you were under siege you couldn't leave the tata, the walls couldn't be crossed once the guns were firing, hitting the walls. That is why Samori laid siege on the villages, nobody could leave and when you were starving from hunger without food, you finally surrendered."[85]

Eventually, toward the end of the dry season in 1887, the rebellion was crushed. And having secured treaties with the French in 1886 and 1887 establishing the frontier between their respective territories, Samori now sought to eliminate the largest threat on his eastern boundary, the Kenedugu state. Although Samori's armies possessed superior weapons, the king of Sikasso managed to overcome the arms gap through the construction of a massive mud-wall fortress known as the Tata of Sikasso, perhaps the largest of its kind in West Africa. Unable to breach the walls, Samori hoped to starve out the population, constructing a series of small wooden forts on the plains and hills around Sikasso, from which he launched his raids. As the siege dragged on, Samori relied upon heavy exactions from his imperial subjects to feed the troops. Binger reported that hundreds of porters arrived at Samori's camp each day carrying grain, yet despite this enormous war effort his soldiers were desperately hungry. Sikasso, on the other hand, still had its agricultural hinterland to the east and south, as Binger observed: "The besieged are so unworried that they are out farming. . . . [Tieba] does not lack food as his states are more populated than those of Samori and he can still obtain foodstuffs . . . the country of Samori is poor, absolutely depopulated and depleted."[86]

While Samori's soldiers faced incredible hardship, it was the people upon whom he had depended to provide grain supplies who suffered the most. Those who were unable to flee were rounded up and used as porters or placed in fields under surveillance to produce grain until they collapsed. An even larger portion was sold off to obtain horses and guns. As Binger was preparing to cross the Baoulé, he passed waves of refugees heading north to seek protection under the French. He described the scene of refugee flight:

> On the right bank, where I camp, I discover people coming from
> the battle lines. All are in a deplorable state of health, and among
> them are the dying. . . . Most of them are extremely weak; they
> have been feeding themselves for a whole month on corn stalks,
> leaves, and raw vegetation. . . . [But] in two or three days they
> will have escaped certain death, because they will have left the
> deserted zone separating the Baoulé from Sikasso. Children jostle
> at the adults without strength and force them to stumble into the
> river. It is indescribable. Others are seated on the banks and do
> not even try to cross; they await death. . . . they do not have the
> strength to make it to the other side of the river swimming. . . .
> There are skeletons and cadavers in large number. . . . It's
> horrifying. Those who are living seem dead standing up, a cane in
> hand, emaciated from hunger, eyes expressing no consciousness,
> nor astonishment, no longer having awareness of what they're

doing; they drag themselves painfully along the paths until they fall from starvation. . . . They no longer have the strength to articulate a syllable. They have the grimace of death on their lips.[87]

This deserted zone from which the refugees fled became a landscape of ruins, mass starvation, and death. But as famine and suffering spread along the trail of misery connecting Sikasso to Bissandugu, murmurs of rebellion once again circulated. As we have seen, the hardships of war-time and the rigid imposition of religious policies were likely at the root of people's discontent. The next revolt was also fueled by the rapid dissemi-nation of rumors of Samori's death, partly engineered by French polit-ical agents but also spread through the marketplace by traders. In 1887 the first defections started at the periphery of the empire in Jula market towns, such as Tengrela, indicating how far Samori's actions had alien-ated fellow Muslims. Soon, large-scale insurrections erupted in Wasulu, the weakest link in Samori's supply chain. The revolt immediately severed communications and stranded Samori's forces in the depopulated wasteland east of the Baoulé. With time running out and desperate from hunger and imminent defeat, Samori retreated, pillaging and attacking villages en route to secure slaves and food. One informant recounted as follows: "After being defeated at Sikasso, Samori fled, attacking Tiefala. But then he was dealt a defeat at Diandouba. . . . Samori continued on his path towards Banan. Without reason, Samori was attacking the villages throughout the province, only to impose his domination. At this time, he, himself, took control of the troops and pursued acts of pillaging and enslavement." Suppression of the Wasulu revolt was quick and severe. Samorian armies attacked villages without warning and engaged in scorched-earth practices and public displays of mass executions of rebels. One of the bloodiest scenes was the massacre at Samamurula, where the insurgents, numbering in the thousands, were rounded up and decapi-tated in the plains behind town. No one was left alive.[88]

In local oral traditions, the revolt in Wasulu and the subsequent suppression have been remembered as defining moments in the region's history. Even today, many villages still hold grudges against others based on the sides they took during the conflict. As informants recalled, a war chief from Jelifin named Filifen Bu captured Samori during the revolt of 1887–88 and then let him go when Samori paid him in gold and promised to make him the war chief of the region. At the time, Basidibé was split in two factions led by Ya Sidibé, chief of Yanfolila, and Filifen Bu of Jelifin. When Wasulu revolted, Ya Sidibé led the insurgents, while Filifen Bu remained stubbornly loyal to Samori. Then, following the suppression of the insurrection, Filifen Bu was appointed as the region's chief. As Suleyman Sidibé explained, "It thus became Filifen Bu who collected tribute in Wasulu and gave them to Samori and then he kept the rest. Such was the agreement with Samori . . . It was the same Filifen Bu who plotted against our grandfather and killed him. Filifen Bu was convinced that if he did not kill our grandfather, Samori would end up plotting against him, killing him and giving the country to our grandfather. So that was how Samori turned us against each other and continued to massacre our people." The upshot of Filifen Bu's releasing of Samori was that tens of thousands of people were killed or enslaved by Samori following the revolt of 1888. Some people in Jelifin deny that their ancestor betrayed Wasulu, but many remain silent on the subject. The burden of history weighs heavily on Jelifin, whose people, for whatever actual historical reasons, are often viewed as the region's pariahs on the basis of the purported betrayal of their village's ancestor.[89]

SAMORI'S ISLAMIC LEGACY

The conquest and occupation of southern Mali by Samori's armies overlapped temporally with the theocratic episode, when the Samorian state took steps to forcefully proselytize imperial subjects. Hence many of the worst instances of religious violence occurred in this region. This means that measuring Samori's Islamic legacy based solely on data from southern Mali distorts the image of Samori's religious policies, creating an impression that the militant jihad component was perhaps more prominent than it was. Nevertheless, as evinced in the revolts of 1885 and 1888, Samori's attempts at establishing Muslim political hegemony were rejected by the inhabitants, forcing Samori to reconsider his pursuit of a theocratic state. According to Person's informants, Samori had, in fact, concluded that compulsory conversion only served to weaken his state. Thus, after 1888, the theocratic approach was abandoned in favor of a more pragmatic one. Animist associations and practices were now officially tolerated across the empire, and overnight the network of Qur'anic schools and religious officers disintegrated.[90] Even as Samori was discontinuing his religious

policies, however, the French pushed inexorably into the Guinean hinterland, marching on Siguiri and later Kankan and Bissandugu. By 1892,
with his empire crumbling from within and without, Samori was forced
to flee to the east. Passing through Wasulu, he ordered the mass relocation
of entire villages. Some villages, among them Tenetu, refused to move and
paid the price as the men were massacred and the women and children
were led away in slavery. Samori quickly abandoned Wasulu and continued
his retreat to northern Ivory Coast.[91]

Although the wars of Samori destabilized the religious landscape of
southern Mali by uprooting communities and cutting people off from religious sites and practices, most of my informants were clear that Samori
did not succeed in converting people to Islam. In Fulala, one imam said,
"Samori was an ambitious man who justified his conquests as part of a
jihad that he would lead against the infidels in order to capture slaves. . . .
He had chosen as a pretext for his conquests that he would convert all the
infidels to Islam. If he really had this single ambition of converting the
region to Islam, it is certain that Islam would have remained afterwards
in such or such a village, where the people could even right now show
you by saying 'there, you see, such or such village was converted to Islam
by Samori.' But, there doesn't exist any such village, not even one village!"[92] Certainly, I would not want to give too much weight to single testimonies. However, this account is very representative of the views of my
informants, few of whom were willing to give much credit to Samori for
introducing Islam into the area.[93]

In explaining why Samori had not succeeded in his mass conversion
efforts, Muslim clerics cited the "No Compulsion" verse from the Qur'an,
while condemning Samori's actions.[94] Even those who were not religious
specialists, such as one informant in the village of Niamala, echoed this
idea: "Samori killed in ignorance. He imprisoned people up in their
villages until they died of hunger. Does a Muslim holy man do such
things? In this case, Samori was a powerful man, but he was not a real
believer. On the path of Allah, there is no need for forcing Islam on
people. After the descent of the Qur'an, Allah said that there is no more
compulsion in religion. This cannot be done."[95] Indeed, for practicing
Muslims there was no theological rationale for the Samorian wars. A
few informants said even that Samori had been possessed or guided by
a Satanic spirit that drove the destruction.[96] Indeed, given the theodicy

of local religions, evil (*jugu*) was the only way to explain the wars and associated terror. Some informants suggested that Samori was secretly a fetishist and that his power came from power objects rather than Islam. They also cited his lack of Islamic knowledge and his inability both to read or write properly in Arabic and to conduct prayer correctly. In further distancing the wars of Samori from Islam, informants pointed out how Samori killed fellow Muslims, citing the example of Samori's siege on a mosque in Kong. As one informant said, "Samori began his war with the idea of holy war. He was given the mission to kill all the infidels of planet earth. But, he was not able to do it. When his reign was close to ending, he went to attack Kong. He laid siege to the people in the mosque. So, at this moment he had diverged from the main reasons for his wars. It was no longer a holy war."[97]

In the distinct minority, there are a few who credit Samori with laying something of the Islamic groundwork in Wasulu. One informant said, "I suppose you could say that Samori propagated Islam in this region. Samori had begun his wars as a holy war. And when he arrived in this country, he gathered certain numbers of children and entrusted them to Qur'anic schoolteachers, so that the children would learn to pray and propagate Islam."[98] Samori's Islamic legacy would also be a function of the more general impact that his conquests had in redistributing people, such as slaves, throughout the region. However, in the short term, there was little enduring enthusiasm for Islam, considering the misery and destruction caused by its most powerful proponent in the region.[99] Indeed, Islamization from above seemed to have won few willing or lasting converts.

As we have seen, there was much dissent even within Samori's inner circle. And given his lack of scholarly authority and legitimacy in clerical communities and the long historical presence of a more quietist tradition, Samori's religious justifications for conquest and enslavement likely fell on deaf ears or at least produced serious debate.[100] In another context, as John Hanson has shown, there was considerable disagreement and debate over the uses of violence in the jihad of El Hajj Umar Tal. As warfare and pillaging undermined religious justifications and generated a major "commitment crisis" in the ranks, dissenting voices grew louder and outright internal resistance spread. Just as Muslims today have been careful to distance themselves and their faith from the violence of the Samorian years, it is possible that in disrupting social life so severely, Samori's wars generated discussions among Muslims about the negative role of violence, including the violence of local war chiefs and slave raiders. A movement away from militant jihad and reassertion of the more pacific Suwarian interpretations, particularly as the region came under infidel French rule, helps to explain why slaves and others would be open to embracing Islam. However, in the immediate aftermath of war and given the freedom to choose their religious practices after years of persecution and exile, displaced peoples reembraced their traditional non-Muslim religions.[101]

CHAPTER 2

Reconstructing a Fragmented World

REFUGEES, RELIGION, AND COLONIAL ORDER, 1893–1905

In the village of Koniba-Barila, a blind and elderly Yusuf Sidibé recounted a village foundation narrative. He told how the mythic blacksmith Numu Fayiri had descended from the sky by chain (*jòlòko*), coming to earth "to shape iron," and how pastoralists from Futa Jallon later settled in the region. He talked about *fadenya*, or lineage rivalry, internal wars, and invasion by mercenaries from Segu. Then, seemingly appending to his words, he lingered for awhile on stories of refugee return before explaining how the current village was actually created during colonialism.

Yusuf's grandparents, originally from Barila, fled their village in the early 1880s and took refuge near the French post in Kati. Their intention had never been to stay long, but the wars of Samori continued, and famine was widespread.[1] A decade later, when rumors of Samori's defeat circulated, the Sidibé family headed back to their homelands, where, in the absence of cultivators, their fields had reverted to bush and been repopulated by wild animals. Their huts had collapsed and were overtaken by thickets. The landscape had changed so much that the family could barely recognize their village. And there was another surprise: refugees from a different lineage had stumbled upon their deserted village and decided to settle.

In 1896 the French visited the newly "pacified" territories, and purportedly a military official asked, "What is the name of this village?"

The refugees did not know. Then, according to village traditions, the Frenchman declared, "Okay, there is a stream [ko]. This plain must lead up to the river [ba], somewhere. There is a stream, and there is the river. Ko-ni-ba, stream and river." So Koniba it was. A couple of years later, when the Sidibé family found their village of Barila inhabited, they decided to chase the strangers away. But an elder in the family, Ali Jan, counseled, "Let them cohabitate with you. They are your brothers. You don't make war on your brother." Henceforth, the two groups of refugees would share the village, Koniba-Barila, and its lands. As Yusuf explained, the area had been so thoroughly depopulated that they needed every extra bit of labor they could find. Besides, there had been enough violence. Now it was time for peace and reconstruction.

Beyond establishing village names, the rebuilding of communities involved the reconstitution of political authorities, no easy task. Each wave of refugees brought with it competing parties who sought to establish their legitimacy by force of arms or genealogical precedent. Despite the emergence of communities of shared suffering and support and the necessity of refashioning kinship ties to accommodate refugees, precolonial systems of political authority and landlord-stranger reciprocities had been thrown into disarray. Displacement had also fostered social mixing and the breakdown of local particularities. The old order, already disintegrating on the eve of conquest, now fell apart. The postconquest world was a profoundly altered one: refugees were not traveling back in time, they were starting over in radically different political and environmental contexts.

RECLAIMING THE LAND

The landscape changed over a decade, as nature was quick to fill the void left by human absence. Mud huts, left unattended, were worn away by the rains and crumbled to the ground. The extensive webs of intervillage pathways, stretching out in every direction, were covered with grasses and shrubs. Tse-tse flies and mosquitoes enlarged their zones, carrying with them their fatal diseases. Without the everyday human effort of domesticating nature, once-settled lands became inhospitable. As informants recalled, the great bush (wulaba) was enlarged. This made reconstruction and basic agrarian tasks like farming and finding wood and water all rather labor intensive. Effectively, much of the region had been left fallow, and in the absence of hunters various wild animals (*kungofɛnw*) such as elephants, buffalos, lions, and snakes expanded their territories, making resettlement perilous as well as arduous.

Previously, hunters had been able to protect their people and crops. But village hunters died in the wars of Samori, and these crucial agents in establishing ecological control over the lands were lost.[2] The French military explorer Louis Binger noted that after hunters were killed in the wars, elephants reclaimed territory and destroyed crops, so that by 1888 nobody in the region "dared to hunt them."[3] In early census tours, colonial officials also remarked on the numerous wild animals that inhabited the region. One report stated, "Elephants literally pullulate the region, [but] nobody hunts them. . . . In certain districts you cannot go one hundred meters without seeing the paths of elephants."[4] Even while living off the land the residents began reclaiming it, which meant securing villages from wild animals, a process that took several years. As an elder in Wasulu explained, "The people were forced to be hunters because there were too many wild animals that destroyed the fields, and too many wild animals killed people here in the village." He noted that this process was partly aided by the greater stock of firearms following the wars of Samori. More men were now able to hunt individually rather than in groups using nets and spears or bow and arrow.[5]

Battling such adversaries in the bush was not just a question of action in the material world. It also required occult knowledge. One hunter's bard told the story of battles between hunters and evil beings (*fenjugu*) during this process of reconstruction. Although such tales are often mythic in nature, his account provides a useful depiction of the world of the *donso*, or hunter, and how locals may have perceived environmental threats. What immediately becomes clear in such accounts is that the bush was alive with spirits and occult forces. It was a place of considerable nyama, or energy of action, as well as dangerous beings. Doulaye Koné said, "When the wars of Samori had ended, the brave warriors were not just engaged in pursuing game. They fought against the 'shape shifters' [*mɔ̀gɔ̀ yelema*] and other spirits [*jinɛ yelema*] that attacked people in the bush and in the fields. Many hunters lost their lives during these battles. These perilous battles were not for amusement, because the animals transformed into 'earthen shape shifters' [*duguma yelema*]. When the hunter went to kill these animals, they changed into rocks, trees or dust.

[They] had to have the ability to recognize them in all of these states of change. . . . Because these 'bush dwellers' [*kungofenw*] changed into inert things, it was a question of knowing how to confront them."[6] In such circumstances, more men participated in the hunters' associations in order to acquire the requisite esoteric knowledge. Although there is no way of knowing how such activities connected to religious changes, it is likely that the wider involvement in hunters' associations and the mastering of occult skills gave a boost to bamanaya. Again, religion was not a discrete domain of activity. Hunting and farming were inseparable from more formal religious rituals.[7]

Refugee communities in exile sent scouts ahead in small groups to resettle before displacing everyone, thus minimizing the risks of mass starvation or kidnapping en route. In 1896 one colonial official observed this trend: "Scouts have returned to their villages to construct huts and reclaim the land, but the masses have stayed in Kati." Then, after the harvest, they "called the rest of the family." At first, camping out in the ruins, the refugees survived by hunting, fishing, and gathering wild fruits, roots, and plants. Then, as resettlement proceeded, more and more people returned at the beginning of each rainy season. One colonial observer noted this seasonal dimension: "The movement of refugees from the right bank appears to be momentarily stopped. This stop is caused by the difficulties of the trip in the full rainy season and also by the necessity imposed on the population to stay where they are in order to farm." While hunting and gathering, the refugees planted small fields, with the aim of using much of the harvest for seeds the following year and thus slowly rebuilding the subsistence base.[8]

According to early census reports, the population of Buguni in 1896 was measured at 13,814, while four years later it had skyrocketed to 90,096. Although these numbers are far from accurate, they do convey a sense of the scale of things. Evidence suggests that the population was out of balance in terms of gender. One report stated, "There is a shortage of women in many of the villages," while another noted, "Very few women have been able to follow the exodus." Aside from the practice of sending scouts ahead to resettle, another reason for the gender imbalance was that more women than men had been enslaved. Some of them later returned at the end of slavery, but many did not. Although statistics on births are rather unreliable for this period, it stands to reason that demographic recovery based on reproduction as opposed to return migration was slow in coming. Many of the children observed at this time were probably born in exile rather than in the war zone.[9] Beyond these generalizations, however, little else can be asserted given the paucity of sources on the demographic history.

Despite commonalities in the refugees' experiences, the impact of the Samorian wars varied. One of the most devastated regions was Wasulu, in the northwestern quadrant of the district. Further to the west, along the eastern frontier of the canton of Jallon-Fula, all of the villages were reportedly deserted. However, in the southwestern quadrant, which included the northern parts of Gwanan, the country was described as "less ruined and rather less deserted than that of Basidibé."[10] Cattle and other livestock, a rarity at this time, were even observed in Gwanan, the only kafo with a Muslim chief, Farabalay Jakité, who had allied with Samori. Many villages in this region had submitted to Samori and had been spared the worst of the warfare and pillaging. From Koloni to Buguni was the large canton of Cémala, which had "not suffered, or very little, the wars of Samori." It was situated along the Baoulé River corridor, just across the river from Gwanan, and had remained loyal to Samori during the revolt of 1887–88. Although Cémala resisted the forced relocations of 1893 and had occasionally pillaged Samori's millet caravans during times of famine, the Jula of Garalo were early collaborators with Samori and hence preserved the peace in their kafo.[11]

In the northeastern quadrant, Banan was "horribly ravaged by Samori and abandoned during a lapse of time." For three years, colonial officials saw almost nobody, except for a few people "hiding in fear, here and there, in the high grasses that surround their temporary habitations." According to colonial officials, the most devastated region in the district was the southeastern quadrant, which had served as the buffer zone and battleground between Samori and Tieba. It was completely denuded of resources and people. There were entire cantons "without a single sheep," notably Fulala, which was described as "the poorest canton in the district and . . . the most devastated." One official reported on the plight of Fulala: "The natives are almost all in a state of misery impossible to describe; the great majority do not wear any clothes. . . . Everyone wears a loincloth or a simple scrap of cloth that covers their buttocks. Other than clothing, the huts are empty, they hardly have cooking utensils. It is complete misery."

The subsistence base in Fulala had been stretched to the breaking point, as famine and disease stalked the land. This was exacerbated by the constant influx of refugees, which strained the region's food security. But through it all communities continued to accommodate strangers. What brought refugees back to their homelands was "the love of their native soil."[12]

THE UNSTABLE COLONIAL FRONTIER

In 1893 Lieut. Col. Eugene Bonnier, a native of French Reunion and just returning from military missions in French Indochina, was instructed by the outgoing *commandant-supérieur* of the Sudan, Louis Archinard, to form an expeditionary force and extend the military frontier south of the Niger River. Then, within days of defeating the Samorian forces and establishing a garrisoned post, he dashed off to conquer Timbuktu, where he would die in a Tuareg ambush.[13] From the post in Buguni, the colonial frontier, or the zone of occupation, as officials called it, expanded slowly over the next decade, as refugees returned from exile and commercial avenues opened up. Famine was still widespread, though, and the hardships far from over. The modest policy toward refugee repatriation aimed simply at repopulating villages along the main road from Bamako and creating a corridor of settlements that could be used as local labor reservoirs for building the new colonial infrastructure. Most of the refugees moved freely, but some were sequestered in refugee centers under French control or forcibly settled in roadside village conglomerations. Villages that had been loyal to Samori were relocated, consolidated, and kept under surveillance by the administration. Most villages had been reduced to ruins, and many were in such a state of destruction and "filled with rotting corpses" that they had to be abandoned. Over time, officials conducted tours further out from Buguni, holding palavers and patrolling the trade routes. When refugees were encountered searching for their homelands, they were intercepted and sent to the post. Everyday, officials reported large numbers of arrivals, but many were quick to move on, venturing out beyond the sphere of French protection.[14]

French rule was aimed not at altruistically freeing the people from Samori but at establishing a colony. From the beginning it sought to impose order by resettling people as hastily as possible, while preventing excessive reshuffling and armed rebellion. In order to do so, populations had to be made legible to the colonial state, that is, settled in easy-to-find places for purposes of tax collection, census taking, labor recruitment, and punitive operations.[15] As the colonial frontier expanded, expeditions were sent out to "bring back to their villages of origin populations taking refuge in other districts." This task was delegated to newly appointed village chiefs who traveled around informing other chiefs in exile that they could return. Strict instructions were given to prohibit refugees from "dispersing into the bush [and] hiding with the goal of escaping the authority of their village chiefs and taxes." The administration took its first steps in expanding administrative control beyond its immediate surroundings, while allowing the resumption of commerce. The French also set up an informal local intelligence service aided by "secret village agents" who patrolled key routes and river crossings, keeping an eye on the goods and traders passing through the district.[16]

Soon refugees were coming back from every direction, the largest numbers returning from Bamako, Segu, and villages in northern Ivory Coast. The majority of the returnees never visited the French post, spurring colonial officials to send out political agents to collect information on their whereabouts. Warfare and pillaging were still widespread. Above all, the kafo of Niené was in a desperate situation. Many of its villages had been uninhabited since the clashes along the Bagoé River. Then, after 1888, with the withdrawal of Samori's forces, Kenedugu extended its sphere of control, pillaging Niené for slaves. By 1894 Samori had reinvaded the region from his new base in northern Ivory Coast, thus effectively forcing the refugees to flee north or risk capture. Samori and Babemba, the new king of Sikasso, then contended for hegemony in the region, battling over the remaining resources in the no-man's land. Colonial officials noted that the region had been "transformed into a hunting grounds" for slaves, grain, and livestock. By the dry season of 1896, all the villages within a twenty-five-kilometer radius had been deserted, "most of the inhabitants having disappeared, either taken by the cavalry of Babemba, and the rest fleeing as refugees." As the rains came and people cautiously began farming, warrior bands from Sikasso attacked Senufo villages around Tiongi and Tengrela.[17] Further to the south, nine years had passed since the refugees had fled Fulala and Céndugu. Now their safe haven in Maàle was also under attack. According to oral accounts, Samori cordoned off the village, maintaining a state of siege until the village capitulated. Most people ended up being enslaved or massacred.[18]

In early 1898 the French conquest armies reached Sikasso and battered the renowned fortress with artillery, sending the city into disarray. People tried to flee, but many were captured and sold into slavery. Everyone in the colonial army joined in the pillaging. Yusuf Sidibé told of how his grandfather was rewarded for serving as a soldier in the siege of Sikasso: "My grandfather, Jebi Missa, encountered the French and pawned himself to them. . . . He helped the French demolish the *tata* of Sikasso and that was why he was rewarded and our house became filled with slaves."[19] In the aftermath of Sikasso's fall, refugees and runaway slaves from Sikasso streamed westward back to their homes. Soon after, once Samori was captured in 1898, further waves of refugees fled his crumbling empire. Many others returned years later, often intermingling with freed slaves.[20]

When the new governor of the French Sudan, Albert Grodet, issued decrees prohibiting the slave trade in 1894, the administration in Buguni began stopping trade caravans and confiscating slaves. As the decrees were posted throughout the colony, slaves began fleeing their masters. By 1895 many runaways were reportedly escaping from slave markets across the Sudan, seeking refuge at French posts, in the so-called liberty villages.[21] One such liberty village was established in Buguni in May of 1894, and colonial documents reveal that there was a steady stream of runaway slaves passing through over the next decade, seeking certificates of freedom. While residing at the French post, they provided labor for the colonial administration. Oftentimes men would park their families in the liberty village temporarily as they built up their resource base. Thus, it served as a halfway house and staging ground for resettlement.[22] From the south, runaway slaves were coming from Ivory Coast, where abolition was accomplished through the exigencies of military rule. When slave caravans were intercepted, the slaves were liberated on the spot and recruited as military porters. Further to the north, runaway slaves fled localities in the Sahel and along the Niger River, blending in with the groups of refugees heading south. This process would only accelerate after legal abolition.[23]

Buguni was no promised land. Refugees and runaway slaves were often reenslaved en route or kidnapped upon arriving in their homelands. Villages were split along partisan lines, resulting in local wars of enslavement. As one official reported, "In the south, and the southwest, many regions escape our actions because of their remoteness. Almost every-where the population is divided between partisans. . . . The result of these wars is the removal of a large part of the population that slave raiders lead away as slaves."[24] Indeed, as the French were expanding southward, effectively blocking Samori's access to northern markets, slaves were being sent south. Samori supplied Baoulé traders with slaves on "a mas-sive scale." The price of slaves was dropping so low and the flood of cap-tives was so great that virtually every Baoulé household was able to obtain them. Toward the end of Samori's reign, his forces were selling slaves for chickens, goats, yams, and manioc just to stave off starvation. These slaves usually worked in the goldmines, labored in cotton textile produc-tion, served as porters, or produced palm wine, rubber, yams, and other foodstuffs.[25]

The capture of Samori did not end the slave trade or the dangers of being enslaved. In the immediate postconquest years, people were moving about precariously in a landscape decimated by war. Given the shortage of able-bodied laborers, many villagers resorted to kidnapping. Women were especially valued as agricultural and domestic workers and as wives and mothers. As local slave raiders entered the fray, the regional clandestine slave trade continued for many years. One elder recounted how people were kidnapped from their fields as they worked: "After the French first arrived, people were still afraid to be alone in the fields because warfare continued. One could come and take you away and bring you far away from your field, to go and sell you. At this time, people 'fed themselves' off other people. They began enslaving each other to survive. Solomanin-Jan, who was in Kola at this time, his father apparently had just gone out to go cut and harvest his millet when he was enslaved."[26]

Enslavement was opportunistic. Small bands of raiders traveled around kidnapping women, children, isolated farmers, and anyone they encountered. As late as 1900 one official stated, "The countries ravaged by Samori are in effect currently traversed by a multitude of natives, sort of pirates of the bush."[27] Fugitive slaves escaping Samorian control were intercepted by marauders, while refugees dying of hunger were purchased in the markets "for a cheap price."[28] Villages that resorted to kidnapping to obtain labor supplies even preyed upon their neighbors, as one elder recalled: "At this time, it was not only foreigners who committed these acts, sometimes it was your nearby neighbors who did. The people were

constantly kidnapping each other."²⁹ Broadly, during the period of instabil-
ity following conquest, while the French military sought to end the slave
trade, small-scale enslavement and kidnapping continued throughout the
region. Even so, from the earliest years the administration began laying
the groundwork for colonial rule.

JÒNYÀJÙRU: PAX GALLICA AND COERCED GRATITUDE

In *L'Étrange destin de Wangrin*, Amadou Hampaté Bâ recounts the story
of a wily colonial interpreter named Wangrin, hailing from the district of
Buguni.³⁰ In telling how Wangrin became part of the colonial administration, Bâ notes the incursions of Samori that led many people to accept the
Pax Gallica: "His country was the sad arena where conquering Yorsam
[Samori], who sought to carve an empire for himself by fighting against
Nubigu [Buguni], engaged in lengthy conflicts, waging war at the same
time against the French so as to protect the domains he had already
conquered. The senseless atrocities inflicted by Yorsam encouraged the
people of Nubigu to welcome the French conquerors with open arms."³¹
As Bâ suggests, Buguni was one of the regions that suffered most heavily
under Samori, a fact that led many people to initially embrace the French.

After conquest, ritual idioms expressing notions of protection and
dependency were employed in colonial encounters; chiefs sent emissaries
to greet the French commandant and ask for "friendship and protection in
the fear of being attacked by Samori." In 1894 colonial officials confidently
stated that inhabitants were grateful for their liberation from the clutches
of Samori. Five years later, an official stated, "They appear in general to
be grateful toward the whites for having saved them from Babemba and
Samori."³² Namakoro Bamba, who had performed forced labor and was not
an apologist for colonialism, tried to explain the acceptance of French rule:
"It was the French that came and stopped Samori, this bloodthirsty king.
You see why we had a lot of respect for the French at this time? We no
longer heard the firing of guns. The work of Samori had been killing,
but the French stopped him and said that they did not permit anymore
murdering of people. . . . That is why we paid homage to the French and
stayed behind the French."³³

The Bamanankan term often used for colonialism, *jònyàjùru*, literally
means the rope or debt of slavery, suggesting that people became the slaves
of the French, to whom they owed their lives for the defeat of Samori. No

one could have predicted what colonial rule would become, with forced labor, military service, and so forth. But the reality that the French had replaced Samori as the new overlord eventually became clear. At first, villagers gave gifts as symbols of gratitude, usually chickens or eggs, and the gifts evolved into forms of tribute, like the containers of millet and honey (*disongo*) they had given to the rulers of Segu in the mid-nineteenth century. Then tribute became taxes, or the appropriately named *nisòngò* (soul price). As Solo Sanogo noted, "They imposed *nisòngò* on our people. They called it the price of one's soul because when the French had come and saved us from the other invaders, we owed them our lives."[34] Despite the crushing poverty of refugees, the administration started levying a head tax of one franc in 1895. Then, in the following year, the tax was increased to two francs, and taxes would increase incrementally over the next several years.[35]

To ensure that taxes were paid and that the debt was continually acknowledged, colonial officials held palavers, reminding the people of how they had been saved from Samori's bloodletting wars. For example, in 1902 an official repeated a typical refrain: "The natives are beginning to understand the benefits of our civilization, in all parts of the district, and above all from the point of view of security, because the memory of the numerous exactions committed by Samori and Babemba is far from extinguished from their memory." The coerced gratitude served the immediate needs of colonialism. In the "moral memory," Samori was kept alive at the local level; administrators demonized his name in justifying the colonial project. It became part of the colonial ideological apparatus, a means of establishing legitimacy and hegemony.[36]

In a more practical way, chiefs who had collaborated with Samori were arrested and kept under house arrest in Buguni. For example, Moriba Diakité, a Samori loyalist whose father had been the chief of Banimonotie, was imprisoned. Similarly, in the canton of Kurulamini, Karamògò Samaké, a Muslim who had served in Samori's army, was, like others, divested of his power and imprisoned.[37] The rare exception was in the canton of Gwanan, where the administration decided to ignore the Samorian past of Farabalay Diakité and restored him to power. Described as a Muslim marabout of the Qadiriyya brotherhood, he was considered an excellent chief.[38] In cantons that already had Muslim chiefs, the administration was undoubtedly more interested in effective governance than in disrupting religious life.

FORGING POLITICAL ORDER

Following Richard Roberts, one might think about how "landscapes of power" in early colonial Africa were highly variegated over space and across the social field, and how "established forms of power and authority were often eroded, only to be replaced by new or reconstituted forms." In such circumstances, African chiefs, functionaries, traders, and peasants continually probed and tested the limits of colonial power, which was structured around both precolonial and French political institutions. But also, depending on geographical location—whether remote rural hamlets, isolated cantons, roadside villages, market towns, or the district capital— the effects of colonialism could be quite uneven spatially.[39]

As French officials rarely set foot in most villages, colonial encounters usually took place in the administrative capital or canton capitals. Yet even more important than these colonial contact zones were the indigenous agents, such as canton chiefs, village chiefs, district guards, soldiers, interpreters, canton representatives, and other civil servants, who mediated the encounters. As scholars have noted, indigenous agents of colonial rule were not simply collaborators, in the sense of being mimics mirroring the interests of French officials. Rather, they represented a complex nexus of intersecting and diverging interests. In mediating colonial encounters and transactions, they gathered considerable power and resources in their hands, capital which could be redistributed or concentrated according to both indigenous and colonial logics. And since the number of European personnel was always rather small and their turnover rapid, the everyday and local business of empire was largely the work of these political figures. French commandants came and went, but chiefs and other intermediaries remained in place for decades.[40]

The colonial administration based its territorial organization on the French model of departments. But it also parasitically followed the imperial contours of the Samorian state, while deriving cantons from precolonial kafow. In a sense, French empire was built on top of previous empires.[41] But where Samori's power had been weak or where precolonial kafow had not existed, disparate villages were lumped together around the nearest trade town with the canton taking the name of its nominal capital. In some cases, the capital rotated between key villages in a sort of power-sharing agreement. But generally, clusters of villages and prior networks of alliances were cobbled together into units based on geographical and administrative conve-

nience. Given the French concern to appoint legitimate canton chiefs, colonialism in Buguni was in certain ways a form of indirect rule. As in other
colonial settings, the administration was cost averse and chronically short
of manpower and therefore sought to appropriate indigenous institutions.
In practice, the local functioning of empire warranted frequent departures
from the ideal, often to compensate for the state's basic weakness.[42]

Like any institution, the chieftaincy was constantly evolving. To begin,
chiefs of noble lineage were difficult to identify, either because there had
never been one or because, given the prevailing war-based nature of the
previous system, the position was thoroughly contested. Rarely did canton chiefs actually possess all the desired qualities, such as uncontested
legitimacy, nobility, French literacy, and efficiency.[43] In any case, after conquest, canton chiefs were appointed in an ad hoc manner and frequently
dismissed as more legitimate or effective intermediaries emerged. Early
colonial personnel files for the canton chieftaincy are rather scant on
detail, at least until 1903, when the colonial legal system was promulgated
and considerable effort was invested in recording and codifying customary law.[44] Therefore, most of the political wrangling from 1893 to 1903
was never recorded. In Fulala, however, chieftaincy genealogies provide a
small glimpse of how things may have played out. According to colonial
documents, Fabala Suntura was the first official canton chief.[45]
However, Fabala had not been the first canton chief. Informants said the
first chief was a man named Joba N'Piyé, who was appointed as an
interim. Although he was not from the Suntura ruling lineage in Fulala,
he was put in charge temporarily until an appropriate elder could be nom-
inated. Then, when more refugees returned, "Joba N'Piyé called a meeting
with the Commandant from Buguni. He said to them, 'The French came
to our country when the war decimated our lands. This white man gave
me the power. But I do not want the power, either today or tomorrow.
Give the power to whomever you wish. I'm releasing the power from my
hands.' The elders consulted together and said, 'The oldest among us now
is Fabala.' That was how he was elected as the first canton chief."[46] While
Fabala was seemingly the right choice, given his seniority and lineage, the
administration was largely dissatisfied with his performance. Later, he
was described as being a powerless chief who, at eighty years of age, was
too weak to perform his job and entirely uninterested in clearing the bush
pathways or looking after the rubber plantations.[47]

During the immediate postconquest years, the French depended heavily on colonial soldiers and numerous political agents to run things. This newfound power was not only bequeathed to Africans from above. In many cases, as new openings and opportunities emerged, various intermediaries slipped into power vacuums and used the colonial state to increase their power and wealth.[48] Sometimes the French were duped, as the classic story of Wangrin suggests, and indeed the administration frequently caught and punished individuals who abused their authority. For example, in 1897 one of the most powerful political agents in the district of Buguni, Nonbougare Soumasurou, used his position to swindle people and was convicted of abuse of power, abuse of confidence, engaging in the slave trade, and treason. He was sentenced to death. Often such opportunities for accumulating wealth were found in the colonial frontier regions. In one representative case from 1898, a former *tirailleur* (African colonial soldier) tricked villagers in a village at the outer limits of the district into handing over their slaves, women, and livestock, but he was ultimately arrested and executed when a village chief reported the incident to the administration. Two years later, a colonial administrator reported on another case involving a tirailleur and remarked that such instances were not isolated.[49]

The authority of village chiefs was constantly being undercut by tirailleurs who used their power to wrench exactions from communities, a theme that would recur frequently over the span of colonial rule. The administration often found itself in a double bind, needing legitimate authorities, who were usually elderly, but also literate, competent civil servants. One official wrote as follows about the problems in governance: "The attitude of the chiefs is generally bad owing to their old age, which prevents them from assimilating our way of doing things, and their infirmity, which forbids them from traveling. On one hand, they do not know their cantons and are not obeyed there because they cannot show any authority. On the other hand, they are unable to come to Buguni, so therefore they do not know us." Many of the elderly chiefs were blind or senile, spurring officials to suggest that they be replaced by more competent leaders or at least be aided by their sons. In such cases, the elderly chief would remain merely as a symbolic figure while his son or nephew, as a sort of deputy or representative (*lasigiden*), functioned as the actual day-to-day local administrator.[50]

Across French West Africa, the sons of chiefs were commonly sent to French primary schools in order to learn the requisite skills for mediating colonial encounters. However, it was not until 1903 that the governor general of French West Africa, Ernest Roume, created a federal school system aimed at providing education for African subjects. As Alice Conklin has explained, although Roume had initially rejected assimilation of Africans into Frenchmen, viewing it as politically dangerous, he agreed to adapt schools to local conditions. Rural primary schools offered short courses of study focusing on French language, reading, writing, arithmetic, and vocational training in modern farming techniques, that is, an education designed to produce a class of literate auxiliary personnel to serve the needs of the administration.[51] From 1895 on, students had been sent from Buguni to study at the School for the Sons of Chiefs in Kayes, a policy perhaps not unlike Samori's sequestering of chiefs' sons in Qur'anic schools. But the numbers remained small. In 1903 the first French school in Buguni had only twelve full-time students. Unlike other parts of colonial Africa, Buguni had no missionary presence to play a role in education.[52]

In time the French set about codifying and reinforcing the chieftaincy, handing unprecedented amounts of power to colonial intermediaries. Among decentralized societies this concentration of power in the hands of one person was antithetical to local notions of governance and in certain contexts had the potential to incite rebellion. Yet despite fears of unrest, the district of Buguni remained remarkably peaceful during the entire colonial period. Still, there were routine acts of indiscipline, chronic tax evasion, and census dodging. The northern province of Banan was notorious for this sort of everyday resistance. Whenever political agents, colonial officials, or guards were sent out to collect taxes or administer justice, the entire population fled into the forest. The resistors were then arrested and imprisoned until their taxes were paid. Banan also became a refuge for "pillagers, brigands and former slave raiders that used the remoteness from the post to commit all sorts of crimes as they almost totally escape surveillance." Even chiefs who were supported by the colonial administration were themselves terrorized by the brigands.[53] Slowly, these lawless pockets of non–state space, or "zones of refuge," would be absorbed more completely into the administered and tax-paying "fiscal population."[54] The colonial state would remain rather weak nevertheless, concentrating most of its power along major transportation arteries and at resource catchment sites. In this respect, power was much more "arterial" than "capillary," although even in rural areas, where colonial rule was crudely deployed and incomplete, new commodity markets and commercial networks were facilitating the wider diffusion of Jula traders and spurring mobility.[55]

RUBBER, MOBILITY, AND THE RURAL EXPANSION OF MUSLIM TRADE NETWORKS

Within the span of a decade after conquest, the rubber trade effectively integrated many rural households into the world economy as rubber producers. And over the ensuing half century, the district of Buguni slowly shifted from being a producer of "foraged" crops, such as slaves, gold, and rubber, to that of agricultural crops.[56] In the short term, however, the Pax Gallica enabled merchants to widen their spheres of economic activity, drawing more villages into regional trade and triggering greater mobility. As one official reported, the colonial economy was forcing "natives to move about."[57] Displaced peoples tapped into the rubber trade as an early source of income, which helped considerably in the rebuilding process, especially as fields had become overgrown with bush. Indeed, because there were few agricultural inputs aside from labor, rubber collecting rewarded mobility and was "particularly attractive to people in transit."[58]

Until the worldwide price crash of 1913, most people paid their taxes by selling rubber collected from vines. For refugees, who lacked seed and special tools to grow cash crops, rubber served as an accessible foraged crop that was converted quickly into capital. Recently, scholars have drawn more attention to local initiative in producing cash crops, such as peanuts, cocoa, and gold.[59] In neighboring French Guinea, for example, Emily Osborn has examined the decisive role played by Jula traders in the growth of the rubber market. Osborn shows how, long before French commercial houses entered the business in 1889, Jula traders were buying rubber in the interior and transporting it to Freetown, Sierra Leone. Eventually, the colonial state intervened more directly, as it sought to redirect the rubber trade to Conakry, building a railroad and recruiting forced laborers to accomplish this task.[60] By contrast, the administration in Buguni was much more instrumental in initially starting the rubber trade in a region where the inhabitants had never exploited the product. Still, the rubber trade was comparatively slow to develop, largely owing to the unstable nature of the district and its great distance from coastal port towns. The administration had targeted rubber as early as 1894, and peasants were reportedly being encouraged to seek out rubber sources.[61] Finally, a decade after the French post was established, the commandant could state, "The district, which until now was completely disinterested in this harvest, is now producing [rubber] in strong quantities, such that merchants are coming to Buguni to buy this product."[62]

Generally, peasants carried their rubber directly to the administrative headquarters, where French buyers facilitated transactions. Depending on where a village was located, the round trip could take a couple of weeks or more. While some villages were lucky to find rubber vines near at hand, most peasants had to travel extensively in search of the commodity. As in other regions, in Buguni the rubber frontier was always moving; as vines became depleted, the collection zone expanded. Colonial officials were aware of this process and encouraged people to cultivate rubber vines near their homes. In fact, the earliest colonial interventions into local farming practices constituted efforts to curb the practice of dry-season burning in order to protect rubber vines.[63] In 1900 a decree was signed in the interest of protecting the forests from overexploitation, which extended certain forest laws stipulating that rubber harvesting should be done in a manner that did not destroy the vines.[64] It is impossible to know the extent of enforcement of such forest laws or the precise effects such interventions had on indigenous farming practices or rural livelihoods. But one report did suggest that some level of coercion was involved: "The natives burn almost all over, without caring about the damage. . . . [It] will be necessary to send, without delay, a district guard or at least a political agent, to spend some time in each canton that produces rubber with the mission of forcing the natives to clear the land around each vine to protect it from burning, and to notify the Commandant of all the village chiefs who do not conform to the instructions."[65]

Although the wild rubber trade would never approach the productivity or brutality seen in the Congo under King Leopold or in French Equatorial Africa, the region finally seemed to be producing something of value. The French Sudan had been an economic backwater until the arrival of the railway line from Kayes in 1904, which effectively "grafted a colonial layer" onto the regional economy. From this point on, there were more aggressive efforts to channel rubber toward Bamako. By 1908 rubber already accounted for over 90 percent of the total export value from the French Sudan.[66] Eventually, European traders set up shop in Buguni with the aim of tapping into the lucrative trade. Concessions of land were granted for the building of stores, and the colonial administration gave French traders certain buying advantages. Merchants were also expanding their operations by opening small collection sites dispersed along the trade routes. Despite the administration's efforts, much of the product ended up being sold to Muslim traders such as the Jula, Soninke, and Kooroko, who advanced merchandise on credit to village and canton chiefs. Many of these traders came from Guinea, especially Kankan, where ties to the coast provided easy access to manufactured wares circulating in the world economy. But a few, such as the Kooroko, were indigenous traders. Former soldiers and porters traveled from Siguiri and Kankan to remote villages to buy rubber, outmaneuvering European rubber traders based in Buguni and Sikasso. To level the playing field, colonial soldiers were occasionally sent out to arrest Muslim traders for not having permits. Furthermore, customs posts along the borders with Guinea and Ivory Coast were set up to monitor cross-border transactions.[67]

To encourage trade and establish greater control over the territory, the French paid attention to the construction and maintenance of roads, paths, and bridges. From the early colonial period, the creation of a better system of roads, albeit built with forced labor, was viewed as part of the humanitarian wing of the civilizing mission. Eventually, as a wider system of roads and footpaths took form, Muslim traders began visiting more remote localities, and more villages were drawn into the rubber trade.[68] Finally, local transportation arteries were being opened for traders to "infiltrate throughout the region and pass from village to village plying their merchandise, exciting the desire of the population." Officials hoped that such merchandise, "glittering under the eyes of natives," would ignite new consumption habits, resulting in the production of more agricultural surplus. Aside from local paths connecting villages to trade towns, a main road from Bamako to Buguni was completed, one that would allow travel by automobile.[69] Years later an inspector sent out to survey the new 139-kilometer road connecting Buguni to Tengrela reported that the major roads would also "serve as the base and means of control" over the region.[70] The colonial administration was seeking to ensure their ability to broadcast power effectively in the event of a revolt, particularly as tensions mounted in Europe and the specter of Pan-Islamism appeared on the horizon.

COLONIALISM AND THE MUSLIM FRONTIER

In the colonial imagination, the district of Buguni occupied a kind of frontier zone separating the wider world of Islam from regions hitherto nominally fetishist. In some ways this frontier was real, in that there were religious contact zones. But for some colonial observers the zone was posited more as a static boundary.[71] Maurice Delafosse, for example, emphasized how after Islam's dramatic march in the nineteenth century, the "conquering faith" was now stationary, halted by French rule. He argued that with the disappearance of Muslim states, the rationale for conversion had vanished overnight: "The animist peoples, feeling that their conversion to Islam—which was a political necessity in the empires whose chief was Muslim—no longer brings them any advantage, and benefit from what our protection extends equally to all in remaining faithful to their ancestral religions."[72] Regardless of whether or not the frontier was moving, it represented an important and recurring trope that informed the practices of local administrators. The colonial ethnography of Islam and indigenous religious life was deeply politicized.

In an important colony-wide circular, Governor General Roume characterized Muslim proselytization efforts as a "constant threat to the tranquility of our domination."[73] Thus the spread of Islam and the potential political role it might play would become a central focus of the colonial administration. This is not to say that views of Islam in French colonial imaginaries were monolithic or static. In fact, during the early years of colonial rule, administrators and scholars in North and West Africa often held quite ambivalent views on Islam and learned and adjusted as they muddled their way through.[74] Many influential observers and policymakers even held favorable opinions of Islam. For example, Binger, who, as we have seen, witnessed the wars of Samori in southern French Sudan, nevertheless espoused a favorable, or at least not an overtly hostile, view of Islam. Later, as the director of the Africa Department of the Colonial Ministry, he advocated for a policy of neutrality vis-à-vis Islam, arguing that allowing intolerance and persecution of Muslims to guide colonial decisions would result in failure. Alfred Le Chatelier, who produced the most important early study of Islam in West Africa, also tended to see Muslims as superior to fetishists and recommended forming strong alliances with Muslim notables. In any case, within the district of Buguni, with its recent history of campaigns against Samori, French military officials initially viewed Islam as a threat. District guards routinely detained and imprisoned Muslim traders, usually for illicit involvement in the slave trade. Every appearance of a marabout in the district produced flurries of paranoid reporting.[75]

At the same time, key Muslim notables in Jula trade towns sent emissaries asking for friendship. For example, Mady Sylla, chief of Bole, and the marabout Almamy Sylla came "declaring their good intentions regarding the French and bringing a chicken as a gift." The thawing of relations owed something to the fact that many of the first interpreters and political agents, such as Abdulaye Traore from Bamako, were Muslim. For the French, Muslim traders were also an important source of information. They brought back intelligence on various economic and political developments, and, as the administration discovered, the Jula had not all been uniformly loyal to Samori.[76] Jula traders and clerics seem to have accepted French rule, perhaps seeing the benefits of peace and regional security after the Samorian wars had so disrupted commerce. Indeed, as Robert Launay has noted, acceptance of infidels as temporal rulers was nothing new. Drawing on the Suwarian tradition and their long history of adapting to non-Muslim rule, the Jula developed a "peaceful modus vivendi" with the French administration and just went about their business. From their perspective, free circulation simply enabled the further extension of Muslim influence into the bush.[77]

The atmosphere of peaceful cooperation, however, was occasionally shaken by evidence of potential rebellion. For example, the grand marabout of nearby Sambatiguila, Konya Mambi, stridently opposed colonialism. When he was invited to meet with the French envoy, apparently unnerved about the stopping of caravans and confiscation of slaves, he sent his griot to fulminate against the new imperialists: "The whites are our enemy, they are coming to pillage us. . . . We do not want them to come here among us, we will chase them away like dogs."[78] Certainly, in the spotty reporting on postconquest relations, these words, coming from an ardent supporter of Samori, represented a rare voice of dissent in the region. Yet it was evidence enough to administrators of what Muslims might really be thinking. Baseless or not, there were recurring anxieties about fifth-column Muslim threats.

In the short term, there was nothing to suggest an anticolonial jihad was brewing. And there were few signs of Islamization. Colonial reports on the spread of Islam were based on two specific indices: the number and size of Qur'anic schools and the presence of influential marabouts. Officials were looking for identifiable leaders who might incite a rebellion and for institutional structures that might serve as sites of dissidence. The number of Qur'anic schools was very small and would remain so throughout the early colonial period. In 1899 there were only three such schools in the entire district; the largest Muslim community was in the Jula town of Garalo, which boasted a mosque and an imam literate in Arabic. Six years later, there were four schools, including one in the administrative capital of Buguni, which had only nine students. Outside of these Muslim communities in roadside trade towns, the majority of the population was described as Bambara fetishists. Indeed, Muslims were "drowned in a crowd of fetishists" and therefore enjoyed "little success in proselytization."[79]

Some administrators argued that Islam was in regression in the region. Typically, conversion was viewed as a byproduct of violence. The Religion of the Sword thesis, which had been around since at least the time of the Crusades and had been reinvigorated during the nineteenth century as modern European imperialism in Muslim lands began, was the most widespread explanation for the spread of Islam.[80] It seemed to fit with the image of Samori as a bloodthirsty conquering warrior who had left no legacy, only a bad memory. Fittingly, officials asserted that Africans were instinctively resistant to Islam. One reason was their love of dòlò, or millet beer, and another was their worship of fetishes. The administration championed these beer-drinking cultivators for their robust attachment to a practice that did not "accord well with the principals of Islam." The fermented beverage served to inoculate people against the perceived contagion of Islam. But officials also frequently complained about the drunkenness of chiefs and the fact that people wasted their surplus grain on "stupefying themselves with dòlò." Colonial officials saw dòlò as a superficial luxury whose overuse could lead to social anomie and the "plague of alcoholism." Although certainly attuned to the place of wine in the local cultures of France, colonial officials could not appreciate the complex social role of dòlò in African ritual life. Rather, they saw it in relation to other concerns, such as assuring that peasants paid their taxes, conserved enough grain to plant the following year, and did not backslide into unruly, out-of-control behavior.[81] Still, dòlò indexed fetishism in the colonial mind, and it was a hedge against the spread of Islam.

Although the administration repeated its mantra of fetishist imper-meability, Muslim holy men were beginning to operate as purveyors of religious services and amulets in rural areas. Most of these holy men were Sufis, according to an early report on Islam in Buguni. However, officials struggled to see emergent forms of rural Islam, in which the typical traits, institutions, and authority figures were largely absent.[82] In 1899 one report on Buguni described how rural Sufis were roughly Qadiri and how they showed tolerance, and an interest in charity. But they were Sufis who had no zâwiya (Sufi lodge) or tombs of venerated saints, and they lacked direct connection to a muqaddam (regional Sufi deputy tasked with initiating people into the order). Furthermore, none of the marabouts in the district had done the hajj, few of them had knowledge of Arabic, and they did not make tours to collect hadîya (gifts).[83] Nevertheless, there is evidence that Muslim holy men were expanding their influence. In 1905 most marabouts, or moriw in Bamanankan, were reportedly natives of the district who farmed for a living. But these preacher-farmers were precisely the kind of grass-roots religious figures that would later have success in rural areas.[84] While perhaps unsuccessful in converting people, they were certainly having an influence on religious life. In the decade after Samori's defeat and the beginnings of colonial rule, the resistant "pure fetishists" were finding something useful in the services being offered by more peaceful and tolerant holy men. One official reported as follows:

> The population of the district includes the Bambara and the Wasulunké, in general all fetishists. The efforts by the marabouts to convert them to the religion of Muhammad have had few results until today. . . . One could say that the inhabitants of the district are pure fetishists. Superstitious to the excess; like all the blacks elsewhere, they believe in good or bad spirits, in sorcerers, and they cover themselves with amulets for protection against numerous evils. . . . They do not believe in any divinity and for them after death it all ends. But even as fetishists, they get aid from marabouts when they are sick, and they buy amulets from them to protect against new afflictions.[85]

Even though people were not necessarily "doing Salam" or publicly displaying their Muslim faith, there was growing acceptance of magical Sufi practices known as moriya in addressing such concerns as the lack of rain, crop failure, illness, and infant mortality. As we have seen, amulets and power objects were already part of bamana material culture; and there were ritual specialists, such as blacksmiths, who were experts in their fabrication. Thus, moriya did not represent a major conceptual break. But in the wake of the Samorian wars, owing to the shortage of ritual specialists, local practitioners of moriya were playing a role in the religious reconstitution of communities.

BAMANAYA, TRANSLOCALISM, AND COLONIAL ORDER

As I stated earlier, the lack of solid baselines from which to measure religious change makes it rather difficult to track shifts in bamanaya. In contrast to the early colonial surveillance of Islam, there was little comparable effort to produce intelligence on fetishist notables. Correspondingly, the result has been that scholarship on French policy toward non-Muslims has been rather slow in developing. Later, with the wider shift to policies of association, in seeking to preserve and reinforce traditional authority structures the colonial state expended considerable energy on collecting information on subjects like the "Bambara religion."[86] In any case, even with the crucial complement of oral traditions, the gaps in the evidentiary base leave one with only provisional sketches of the religious landscape. Keeping this caveat in mind, I want to examine the resurgence of bamanaya and the expansion of translocal religious networks in the postconquest era.

In the wake of war and dislocation, the religious habitus integrated new historical experiences, events, and ideas into its local reproduction. These experiences included violence, enslavement, and mass displacement, which resulted in widespread social mixing. Formerly, as one informant explained, "each region or ethnicity [siya] had its tribal scars [fonw], and the people were recognized by their scars."[87] These embodied markers of identity represented local differences in cultural practice, language, social affiliation, and political belonging. However, after war and years of exile, scarification and other distinctions encoded in social practice lost their meaning. As another elder noted, "People from different regions were forced to mix with those of other regions."[88] The result was a breakdown of local particularities. Older distinctions, signified by language and family clan names and often representing ecological and territorial boundaries, eroded. Social mixing in connection with the absence of women resulted in the weakening of rules governing marriage practices. In many villages, the lack of women forced people to transgress traditional taboos on inter-marriage, such as the restrictions on marriage between people of caste and nobles. When asked when and how people began intermarrying, Broulaye Doumbia explained, "The changes that brought about this intermarriage were caused by the fact that there were no people around after the wars of Samori. War had come and dispersed the people . . . and cut the men away from their women."[89] The breakdown of normative social rules govern-ing marriage had long-term cultural consequences. As households and communities accommodated cultural others, social rules and norms were reconfigured. And the integration of stranger women meant that the local habitus, in particular the upbringing of children, would be inflected with new cultural ideas and patterns of everyday life.

Despite the changing markers of localism, returnees sought to revive bamanaya. As one elder in Wasulu explained, "These people were not big innovators. They wanted to simply preserve their traditional values that they had been forced to leave behind them. . . . When the people came back, they came back to reclaim their customary practices, they did not want to modify them."[90] Indeed, following years of violent imposition of Samori's religious policies, there was a widespread resurgence of indigenous practices. One informant summed up as follows: "At the end of conquest, the people regrouped themselves, and as a result bamanaya was practiced freely among the populations according to each person's convic-tions. Those who had been forced by Samori to convert and abandon their power objects readopted them and venerated them as they had before."[91] The resurgence of bamanaya was given added urgency in the immediate postconquest years owing to the precariousness of life and the generally fragmented social and political circumstances. Reconstructing village communities was not only about clearing land, hunting, and defending against external threats. Reclaiming the land had supernatural dimensions and required strenuous ritual work.[92] One colonial official observed how villagers returned to old rituals tied to farming: "[Samori] had always been opposed to this ceremony. . . . Each family designated one of its members who participated in the ceremony, excluding women. Each brought with him a white chicken, some kola nuts and pounded millet. . . . The spirit of the locality was asked to give prosperity to the collectivity, to protect its members from epidemics, and the harvests from natural scourges, and to render their women fertile. All the chickens were then killed over the stone itself on which the blood spread out . . . everyone promised to be obedient and faithful to the divinity of the locality. . . . The meal lasted the whole day, and dòlò was consumed in abundance."[93]

Given the centrality of fertility-based rituals, blacksmiths were crucial in returning villages to a healthy state of agricultural production. Their efforts and sacrifices were central to restoring harmony with the land, the spirits, and village ancestors. Because many village blacksmiths had been enslaved for use in the Samorian munitions industries, while others had been killed and still others had fled as refugees and never returned, there was a relative deprivation of smiths in many communities.[94] In certain communities, people resorted to forms of moriya in the absence of black-smiths, as bits and pieces of Islamic religious culture slowly found wider acceptance. Most communities, however, simply sought out blacksmiths from neighboring villages. There were also blacksmiths who traveled from village to village providing ritual services. In the village of Tenemakana the traditional blacksmith quarter was abandoned during the wars of Samori and never again resettled. Therefore, villagers became dependent on a powerful blacksmith from a neighboring village.[95]

Out of necessity, then, communities and families invested in translocal religious relationships and sacred sites. This is not to say that religious translocalism was new. Ritual sites and experts had long been situated in wider regional networks of territorial cults.[96] However, with the improved security under French rule, villagers were now free to travel without exposing themselves to danger. This enabled them to gain access to power objects, renowned healers, and many diverse sacred sites, tombs and magic in more distant localities.[97] In Wasulu, there were numerous such places, arrayed within extensive networks, and structured around hierarchies and gradations of power. Two of the most important sacred sites were the tombs of Sabu Satigi (canton of Basidibé) and Tumani (canton of Gwanan), which would remain popular well into the late colonial period.[98] One elder recalled the tomb of Sabu Satigi in the fields between Solona and Gualala: "In Numu Foro, there where we have the banana trees, the stream there was called Numurilako, in the hamlet, the people would go there to entrust themselves to the power object (jo). The person whose tomb they would go to do the sacrifices to the site, he lived between our garden and the village. It is not far. He lived right here. They took a stone from here to put on his tomb to immortalize him with this stone."[99]

Of course, beyond sacred sites, one of the most important religious institutions was the kòmò society, which helped to reestablish political order in an unstable era. Because of the lawlessness in Buguni and the absence of intact authority structures, the kòmò served as a judiciary and police force and as an antisorcery watchdog in precarious times. Furthermore, as the most central of men's power associations, it was instrumental in reproducing the religious habitus through its involvement in life-crisis rituals and rites of passage.[100] As an expression of a reconstituted bamanaya, however, it was more than just a village affair. Kòmò societies often extended beyond "their ethnic limits," while still functioning "in an essentially local context."[101]

Many sacred kòmò sites had been destroyed or lost during the wars, but returning refugees introduced new power objects they carried with them from distant localities. For example, refugees returning from Ivory Coast reintroduced kòmò power objects into Tenemakana, and in time the kòmò of Tenemakana regained its reputation as one of the most powerful in the region. People were known to travel even from Guinea and Ivory Coast to ask for help from the kòmò of Tenemakana.[102]

Based in the spirit of independence of these associations, there was intense competition between kòmò societies. Thus, even as religious life became more translocal, there were deep divisions between lineage-based cults. Informants spoke of "wars of sorcery" between rival kòmò societies, as religious authorities mobilized their initiates to operate in the interest of the community. This could include involvement in disputes over land use rights, anti-witchcraft crusades, and contestations over the chieftaincy or control of labor during the clandestine slave trade. In Fulala, competition over the canton chieftaincy found expression in turf battles between rival kòmò societies.[103]

One of the rivals of Tenemakana's kòmò was a powerful oracle named *mógóyiko*, which had been introduced into Niamala by a ritual priest named Jékura after the wars of Samori. Peasants in Fulala knew mógóyiko for its power to heal and resolve crises. One informant remembered it: "The people brought sacrifices to resolve their problems, going to the sanctuary, to the tree. . . . When you arrived there, you would recount everything before resolving your problems."[104] Interestingly, oral traditions around mógóyiko and its role in securing and blessing the village of Kolondieba are still quite vivid. As the local story goes, after the

Samorian wars the people began consulting mógóyiko, and the oracle told the community to sacrifice a spotted bull and to engage in an all-night dance. When the bull was killed, they divided the meat into small pieces, and poured the blood and the stomach contents into small holes. Tree branches were placed over the holes. Then they took parts of the bull, mixed with fonio, and distributed portions around the village. The people "scattered the mixture as far from the village as possible," to small hills and clearings, where "the hunters had begun setting their traps and pursuing their game." This ritual would enable Kolondieba to expand into a large village, as people would periodically repeat the community ritual. Such accounts convey how locals viewed their historical connections to sacred sites and rituals.[105]

In an era of freer mobility, particularly as kidnapping and enslavement waned, communities sought out power objects located outside the canton. One of the most powerful kòmò was in the village of Zaniena in Ganadugu. Its appeal to people from Fulala and surrounding cantons was in part due to its location; visiting the kòmò of Zaniena was an act of pilgrimage. For pilgrims, this included "crossing the river" into a zone where people's huts were constructed differently and people spoke different dialects of Bamanankan and Senufo. Many people believed that if its reputation reached across the river, then its power must be enormous. As one informant remembered, "We used to go all the way to Zaniena to sacrifice chickens to the kòmò. Ever since I was a baby. Chickens would be killed, sacrificed to the kòmò of Zaniena by our family, for protection."[106] Most sacred sites were less visible to colonial observers than mosques or Qur'anic schools, but because of its renown the kòmò of Zaniena appeared in archival sources. During a census tour in 1912, a colonial official witnessed pilgrims heading to its site: "[We] encountered natives going to make offerings to the kòmò of Zaniena. . . . The sorcerer, who is very reputed, lives in the canton of Ganadugu . . . at more than eighty kilometers from the cantons of Molodiana and Fulala, from where he draws clients and dupes."[107]

Indeed, colonial administrators often characterized indigenous religious leaders as charlatans engaged in duping the population. Such institutions and their leaders could also represent a threat to colonial political order. Writing about religious associations in his *Haut-Senegal-Niger*, Maurice Delafosse identified key secret or semisecret indigenous institutions that could potentially cause problems. He admitted that usually these associations did not have political goals, but he cautioned, "Certain diverse sets of circumstances could, very certainly, bring about a change of orientation in the primitive goal and make these associations more dangerous than even the Muslim brotherhoods." Whereas the Muslim brotherhoods were kept under tight surveillance and were far more legible, indigenous power associations were characterized by intense secrecy. What troubled Delafosse most of all was the potentially territory-wide nature of these religious associations, which spread through rumor and could explode "like a powder keg." Certainly, the concerns Delafosse expressed were not unique, as numerous regional millenarian religious movements were taking place during the first decades of colonial rule.[108]

Expressing a kind of theodicy in times of duress, these movements combined indigenous religious idioms and more translocal forms of millenarian prophetism. Most of them spread quickly and then disappeared, leaving few traces. But in the district of Buguni, colonial administrators occasionally reported on such processes. For example, one movement began in the spring of 1903, when, as people began preparing for the rainy season, a man "fell from the sky," as in common indigenous creation myths, and called on local religious and political authorities to make sacrifices at a powerful sacred site to ensure an abundant harvest. The holy man was described as "an enigmatic personality who travels a lot." It is unclear whether he was Muslim or not. But, then, as Peel has noted, when such cults moved into new areas, they might take on "new attributes or lose old ones," depending on the needs of the community.[109] Thus, regardless of the man's religious designation, the majority of local religious authorities and canton chiefs in Buguni sent emissaries to greet the man. Chickens were slain in his presence, blood poured on a sacred object under a tree. The prophetic figure invoked "his God," asking for good luck in the lives of the families of the gift bearers. He assured them that they would have rich harvests and that the locusts would not cause any problems. As the man spoke, he told the emissaries that immediately after returning to their villages they should take care of the poor and sell everything they owned, especially their slaves.[110]

As an ecologically oriented movement of reform, the holy man generated a following by emphasizing key themes: avoiding natural calamities, taking care of the poor, getting rid of slaves, promising good harvests, rain, and no locusts. As we have seen, the issues of poverty, slavery, and food security were central to the reconstruction process. But in hearing about this holy man's peregrinations and preaching, colonial officials were less than understanding: "This clever personality appears to be very mobile. . . . My information permits me to believe that he is simply a swindler, who takes advantage of the credulity of the blacks of this country, who are essentially superstitious. He has benefited from the approach of the rainy season, threatening numerous calamities in future harvests." When rumors circulated that people were selling off their cattle in the markets, the colonial state stepped in to allegedly protect the people. A secret agent was sent to follow the holy man and to monitor his actions and send in reports. A month later the commandant summoned all of the canton chiefs who had visited the man to Buguni. After "having severely admonished them," the commandant explained how their excessive trust had brought about a loss of revenue, which was particularly egregious because "their taxes were far from being paid."[III]

In the neighboring district of Sikasso, the colonial state intervened even more directly against indigenous religious institutions in the interest of protecting villagers from the exploitative and nefarious practices of sorcerers. The administration had learned of "practices of witchcraft that accompany the ceremonies of the kòmò" and immediately warned that "these acts will be repressed with the utmost rigor. The culprits should be denounced before the Justice and pursued before the Tribunal of the district for the crime." Colonial officials justified their repression of kòmò ceremonies as condemning the practices of "cannibalism and human sacrifice under the cover of darkness, at night, by the witches, under the masks of the hyena." It is unclear what threat the kòmò actually posed to local communities. Even the colonial official reported that "the native seems to have faith in these practices. . . . The families who provided us with the testimony on this subject appeared surprised that we accorded it so much importance."[112] The colonial state made it clear nonetheless that it would not tolerate any religious practices deemed barbaric or morally offensive to French standards of civility.

In a related incident, two men were put on trial for charlatanism. Before a large crowd an administrator directed soldiers to throw numerous fetishes into a bonfire. As the objects were burned, the official announced, "The kòmò has been killed. Now it can no longer be

harmful." The justification for this action was again that "certain charlatans had for a long time been stirring up fear in their villages, using
charlatan practices to which they have dedicated themselves in order to
terrify the inhabitants of their predictions."[113] There is no record of how
such actions were received by locals. But the intervention against indigenous religious authorities and the public burning of power objects and
masks by colonial officials must have sent mixed signals to the inhabitants. In Buguni, the threats posed by the ceremonies of secret societies
like the kòmò would later be punished under a law code which stated that
anyone found guilty of organizing or participating in secret gatherings
could be put to death. The justification was that "these gatherings have
the character of subversion aimed against the village headmen and reveal
themselves to be very severe with respect to those who dispossess those
in power."[114]

In one's assessing of the broader relationship between French empire
and religious difference, such evidence of state interventions against
traditional religious institutions calls attention to the highly ambivalent
and pragmatic manner in which colonial order was maintained. Even
as refugees were reconstituting their religious lives along new translocal lines, the colonial administration sought to domesticate indigenous
religious institutions, while eliminating practices which were morally
repugnant to Europeans. And even as the state sought to limit processes
of Islamization, its own actions contributed to the inadvertent weakening
of indigenous religious authorities. However, the habitus was also in the
process of changing, such that Muslim holy men were able to fill certain
religious needs in communities. And as the political economy shifted and
new openings facilitated greater mobility and wider commercial transactions, religious change took on a more translocal character. Itinerant
Muslim holy men and traders tapped into these social networks, grafting
their own institutions, interests, and bases of authority onto emergent
webs of religious affiliation. These processes would only deepen during
the era of emancipation, when tens of thousands of slaves returned to
their homes, carrying Muslim prayer with them.

CHAPTER 3

Slave Emancipation and the Expansion of Islam, 1905–1914

Tumani Danyoko has been credited as the first practicing Muslim in the village of Tenemakana. Long before this local beginning of "prayer," Tumani had been a slave in a Muslim household in northern Ivory Coast, where he came of age in a world punctuated by the daily rhythms of Islamic culture. In time, he learned the basic prayers and was inculcated with new values and beliefs. As a portable way of being Muslim, this new religious habitus constituted a set of practices and manner of bodily comportment that could be adapted to different social milieus. Thus, in the aftermath of slavery, when Tumani returned to his homelands, he carried prayer with him. Although the village was still dominated by the kòmò society and Muslims could not pray publicly, Tumani retained his new faith.[1]

The story of Tumani resonates in other village and family religious histories, which emphasize the ways in which Islam expanded into rural areas at the end of slavery. As a mass of so-called converts, slaves formed the nuclei of future Muslim communities. In time, their daily religious practices would help soften the ground for later, more profound and enduring religious changes. Although returning slaves were the largest social group attributed with introducing Islamic prayer into their rural villages before the First World War, there was a plurality of paths to Islam. As one informant said, "Each village has its story of how it came to prayer."[2] Colonial soldiers, holy men, traders, slaves, and migrant workers have all been credited with playing this role. However, these social categories often overlapped: a former slave may have become a colonial soldier, migrant worker, trader, or even holy man. The multiple itineraries and permutations of individual lives within larger contexts of mobility defy strict correlations between social categories and processes.

By 1912 the canton of Fulala, where Tenemakana was located, had roughly fifty Muslims, or two or three per village. Although they lacked a Qur'anic school and Sufi muqaddam, Muslims were described as adhering to the Qadiriyya.[3] Sufi influences were penetrating the canton, which was far removed from major commercial routes and trade towns. In this process, returning Muslim slaves like Tumani Danyoko were crucial agents in the dissemination of Muslim practices into areas that had been largely untouched by holy men or traders. Then, as small clusters of first-generation Muslims began to form, holy men extended their networks further into uncharted areas. Based in a culture of orality and rather simple theodicy, their religious influence would grow among peasants.[4] Muslim holy men performed rainmaking prayers, fabricated amulets, practiced forms of divination, or sand writing, preached, and tried collecting gifts. They also enabled local Muslims to tap into wider Sufi currents.

By way of contrast, around the time that hundreds of thousands of slaves were returning to their homelands and Muslim holy men were gaining wider acceptance, the lieutenant governor of the Sudan, Marie-François Joseph Clozel, predicted that the end of slavery would lead to a weakening of marabouts and even "regression" of Islam. In 1909, as the slave exodus was underway, Clozel confidently outlined his ideas: "Islam has always been, and continues to be, prosperous in the countries where slavery raged. . . . Now, our occupation in the black countries has had precisely the effect of definitively ending slavery and freeing the population from all politico-religious subjugation. It should logically have the result of a regression of the Islamic faith. . . . I would estimate that the activities of marabouts will henceforth no longer constitute a serious obstacle to our political supremacy."[5] Echoing the views of the new governor general, William Ponty, whose involvement in the campaigns against Samori had alerted him to the perceived dangers of jihad, Clozel believed they were dealing a definitive blow to the old feudal system dominated by Muslims. He also fashioned himself as a defender of fetishists against the threats posed by alleged Muslim fanatics, setting up surveillance networks to monitor the activities of Sufi holy men and bolstering the authority of traditional chiefs.[6] Despite its official stance of religious neutrality, the colonial administration actively sought to thwart the expansion of Islam into zones categorized as fetishist. While partly a program for intervention, Clozel's prognostications were ultimately off the mark.

The exodus was no fringe social phenomenon. The mass return migrations lasted a decade, with as many as one million slaves leaving their masters across the French colonies of the Sudan, Guinea, and Senegal.[7] Although similar processes were occurring elsewhere in Africa, the slave exodus in the French Sudan was unequaled in its size and geographical breadth. And as colonial documents reveal, southern French Sudan was the single largest recipient of former slaves.[8] Within these decentralized societies, slave holdings had been generally small. However, as we have seen, they had also been the zones frequently targeted for enslavement. Therefore, most families would experience slavery, either directly or indirectly through the loss of kin. Owing to the high proportion of enslaved people, as opposed to those born into slavery, hereditary slave status would be relatively unimportant in the aftermath of slavery. Emancipation in Buguni represented a cleaner rupture with the past than in most regions in the French Sudan, as families and villages reconstituted themselves in their homelands.[9] Ironically, then, although it was a leading source of slaves, most vestiges of slavery, such as the lingering forms of obligation based in a sort of kinship, that were so prevalent in the Sahara and Sahel were rather diluted. Because of the exodus, descendants of slaves shed the socially embedded dispositions of being a slave, the public deference to masters, and the identification of belonging to a low-status group. Slave status, which had been experienced in exile, was a temporary marker of identity. Their "social death," as it were, had been transitory, leaving few traces in the status of their descendants.[10]

Historiographically, studies of slave emancipation in Africa have tended to focus on colonial policy, exploring the transition from slave labor to free wage labor, and on the complex interplay between metropolitan interests, ideologies, and the initiatives of African elites.[11] More recently scholars have sought to reframe the analysis of emancipation processes, expanding the temporal boundaries and incorporating questions of race and citizenship.[12] Yet, according to Martin Klein, the "biggest weakness" still remains the "failure to recognize slaves as actors."[13] Furthermore, Kristin Mann has called on historians to push beyond the accomplishments in the field, noting, "Ideas, information, and movements circulated not only among members of the ruling classes, but also among the ruled. This phenomenon too cries out for more research."[14] Focusing on slaves as historical actors, I explore processes of Islamization, agrarian change, and shifts in political authority at the end of slavery.

PATHS OUT OF SLAVERY

The descendants of former slaves speak of *jònnabila san*, or "the year that slavery ended," in reference to the end of legal slavery by decree in 1905. However, as we have seen, many slaves fled long before the abolition decree, often blending in with streams of refugees. Others would return home much later, after the First World War. And most slaves, especially women, would never return.[15] The most dramatic era of mass exodus began in the spring of 1905, when slaves in the Sahel trade town of Banamba started leaving their masters. A year later, as the rains approached, once again slaves prepared to leave. Soon the exodus spread to other towns.[16] For those heading for their homelands, it was a long walk, sometimes a couple of hundred kilometers or more. En route, freed slaves confronted privations of all sorts, often relying on famine foods and French "liberty villages" to survive. They frequently took long detours in returning home, farming peanuts in Senegal, working in Bamako and Kayes, or settling in new communities along the French supply lines. Many slaves would end up as soldiers in the colonial army.[17] Through it all, kinship and information networks facilitated what was otherwise an arduous process fraught with uncertainty.

Archival sources indicate that the district of Buguni was one of the main destinations of freed slaves. A report issued from Bamako stated, "The exodus of slaves has taken place with remarkable calm and order. . . . Most of them were former inhabitants of the district of Buguni. . . . [They] show great joy at being able to reintegrate in their country from which they had been taken, hardly fifteen years ago, to be sold in entire villages to the Maraka, suppliers of horses for the armies of Samori."[18] On the receiving end, an official in Buguni observed, "As the inhabitants know that they can rebuild their homes without fear of being one day pillaged or led away in slavery, they are coming back to their villages."[19] While slaves wishing to leave were officially required to notify the local commandant and pay their taxes before departing, many returned undetected by the French administration. As one official noted, these departures were "at times numerous, but have not been generally reported by the natives to the Commandants. . . . The result is that the real number of departures is far greater than those officially reported."[20]

Nevertheless, the official numbers establish the approximate scale of the process. In the district of Buguni, the population increased from 95,592 to 162,343 between 1905 and 1913, the most active period of return migration.[21] In the canton of Fulala, the population grew from 980 to 2,655, largely as a result of "slaves, taken during the wars of Samori, returning to their country of origin." On a slightly broader level, in the southeastern quadrant, census tours recorded a population increase from 8,052 to 12,779, the majority of which were freed slaves returning from the Niger River region.[22] Other cantons reported varying rates of population increase, which fluctuated over time as the exodus from Banamba was reproduced throughout the colony of French Sudan. By 1908 the wave of liberation had spread to Segu and beyond, moving from west to east and fanning out from the Niger River, with slaves returning from distant Sahel localities in Nioro and Gumbu. As late as 1910, slaves were leaving the regions of Kita and Bafoulabé, part of an "exodus of former slaves towards the south."[23]

As Klein has emphasized, most slaves would remain in exile rather than return to their former villages. Female slaves, in particular, had often been married and integrated into households. Their children, born into servitude, had no memory of their mothers' former villages. These younger slaves often felt at home and decided to stay and renegotiate relations with their masters, hoping to assert greater control over their labor. Other factors mitigated their departure, such as their masters' use of violence and intimidation, poverty, illness, old age, and lack of knowledge of their homelands. Still, those who stayed often sought more autonomy by founding their own villages and farming hamlets.[24] One report from Gumbu stated, "[A] large number of slaves born in the country and who would not have any advantage in emigrating, benefit from their freedom to separate themselves from their masters, founding new villages and creating new fields." Slaves who stayed put often did so for "reasons of personal attachment" or because they had "no other family other than their master." They were free but continued to provide services for their former masters.[25] Often they were woloso slaves, or those born into slavery. In the Senegalese peanut zone, former slaves provided tribute labor, paid an annual tax to their former masters, demonstrated public deference, and performed ritual services. Elsewhere, in the Upper Senegal River Valley, slaves served as soldiers or forced laborers in the place of nobles' sons and stayed on as serfs, working their former masters' land.[26]

While most slaves renegotiated relations with their masters or fled back to their homelands, a few emigrated and found wage work in neighboring colonies. Kankan, one of the early destinations, had a large "floating population" of migrant workers and former slaves. Because of Kankan's proximity to Wasulu, many of these workers were from the district of Buguni. Indeed, workers on the railway line in Guinea were described as Bambaras from the French Sudan. Gold-mining centers in Guinea were also "a noticeable attraction" for people from Wasulu. In Ivory Coast, administrators and traders recruited workers "among the countless foreigners coming from the Sudan, or from Guinea, who, without the means of subsistence, wander around." Hundreds of these supposed vagabonds were employed as porters in trade towns.[27] Oral accounts suggest that former slaves worked as porters or in the gold and diamond mines in Guinea. Some slaves were able to take advantage of social networks forged in slavery to tap into long-distance trade or used their experience, connections, and knowledge acquired from working as slave porters to engage in the kola trade.[28] Many freed slaves went to Senegal or the Gambia, where they grew peanuts. Colonial officials even noted the emergence of what they called a "new social class" consisting of "free and waged agricultural workers."[29]

As tens of thousands of former slaves returned from distant localities, they carried with them the news that slavery had been abolished, which set off chain reactions of local liberation within the district of Buguni. Most departures occurred before the rainy season started. Then, once the rains arrived, slaves who had not left would usually stay put for another year. However, in local processes of emancipation, since slaves were often from nearby villages, they just fled whenever they could. As we saw in the previous chapter, the clandestine slave trade had continued in the postconquest era, resulting in widespread kidnapping. Now, many of these recent local captives began returning home. One official reported that following the Banamba exodus slaves held locally began "asking for authorization to return to their respective villages." Apparently, former masters "watched as dozens of their slaves left," without showing "any surprise" and simply accepting it "without protest."[30] Another official observed that because families had "similarly experienced this terrible institution," slave owners were more "inclined to understand the sad situation of the slave as he himself awaits the return of a father or a brother, disappeared since the wars of Samori." Furthermore, since many of these slaves had been kidnapped rather than purchased and were being replaced by returning family members within contexts of domestic slavery, masters appear to have been less motivated to use force in maintaining their slaves.[31] The exception, however, was female slaves, particularly those who had been married and whose stories have been brought to light in colonial court documents.[32] Still, the colonial archive is mostly silent on the experiences of freed slaves.

"ISN'T THAT BECAUSE OF THE WILL OF PEOPLE?": HUMAN AGENCY AND KINSHIP NETWORKS

Slave return narratives have value as representations of the subjective experiences of emancipation. They reveal local perspectives on large-scale historical processes that often get lost in archive-driven narratives. To begin, the accounts normally provide only skeletal chronicles of families being dispersed and resettled, narrated around a lineage head, the pivotal figure in family histories. There are common motifs, such as the reliance on family networks of support, neighbors, and the wider community and the ways in which families were reunited. One informant told of his grandfather's experiences: "Ba Nankuma came back and found that none of his family members were here. So he went to stay with the family of Ba Teneman. He added himself to them. He did everything there with them. My father's father, he died. But all his children came back to the village at the end of slavery. Ba Nankuma received them, and slowly our family was resurrected from the ashes. Ba Nankuma became the head of the family."[33] Slave return narratives also reinforce the fact that slaves, even those from the same family, were returning from disparate localities. In many narratives, there are references to the ways in which the exodus was staggered over time, as wave after wave of slaves returned. Broulaye Doumbia recounted his family history: "The affair of slavery was ending. . . . For us, our own fathers, Koro and Bakoniba, they had been in slavery in Maàlé. For Maba, it was near Korhogo. They were all in different places. What

I've been told, as for the father of Basibiri, his slavery was in Gouni. . . . Among those who came back first to the ruins, the news of Maba was known, [and] it was his brother, Bakoniba, who went to search for him in Korhogo. . . . And, at this time, more people were coming back. . . . There was a stream of people all the way from Segu to the village here. Now isn't that because of the will of people?"[34]

As in the case of refugee return, reintegration proceeded with considerable reshuffling, resulting even in the settlement of new villages. Families often followed circuitous paths to their homelands. Such was the case of the Diakité family, originally from eastern Guinea. When their village, Nénéjana, was destroyed during the wars of Samori, most of the family was sold into slavery. Lamine Diakité recounted the story he heard from his grandmother, a former slave: "When they said that slavery was finished, each person rejoined his country of origin. And my parents, my grandfather and his family were in Kayes. They returned to Wasulu . . . my grandfather walked with his family from Kayes. . . . They wanted to return to Nénéjana, but on the road home they stopped in the village called Hajilaminina. They were Diakité, like us. But when they saw their brothers passing through on their way to Guinea, they said, 'No, you should stay here. You are not very numerous. When you go to construct your huts, you do not even have enough people to put up the roof, you must be more numerous."[35] Therefore, they decided to stay in Hajilaminina until they had stored up enough resources to resettle their own village.

Rather than allowing freed slaves to settle wherever they chose, the administration created roadside villages, which were easier to visit for purposes of taxation and political control. At the same time, officials pursued a policy of restrictive resettlement to avoid "disorder and confusion." Although people were attached to their homelands, officials hoped that the younger generations would adapt to new colonial settlement patterns. In Guinea, where many slaves from Wasulu ended up, one report stated, "The black forgets only with difficulty the village of his ancestors, which is for him the true and only homeland. Also many in their village today think of this former home and come to the post to ask for authorization to return there. . . . In questions of changing villages, it is necessary therefore to maintain much reserve. Permission given would lead to a mass of others and if we continue along this path the country will find itself in disorder and confusion. . . . Only the elders, moreover, remain truly attached to the former villages, the young adapt to their new milieu. . . . [It] will be the work of a generation."[36] Although colonial administrators preferred to resettle people within their own jurisdictions, they could not control the movement and settlement of new villages. Communities of former slaves were frequently held up in transit for years before reintegrating with their families. Indeed, resettlement lasted well into the interwar period, as one colonial official reported in 1923: "Entire families, barely out of the state of slavery, have still not been able to resettle in their homes."[37]

When villages were reconstituted, the first bit of information utilized pertained to the location of missing family members. Many slave return narratives, therefore, contain stories of news received about a loved one's whereabouts and the subsequent journey to retrieve them.[38] An informant in Balanfina explained as follows: "The first people to come back from slavery, they helped to retrieve the other members of the family, until eventually the population grew. These people had a lot of sympathy for each other. Even if you heard that your brother was all the way in Guinea, you would travel to go find him." Unfortunately, sometimes it was discovered that their loved ones had died or been integrated into a new household and were unable to leave.[39] In Guinea, a colonial report stated, "There are people from the Sudan who search for their women or their sons for ten years and find them one day, provided with a new family, deep in a far away village."[40] And while many people in Wasulu went searching for family members in Guinea, those in the cantons of Fulala and its neighbors went south to Ivory Coast. For example, Bakary Diarra talked about how three brothers of his family returned from slavery and then immediately set out looking for their mother: "They were coming from Soninkelen, near Tengrela. Their mother had disappeared, so they arrived in this country to look for their mother. When they found her, she threw herself on them. They had been separated from their mother following the wars of Samori and been in slavery."[41] Aside from news of family members, slaves also carried other useful information and knowledge, which helped in the rebuilding of communities.

THE THINGS THEY CARRIED: CROPS, INFORMATION, AND KNOWLEDGE TRANSFERS

A local proverb in Buguni says, "The slave belongs to you, but his knowledge and his spirit belong only to himself." In interpreting this proverb, an informant explained, "You can succeed in reducing someone in slavery in the kitchen of your mother. But you better get it in your head that the slave might have supernatural powers that you have ignored." Although slaves were valued primarily as workers, they represented more than just labor power; slaves carried with them their knowledge, beliefs, and practices.[42] Returning slaves introduced a diverse set of ideas into their villages, which became part of a larger store of knowledge. The kinds of innovations they transplanted to their homes depended on the location and context of their slavery, as Bourama Dembélé explained: "The people had all been dispersed, they were not in the same place. . . . So, when they were taken away, those who ended up among followers of Islam, they came back with religion [alasira]. Those who were in other places, they came with some other sort of work. Those who found some way to earn money, they came back with the knowledge of that."[43] Much of what slaves learned was based on their travel experiences, which had broadened their horizons. They acquired new ideas and gained a sense of their village's place in the wider world. They were exposed to different landscapes, trees, and kinds of wildlife; they crossed ecological boundaries that had once seemed dangerous. They were immersed in different languages and customs.[44] As Doulaye Koné recalled, "Ba Jeefe came back from slavery in Koyaga country. He could never rid himself of the Koyaga language, and he could never really speak the language of here correctly. He even came with his Koyaga wife and two girls, the oldest of which was married in Siten. She was exchanged for my mother actually. . . . So there you have it, you know what I was told. Ba Nankuma only had one wife, my grandmother. Ba Jeefe who came back from Koyaga country had sons here."[45]

Slaves were sometimes responsible for bringing back new agricultural ideas and crops.[46] Seeds for various kinds of millet, rice, and maize were introduced, and some people even tried growing kola trees. Adama Diallo of Niamala explained that the wider mobility of people at the end of slavery led to the transfer of new varieties of crops: "After the time of Samori, the world changed so that people could travel from place to place and visit each other. Before this time nobody would go travel to visit other people because they were too afraid. They were afraid of being captured. The people brought with them peanuts to plant, and others brought back some kinds of potato, màsàku, woso, and manioc [bànànku]. There were many kinds of yam. . . . So these people left the region for other places, they learned about other crops and they brought these new seeds [si]."[47] A census tour report of southern Wasulu similarly reveals that crops were in the process of changing at the end of slavery, whether carried by slaves, porters, or traders. In certain villages, millet and sorghum were slowly being replaced by rice and fonio, and large fields of manioc were being planted everywhere.[48]

Many returning slaves brought back fruit trees in the form of seeds, pits, and cuttings. In Fulala, one informant told of how the mango was introduced into his village: "What our father told us was that the mango was introduced from Guinea. When Samori ravaged the country, many people who ended up in Guinea, they found that the mango was in great quantity there, so our people began the history of mango trees in this fashion. Our mango trees were brought back from there, it was our people who brought it back and planted it."[49] Of course, slave return migration does not explain all of these innovations. General regional security enabled people to move around before and after emancipation. For example, the villages of M'Pagnala, Fulala-Ba, and Manankoro acquired banana and citrus trees when villagers imported them from Ivory Coast. Often village chiefs and traders invested in fruit trees. In one village, colonial officials reported that the village chief was "importing each year orange trees from Sokoro, Ivory Coast. There are presently eight orange trees in this village, of which two are producing." In explaining the way in which the fruits trees arrived in these villages, the colonial official noted broadly, "The importers of these plants are all natives."[50]

Some slaves had been weavers or blacksmiths and had learned new skills and techniques they could use in the marketplace. One informant's father had worked as a slave-weaver of cotton textiles. Upon his liberation, he was able to continue weaving and managed to pay his taxes from practicing the craft. Those who were enslaved in regions that were more directly tied into the world economy gained knowledge about the kinds of products that had a high exchange value, such as rubber and ivory. Many slaves returned with the knowledge that gold and diamond mines in Guinea were lucrative, that tree felling and hunting were sources of money in Ivory Coast, or that farming peanuts in Senegal was remunerative.[51] And as more slaves arrived with new crops and knowledge, many began venturing out to settle new lands.

THE EXPANSION OF AGRARIAN FRONTIERS

In the hills between Tenemakana and Wakoro new land was cleared in the decade after the exodus. Men and women, putting their hoes to work in the virgin land, farmed together and expanded their fields. Informants told how their former lands near the village ruins had become tied (*siri*), or infertile, and were teeming with malevolent spirits. Therefore, groups of families constructed huts outside the mud walls of the village and formed agricultural hamlets and fields further away from the village. As this process was underway, elders had warned, "When they leave to the exterior, the eating place will be too far away for everyone to put their hands in the same bowl. This will hopefully not ruin the relations between us all." Still, more people continued to settle on the village frontiers. In time, a dispersed new village, called *sokura* (new home), was formed.[52] Broulaye Doumbia explained: "When they went to construct *sokura*, that started to risk ruining things, and the village first began to break apart. When Bassori came back from slavery in Kayes his family made fields near the ruins of the banan tree. People coming back went to the west to resettle [toward Wakoro]. But Bassori and his group went to the east. Our people did not go there because the ruins of the banan tree. . . . The spirits there were really mean."[53]

Broadly, one of the more salient changes in the aftermath of slavery was the expansion of village agrarian frontiers. People relocated owing to the lack of potable water, diseases, political conflict, or bad spirits. However, most people were lured by the prospects of fertile open land and greater independence. Formerly, villages had maintained their fields close to the village, all of the inhabitants residing within the protective mud walls to defend against the attacks of slave raiders.[54] With the broader security established by French rule, people were able to venture out in smaller groups, clearing land in distant localities and even establishing new hamlets. In a colonial monograph on customary land practices, one official noted, "The natives maintain that this fact results from the peace in the country, even more than these routes of penetration, because formerly they did not cultivate but small tracts; it was that there was the necessity to assure the protection of the harvest with armed men."[55]

This process had begun in some villages during the era of refugee return. But the clandestine slave trade had forced villagers to be more cautious in unsettled areas. Then, once the news circulated that slavery had ended, villagers started venturing out with less trepidation. In this way, villages expanded into clusters of hamlets spatially arrayed around the old village (*sokoro*) but dispersed further into the fields. One colonial official commented, "A large number of refugees or freed slaves, having returned to their villages of origin, have shown a marked tendency to abandon the large centers and to settle themselves, permanently, at noticeable distance from the villages, in the middle of the fields in which they farm."[56] The expansion of agrarian frontiers was also observed in Sahel regions. In one report, an official noted how "the vigorous impulsion given to farming by the freed slaves of the Sahel who have remained in the country" had resulted in "beautiful fields that one can admire at several kilometers in the surroundings of the villages."[57]

In terms of technique, agriculture was a rather stable form of human activity until the introduction of plows and the shift to private or slave fields (*jònfòrò*). Bamana farming was part of a larger agrocultural complex that had particular rituals, myths, tools, and techniques. People generally farmed their lands for anywhere between three and seven years, followed by a medium fallow period. The controlled use of brush fire (*binjeni*) was commonly practiced toward the end of the dry season, when farmers also hunted for small game, such as bush rats (*kònyina*).[58] This Bamana system included such practices as shifting cultivation, intercropping, collective labor, and building mounds (*ntugun*) and furrows (*walan*) for planting. As one man explained,

> Before, we worked with the big hoe, bent over together
> making mounds, now lost from view. We passed the whole day
> competing together. . . . There were few modifications, even
> with the farming of maize; they planted the maize fields, one
> mound for one or two stalks of maize. But when the fields were
> harvested, the yield was not great, so one would harvest a small
> quantity and hang this quantity in the branches of a tree. In this
> method, one would then plant beans at the feet of the maize. . . .
> You could farm grains, gourds, and beans all in the same field.
> When you cut the maize, there would be the beans left, which
> would be an extra gain in your production. When you harvest
> the gourds, you could keep them or use them right away as food.
> That only increased your quantity of food to eat for the year.[59]

Aside from agriculture, there were other movements of ecological frontiers. As communities grew and commercial transactions expanded, hunters pushed into new territory. And with the spread of firearms, individual hunting became more common. According to one colonial observer, individual hunting was practiced everywhere "with firearms, bow and arrow, and traps, except in certain reserved places, like ponds, bends in the river, and certain parts of the forest."[60] Although hunters often evaded state claims, there is early archival evidence of their importance in the colonial economy. In the cantons of Cemala and Nienandugu, for example, one official observed, "Hunters are numerous in Nienandugu, and large game are abundant: antelopes of all kinds, buffalo, hippopotamus, and elephants. One inhabitant of the village of Niako claims to have killed nine last year, the sale of which would bring him three thousand francs. Lions are also numerous."[61] Hunting was practiced in specified zones and during specified times. Hunters working alone could dispose of the meat as they saw fit, but out of custom they would usually give the local landowner a shoulder of the animal killed, and in the case of elephant, one of its tusks. Often hunters from neighboring villages would come together on communal intervillage hunt days. All the game that was killed would be shared between the hunters, the hunter who had actually killed the animal taking the horns, teeth, claws, or one of the tusks. An exception to these rules was when hunters ventured into the zones considered empty bush (*kungokolon*) or faraway bush (*kungojan*), where they would not owe parts of their game to anyone. Hence there was incentive to hunt individually in such deserted regions.[62] Although hunting provided income for people, it was also a necessity in depopulated zones that were being resettled. Nevertheless, the state saw such mobility and shifting settlement patterns as a threat to order.

STABILIZING AUTHORITY: THE CHIEFTAINCY AND SHIFTING POWER RELATIONS

From the perspective of the colonial administration, the dispersal of people into remote farming hamlets was a source of political anarchy. As more slaves returned, canton chiefs struggled to prevent people from "disappearing into the bush."[63] Given the state's efforts to render the population more legible, constant movement was a bureaucratic nightmare. Moreover, it was interpreted as willful evasion of the state, as one official noted: "The natives dissimulate . . . rendered very easy by their infinite dissemination in the farming villages."[64] When such perceived dissimulations were detected, the administration was quick to act. For example, after people from the village of Fulala-Diassa settled a village "without authorization, in order to escape surveillance," the canton chief reported the incident, and soon the commandant sent out guards to destroy the unauthorized huts.[65] Because of the constant flux, village names and canton boundaries were always changing. Even family surnames were unstable. Slaves took the names of their masters and then later tried to change back; people switched surnames to integrate into new communities; others did so to advance claims on land or to leave their low-status pasts behind. In many cases, individuals or whole communities adopted praise names for political reasons, vying for the chieftaincy, or to indicate ethnic shifts based more in occupational or religious changes. Such "identity conversions" were widespread in southern French Sudan, in large part due to the histories of displacement and ethnic mixing. With respect to Buguni, Jean-Loup Amselle notes, "Identity change always occurs in terms of power relations. . . . The different categories of names (nickname, praise name, ethnonym) form a central element in the ideological stakes proper to a given political arena."[66] Yet name changes also resulted from identity assignments from above, owing to basic "state simplifications" aimed at bureaucratic efficiency. Rather than dealing with an overwhelming mess of vernacular names, many locally specific surnames were conflated with others and fit into more general, but permanent, surname categories.[67] For example, as one informant explained, "When we were in slavery in Segou, in Marakaduguba, we were Djiré. After slavery, when our father, Ba Céblen Djiré, arrived here, his name was transformed into Diarra. . . . There were many other Diarra families here, so when the French did the first census, he transformed our name from Djiré into Diarra."[68] But even as the administration sought to fix the population in categories, names, and villages, it struggled to stabilize the chieftaincy.

Officials routinely reported cases of villagers refusing to obey chiefs; and the abuses of chiefs filled monthly reports and colonial court records. It was easy for local administrators to blame governance problems on elderly or illegitimate chiefs.[69] However, one touring inspector also cited other reasons: notably the infrequent tours and palavers and, most important, the discontinuities in European personnel. He summed up as follows: "The lack of adequate [French] personnel render inefficient and even illusory the control of the administration."[70] Owing to the high turnover of European civil servants and officials, the so-called administrators' waltz, each new commandant struggled to establish his authority, as African intermediaries and canton chiefs probed the limits of the administration's power. In such circumstances, chiefs were quick to seize on opportunities, finding ways to profit from the gaps in authority.[71]

The chieftaincy was a certain path to enrichment, which came at the expense of peasants. Chiefs commonly requisitioned crops and livestock, conscripted laborers for their personal fields, and illegally seized women. They were also instrumental in codifying customary law and rewriting local histories to benefit their lineages. This enabled them to assert greater control over female and junior male labor. Usually, they simply overtaxed the population and kept the surplus. Most transgressions and local forms of corruption went unreported; misdeeds that did not challenge French authority and legitimacy were forgiven. But after repeated reports of canton chiefs siphoning off revenue and inciting village unrest, the commandant in Buguni assigned African "tax intermediaries" to approach village chiefs directly. Over time, these agents, too, became "the cause of conflicts or disputes between cantons and villages."[72]

Even as canton chiefs and indigenous functionaries squeezed the peasantry, the people pushed back. Although chiefs were "decentralized despots" in many ways, there were limits to chiefly power; it was not nearly as totalizing as some have suggested.[73] As Thomas Spear has argued, the colonial state was less than hegemonic and far from successful in normalizing the exercise of power at the local level. Struggling to build its institutions of governance on certain indigenous logics, it was never able to truly stabilize the chieftaincy.[74] At times this breakdown was due to the sheer incompetence of the administration, while at other times it resulted from resistance and peasant initiatives from below. For example, in response to overtaxation by chiefs, many villagers circumvented the canton chiefs and other intermediaries and began delivering their taxes directly to the French post in protest. This practice was reported: "The tendency, which was initiated in the villages, of paying taxes to the district post without first passing through the canton chief increases more and more. . . . They cite as the principal reasons the exaggerated demands made by their canton chiefs."[75] Three years later, when this initiative by peasants was embraced on a wider level, one official remarked how such practices would serve to establish direct contact with African subjects: "The population realizes in effect the advantage that they have in liberating themselves from the intermediary of the canton chief and to address themselves directly to the Commandant for the payment of taxes. . . . When these tendencies manifest themselves, they are always favored, because of the primordial interest that is attached to the wider development of direct relations between the natives and the administrator."[76]

This policy of weakening canton chiefs would later be embraced across French West Africa under Governor General Ponty, who had begun his colonial career as an aide in Colonel Archinard's conquest army in the Western Sudan. After participating in campaigns against Samori, through which he developed a hatred for such Muslim "feudal potentates," Ponty became a district commandant and eventually, in 1904, the lieutenant governor of the French Sudan. His conviction that the French were liberators was carried over into his native policy. For example, in Ponty's circular of 1909, which outlined this so-called *politique des races*, he emphasized the importance of refraining from appointing Muslim chiefs in fetishist zones.[77]

In Buguni, canton chiefs were often characterized as local tyrants who abused their positions of power by wrenching exactions from peasants. But after years of propping up the canton chiefs, French officials were now discrediting them: "It is fitting to note that the institution of canton chief is not an integral part of native social constitution. Certain races, the Bambaras in particular, support it only with difficulty, and have a marked tendency to live in villages under the single direction of the head of this grouping."[78] There were local consequences to this attempt at the structural overhauling of power hierarchies. As feared, increased political anarchy was reported in Buguni. Furthermore, the commandant was suddenly swamped in a welter of petty problems, dealing with over eight hundred village chiefs as opposed to just fifty-two canton chiefs. In many villages, the problem was further exacerbated by the fact that previously there had been no traditional village chief that corresponded with the sort of chief the French had in mind. There had been lineage heads and councils of elders and in some villages a symbolic senior chief, or *dugutigi*. However, the notion of a single man with immense powers over others was alien to the political culture of many communities.

The result was constant contestation over the chieftaincies. And as more people returned from slavery, the local balance of power continued to be tested. Local disputes over the chieftaincy were common: "As soon as the first harvest of millet is assured, now the rivalries of the families begin, each aspires to impose one of its family members on the others as the choice to fill the functions of chief. Thus, it explains the disintegration of many villages: one family or grouping, settles definitively in the middle of the fields, where previously there had only existed a temporary shelter, in order to escape the influence of the chief whose authority they refuse to recognize."[79] Later, as the First World War loomed on the horizon and famine raged across the French Sudan, efforts were made to reel in Ponty's reforms, which included changes in the legal system in 1912. The French ethnographer and head of Native Affairs, Maurice Delafosse, came out strongly in favor of strengthening the chieftaincy, pointing out the consequences of promoting Ponty's "direct contact" approach. By the end of the war and through a quick succession of wartime governor generals, the administration was again reinforcing the authority of canton chiefs to prevent future rebellions and implement plans for economic development.[80]

Beyond chiefs, the social field shifted to the benefit of former tirailleurs, who were powerful actors in local political arenas. Because of their proximity to French rule and their more instrumental roles in the maintenance of colonial order, tirailleurs were in a position to make claims on canton and village chiefs and even lobby for appointment as chiefs themselves. And their outsized influence was considerable in Buguni, a district that had a disproportionately large number of veterans. One official remarked, "Buguni is presently, I believe, the district of the Sudan that possesses the largest number of tirailleurs, retired or not. I regret to point out that they are far from rendering us the useful services that Colonel Mangin had expected. For only a small number among them actually show themselves deferential and useful; the majority consists of big drinkers of dòlò and pernod, and ignore, in principle, all of the black chiefs.... They can, in certain circumstances, paralyze the action of an isolated district guard.... [It is] necessary to enter into contact with them ... [in order to avoid] 'Carthage going into the hands of the mercenaries.' "[81] The colonial administration had invested heavily in the power and prestige of tirailleurs. Now, as the above report suggests, that investment seemed to be backfiring. There were many cases of tirailleurs mobilizing private campaigns to have canton or village chiefs dismissed in their favor. On occasion they did manage to finagle their way up through the ranks. In the interest of maintaining order and preventing an avalanche of politically motivated complaints directed against chiefs, the French usually backed up sitting chiefs in such disputes. Only in the most egregious criminal circumstances did the colonial administration remove a canton chief from power.[82] But just as soldiers and interpreters forced changes in the political arena, emergent religious actors, such as Muslim holy men, contributed to subtle shifts in chieftaincy disputes and the more general religious complexion of localities.

OBSERVING ISLAM: MARABOUTS AND PATTERNS OF COLONIAL INTERVENTION

During the postconquest transition to civilian rule, Muslim traders and the French administration settled into a peaceful modus vivendi. At the same time, owing to the perpetuation of the belief that the inhabitants were naturally fetishist, colonial officials disregarded the importance of Islam, summing up the perceived Muslim question with the ubiquitous phrases "Nothing to report" or "Insignificant." But soon, as unrest across the wider Muslim world grew in the years leading up to the First World War, officials took a keener interest in itinerant marabouts and other so-called foreign influences. While administrators did not see any potential for rebellion in Buguni, circulars from Dakar and reports from surrounding districts in the French Sudan and elsewhere colored local perceptions of Islam.[83] In a more instrumental way, such reports added a sense of urgency to efforts to stop the spread of the "conquering faith." Couched in the language of disinterested anticlericalism, the reports of the administration tried to project an image of neutrality and not taking sides between Muslims and fetishists. Yet in local disputes, administrators clearly weighed religious difference as a crucial variable in their political calculations.

As Christopher Harrison and David Robinson have shown, leading up to the First World War the general administrative mood with respect to Islam was one of fear and suspicion. While there were numerous incidents across French West Africa during these years, a signal turning point was the murder of Xavier Coppolani, an early architect of French Muslim policy. After optimistically lobbying for the establishment of a protectorate over Mauritania, Coppolani had ventured eastward into the Tagant interior, at the outer limits of French influence. There, in a desert encampment in Tidjikja, where the proadministration networks were more diffuse, a rival faction assassinated Coppolani, thus discrediting his "peaceful pacification" approach to conquest. At the same time, international political developments in the Middle East between 1905 and 1914 served as a compelling backdrop for French officials striving to determine the shape and direction of political Islam. Such events, in conjunction with reports of local rebellions and rumors, kept local officials on their toes, chasing chimeras and imagining far-reaching Muslim conspiracies. In French West Africa, there had been considerable internal debate over the most effective Muslim policy and disagreement regarding the role of Sufi brotherhoods in colonial governance. Building on the Algerian experience, Coppolani had focused heavily on the brotherhoods, which, he argued, required tight surveillance and direct control, even going so far as supporting subsidies for Qur'anic education, mosques, and pilgrimage. In contrast, Alfred Le Chatelier argued that the Sufi orders were only loosely organized in West Africa and that Islam could still spread through the activities of unaffiliated itinerant marabouts. Such debates on the merits and character of Islam would span the colonial period.[84]

By 1905, and stemming from the prevailing political currents, marabouts and their practices, known as *maraboutage*, emerged as rather shadowy figures, filling reports with fears of Pan-Islamist plots. In contrast to the "Grands Marabouts" of Senegal and Mauritania, marabouts in Buguni and Sikasso often conformed more to the French image of small-time religious charlatans and amulet makers. Harrison has usefully pointed out how, given the anticlericalism of the French state at this time, these marabouts were viewed as being akin to the parasitical Catholic priest in rural France, who duped ignorant believers through magic. Just as there were constant rumors of Jesuit plots in France, the Muslim marabout, as a sort of local *mahdi*, was believed to be tapping into religious fanaticism and engineering territory-wide jihads.[85]

According to local colonial observers, marabouts in Buguni were having little success "trying to convert people to the religion of Muhammad," whereas in Sikasso marabouts sought to undermine the authority of canton chiefs and even led a "very serious" Islamic movement. By 1906, in response to Dakar's request, colonial surveillance efforts eventually brought Muslim notables into greater focus. In Buguni, the first to appear on the radar was a man from Segu who had been invited by a local chief to set up a Qur'anic school in the canton of Danu. But by the following year, and after "active surveillance" of such figures, the administration dismissed the importance of any "political and religious action." The upshot was that while most districts provided personal files on key marabouts, officials in Buguni responded with cursory dismissal of their importance.[86]

Administrators in Sikasso, by contrast, frequently reported on the district's marabouts, who benefited from both a large population of Jula traders and the town's location along the main trade artery from Segu to Korhogo. Most of them were linked to the Qadiriyya and had direct contacts with the Kunta of Timbuktu, although one of the leading marabouts had done his studies with Shaykh Muhammad Mokhtar in Nioro, among followers of the Tijaniyya.[87] Even when such figures had no direct linkages to the Sufi orders, the theme of amulet makers as a threat to the population was common. Thus, the administration maintained surveillance of such figures to thwart machinations against local victims. It also continued to be on the lookout for attempts at forced conversion. In one case, Niama Diabaté, a marabout from the village of Koloni, went on a reportedly crazy rampage, destroying idols and raiding sacred sites. He first imposed new Muslim names on his family members and then set out "to convert all the inhabitants of his village to Islam." But when he tried building a mosque, he was "chased away by the inhabitants, all fetishists." He eventually took to the road and led a band of followers across the river, to a village where "he and his followers destroyed all the fetish huts of the village, burning all the fetishes." When farmers returned from their fields at the end of the day, they immediately attacked the intruders, killing and wounding several. While the incident was considered "the work of a crazy man," it nevertheless sent a message that itinerant marabouts represented an ongoing threat to the political order.[88]

It was relatively quiet for the next few years, and administrative reports simply recycled hackneyed phrases until Ponty renewed his call for more information. Soon, just as new legal reforms were taking place in 1912, Paul Marty, as the head of the Bureau of Muslim Affairs, synthesized the data collected by district-level administrators on the Muslim question in the production of numerous region-specific volumes. In a broad effort to construct a virtual intelligence database on Islam in Africa, most of the focus was on Muslim personalities. Marty also documented other indices and bodily signs of Islamization, such as prayer styles, beards, facial scarification, and the wearing of different amulets. He concluded that pre-Islamic cultural practices were still far more important than normative Islamic traditions in determining religious identification. Furthermore, African Islam was described as fundamentally docile and localized. As such, Marty reinforced the notion of *Islam Noir*, or "black Islam," as an inferior form of Islam, corrupted by African cultural practices and steeped in fetishism. But even in heretical form, Islam Noir was considered more governable, as long as it was protected from nefarious Arab influences. Indeed, politically, Marty warned of the unforeseen dangers of "religious neutrality," pushing for more proactive safeguard measures to preserve "animism."[89]

In Buguni, from 1911 to 1914, there were copious reports on suspicious characters. Given the fearful state of administrative writing, it is difficult to know the actual roles marabouts played in village communities, but the reports do provide some useful information. In the most detailed portrait of an itinerant marabout in Buguni, one report described an individual named Mamadou Gassemba, a native of Futa Jallon. The holy man carried with him a "bundle of spare things," including a bottle of black ink and a small sack made of animal skin containing a collection of "loose pieces of paper covered with Arabic writing and drawings." There were several gazelle horns decorated with leather, a shell with "a cluster of horsehair," and six cowries. It was determined that in the course of his traveling he was engaged in "the making of amulets and the art of divination." The man had no other resources and no other way of making a living. He was simply "feeding himself freely along the route." In principle, colonial officials tolerated such holy men as long as their influence remained strictly local.[90]

In accord with the ethnic particularism of Ponty's *politique des races*, the administration sought to buttress the power of fetishist chiefs in its political moves against Islam. To this end, palavers were held with village and canton chiefs, who were employed more directly in the struggle to prevent or at least slow the spread of Islam. Regardless of the intentions of traveling holy men, the administration warned chiefs of such people. One report stated, "We have explained to them that these latter, after having made their profitable collections, disappear, leaving the inhabitants with the responsibility to the administration for the seditious activities. . . . Village chiefs have declared to never receive among them foreign marabouts." In some cases, local chiefs intervened directly, preventing Muslims from settling in their villages by simply chasing them away. In other cases, marabouts were arrested after villagers complained of their actions. For example, in 1911, a young woman went to the administration to protest being forced to marry a visiting marabout, Lae Diakité. The holy man was originally from Ivory Coast but had been traveling around and living "from the small gifts that were made to him." The marabout had inspired such terror in one village that the administration stepped in. Interestingly, when the marabout was arrested and imprisoned, the villagers expressed shock because they had "believed the whites to be the friends of marabouts."[91] Indeed, as the administration muddled through in mediating local disputes and controversies, their religious allegiances were far from apparent. And with colonial bureaucracies staffed mostly by Muslims, local people may well have believed local rulers represented a "Muslim power" in some sense.[92]

Although officially the French sought to maintain a position of neutrality in many widely circulated statements, an assessment of local interventions to bolster the authority of fetishist chiefs and sketches of district-level policy statements reveal that officials sought to stop the spread of Islam by reinforcing traditional authority structures. Although it was considered impossible to force Muslims to "return to fetishism," the administration mobilized village chiefs, lineage heads, canton chiefs, and councils of notables in the "fight against bad Muslims." In Sikasso, the commandant outlined his marching orders for chiefs: maintain surveillance of marabouts, reinforce fetishist society, prevent Muslim infiltration, and stop all intrigues against fetishism. He stated,

> Insisting on the necessity of fetishist society, based on a strong
> family, in which the authority of the chief is all powerful; to
> remain organized and to have the heads of family obeyed and
> respected, we are trying, during the palavers, to explain to
> the populations, that their happiness depends on this strong
> organization . . . [and] that Muslims who infiltrate among them,
> are searching in general to bring about dissension in their

family, and to combat and annihilate their chiefs. It is therefore
necessary for them, and they will be given wide latitude in this, to
prevent Islam from attempting this breakdown. . . . The Council
of Notables, by intermediary of the village chief, is responsible
for the execution of these measures stipulated in the interest
of fetishist society: obligatory declaration of all marabouts
in residence or in transit in the district; denunciation to the
administration of all intrigues or attempts against fetishism;
absolute prohibition of opening schools or building a mosque
without the approval of the Commandant.[93]

Although there is no exact outline left behind from the administration
in Buguni, there is evidence that a similar course of action was pursued.
To begin, in 1912 one official reported, "The prestige of the fetishist local
chiefs must be enhanced if we wish these chiefs to be of some help to
the Commandant in the surveillance of Islamism." Furthermore, political
agents and spies traveled throughout the district visiting towns aimed at
curtailing the influence of marabouts. These agents reported when marabouts entered the district from other regions, such as Guinea, Ivory Coast,
or northern French Sudan. When attempts were made to build Qur'anic
schools or mosques, the French would respond by dispatching soldiers
to demolish them.[94] For example, an itinerant marabout named Ibrahim
Diarabi from French Guinea arrived in the canton of Nienandugu and
had a Qur'anic school built. The French quickly sent out district guards to
Mafélé, and they "proceeded to demolish the religious edifice which had
been constructed without authorization."[95] In the village of Kona, a marabout constructed a mosque without authorization but with the consent
of the village chief. The result was the same as in other villages. A report
stated, "From the moment it was brought to my attention, I ordered the
village chief and the marabout to the district capital, on whom a punishment was inflicted. The mosque was demolished without problems."[96]

Pursuing a policy of containment, colonial interventions also included
the surveillance of books and written materials in Arabic. Particular
emphasis was placed on cordoning off the district from Arabic literature
coming from surrounding districts or colonies. For example, when a
man arrived from the district of Segu to settle in the town of Garalo and
distribute Arabic literature, usually just making copies of the Qur'an and

leading prayer, he was arrested and punished.[97] Then, as the First World War approached, more political agents were sent out to scour incessantly through villages under orders to "exercise active surveillance on all Muslim subjects of the district." These agents collected all the scraps of paper with Arabic writing they could find to monitor the communications traveling across the Sahara. Often, as it was noted, such bits of paper contained no seditious material, only verses from the Qur'an.[98] But in the end, largely invisible to colonial observers, the grass-roots expansion of Islam was already underway, driven partly by the mobility of freed slaves.

EMANCIPATION AND ISLAMIZATION

Despite the long, intertwined history Islam has had with slavery in West Africa, few scholars have examined in depth the linkages between slave emancipation and the dissemination of Islamic practices. Martin Klein alludes to conversion at the end of slavery, noting that "former slaves, who had little instruction and often clung to traditional cults, converted or became stricter Muslims." And Humphrey Fisher has speculated that freed slaves "may have carried the seeds of Islam with them, home to fields hitherto unsown." James Searing has also drawn attention to the role of former slaves in Senegal. Emphasizing the "religion of social liberation" thesis, Searing demonstrates how Murid Islam brought with it a liberating ideology of equality, which spurred slaves to flee slave-owning Wolof aristocrats for Muslim communities.[99]

Most colonial observers in the French Sudan correlated emancipation with a decline in the Muslim population. Armed with statistics on Qur'anic schools, Clozel argued that marabouts who had previously depended on slave labor to underwrite their religious and scholarly pursuits were now forced to farm for themselves. Based on the theoretical incompatibility between farming and monotheism, he stated, "Islam is in clear regression. . . . [It] loses territory among the cultivators." Then, following the racially and environmentally determinist theories of Ernest Renan, Clozel pursued an argument common among colonial officials, namely, that herders, nomads, and other mobile groups, such as traders, were naturally inclined to thinking about existence, hence the preponderance of monotheism among them. By contrast, sedentary cultivators were purportedly fetishists by nature owing to their close connections to the land: "Perpetually bent over towards the nourishing land whose inexhaustible fertility and expanse without limit has assured the black cultivator, for infinite generations back, the happiness to live without struggle, without fatigue or constraint of any sort. He naturally envisions his future in a positive light, lacking any metaphysical speculation and not having any connection with his moral responsibility. His present divinity and faith are above all in this world that nourishes him and provides him with all his needs."[100]

Clozel, Delafosse, and others noted that even Muslim Maraka slave-holders had been forced to return to their pre-Islamic ancestral religions. Bereft of their slaves and forced to work the fields, slave masters "progressively abandoned the Muslim faith in order to adopt the fetishist ideas and practices of the Bambaras who surround them."[101] Although such supposedly natural laws were highly reductive, there may have been some truth to the observations. Richard Roberts has shown how the Maraka, having lost their place as former slave owners and traders in the economy and society of Banamba, allowed their "commitment to Islam" to wane and blended in with their pagan neighbors. Robert Launay and Benjamin Soares, with their foci on Korhogo and Nioro, both Muslim merchant centers, agree that the abolition of slavery delivered an economic "crushing blow" to Muslim elites. More recently, Soares challenges the "regression thesis," stating that colonial "assertions and predictions" positing a decline of Islam were "fanciful."[102]

On balance, it is moot to propose a generalized decline or expansion of Islam, particularly as the relations between former masters and slaves in Nioro, Korhogo, Banamba, and Buguni were all very different. One thing is certain: the end of slavery and the wider changes in the political economy forced social adjustments with profound religious consequences. Thus, while there may have been a slight weakening of Islam in high-density slave systems located in and around the market-oriented towns of merchants and traditional Muslim elites, the evidence suggests that there was a countervailing current of Islamization in regions of low-density slave systems. While former slave masters were "obliged to devote themselves to work" and did not have "much time or enthusiasm for praying," as Marty observed, farming did not necessarily translate into fetishism. As we shall see, there were still plenty of Muslim farmers, even rural holy men, who saw no fundamental contradiction between being Muslim and working in the fields.[103]

The first generation of Muslim converts who had been in slavery are now long deceased. Therefore, the "moments of conversion" and the individual motivations behind conversion remain obscure.[104] In that these people were the first generation of Muslims, their conversion represented the initial steps in gradual processes of Islamization characterized by considerable religious flexibility. Communities were incrementally drifting in the direction of being Muslim rather than making decisions to move unambiguously across an imagined religious boundary. Nevertheless, religious changes were occurring. While most colonial administrators were blind to the role of slaves in introducing Islamic practices into their home villages, a few astute observers, such as Marty, were able to see contradictory processes. Marty noted that recently converted slaves were bringing Muslim prayer back to their home villages at the end of slavery. He summarized as follows: "In most of the fetishist villages, there were at least one or two natives returning from slavery and performing Muslim prayer. These Muslims certainly are not very fervent, nor very convinced. But nevertheless, wittingly or unwittingly, they are preparing the ground, more favorable for Islam."[105]

The first Muslims embraced prayer not as a part of larger processes of "communal conversion" or as a result of institutions of Islamic education, but as individuals in disparate localities unified by the common experience of slavery.[106] Because many of the first Muslims had been enslaved during childhood or adolescence and spent their important formative years in captivity, cut off from the religious practices and structures of their home villages, they discovered alternate forms of ritual and identification in Islam. They took on the religious habitus of the locality. Tumani Danyoko, for example, passed his formative years in exile, missing important initiation rites, which normally lasted seven years, and never belonged to the kòmò society.[107] Being excluded from local religious hierarchies was an important reason conversions held upon return. There must have been many returning slaves who did abandon Islam once they reintegrated into their home villages, but in plenty of cases their new Muslim habitus could not simply be removed through ritual ablation, as the first Muslims had spent "part of their lives living among Muslims as slaves."[108] In contrast to refugees, who lived in transplanted communities in exile, slaves were often displaced as individuals, meaning that their assimilation into local cultural norms and practices was more thorough. In terms of statistics, in the aftermath of the slave exodus, there were 13,710 Muslims in Buguni, of the total population of 157,435. Although such numbers on religious identity are far from accurate, this represented an official increase of roughly 11,000 Muslims in the years after the abolition decree of 1905. As there were only five Qur'anic schools, with seventy-eight students, limited to four Muslim trade towns, it seems unlikely that the early expansion of Islam was the result of Qur'anic education.[109]

Oral accounts emphasize the role of returning slaves in this process. In Fulala, Drissa Diallo recounted, "It was the return of slaves, above all, that gave Islam the force necessary to expand here as it did. After the liberation of the slaves, people reintegrated with their families, bringing this new Muslim religion with them. . . . There were five men related by maternal bloodline . . . who introduced the Muslim religion here in N'Golobala at the end of slavery. In our family, it was our father, Kojugu, who first introduced Islam."[110] Testimonies of elders in neighboring villages of Fulala reveal similar histories.[111] And comparative case study material reveals that across the district of Buguni slaves returned with prayer. Informants in the canton of Céndugu reported that the first Muslims were often returning slaves.[112] Similarly, informants in the canton of Basidibé told of the end of slavery playing a decisive role in the spread of Islam. Colonial documents substantiate this link, as one observer reported during a census tour that most of the Muslims were either former slaves or colonial soldiers.[113] In the canton of Gwancédugu, south of the Banifing River, informants reported that the first Muslims in their village were returning slaves. In Tienaga, Zoumana Koné explained how Islamic prayer was introduced into the village: "The person who brought religion [alasira] here was our uncle. But there were actually two people, two people who prayed in our village here, otherwise nobody else prayed here. But these two people, they came back from slavery, bringing prayer with them. One of them had been in slavery in the region of Segu. The other had done his slavery among the Maraka. So these two people were the first people to pray here."[114]

Slave return and reintegration lasted over a decade, so it took time for the first Muslims to realize that they were not alone in their new faith. As more Muslims accrued to local communities, Muslim subcommunities and networks emerged; people slowly connected with Muslims in surrounding villages and began praying together. Imam Drissa Diallo spoke of this process: "Kojugu brought religion here after slavery, and he began to pray alone until some others came to enter the religion with him. They went to congregate among the people of Tenemakana, with Tumani and Bassori, those who had brought prayer there. . . . After that, N'Jignana Baji and Ba Cékoro came back. . . . Then, the father of Sidi Ba Lamine came back. And after that Gnama and Bakoroblén came back with prayer from slavery and added to the others. So at this time, Islam came little by little."[115]

As such testimonies suggest, those credited with returning from slavery with prayer were all men. Yet most slaves in the French Sudan were women. Certainly many female slaves did not return to their home-lands during the years of exodus. As wives or concubines, they had been easier to assimilate into the household culture, and most had created fam-ilies.[116] But there were many female slaves who did return to their homes. Furthermore, colonial court records reveal that numbers of women, often seeking divorce or involved in bridewealth disputes, had Muslim names. For example, in 1910, an apparently Muslim woman, Fanta Koné, sought her freedom from her husband, Mamadu Fofana, claiming that although they had a child together she had been kept in captivity against her will. The court decided that she must be freed.[117] Indeed, there was likely a sizable population of Muslim women who were former slaves alongside their male counterparts, considered the first Muslims. And women would have passed rudiments of their faith onto their children. However, owing to gender biases in oral accounts, few women are credited with introduc-ing Islamic practices into their villages; and given the nature of household gender relations, women could officially embrace Islam only after their husbands or fathers had done so.[118] Nevertheless, as Muslim communities grew in size, Muslim families demanded that their sons marry Muslim girls or at least ritually convert a non-Muslim girl before marriage; con-versely, a Muslim father would never allow his daughter to marry a kafir. However, much research remains to be done on the question of female slaves and the expansion of Islam.

HIDDEN PRACTICES, SOCIAL NETWORKS, AND PUBLIC MANIFESTATIONS

Although the first Muslims were not necessarily social subordinates, their new faith represented a sort of dissident subculture. The ideological and ritual underpinnings of Islam ran counter to bamana

practices, such as the consumption of dòlò, eating bush pig, and sacrifices to power objects. The dominant religious group, led by the village
chief and the head of kòmò power association, effectively policed village
public culture, forcing Muslims underground. In some ways, the cultural
survival skills employed by Muslims represented a "hidden transcript."
Their secret lives were largely conducted "beyond the direct observation
of powerholders." In contrast to the model developed by James Scott,
however, in this case cultural practices should not be narrowly construed
as forms of resistance, in the sense of opposing the claims or actions of a
dominant group.[119]

When they first returned, Muslims were forced to hide their prayers,
as one informant reported: "Muslims were not very numerous at this time
... because the problem of the kòmò was widespread in the village. At
this time, nobody dared to discuss building a mosque in the village. The
followers of Islam were forced to hide themselves when they said their
prayers."[120] When young Muslims tried to perform public prayer, they
were often attacked or even arrested by the chief. In one suggestive case
from the colonial archives, a recent convert to Islam whose parents were
fetishist tried to pray publicly, and the village chief had him arrested. In
a deposition, the chief's official statement read, "Since this individual
has become Muslim, he has sought to make trouble in the village. I put
an end to his intrigues, which have attempted nothing less than the
disappearance of our fetishes. I have forbidden him from calling prayer
in the village, in which, all fetishists, we want to remain fetishists like our
fathers, rather than becoming bad Muslims, like him. I had him arrested
recently for his pranks, and sent him before the Commandant."[121]

Because the social field was so thoroughly dominated by traditionalists, early Muslims sought to break out of isolated, village-level niches
and the clandestine religious lives they lived by investing in translocal
social networks. Such Muslim networks were central to religious dynamics during the early colonial period. They were not only conduits for the
transmission of information, but also "active networks" through which
ideas, beliefs, and practices were reproduced and transformed.[122] And,
as we have seen, these networks would be grafted onto preexisting webs
of bamana cultic affiliation. They were also expanding through the acceleration of commercial transactions and the wider dispersal of Muslim
traders into rural areas. As such, translocal links were facilitated and

strengthened through intervillage prayer associations and forms of social obligation and religious friendship. In many instances Muslims drew on connections with their mothers' natal villages, forging ties through their maternal bloodline. Furthermore, Muslims used the practice of bride exchange (*falen-ni-falen*) to form alliances with other Muslims in remote villages. Such connections enabled them to gain strength in numbers, a development that was not possible within the confines of the village itself.[123]

Muslim subcultures reproduced themselves in specific sites. Communal prayer was performed with groups of Muslims drawn from neighboring villages, often in someone's home and preferably in a settlement removed from the centers of traditional power. In this way they could benefit from the more dispersed settlement patterns, in which village hamlets were at a safe distance from the chief's residence. Thus, even before a mosque had been built or the position of imam designated, local Muslim leaders like Sangaré Cémogo and Tumani Danyoko in Tenemakana and Kojugu Sountura Diallo in N'Golobala stepped forward and brought people together in their homes. The imam of N'Golobala explained, "Before Kojugu became imam he led the people in prayer, and that lasted quite a long time. The inhabitants of the village came and added to him, and they prayed together at the prayer site, everyone going to his house."[124]

Muslim rituals were still rather rudimentary in these days. Prayer focused on simple repetitive chanting of what informants called the *kalima*, also known as the *shahada*. Bits of Sufi litanies were also chanted. Adama Diallo, an elder from the village of Niamala, said, "People would chant the kalima. At this time, the people did not have a big desire to study."[125] From the standpoint of contemporary Muslims, the prayer these pioneers engaged in was incorrect: they did not know all the protocols or the correct way to pronounce Arabic words. As a result, the first Muslims are referred to as pretenders (*an yé ka do ké*), or those who manifested only external signs of Islam and whose prayer was not clear (*jelen*). As it was said, "They knew there was some sort of God, and so they prayed in their own manner."[126] The fact that they prayed symbolized that they were Muslims. The role such figures played in opening a door to a deeper understanding of the relationship between their village and Allah placed them beyond scrutiny. Tumani's grandson explained: "Tumani knew that something had put everything in the world into existence. There was no Qur'an at this moment. There were no marabouts. But Tumani would pray, very simply, he would pray to Allah."[127] Indeed, compared to the normative traditions of Islam, the practices of the first generation of Muslim were fraught with mixing. Colonial officials frequently commented on the religious hybridity of local Muslim rituals. But they were also rather dismissive of African Islam, which, they thought, was so thoroughly deformed by indigenous cultures that it was virtually a different religion. Officials often denigrated the "so-called Muslims" with their cultural promiscuity and messiness. An exemplary passage from one report reads as follows: "[Muslims] know Islam only in name; they do 'Salam' without knowing why. . . . They claim the profession of faith without great conviction, their forehead stained with dust attests that they perform prayer, but they do not understand the meaning of what they say in their invocations to Allah. They ignore fasting . . . but they participate gluttonously in the feast at the end of Ramadan and at Tabaski. They do not seem to give gifts to marabouts, and that is the main reason ambulatory marabouts avoid this district."[128]

On a discursive level, the idea of a discrete Islam Noir reproduced certain categories and negative stereotypes. Setting aside the value-laden judgments, one can see that such accounts do convey a sense of the local religious practices at a time when there was much religious overlap. Early Muslims did practice attenuated and hybrid forms of Islamic rituals. Qur'anic students did focus on simple memorization of the opening of the Qur'an, or *Fatiha*, without understanding it in Arabic. Many early Muslims did participate in community rituals without the sort of interior piety characteristic of many Muslim societies. Such accounts also suggest that while secrecy shrouded the lives of the first Muslims, they were occasionally allowed to bring their faith into public view, such as during the celebration of Muslim holidays: the month of fasting, or Ramadan (*sun kalo*), commemoration of Ibrahim's sacrifice of the ram (*tabaski* or *seliba*), and the celebration of the Prophet Muhammad's birth (*donba*).

There was a tacit understanding between Muslims and traditionalists that the new faith would be tolerated on occasional public manifestations so long as Muslims did not encroach on certain domains of indigenous religious and political life or challenge the authority of the heads of the power associations. There were clearly demarcated limits to these manifestations: "When they were allowed to pray, it was Sangaraje

Cémogo who led the prayers. He led the prayers the whole year, including Ramadan. But when it was time for public prayer, Sangaraje Cémogo
said to his followers, 'I can lead prayers during the month of fasting, but
I cannot organize the public prayer because I do not want to be killed.' "[129]
Traditionalists did more than just tolerate the celebrations, however;
everyone partook in the festivities, enjoying the feasts, dances, and "mixed
sacrifices." Practitioners of local religions would use the opportunity to
make sacrifices to power objects or to their ancestors, while Muslims
would perform sacrifices to Allah (*saraka bò Ala ye*).[130] Colonial officials in
Buguni commented on the celebrations surrounding Ramadan, reporting,
with an air of amusement, when non-Muslims joined in the festivities. In
1907, one official described Ramadan: "The end of Ramadan gave place to
certain rejoicing to which the fetishists took part in as large a part as the
Muslims. Some hastened to seize the occasion to permit them to make
noise and give free rein to their voracious appetites."[131] The year before, it
was observed that Ramadan was "being celebrated in grand style by the
natives, who indulge in their ordinary gatherings. Numbers of guns being
fired at the appearance of the moon and abundant libations during the
three days that follow."[132]

In addition to such isolated public manifestations, a space of mutual
borrowing emerged on a more everyday level. Informants frequently
spoke of pragmatic appropriations and complementary practices which
blurred the boundaries between Islam and bamanaya. Peasants were
consulting Muslim holy men to deal with various misfortunes and buying
amulets for protection. What officials described as an "ensemble of crude
superstitions" was, in fact, an emergent religious formation, characterized
by interdependence and interplay between adherents of local religions and
Muslims. It was facilitated by certain commonalities such as the belief in
local spirits and a single transcendent supreme being, ritual sacrifices,
the use of plants in healing, and an array of other practices.[133] Muslims
integrated indigenous forms of knowledge into their larger repertoires,
and, conversely, traditional healers would often use Muslim benedictions
in their rituals. Even after Islam had been introduced, people continued
making sacrifices to ensure the fertility of the land.[134]

Certainly one of the most important spiritual roles that any religious
leader played in the village was that of rainmaker. The heads of traditional
power associations had filled this role. And rainmaking ceremonies were

some of the most vital and collaborative rituals of the community. In Wasulu it was recounted as follows: "Before the spread of Islam, we had a stream here. When there was a problem of rain, there was a sort of music here, a music that unfortunately no longer exists. We called it *Buru*. So this *buru* was played with the *yabara* [a sort of calabash drum]. When one started to play it, all of the men and women would put themselves in white earth. Nobody would wear black. They did this music while walking down to the sacred stream. That was done when it did not rain at the beginning of the rainy season, when the stream was at the point of drying up. When they started the libation ceremony, the same night of the ceremony it would rain abundantly until the sacred stream started to overflow! One could say that it had nothing to do with Islam, but it was a form of *Aladeli* [invocation of Allah]."[135]

Islam introduced changes in rainmaking rituals. While traditionalists were performing their libations and music on the banks of sacred streams, Muslim rituals focused on group prayer, chanting of the kalima. Muslims also sought to fill this role of rainmaker using forms of divination and geomancy. An informant in Fulala explained it as follows: "For the *mori* [holy man] it was prayer. If the problem of rain became very difficult, they would prepare their things there, put the toad there and do their things, and if the toad jumped across it, then this day there it would rain. There were others who would do it near the termite mounds. Even during the dry season, when you put it near the termite mound and raised it above, you would hear the rumblings of thunder."[136] Evidence suggests that the most powerful, last-resort ritual was performed by the women's power association. According to one imam, when the prayers of Muslims failed to bring rain, "Women would come and do their special ceremonies, and thanks to the combining of the different prayers together Allah would make it rain." When asked if the women's ceremony was tied to Islam, he responded abruptly, "No." But then he added, "Though it had nothing to do with Islam, the two complemented one another, so if both of them helped the people to have what they want, we could say that the religions are complementary."[137]

Two of the most profound social transformations in the district of Buguni and in the entire French Sudan were the end of slavery and the spread of Islam. The case of Buguni was unique in that the end of slavery in the French Sudan was a much more dramatic event, characterized by

mass exodus and massive numbers of people. In contrast to other localities, such as the Wolof kingdoms in Senegal, Islamization in Buguni was
more of a territorial or geographic expansion; the religion was spread
spatially through the diffusion of people migrating away from Muslim
centers. On a social level, slaves who returned as Muslims to their villages
in Buguni were forced to contend with a non-Muslim religious majority,
whereas runaway slaves in Senegal joined Muslim communities.[138]
Furthermore, as we have seen, the violence, terror, and displacement
during the late nineteenth century were greater in southern Mali and
contributed to wider social dislocation. These particular logics determined
the ways in which village localities worked out the details of religious
change over the course of the colonial period.

Slavery and its demise had a leveling effect; there was an erosion of
the old hierarchies, idioms, and ideologies of inegalitarianism based on
"caste." A decade before, the displacement of refugees had attenuated
certain social distinctions and markers of local difference. In a similar
way, the dislocation caused by slavery would deepen this process of caste
fragmentation, engendering a greater sense of equality and shared suffering. As a result, with few hereditary Muslim lineages, as in the Sahel,
the expansion of Islam occurred in an environment in which virtually
anyone, regardless of prior caste or social position, including slaves and
blacksmiths, could benefit from subscribing to the new faith. The religious repercussions of this leveling process would not be palpable in most
villages until decades later. However, the end of slavery and the attendant
social adjustments set in motion a multigenerational religious drift.

CHAPTER 4

Coping with Colonialism

CONTINUITY AND CHANGE IN THE INTERWAR YEARS

In 1928, upon the death of the canton chief, a succession dispute erupted in Fulala. With numerous claimants throwing their hats into the ring, the French commandant tried to quiet the row, while steering his hand-picked candidate, Wakoro Suntura, into power. As the incumbent canton "representative," and the chief's nephew and interpreter, he seemed the ideal choice.[1] But Wakoro had used his position to virtually enslave people, singling out rival villages for harsh treatment, rigorous tax collection, and forced labor.[2] For some, such chiefly actions and forms of predation were synonymous with slavery. And, indeed, across the district, chiefs and their intermediaries were using their positions as big men to accumulate pawns, seize livestock, and recruit young men to work in their personal fields. Later, in 1946, when African delegates went to Paris to lobby for the end of forced labor and to contest the citizen–subject divide, they too invoked the image of slavery. As it turns out, these claims were more than rhetoric. They resonated with the daily experiences of colonial subjects toiling across France's African empire.[3] For this reason, the stakes were high in contestations over institutions of local governance. Just as administrators embraced policies of association and increasingly sought to reconstitute the chieftaincy while encouraging closer collaboration between chiefs and new colonial elites, the fundamental contradictions inherent in the civilizing mission were becoming more apparent.[4]

The violence and coercion associated with the chieftaincy and the system of summary justice, or the *indigénat*, were not expressions of purely local interests and power relations. They also represented state-effects of colonial policies. Before the First World War, France had yet to tap into what colonial officials believed was the French Sudan's enormous potential for rational economic development. Then, the war provided the context in which the colonial state's capacity for top-down planning was greatly enhanced, while advancing technology and revolutionizing the management of labor.[5] After the war, there was renewed interest in the colonies as producers of raw materials for the metropole, which led to the initiation of grandiose public works projects, the rationalization of agriculture, and a systematic use of forced labor. Such colonial interventions, along with the combined shocks of the Depression and devastating famines, forced permanent shifts in subsistence practices and village social relations. In these circumstances, peasants increased their production of cash crops and left their homes as migrant workers.

I want to focus on how people coped with the everyday demands of colonialism. Most of the chapter explores the economic and material realities that framed the strategies and life chances of communities and individuals. As colonialism was consolidated and routinized, structures were put in place and processes were set in motion that would fundamentally reshape the social landscape of Buguni. In establishing the historical linkages between changes in religious practice and rural social life, I need to account for larger political and economic determinants. In particular, the role of the colonial state must be factored in as a force that generated social change. For societies so recently removed from slavery and still within living memory of precolonial village life and the wars of Samori there were important continuities that gave colonialism its unique character in Buguni.

There were also important political changes after the war, as tens of thousands of soldiers returned from Europe with an altered view of empire and their place in it. In the rancorous conflict in Fulala, one of the key players was Samba Diarra, a forty-year-old decorated veteran and former slave. Samba had been born in the village of N'Golobala to the Suntura lineage. When Samori's forces invaded Fulala, he and his mother were captured and sold into slavery. Passing between the hands of Maraka traders, they ended up in Segu, where Samba, adopted as the slave master's son, remained through the period of emancipation. When the First World War broke out and families were asked to volunteer their sons for military service, Samba was offered up. After the war, he returned to the French Sudan as a Muslim convert and became an interpreter, taking a position in the district of Buguni.[6] This sort of social mobility was not unusual. Oral and colonial sources are replete with cases of former slaves serving as soldiers and functionaries. Slaves even became chiefs, as one report in Buguni noted: "Many of the chiefs are not 'chefs de race.' They are, for the most part, men of servile origin."[7] In any case, Samba Diarra did not lobby for his own candidacy, but he was involved in the behind-the-scenes wrangling aimed at bringing his kin from N'Golobala to power. As a literate functionary, he wrote numerous letters and even presented his village's case to the lieutenant governor in Bamako. At the same time, there were other, more inchoate forces at work. Lurking in the local shadows, the head of the kòmò society in Tenemakana and a powerful bard fought hard to outmaneuver Wakoro by bringing religious pressure to bear in the dispute. In situating political struggles in local arenas, one must take into consideration certain structural continuities, religious processes, and cultural idioms.

ISLAM, COLONIAL GOVERNANCE, AND THE CHIEFTAINCY, C. 1920S AND 1930S

On the heels of emancipation young men were conscripted in droves to fight for France. As the story of Samba Diarra suggests, colonial military service was one of the paths out of slavery. Whether woloso or jòn slaves, roughly 180,000 tirailleurs served in the First World War, many of whom fought and died in the trenches to defend French soil.[8] In Buguni, as we have seen, the local sentiments of debt to the French likely made recruitment easier among supposedly grateful subjects. But also, given the region's historical links to slavery and its position as an emerging labor reservoir, Buguni had "the highest proportion of ex-tirailleurs" of any district in the French Sudan.[9] Even for noncombatants, the war represented a historical rupture. On the home front, peasants were asked to contribute grain and other commodities such as cotton, rubber, and sisal. In certain regions, the requisitions and hardships brought to the surface long-simmering anger among chiefs over being stripped of their precolonial power and authority. With the diversion of colonial troops to France, disgruntled chiefs seized the opportunity and fought to reclaim their autonomy. These revolts were brutally suppressed.[10] However, they sent a signal to the administration. After the war, Governor-General François Clozel moved to shore up the authority of chiefs. In a reversal of the trend established under Ponty, the chieftaincy would henceforth be decided in rigorous conformity with local traditions.[11]

From the standpoint of French governance of Muslim subjects, the war put to rest concerns over imminent Pan-Islamic jihads. Large numbers of Muslim soldiers from West and North Africa fought bravely and died for France, and leading Sufi shaykhs publicly supported the French war effort. For example, shaykh Sidiyya Baba backed the recruitment of African soldiers, wrote prayers for the troops, and theologically decoupled "Ottoman actions from Islamic obligations," hence clearing the way for Muslims in the colonial army. In exchange for greater autonomy in his religious activities, Malik Sy pledged his loyalty and paid an enormous sacrifice when his oldest son died in combat. Amadu Bamba, the founder of the Murids, recruited hundreds of soldiers for the French and made public pledges of loyalty.[12]

Although strands of association policy had been in circulation for decades, the interwar years saw its greatest crystallization in practice. One of the strongest advocates for a native policy based on traditional authority was Maurice Delafosse. In 1912, although he warned against viewing Islam as an evil, Delafosse argued that Africans and their institutions of governance should remain firmly rooted in their animist faith.[13] In time, Delafosse found a reliable ally in Jules Brévié, the governor general of French West Africa from 1930 to 1936, who had actually started his career in the French Sudan, serving as the commandant of Bamako. Later in life, he was the governor of Indochina and finally the minister of the colonies under Pierre Laval's Vichy government.[14] Brévié's views on religious policy, which was tightly linked to French conceptions of indirect rule, were summed up in his provocatively entitled book *L'Islamisme contre 'Naturisme.'* Reflecting the sociological currents of the day, especially that of Emile Durkheim and Lucien Lévy-Bruhl, Brévié embraced an essentialized pre-Islamic "naturism" as the foundation of his native policy and theorized that conversion to Islam would lead to political and social disorder. In short, Brévié saw French secularism as being engaged in a political battle for the souls of Africans, whose primitive religious lives and "organic solidarity" had to be protected from the disruptive threats of Islam.[15] He was not unique. Around the same time, the French administration in Morocco was similarly seeking to preserve pre-Islamic Berber custom against putative foreign Arab contamination, which culminated in the Berber *dâhir* of 1931 separating Berber from Arab custom. In short, religious policy was inextricably linked to methods of colonial governance aimed at maintaining political order and control.[16]

Despite the efforts to reinforce tradition, the expansion of Islam was given a boost by wartime mobilization, which necessitated more extensive travel and improved communications. Compared to most rural communities, the French colonial army, with its camps and transit stations, served as a sort of religious crucible that accelerated cultural change but also impressed conformity. In time, the colonial army even facilitated prayer, pilgrimage to Mecca, and wider access to religious materials. In 1916 the lieutenant governor of the French Sudan drew attention to tirailleurs "leaving as fetishists from their villages of origin" and returning to their families to "announce their conversion to the religion of Muhammad."[17] Many of these soldiers would later move on to positions in local bureaucracies, as the story of Samba Diarra suggests. Although there was an undoubted link between military service and a wider embrace of Islam, however, conversion was not a foregone conclusion. Furthermore, during the First World War, at a time of considerable fear of Pan-Islamist plots, military officers often exaggerated the supposed internal threat Muslim soldiers might pose. Although military service did not necessarily translate to conversion, viewed from the perspective of such districts as Buguni, veterans represented an important social group of returning Muslims, Muslims who would accrue considerable political influence.[18]

Across French Sudan, Muslim functionaries were becoming dominant in administrative centers, as they entered the state apparatus and made Islam the default religion of the bureaucracy. Delafosse had expressed fears that conversions were resulting from the influence of Muslim intermediaries. And Marty had advocated for the elimination of Arabic from use by African intermediaries in order to avoid a more generalized spread of Islam.[19] Archival sources in the French Sudan similarly suggest that Islam was becoming a powerful marker of social prestige among colonial functionaries. One report stated, "In this connection, one must note the action of the native functionaries who, by their example and sometimes their words, make themselves, in a way under our cover, the propagators of Islam. . . . In general, its progress reaches the elite natives first. To pray constitutes a sort of certificate of evolution and a certain snobbism."[20] Nevertheless, the influence of Muslim elites was often limited to small urban enclaves in an overwhelmingly rural world. Only later, as we shall see, when census tours became more regular and agricultural monitors spent more time in villages, would the bureaucratic tentacles of religious pressure begin to grow.

Whether the troops were Muslim or not, as Gregory Mann has shown, soldiering became one of the definitive paths to power. Previously, many villages had sent their undesirables, such as slaves and orphans, to serve as soldiers. After the war these low-status men returned home and found work in the colonial government, most occupying the lower ranks of the administration as office boys, gardeners, district guards, and such. Having French language skills and being familiar with colonial methods, they also took up positions as postmen, foremen, functionaries, interpreters, canton representatives, and even chiefs.[21] Still, despite their loyalty in time of war, they became "unruly clients," often suspected of being "mixed up in the intrigues directed against canton chiefs." In certain cases, they competed for and often captured the position of canton chief itself, or at least took bribes and lobbied on behalf of kin. As canton representatives, they took advantage of their canton chief's old age and fragility and became de facto rulers. Once in power, they sought to hold on to it. An official noted the power of these representatives: "I would not want to suppress this institution that still responds to a certain need in the district, where the canton chiefs, for the most part illiterate, prefer to receive our orders through native intermediaries, having their trust, and who are designated under the name 'representatives' . . . some of these auxiliaries have grown in political importance, and not always without inconveniences. . . . In posing as vice canton chiefs, they maneuver to succeed those whom they represent . . . abusing their trust and most often trying to gain support for themselves from the native personnel of the post."[22]

At the same time, alongside soldiering, the expansion of French education served as a pipeline for channeling the sons of chiefs and village notables into bureaucratic positions. By 1935 four French schools had been set up in the district of Buguni, with a total of 446 students, or an average of 8 students per canton. It would appear that elites came to see the benefits of sending their family members to the French schools, as by the mid-1930s it was mainly "the sons of notables, chiefs and those of functionaries and merchants" who made up the student body. Aside from working in the bureaucracy, many returned to rural areas and served as grass-roots agents of modernization and propaganda: "After a few years of studies, they return to their homes. . . . They are just able to translate to the chiefs the notes of the Commandant and send the reports of chiefs on the events in their villages. . . . They propagate around them the advice on hygiene and the good reputation of our administration."[23] The commonly noted irony was that in pushing incrementally ahead with its heavily diluted civilizing mission, Western-educated African elites, or so-called évolués, became the most ardent challengers of traditional author-ity. One official pointed out what had been an issue in colonial Senegal and in urban settings for decades: "Certain natives, more or less évolués, have a marked tendency to free themselves from the previous social constraints, replacing them with individualistic aspirations, and it is this [group] that presently disputes the authority of certain chiefs."[24]

Informants noted how such new elites derived their power from the "work of paper." Indeed, there was a proliferation of "administrative literature," as auxiliary figures like interpreters produced and deployed written documents in contestations over the chieftaincy.[25] The entrance of the bureaucratic work of paper into political disputes occurred at a time of increasing scriptural authority, represented by the slow expansion of Qur'anic schools and the symbolic capital that accrued to those who could claim Qur'anic knowledge. This highlights the complex political nexus in which the oral and written intermingled and reframed bases of power.

In the dispute over succession that arose in Fulala, notables were called to the headquarters to resolve the political impasse in 1929. When Samba Diarra caught wind of Wakoro's continued pursuit of the chief-taincy, he sent a letter to the commandant telling of Wakoro's plot to have his rival discredited by charging him with adultery and swindling. Ignor-ing Samba's accusations, the commandant went ahead and sentenced the accused party to prison. Samba then carefully crafted another letter and sent it to the head of French Sudan's Political Bureau in Bamako. In the letter, after a foundation narrative of Fulala and brief genealogy, he ended as follows: "After this war [Samori], it was Fabala of Kologo, then Bafing of Massala, who died in 1926, then Famodié Suntura in Sekan, it is thus that the command has passed. Now, the turn for N'Golobala has arrived. The population has designated Numucé in N'Golobala to be the canton chief. Wakoro wants to be elected, but the population [has refused him]."²⁶ Indeed, historically, the chieftaincy in the kafo of Fulala had been shared among five villages: Massala, Sekan, N'Golobala, Niamala, and Kologo. And during the colonial period the canton chief was drawn from these villages in order of their foundation. Since Famodié was from Sekan, the next in line would logically have been someone from N'Golobala. Samba followed up his letter by traveling to the capital for a meeting with the lieutenant governor. The immediate results of Samba's efforts were mixed. While an official was dispatched to Fulala within days to investigate the chieftaincy dispute, Samba had made himself an enemy of the local administration by going over their heads. After being outflanked, the commandant wrote to Lieutenant Governor Jean Henri Terrasson de Fougères: "[Regarding] the position taken by Samba Diarra in the affair of the canton of Fulala, it remains only to inform you of the new attitude adopted by Samba Diarra since his last trip to Bamako. Samba, who had previously appeared to be a calm and simple 'good boy,' has brusquely revealed himself to be a knucklehead, aggressive, and instigating. His actions are to be watched."²⁷

In his investigation, the lieutenant governor's assistant soon discovered that in addition to lacking a canton chief, seven of the twenty-four villages in Fulala had no village chiefs. This was not unusual. The problem of vacant chieftaincies reached far beyond this single canton. In 1926 almost one-third of all villages, or roughly three hundred, in the district were without chiefs, while in many other villages "command was divided," as "heads of families refused to obey the true chiefs." Part of the problem was the continued disappearance of peasants into remote rural hamlets. As agrarian frontiers expanded and small villages proliferated in outlying areas, problems of command and order were exacerbated. In remote cantons along the border with Ivory Coast or in the inaccessible northern region of Banan, distance too made colonial governance difficult. Employing their usual state-distancing strategies, many rural communities were able to completely evade the state. In response, the administration made a push to "regroup stray villages," although the colonial state would remain rather weak in many rural areas until the so-called second colonial occupation after the Second World War.²⁸

In theory the canton chief appointed village chiefs. But, unlike other colonial settings, such as Senegal, in Buguni there were no foreign or provincial chiefs in power. Chiefs were drawn from within their villages. In order to avoid lengthy, unresolved disputes, one official suggested, "The village chieftaincy should be designated by the canton chiefs instead of by the notables involved." This method would also restore to canton chiefs "a bit of their former prestige, which will flatter their vanity and incite them to occupy themselves more actively in the villages under their dependence." As colonial big men, canton chiefs were believed to measure their power by their number of dependents, and many of the chiefs, having lived during the precolonial period, were aware of what constituted traditional power. Colonial officials noted that authority problems would probably persist until the older generation had disappeared and a younger, colonial generation of chiefs took over. They would be, or so it was hoped, more knowledgeable of French bureaucratic norms and also more malleable.[29] Even as the administration sought to transfer chieftaincies to the young, skilled, and energetic, communities refused to accept such men as legitimate chiefs.

In the case of Fulala, the commandant struck upon an idea: what about amalgamating Fulala with the neighboring canton of Siondugu, which had an ideal canton chief? He wrote, "I hope to find out the racial affinities that exist between the inhabitants of Fulala and Siondugu, the neighboring canton that is, by chance, commanded by an energetic chief, who, should the amalgamation be possible, would know how to 'break in' [assouplir] the unruly and undisciplined Fulala." In response, Lieutenant Governor Terrasson cast doubt, cautioning, "In order to avoid future disorder or complaints, the designation [of chief] should take place without prejudice and conforming to custom." It was decided that the notables of Fulala would elect their chief. In July, twenty individuals, including village chiefs, tirailleurs, and elders presented themselves as legitimate successors. An election was held, and a new chief was named. But, in a break with tradition, the chieftaincy remained in Sekan; the power stayed in the hands of Wakoro. The result was peasant unrest and near insurrection.[30]

What role Samba Diarra's intervention played in the chieftaincy row is a matter of speculation. What is known is that his kin Numucé was eventually elected as the canton chief of Fulala. Certainly Diarra's direct appeal to Lieutenant Governor Terrasson brought higher authorities into the dispute. A few years later, on Bastille Day of 1934, Diarra, now a retired functionary, received certain awards, becoming even a member of the Conseil d'Administration du Soudan Français, so apparently he had smoothed things over. And, parenthetically, lest one forget who was in charge, on the French Republican day of celebration when Samba was honored, officials commanded demonstrations of respect and loyalty from all the canton chiefs and tirailleurs, while making it clear to the "natives in attendance" that taxation was not "a kind of tribute to a conqueror, as in the time of Samori, but a native contribution to the work of protection, security, and moral uplift."[31] In any case, by 1929 the archival trail ended with respect to the chieftaincy dispute in Fulala. The oral record being the only guide, I turn to local versions of this history, which emphasize the roles played by religious authorities and by peasants themselves, who threatened to use violence in order to prevent Wakoro's investiture. N'waari Suntura recounted, "Wakoro wanted to become the canton chief again, but the people would not have it. The day the Commandant came to designate Wakoro as the canton chief, the people arrived with their machetes and rifles, ready to kill Wakoro if he was appointed."[32] Beyond well-placed kin and the threat of insurrection, there may have been other factors. Indeed, in local understandings the seizure of power was never merely a secular affair. It required the consultation of oracles, sacrifices, and approval from religious authorities. In other words, it involved contact with invisible spiritual domains. This is not to say that Samba's secular letter writing was not seen as magical, representing the mastery of the white man's occult power. But there were clear, well-established religious paths to power.[33] Thus, for informants the decisive moment in this drama was the consultation of the kòmò of Tenemakana and the taking of oracular advice. The following oral account provides an inside view:

> The Commandant called the people of Fulala to Tusséguéla. . . .
> Our father, Numucé, traveled on foot, as the kòmò told him to
> do, even as all the others arrived on horseback. Everyone was
> stunned to see Numucé travel such a great distance on foot. . . .
> They waited until Numucé appeared in the distance, walking
> with the great bard, Jeliba. The people of Tenemakana joined
> him, and the people of Kologo joined him, and the kòmòtigi of
> Tenemakana. Then [seeing the kòmòtigi and powerful bard] the
> other candidates lost all hope. . . . Everyone in attendance raised

their hands for Numucé. The Commandant spoke: "Then it is
Numucé who will make the decisions. Here are four guards to
serve you. Any person who opposes Numucé will be arrested and
spend their life in prison." Then, our father said his oath before
the population of Fulala: "As canton chief, should I betray Fulala,
may my entire line become a line of good-for-nothings, but
should one single person betray me, young or old, they will be
washed away by a torrent of water."[34]

Fulala was not alone in its contestations over the chieftaincy. Nor was
the centrality of religion in such processes unique. Three comparative case
studies, Basidibé, Céndugu, and Gwancédugu, shed light on chieftaincy
politics. In the canton of Basidibé, the fetishist chief Balan Sidibé remained
in power until 1937, when, following protests over his abuses of power, he
was dismissed. The case is instructive in that it provides rare documenta-
tion of the grievances of the peasants. During the proceedings to unseat
Balan, the village chief of Assamorola, Soloman Sidibé, said in his deposition, "Balan's entourage mistreated my people who worked on the road.
He sought to take them to work for him personally, but they fled. He also
manipulated the price of cotton and did not reimburse us." Balan even
reportedly intervened in village politics by naming chiefs, who served him
directly: "After the death of our village chief, Balan appointed a chief . . .
he forced the people of the village to work for him, we did not dare speak
to the *Commandant*." In Koniba-Barila, the village chief, Suleyman Sidibé,
reported, "I wanted to put a canoe on the river, and he made me pay two
cows for that." By 1937, on the basis of grievances like these, twenty-nine of
the thirty-five villages in the canton reportedly refused to obey the chief. An
official reported the predicament: "For two years now, the canton chief has
lost all authority. It is impossible for him to execute any order in the
canton. . . . It is necessary to eliminate Balan or expect, if not serious disorder, at least perpetual anarchy and perhaps mass exodus to Guinea."
At the same time that peasant grievances were growing, the religious
and political landscape was changing. By 1928, in the middle of Balan's
tenure, a census official reported on the expansion of Islam, noting that
mosques were being built and Qur'anic schools were being established.
Furthermore, Balan had tarnished the image of bamanaya and of the kòmò
by associating them with violence, coercion, and the rule of brute force

(*fanga*). On the eve of his dismissal, possibly to curry favor with village chiefs, Balan changed his official religious identity and declared himself Muslim. In short order, however, he was deposed. By this time, most village chiefs among the pool of candidates for the chieftaincy had Muslim names, indicating that multigenerational processes of religious change had reached a point at which nominal Muslims were accepted in local positions of power. In the final vote, Suley Sidibé, a rural Muslim notable, was elected. He had worked in Ivory Coast for years as a trader and shopkeeper before the First World War. Owing to the long-standing connections between trade and Muslim communities, his years in Ivory Coast among Jula traders would certainly have reinforced his Muslim identity.[35]

Elsewhere Muslims were becoming canton chiefs, such as in the canton of Gwancédugu, where the ascension of the first Muslim chief to power was surrounded by political disputes. Until 1938 fetishist chiefs had reigned in this canton. Nakidian Konaté had been in power since 1897, and when he died in 1932 his nephew, Tumani Konaté, also a fetishist, replaced him. Within a year of Tumani's nomination, however, village chiefs began refusing to obey his orders. The state intervened and quickly replaced the disgruntled village chiefs. Then, in 1935, Bakari Traoré, a Muslim chief from the village of Bilendio, began a coordinated campaign and movement of opposition to Tumani Konaté, which resulted in the withdrawal of nine villages from the canton and their refusal to cooperate. Again, the colonial state punished the dissenters and imprisoned Bakari. At this point Tumani suddenly died, ending the rule of bamana chiefs. The upshot was that a Muslim chief, Mori Cékoroba Konaté, was elected. His legitimacy was given a further boost by one of the most influential Sufi shaykhs in the district, Sidiki Koné, who had a large following in Gwancédugu.[36]

In neighboring Céndugu fetishist chiefs had been in power since the beginning of colonial rule. In 1934 the first Muslim, Sibiri Koné, was appointed to head the canton. At the time, the fetishist Daba Koné, a former tirailleur, was in power, although Sibiri Koné, his cousin, had really been in command, serving as the canton representative. Apparently, as an elder Daba lost interest in the chieftaincy and restricted his role to attending a few palavers. Then, upon the death of his brother, Daba inherited the title head of the fetishes in Céndugu, requiring that he step down as canton chief. But Daba Koné did not go peacefully. Within months, he was lobbying to reclaim his position as chief. Soon he was conveniently dead. After consulting a local oracle, his son suspected that Daba had been murdered by Sibiri and brought a complaint against the new canton chief. Sibiri responded by throwing him in prison for "unjustified complaint." This changing of the guard was doubly symbolic as Sibiri was a "practicing Muslim," the first to take the chieftaincy. As long as Sibiri proved himself an effective ruler, much could be forgiven.

A quintessential big man, Sibiri Koné was known to buy up young girls as pawns from poor families and to recruit men to work his personal fields without pay. Forced labor and wartime requisitions were equally tied to his legacy. Furthermore, he was viewed as an illegitimate chief, one who had been imposed on the people by the French. His family's path to power had been via soldiering and service in the colonial bureaucracy. When a group of villages contested his legitimacy in 1937, colonial officials noted, "His nomination to the chieftaincy of Céndugu does not appear to have been based on the normal principles of customary succession. As a former representative in Buguni, he maintained good relations with the native personnel, who appear to have played a main role in his election." Later, because of his association with the wartime hardships under Vichy, Sibiri became highly unpopular, and in opposition to his power many people looked to Niamaba Koné, "the chief fetishist in Kebila" for leadership. In contrast to Sibiri, who was viewed as "the chief for the whites," Niamaba was "in the eyes of the natives the only real chief of the country."[37] Still, the administration took a pragmatic approach and continued to prop up Sibiri, despite his lack of traditional legitimacy. Even as the state championed association and tradition, wherever convenient and possible the administration bolstered the power of illegitimate chiefs and ignored customary practices and certain colonial articles of faith by appointing Muslims to rule over fetishists. In short, there were enormous gaps between imperial rhetoric and local colonial governance. This was particularly the case in questions of labor, as officials often turned a blind eye to excesses of violence in the service of what they called development and progress.

COLONIALISM, COERCION, AND CALAMITY

After the war the French empire-state embraced regulated forms of coercion in pursuing its plans for the *mise en valeur*, or development, of the colonies. For some, forced labor was a requisite disciplinary wringer in the civilizing mission; colonial subjects could be educated and taught to work, but only by force. Although forced labor had been used since the period of conquest, development plans, in both public and private enterprises, now required even larger and more regimented labor inputs. As Frederick Cooper has argued, the colonial state struggled with the contradictions inherent in its labor policies. On one hand, it espoused free labor ideology in ending slavery, particularly as a rhetorical component to justify imperialism. On the other hand, its labor needs were simply not being met through the market. As in most colonies, the French state evoked "public purpose" and the need to open Africa via transportation networks through the provisional use of forced labor.[38]

By 1912, even as the slave exodus continued, the administration authorized the use of *prestations*, a sort of labor tax on all adult men, in the building and maintaining of roads, bridges, colonial edifices, wells, and telegraph lines. Prestations, the most widespread form of coerced labor, required that each family provide able-bodied male labor for an established number of days each year, depending on the requirements of the canton. At the same time, villagers were responsible for clearing village paths and maintaining local roads. Often, one person in each family would be designated to perform prestations for everyone, working several consecutive rotations so that older brothers could farm or migrate to find money. Organized in small work crews, the men served in fifteen-day rotations, although district guards often prolonged the work period.[39]

There was also the *deuxième portion*, or conscripted military labor, composed of reservists left over from military recruitment. They performed longer-term forced labor, usually on major public works projects, such as the railway line connecting Bamako to Dakar, the irrigation project called Office du Niger, and the private plantations of French settlers. The use of military reservists in development projects began in 1928 in the French Sudan and would ebb and flow through the Second World War, when the Vichy government intensified labor compulsion. There were always internal debates and challenges to the system of forced labor, but it remained fairly consistent until its abolition in 1946. Indeed, even when the International Labor Organization adopted the Forced Labor Convention of 1930, the French government voted against its acceptance, objecting to what it saw as international meddling in a national military matter, since forced laborers were technically military conscripts. Later, when the leftist Popular Front government decided to ratify the convention, the only major change was that recruitment became less involuntary. The administration in the French Sudan stipulated, as a cosmetic public relations move, that commandants had only to certify that forced laborers in their districts had volunteered for service. Given the administrative code of silence on the ground, often shrouding local abuses of colonial labor practices, the deuxième portion, prestations, compulsory crop production, summary justice under the indigénat, and violence would continue to be routine aspects of life for African colonial subjects.[40]

As we have seen, the effects of colonial power were felt unevenly across the landscape. Within Buguni, not every canton or village was compelled to perform forced labor with the same frequency or intensity. Certain cantons in which large public works projects were underway demanded more labor, and certain canton chiefs were harsher and more exacting than others in their recruitment of men. In Wasulu, the canton of Basidibé was responsible for building and maintaining the bridge over the Wasulu-Balé River, which, according to one official, "necessitated a considerable effort from the forced laborers." Similarly, in the canton of Céndugu forced laborers built and maintained a bridge on the route from Buguni to Sikasso. Each year, they worked long days repairing the bridge, which was submerged and destroyed during the rainy season.[41] Bakari Koné provided a shop-floor view of the forced labor process: "To build the roads, we worked with our traditional tools. We dug into the ground, beginning with the black dirt all the way down into the red earth, breaking the rocks, and spreading the dirt out on the road.... From here all the way to Bamako, we built this road with our physical effort.... [They] could beat you until you were dead and nobody could do anything. Until you came back, your family would be worried because forced labor included every kind of suffering in it, and often death.... It was the head of the work crews and the guards who tortured us."[42] The degree to which forced labor impinged on a given community also depended on the village's relations with the canton chief. Chiefly patrimonialism and "internal colonialism" had its winners and losers; benefits and resources accrued to the chief's allies, while their enemies shouldered increased burdens. As one colonial official pointed out, "Too often the animosities of chiefs play a role in exercising the designation of the forced laborers." In Fulala, villagers from Tenemakana worked on roads and bridges over the streams when the chieftaincy was based in Sekan. When the chieftaincy was moved to N'Golobala under Numucé Suntura, forced labor exactions were lightened, as Tenemakana was a long-standing ally of N'Golobala.[43]

Performative violence was routine in colonial encounters. Under pressure to bring in taxes, maintain order, and recruit adequate numbers of forced laborers and soldiers, African intermediaries resorted to brutal methods.[44] Although archival sources are silent on the subject, oral accounts tell stories of cruelty and abuse inflicted on men and women in the daily functioning of empire. Sekou Koné recalled what happened to someone who was unable to pay his taxes: "They would beat you in front of your children. It was humiliation, such shame at this time. . . . To be beaten in front of your wife and children and family." In the canton of Basidibé, another elder reported, "Our family suffered so much because of taxes. . . . The guard would come here to the village with the canton chief to collect taxes, and if you did not have the money, they would shave your head, put a metal ring on your head and then a heavy rock. You would sit in the hot sun for hours with this heavy rock on your head." Aside from being forced to sit in the sun with a heavy rock on one's head, informants told of being held under water, or waterboarded in modern parlance, in nearby streams until almost drowning and being beaten with whips. Sometimes a man would be locked in an enclosed chicken hut and hot chili powder would be burned like incense over coals. One man described the incredible suffering as the smoke filled a person's lungs and eyes, causing internal pain and intense vomiting.[45]

Not surprisingly, people fled. In 1928, for example, the villagers of Sirajuba left with their weapons and baggage in protest, resettling in Guinea. And in 1934 an official reported that the native exodus of whole villages was a constant problem. One of the main causes was the "desire to escape from the harassment of chiefs." As in the case of western Buguni, people living in the cantons along the southern border with Ivory Coast often migrated permanently to live across the border. Young men fled to avoid military conscription or forced labor. Usually such flight was temporary, and sometimes village chiefs and heads of household were complicit. This tendency was reported in Fulala, where, as we have seen, the chieftaincy dispute had nearly boiled over into rural rebellion: "A good number of the young men have fled in order to avoid recruitment, and most of the village chiefs fraudulently conceal the workers with the silence of their subjects."[46]

Across Africa colonial administrations pursued policies of forced cotton cultivation to ensure stable supplies to textile factories in Europe. In French Sudan, the colonial state's main focus was a massive irrigation project along the Niger River, known as Office du Niger, where planners dreamed of irrigating one million hectares of land. However, colonial cotton policy also emphasized the importance of rain-fed peasant agriculture. After 1924 the administration anticipated that the district of Buguni would become a major producer of cotton. Usually, peasants were forced to grow cotton on collective fields known as the *champ du commandant* (field of the administrator). One informant described the system as follows: "All the villages provided men according to their population to go cultivate in the collective fields of the canton chief. These men would spend part of the dry season clearing the bush; this field would be the collective field of cotton. Then to harvest this cotton, all the young women and the young men would be mobilized."[47] Eventually the administration decided that local collective fields in every village would be a better way of promoting peasant cotton production. But the impact of forced cotton cultivation depended on location and varied from village to village; roadside villages were easier to access, hence more prone to colonial exactions. Despite the heavy-handed approach to spurring cotton production, there is evidence that cotton cultivation in local fields encountered resistance from villagers. In response, extensive tours of the most promising cantons were conducted, and village palavers were held to stimulate, that is, coerce, peasants to produce cotton. While the cotton regime was not nearly as harsh in French Sudan as in such colonies as Portuguese Mozambique, it nonetheless was a serious imposition on peasant households and meant diverting important labor away from subsistence crops, which resulted in diminished food production and greater dearth.[48]

The psychological or religious repercussions of such forms of coercion are difficult to assess. Far from the gratitude people had felt at their liberation from Samori, they came to resent colonialism. However, oral accounts also suggest that people were shocked or surprised (*kabako*) by colonialism. Informants described how exposure to certain colonial technologies and techniques changed their way of thinking. The mass recruitment and deployment of men and the forms of labor organization and the projects on which men worked were unlike anything people had ever seen or experienced. People became aware that they were building roads to accommodate automobiles and heavy machinery. One informant described seeing certain technologies as "realizing the end of the world had arrived" and how men were rendered obsolete in the face of machines. People had also heard stories from veterans who had been to Europe and come back with a completely altered view of the world after seeing the mass, industrialized killing of the First World War. In short, forced labor may have produced certain phenomenological shocks and reorientations of consciousness stemming from encounters with the transformative power of the colonial system. In the absence of contemporaneous accounts, however, identifying shifts in consciousness or cosmology remains a highly speculative endeavor.[49]

In any case, as we have seen, there were layers of colonialism and a sort of internal or subcolonialism which elevated local rulers into "lords of the bush." In connecting colonial and indigenous forms of power, customary chiefs brought bamanaya and the kòmò society into close collaboration with the coercive hard power of imperialism. Playing a disciplinary role in village life as a police force, the kòmò punished young people who refused to obey the rules. It was used as a sort of local militia in rounding up forced laborers, and those who refused were often killed.[50] Robert Launay has shown how in northern Ivory Coast chiefs used their control over *lo* initiation societies to coerce junior male labor. Rebellious youths and troublemakers were frequently beaten, sent away to forced labor, or faced "mystical deaths" for their misdeeds. It was not until the abolition of forced labor that *lo* societies finally lost their grip over junior males.[51] Similarly, the close association between the kòmò society and the canton chief's recruitment of forced laborers in the district of Buguni generated animosities among young men. It also made the possibility of breaking with bamanaya more conceivable and attractive. Viewed as a form of slavery, forced labor came to represent the arbitrary power of the bamana chiefs. Yet other hardships were also testing the strength and power of bamana institutions.

A series of environmental cataclysms in conjunction with the Depression placed great strains on rural communities. In such circumstances, people questioned the old ways of seeking divine intervention. The failure of bamana priests to bring rain and to predict and prevent environmental calamities served to cast doubt in people's minds. In addition, the violence associated with bamana canton chiefs further alienated people from traditional forms of ritual power. As people lost control over their lives and their ability to ritually manage crises, they became more receptive to other religious practices that were finding wider circulation. The result was a general weakening of the hold that forms of bamanaya had over people's lives and imaginations. Communities facing crises were precisely the sorts that were open to the preaching and ritual services of itinerant Muslim holy men.[52]

Famine always haunted village life. And dearth had many causes, including locust invasions, floods, plant diseases, colonial requisitions as well as global economic strife. But informants singled out drought as the most important cause. In 1926, when drought hit Buguni, an agricultural report stated, "Large portion of the natives of the district, being hindered presently, are forced to resort to all kinds of expedients to find food." Later, when it was clear the harvests had failed, another report described soberly, "There are many natives who presently are feeding themselves only with leaves and roots." Then, after another series of droughts, locust invasions hit the region in 1931, setting households up for prolonged suffering during the Depression. In many communities, people were left with little grain to consume or to use in planting crops, and they resorted to eating famine foods, hunting and gathering to survive.[53] In oral accounts, elders often talked about locust famines in religious terms and described the locust invasions as an extraordinary phenomenon. For some, the locusts were magical beings that appeared apocalyptically as a dark cloud, obscuring the sun before descending on the fields and eating all the crops and leaves. Such environmental events were also interpreted as signs of spiritual degradation.[54] Then, in the wake of drought and locust invasion, the worldwide Depression hit West Africa, and soon there was a drop in commodity prices and worker wages. Struggling to pay taxes and facing famine, people sold their livestock and pawned family members. By 1932 officials in Buguni were reporting that subsistence reserves were severely depleted. The only thing being sold in local markets was grain. With limited access to markets and few local opportunities for earning money, labor migration became an important way of coping with poverty.[55]

VARIATIONS IN MIGRANT STRATEGIES

Patterns of labor migration defy easy typology. Although there were seemingly typical forms and trends, such as migrant peanut farming in Senegal during the interwar period and cocoa farming in Ivory Coast after the Second World War, there was always considerable variation. Certainly, forms of mobility built on continuities; people tended to follow well-worn paths. But at any given moment migrant peanut farmers, gold miners, hunters, wood sellers, and urban workers all coexisted in constantly shifting sets of household and individual strategies. As a recent corrective to the view of change as a sequence of typical forms corresponding to discrete epochs, James Ferguson has challenged certain dualist arguments which posit a transition from an epoch of circular male migration to a final phase of urbanization in the Copperbelt. Ferguson seeks to replace more teleological narratives with the view of a "full house" of variation. Building on Ferguson's work as well as on that of Jean-Loup Amselle, I want to employ this conceptualization in showing how such a "variation-centered" picture of migration might be fruitfully explored in rural French Sudan. But, before examining the plural forms of mobility, I will first establish the household contexts in which such strategies were generated.[56]

As we have seen, families acted within socially constructed ranges of possibility. Given their sense of life chances in planning courses of action, they chose what they perceived to be the best strategies, even when there were few possibilities. Although the household was a constantly changing social formation, it was nominally under the control of the lineage head, or *sotigi*, to whom everyone and everything belonged. His power was an exercise of certain rights in people. Beneath the sotigi and other male elders there were the junior males, who were divided into age-sets. Then within the category of men, meaning those who had been circumcised, there were finer gradations based on marital status, birth order, cultic initiation, and such. Among women, there were also hierarchies, with elder women naturally at the top. Within this typical household hierarchy, each agricultural season the sotigi would assess options, seeking to control risks by diversifying migrant income-generating strategies. Reflecting the concepts behind polyculture and intercropping, the household might send one man to cultivate peanuts in Senegal and others to work in commerce or in the gold mines of Guinea. Not all households were the same. There was much stratification within villages depending on social location.

Furthermore, patterns of social life at the household level were determined by household composition; particular configurations and arrangements depended on the gender make-up of the family. Finally, while the household functioned as a unit, it was shot through with conflict and competition.[57]

While some migrants found work as porters in Guinea or Ivory Coast, increasingly young men were drawn to Senegal and the Gambia, where the booming peanut trade offered possibilities to earn unparalleled amounts of money. In 1910, as the peanut trade started to take off, one report from the French Sudan read, "Young men . . . have left in groups toward lower Senegal and have put themselves courageously to breaking new land along the railway and planting vast stretches of peanuts. With the season over, they gather in large groups and bring back to the country the income from their work."[58] Before the First World War, the peanut zone had been largely confined to the western regions of Senegal, in a swath of land stretching from Saint Louis to Fatick. Soon it expanded to Kaolack and Tambakunda. By the interwar years, the peanut frontier had pushed into eastern Bawol and Saalum and expanded outward from towns in Casamance, such as Bignona. Migrant peanut farmers, or *nawétaans*, migrated during the rainy season. And most nawétaans were coming from eastern and southern French Sudan, although there were also large numbers migrating from northeastern Senegal and Futa Jallon in Guinea.[59]

As scholars like François Manchuelle, Philippe David, and James Searing have shown, the peanut trade did not develop overnight. Since the mid-nineteenth century, migrants from the Upper Senegal region had farmed peanuts in the Senegambia region. Previously, Soninke long-distance traders had established networks connecting the interior to the Gambia River, largely to engage in the salt and gold trade. But it was the peanut trade that attracted Soninke farmers to the region. Soninke migrants working along the Senegal River as sailors, or *laptots*, opened a major corridor for the movement of people, commodities, and information from the hinterland to the coast. Most of these early migrants were nobles and even Muslim marabouts who tapped into Islamic networks to profit from the lucrative trade. After emancipation there was a sort of downward social spread of migration as slaves began migrating to farm peanuts.[60]

Before the 1920s the nawétaans left few traces in the archival record in Buguni, as French officials were slow to recognize the importance of labor migration. According to oral accounts, young men from Wasulu were migrating to Senegal as early as the First World War. Some of these early migrants were tirailleurs who extended their sojourns, working in the peanut basin or in port towns as sailors or dockers. The wartime mobility of soldiers and porters, returning home and spreading the news about opportunities in Senegal, expanded the sending zone, as Wasulu was incorporated into the peanut trade. By 1923 a census report stated that large numbers of young men were away from their villages "procuring money necessary for taxes." Five years later another report revealed that "it is not rare to find fifty percent of the population gone [on migration]." One official explained the causes behind the emerging phenomenon: "Although the native is very attached to his village . . . the constant worry to obtain bride price and also the obligation to pay taxes are the major reasons that incite this migration each year during several months and often for several years." Then in 1930 the districtwide census recorded a large percentage of young men who were farming peanuts in Senegal, Casamance, and the Gambia.[61] Similarly, informants recalled large groups of migrant peanut farmers leaving for Senegal. One elder told what he remembered from his childhood in the 1930s: "Going to Senegal was obligatory. Sometimes twenty or thirty people from each village would go to farm peanuts in Senegal. . . . They would farm during the rainy season. . . . Even in my family, there were men who went to Senegal. There were men who came back, and there were certain men who stayed there."[62]

A watershed in the history of labor migration was the completion of the Thiès-Kayes railway line in 1923, which effectively connected Dakar to Bamako. Yet many migrant workers from Buguni continued to travel on foot, a journey that could last a month. By then they had established networks of support en route to Senegal, which made the trip much more bearable and risk-averse. They traveled in groups composed of fifteen or more men, suffering through thirst and hunger to arrive at the coast.[63] Although most migrants walked, the railway line still served as a conduit of important information, rumors, and news from Senegal, which reached even remote villages within weeks. This enabled households to make more informed decisions regarding migration destinations and timing. In these years, young women sang popular songs, which spread along the railway line and encouraged young men to seek fortune in Senegal. As one informant said, "The young women danced and sang these songs. All the young men fled to Senegal to farm peanuts. That was the reason that so many people flooded into that locality to earn money." The general message was that to prove their manhood, men had to go on adventure to Senegal.[64] David has shown how such songs first appeared in the western regions of the French Sudan, around Nioro in 1925, and spread east. One of the most popular was "The Peanut Boom," sung by women. It evoked images of status, marriage, new clothes, and jewelry and also contained Islamic themes, such as "addressing the prayer leaders," "visiting Mecca," and possessing "gold prayer beads." Thus, while households were pushed to look for tax money, young men were also drawn to adventure and to the allure of new consumer objects—hats, sunglasses, jewelry, umbrellas, cloth, and so forth—and the status and social distinctions they connoted.[65]

Migrants entered a complex nexus of cultural borrowing and social mixing. But when they arrived in Senegal or the Gambia, most young men sought out villages where they had contacts, preferring to work and live alongside those of the same ethnolinguistic groups. Those who were forced to find work through local middlemen often changed their names to obscure their ethnic or religious backgrounds. Sometimes this entailed trying to pass as Muslims. However, it was nawétaans and traders from the Sahel who had originally introduced Islam into many parts of the peanut zone. These Muslim peanut farmers, then, served as cultural agents in carrying the religion with them as the peanut frontier moved southward. Later, from the 1920s, Islam spread to parts of the Lower Casamance as Muslim nawétaans returned home from the Gambia. There were also Jola animists who farmed peanuts in the Middle Casamance who returned to their villages with prayer, after sojourns among local marabouts. The cultural flows were bidirectional between hosts and strangers, both of which contributed to the shape of religious culture in the peanut zone.[66]

As a diaspora of farmers, nawétaans also carried with them their agricultural habitus. In particular, migrants from the French Sudan retained their practice of mounding, which was rarely used by Senegalese farmers in the region. They brought their own tools or had blacksmiths modify ones available in local markets. In fact, their innovations were imitated by local farmers. On the social level, migrants were purveyors of contractual forms and idioms. The word for host (*jatigi*) was of Mandé origin, and migrants were commonly referred to as *baaranyini*, from the Bamanankan phrase *n'be baara nyini* (I'm looking for work).[67] Contracts between the nawétaan and the host, or jatigi, took an established form that was partly based in former master–slave arrangements, in which migrants worked the host's fields in exchange for land, housing, and food.[68] A former nawétaan from the village of Balanfina recalled his contract: "When we arrived in Senegal, the jatigi would hire the workers. In each week, you worked two days for yourself and five days for the host. He would feed you. They gave us the peanut seeds on credit. After the harvest, if you brought in a lot of peanuts, you would reimburse the credit."[69]

Income from peanut farming ranged widely depending on individual effort, the vicissitudes of the market, and rainfall. One report stated that on average nawétaans could produce twelve donkey-loads of peanuts, which meant that after the product owed to the host was taken out, an average nawétaan took home between two hundred and four hundred francs per season. This represented five or six months of labor. When averaged as a monthly or daily wage rate, it was far above what French employers were paying. Furthermore, the migrants' food and lodging were supplied by their host. The workers' only expenses were transportation costs and any customs duties or taxes paid en route, both of which could be avoided by traveling on foot and avoiding the colonial administration.[70] Searing has observed that the "peasant economy" was still dominant at this time, meaning that wage labor based on clock time was a relatively unattractive option for most migrant farmers. Although migrant peanut farmers commonly supplemented their income by finding wage work during the dry season, earnings from peanut farming determined the minimum wage rate.[71]

Besides peanut farming, migrants worked in the wood and kola trades, hunted in Ivory Coast, and engaged in trade in Guinea. Closer to home they worked in the gold mines of Kalana. Unlike nawétaans, these migrants would leave after harvest, spend the dry season working for wages, and return home before the rains. This pattern of circular migration afforded farmers the chance to earn extra money without completely abandoning their villages. In 1923 one official reported how in the dry season young men "migrated around once the farm labor was complete," usually lasting "just three months." Though Ivory Coast would not be a main destination until after the Second World War, circular migration there was slowly beginning. By 1934 workers could expect to make thirty-five francs per month working in Ivory Coast, still inferior to nawétaan earnings. However, migrant workers could earn the head tax of nine francs within a couple of months and still have enough for marriage expenses or investment in livestock. But, again, what made Ivory Coast a choice destination was its proximity, which afforded farmers and households greater flexibility in meeting agricultural labor demands at home.[72]

Many of the first migrants to Ivory Coast worked in the tropical hardwood trade, cutting down trees and transporting lumber to the coast. Bakari Koné described his life as a lumberman: "Our first time going on migration, we walked for twenty days. When we arrived we found work, gathering wood. . . . We would pile the wood on the riverbanks. We slept along the river, next to our wood. The next morning we would load the *pirogue* [canoe]. Myself, I spent two months transporting wood on my head before learning how to work the pirogue. . . . If the pirogue overturned, your life was over. You would travel maybe twenty or thirty kilometers on water. In reality, we earned money in Abidjan. We sold each bundle of wood for one franc."[73] Migrants also mined gold in Guinea and in southern Wasulu, especially during the Depression, when prices for most other cash crops plummeted. As officials noted, migrants were returning from abroad with "more deception than money," as prices dropped in the coastal colonies. Many workers were stranded away from their homes as steady work evaporated. A few even died in exile, broken by poverty. Within this context, people flocked to the gold mines.[74] One of these miners was Tenaiko Bamba, who recalled his experiences as a teenager in the mid-1930s: "I spent nine years working in the gold mines, learning all the techniques to extract gold from the earth. . . . We worked in the mines; they were often old wells that one finds in the bush. . . . The people would dig the pits until they found gold. You would enter the mine at one end, and there were two parts that connected under the ground. Sometimes the mines would collapse on people. This happened to me three times, and each time they carried me away like a dead man. It was dangerous, but it was the only way to find money, despite the difficulty."[75]

In other regions migrants engaged in hunting, traveling far from their homes in search of wild game, especially as nearby populations were depleted. In the village of Tenemakana, one of the most famous hunters was Zumana Danyoko, who, despite his Muslim father's efforts to dissuade him, had been a hunter since his circumcision. His nephew recounted the following story: "When Zumana began the practice of hunting, his father argued with him so that he would stop hunting. He did everything to prevent him from being a hunter. But the family was larger than just Tumani [his father]. It was a large clan [kabila]. At this time, your father was not the one who ultimately controlled you. The sotigi said that Zumana would not cease hunting." As this testimony suggests, the village was still dominated by practitioners of bamanaya, and Tumani's Muslim identity was in the distinct minority. Therefore, gaining support from the community of elders, Zumana was entrusted to an elderly master hunter, Gònbéléblen, for apprenticeship. Gònbéléblen educated Zumana in esoteric forms of knowledge and hunting techniques. Once his master had died, Zumana began hunting alone in the surrounding forests. His wife recalled, "At that time, the bush was still full of game here. You did not need to go very far to kill game. You could kill game right here behind the village, behind your house with not much effort." Soon, however, Zumana was traveling as far as Ivory Coast to hunt large game. His wife accompanied him on these longer trips, and she too became versed in some of the esoteric arts of hunting and healing. Interestingly, in his old age, despite never having become an observant Muslim, Zumana became the first man from Tenemakana to perform the Hajj, paid by his son, Burama, who had become successful in the cocoa trade in Ivory Coast.[76]

In a more general way, as economic hardship fell on the district of Buguni, people began commuting and circulating locally, looking for work, and cobbling together supplementary income. Although no formal statistics exist on the numbers of people practicing short-term internal migration, one official estimated that several thousands of peasants were on the move at any given moment, searching for tax money, engaging in interfamilial or ritual visits and participating in commercial exchanges. Families invested in social networks by visiting kin in neighboring villages, and women often went home to their natal villages in the dry season and participated in harvest festivals. As more roads were built and

automobiles began plying the main trade arteries, commerce and communications quickened. Although the real expansion of "the paved road"
(*goudron*) would not begin until after the Second World War, there were
already large numbers of passengers and cars and trucks of all kinds. And
as migrants stayed away longer, people began using the money order system to send remittances back to their families. Letters from migrant workers were another way that news and rumors passed from distant localities
in Senegal to home villages.[77] In assessing the links between mobility
and religious change, one must acknowledge not only the ways in which
quotidian forms of local migration and short-distance commuting were
contributing to the acceleration of communications, but also how new
forms of transportation made information, news, and money more ambulatory. Along these lines, it is tempting to speculate upon the emergence
of local "modernities," as Nancy Rose Hunt has suggested in the Belgian
Congo, where the "swift mobility of ideas and things characterized a new
and specific, local colonial modernity of the interwar period."[78] However,
it is still far from clear what this modernity meant for peasants in the
district of Buguni, and also whether things were really changing as
quickly as one might think. Certainly, there had been far-reaching transformations since the period of conquest. But migration across great distances was still ploddingly slow. Local commuting or circulation would
not see a major modification until the introduction of bicycles into the
region after the Second World War. Nevertheless, in order to appreciate
the range of indigenous ways of "being modern," one must attend to
shifting and emergent patterns of mobility and to, as James Clifford calls
them, the "lived connections across distances and differences."[79]

GENDER, SYMBOLIC DOMINATION, AND THE HOUSEHOLD ECONOMY

I have noted the insufficiency of data on women in the archival record
and the problems of access to female domains of religious knowledge.
Yet while female informants were reluctant to move beyond normative statements on religious questions, they willingly talked about their
work and marriage. The life histories that I recorded during my fieldwork underscore the agency of women and their crucial contributions to
the social reproduction of families and communities. This should
not obscure the fact that fundamental gender inequalities, expressed
through various forms of social and symbolic domination, structured

relationships. In local understandings, this was often encoded in idioms of slavery.

I draw, first, on a brief ethnographic anecdote from the village of Bunjoba. During an interview, the elderly wife of the village chief appeared and offered him a calabash of water. She dropped to one knee and handed it to him with both hands. I had not seen this sort of deference and later asked the male elders about it. They commented that this was the old way of showing respect for men. I had heard men refer to women as slaves on many occasions. Then, toward the end of my fieldwork, a male elder, describing household relations during his childhood, made a remark that caught my attention: "The women did much more work than the men. In truth, they were nothing more than slaves. They remained unfreed slaves in the household. When your wife gave birth to a baby girl, we would say to the woman that another girl slave had entered the world. We called her slave girl, and as soon as she entered the world she began her slavery in the house of her father, learning all the hard work of her mother. Then one day she was taken and given away to continue her slavery in the home of another man, the husband to whom she was exchanged. She started her life all over again at zero in his household."[80] This elder was drawing attention to the sedimentation of slavery idioms in gender relations and to how, although legal slavery had ended, women were still viewed as slaves. As such, young girls grew up inculcated with the belief that they were slave girls. Taught the correct bodily comportment, their behavior demonstrated their dominated position. These forms of symbolic domination extended to males as well, especially to uncircumcised boys and unmarried men. All social dependents were, in some sense, the slaves of the lineage head, part of his "wealth in people."

This normative view of female dependents as slaves makes even more sense when placed within the context of pawning. Historically, when families were pressed to come up with tax money, they ran through various strategies, converting social capital into cash, looking for work, and selling things. But in poor hinterland regions, where families depended on migrant labor for money and poverty had already decimated the livestock population, peasants had no choice but to pawn family members, usually young girls or boys.[81] The institution of pawning had its roots in slavery. Suzanne Miers and Igor Kopytoff noted in their classic study on slavery that "a lineage in need of money . . . or unable to feed all its members in time of famine, might transfer all of its rights in a person to another lineage in return for goods or money."[82] Indeed, pawning, or *tònòmada* in Bamanankan, was widespread during the Depression. Even so, colonial officials rarely commented on the institution. The only direct reference from Buguni was in 1932, when an official reported, "The native no longer has anything left. I have learned that certain taxpayers have pawned their women or children to find credit. . . . It is a sign of a very precarious financial situation."[83] Although the colonial record, at least in Buguni, is silent on the subject, oral accounts suggest that the practice was quite common. One informant explained the institution: "Pawning was done in times of crisis. If you were unable to pay your taxes, you would be forced to borrow money from someone else. You would go from household to household, from village to village, visiting the rich families to try to pawn your child. . . . The person who was pawned we called simply tònòmada."[84] Most pawns were young women or girls. For example, Madji Konate became a pawn when her father could not come up with tax money during the Depression. She described working "as a slave" until her family was able to pay off their debt. She said that many girls were pawned and ended up in slavery for ten years or for the rest of their lives.[85] In such cases, female pawns often became wives in creditor households. When this happened, the original loan was converted into bride price, usually composed of livestock. Thus, bride price practices were uniquely tied to pawning arrangements, as forms of bride exchange (*falen-ni-falen*) or labor service (*buranci*) were still the most common ways of mediating marriage. And it is possible that the prevalence of pawning, in tandem with the integration of communities into wider commercial networks, nudged marriage mediation in the direction of bride price.[86] In any case, while forced labor and similar forms of colonial exploitation replaced slavery, pawning was more analogous to the kind of slavery that had been widespread throughout the region for centuries. Pawns were usually women, as most domestic slaves had been; and pawns remained enslaved for years, whereas forced labor was a male institution of much shorter duration. Furthermore, the way in which pawn labor was used within the household more closely resembled that of slave labor.[87]

Despite the social inequalities, women played important productive and reproductive roles in their communities. Even male informants lauded women for their contributions. One elder remembered that "in each village we passed through, my wife would learn quickly all the information of this village. When you leave a village, your wife could tell you so many things, this event or this information. But the man he would not even notice any of these things." Indeed, husbands were able to benefit from the time and energy women invested in social networks, gleaning rumors, stories, and information. Women were also remembered as being skilled in the marketplace and innovative in finding ways to make money. Their work often saved men from shame (màlòya) and humiliation at tax time. Men and women collaborated in earning money. In the production of cotton textiles, women spun the cotton into thread, which the men wove into cotton strips for sale in the market. In most villages, men and women also farmed together. Women were usually given sections of the field, according to the cultivation lines (nkala) demarcated by the lineage head. In some villages, there were designated days for women to work in their own fields. In the canton of Fulala, for example, women worked with their husbands in the communal fields five days each week but could devote two days each week to their own work, a pattern that resembled master–slave and host–migrant labor relations. As women became elders, they often had the right to work private fields or gardens. Most women grew vegetables, fonio, or peanuts in their small personal fields. They also processed and sold shea butter, dried fish, cotton thread, and rice.[88] Among the Senufo, in the canton of Niené, husbands were expected to give their wives personal rice fields when they reached menopause. Kapicòri Coulibaly explained: "Your rice field was part of the land of your husband that was given to you. You could farm this land until you died, then the land was given to someone else. . . . [The husband] would clear the land and cut the trees, and the old woman would use this as her rice field. It was like this with our mothers in our natal villages as well as in our husbands' villages."[89]

Gender relations were far from static, as labor migration in particular forced changes in farming and in women's work. As I have suggested, migrant peanut farming meant a loss of male labor in the rainy season, which could lead to a general decline in agricultural productivity. As one official described the situation in 1930, "The considerable exodus of young men to work in Senegal, Casamance, Ivory Coast, and sometimes the Gold Coast has diminished the labor force and, as a consequence, the areas cultivated. . . . It is not deniable that this exodus is harmful to agricultural production of the district." Responding to the unavailability of labor, households planted fast-growing crops, such as manioc and short-cycle grains.[90] Most important, however, the absence of men increased the labor burden on women. Young single women took over the tasks of their brothers, and wives worked in the place of their husbands. Bintu Koné stated, "The men were leaving for Senegal at this time to find money. . . . When our husbands were away, we worked in the fields ourselves." In Wasulu, Kani Sidibé remembered that "when people left on migration, there were no more men here. So the women were obliged to do the work of their husbands to feed the family."[91]

To compensate for the shortage of labor, women resorted to labor sharing and work parties. These work groups were based in more general forms of cooperative labor that were used in overcoming labor bottlenecks and seasonal labor shortages. People engaged in both exchange labor, which was reciprocal and characterized by smaller groups, and also "festive labor," which was normally villagewide, ritualistic, and task oriented. Cooperation was further encouraged by music and singing, as Salimata Diallo recalled in Fulala: "The women helped each other in their farming. We were forced to help each other. We would group together and sing while we worked. We played the music called Ya. One woman would encourage the others; she sang for the collectivity of workers. The women would work harder, in competition." In northern Wasulu, Kani Sidibé said, "We would go to one person's field one day; then we would go to another person's field the next day. This way all the work was done. There was a woman who would sing encouragement as we worked." Among the Senufo, women farmed in work groups accompanied by singers. The praise songs normally focused on a famed farmer named Suruku. The singer would extol the bravery and work ethic of Suruku and thereby inspire the women to work harder.[92] Forms of labor cooperation were often linked to social and ritual groups, such as the ci-wara association, which organized agricultural competitions, mask dances, and annual celebrations. In addition, young men and women formed youth associations called tònw, which used farming to subsidize celebrations. Often the tònw had their own fields (tòn fòrò), which they farmed collectively. These village youth associations could also play an important role in safeguarding against famine and shame. As M'Bemba Sidibé explained, "When someone was incapable of working in the community, the people would come together, they would come and farm in the field of the person to avoid famine. It was brotherly help."[93]

While absent men allowed women to take charge of households and assert greater control over the labor process, informants emphasized how most women still acquiesced without question to the demands and decisions of the household head. And when they tested the limits of their autonomy, whether in marriage or work, they could expect serious consequences. One elderly woman explained that whomever you were given to in marriage, even "a leper or an old man," you were forced to be the man's wife. She added that when a woman refused to marry the man, she would have to run away from her village forever. Women also risked the possibility of domestic violence. Namakoro Bamba explained: "When a woman's father had decided to give her to someone and she refused, her father would attach a rope around her neck and she would be beaten. She could not contradict the decisions of her father. She was beaten by her little brothers, and her big brothers. . . . I witnessed many scenes just like this." Sometimes, resistant women were brought to the canton chief, who would mete out corporal punishments: "They would bring her to the canton chief. They would beat her, and then they would force her to carry her husband on her back all the way to the village, as she said: 'I will never refuse my husband until my death.'" Women were also subjected to violence for stubbornness, shirking labor, or refusing sexual relations. In establishing male domination in the household and legitimating patriarchy, symbolic and physical violence were commonly used.[94]

As we have seen, even as legal slavery had ended, there was a postemancipation emergence of colonial forms of neoslavery. Informants frequently made reference to slavery when discussing pawning, forced labor, compulsory crop production, and even Qur'anic school, indicating the deep social and cultural continuities in local understandings. This is not to say that these forms of labor were uniformly involuntary and coercive. They represented very different labor processes and sets of social relations. And, in most cases, there were no formal master–slave social ties, such as in the Sahel, where struggles over land, labor, and status continued well into the postcolonial period, often spanning generations. However, the degree to which slavery idioms were discernible in society depended on the particular ways in which localities were incorporated into the slave trade and the social patterning that resulted. In Buguni, slavery would remain central to social life, but more as a cultural artifact of the mind. Even as the bonds between slaves and masters were permanently severed following the exodus, slavery continued to be a powerful explanatory metaphor for describing unequal social relations between men and women, chiefs and peasants, and the colonial state and its subjects. Indeed, in the view of some, slavery was not abolished until 1946, when forced labor and the indigénat ended.

CHAPTER 5

Transforming the Village

CIRCULAR MIGRATION AND RURAL SOCIAL
CHANGE, 1940–1960

As the Second World War raged in Europe, recruitment officials arrived in the village of Massala. Coming from around the canton of Fulala, families gathered in the roadside village's central meeting place, where, under a large kapok tree, their sons waited for inspection. The colonial officials worked their way down the list of villages, calling forward household heads and selecting the healthiest for service. By this time, there were few left. Already in 1941, the canton had seen a dramatic decline in the number of able-bodied men. Some had been recruited for service. Even more had left on migration. However, equally troubling, in this canton of 3,744 inhabitants, was that the rate of mortality was extremely high. Due to famine, malaria, sleeping sickness, and other diseases, "entire families had been decimated." Despite such considerations officials were demanding more wartime contributions. When they called on Tenemakana, two families were asked to furnish a son. Broulaye Doumbia was one of them. The young man received benedictions from his father, and then he departed for southern Europe.[1]

This was not the first recruitment drive of the war. Before the fall of France, French West Africa had contributed heavily to the war effort in soldiers and materiel. One hundred thousand tirailleurs had been recruited already, but the initial war in France would be brief. By late 1940, after the imperial metropole itself came under Nazi occupation, those who had not been killed in action were sent to prisoner of war camps or deported back to Africa. Some, eluding capture by the Nazis, joined the *maquis* and fought in the underground resistance. Later, after the Allied landing in North Africa and the shift of allegiance of the governor general of French West Africa to the Free French side in late 1942, the administration redoubled its recruitment efforts. As a part of this second wave, the tirailleurs would figure prominently in the campaigns, comprising 20 percent of the invasion forces in southern France.[2] While in Europe, Broulaye Doumbia stayed in touch with his family, sending letters and money orders back to Tenemakana. After the liberation of Paris, he returned home to find that the woman he had hoped to marry had found another man and that the money he had sent back had been intercepted and squandered. Moreover, his father and mother had both died in the wartime famine. Soon, other changes were occurring.

In 1946 social and political reforms opened the way to African political involvement. Politics, as the more peaceful competition among parties through ruses (*kekuya*), quickly replaced the local politics and brute force (*fanga*) of the chieftaincy. This is not to say that patrimonialism disappeared. Interparty struggles remained deeply enmeshed in lineage-based conflicts (*fadenkélé*).[3] The two largest parties were the anticolonial Union Soudanais (US)—linked to the interterritorial Rassemblement Démocratique Africain (RDA)—and the Parti Progressiste Soudanais (PSP). Within Buguni the proadministration PSP would remain the most popular party until the territorial elections of 1957. It is curious, perhaps, considering the hardships of forced labor, that peasants would back a prochieftaincy party. But the PSP used the chieftaincy to manipulate local electoral processes. At the same time, the RDA, drawing its strongest support primarily from among veterans, civil servants, and traders in roadside towns, simply had no effective grass-roots networks in rural areas.[4] Furthermore, people in Buguni initially opposed the RDA because of its embrace of Samori as a symbolic resistance hero. Not surprisingly, such Samorian evocations could also be a political liability in the bitter rivalry between the US-RDA and the PSP.[5]

Largely in response to African politicking, strikes, labor activism, and wider crises across the empire-state, the French eventually passed a further series of reforms, known as the *loi cadre* of 1956, which gave greater autonomy to French territories in Africa. Within the new French Union, this "framing law" instituted universal suffrage for adults and devolved powers to Territorial Assemblies, allowing Africans more control over domestic affairs and budgetary decisions. It was not all altruism, however. In decentralizing, democratizing, and "territorializing" the political system, the French were also disavowing the notion of assimilation and retracting the offer of full integration of Africans as citizens, with French living standards, while also abdicating responsibility for social welfare and unpopular decisions. Locally, these political changes were felt most palpably in the weakening of the chieftaincy and its eventual abolition.[6]

Perhaps more important than their instituting of party politics, at least in the short term, the reforms of 1946 abolished forced labor and the system of summary native justice known as the indigénat. Bereft of these key institutions, chiefs no longer had their old powers of coercion, and in such circumstances young men and women had greater freedom to migrate and to assert more control over their individual lives. Against this backdrop, Broulaye left for Ivory Coast, where he worked in the booming cocoa trade for the next six years, before returning home to farm and engage in commerce. After his long absence, he observed further changes in the village. A mosque had been built in Tenemakana, and more people were performing public Muslim prayer. Young men were marrying without the consent of their fathers. And they were devoting more time to their individual fields, called jònfòròw, or slave fields, which were farmed in the afternoons and evenings after communal work for the lineage head was completed. Indeed, breaking with a practice that reflected labor relations between masters and slaves, now the former slaves of the sotigi, or household dependents, started to work for themselves.[7]

The Second World War represented a major turning point. Among global realignments, it marked the beginning of the end of French empire in West Africa. And yet, ironically, in its wake capital from the metropole flowed into the colonies, fueling economic development and accelerating the pace and scale of commercial transactions. The colonial state extended its bureaucracy and development projects further into remote regions, in a sort of second colonial occupation. The tying of peasants into more direct relationships with the state and the wider mobility of workers also depended on certain technological changes, such as the building of roads and the spread of automobiles and bicycles. On a regional level, as demand for colonial cash crops grew and forced labor ended more people from hinterland regions migrated to zones of production in Ivory Coast and Senegal. Linked to this system of circular labor migration, new cultural styles and practices emerged which fundamentally reconfigured religious communities.[8]

THE "TRAUMATIZED BUSH": HARDSHIPS ON THE HOME FRONT

While young men served as soldiers in France, hundreds of thousands of their family members performed forced labor or compulsory grain production. With each colony producing particular crops for the wartime empire, the state intensified its use of the deuxième portion, even funneling large numbers of Africans to work for private enterprises in Ivory Coast. Indeed, the war was a high-water mark in the totalizing penetration of colonial power into everyday life. Owing to the imperatives of the war effort, peasants were tied more directly into centralized and regularized state projects. As in the "political dream" so evocatively described by Michel Foucault, the wartime "mechanisms of power," like the state emergency measures to combat the plague, functioned in a more capillary manner than was normally the case. The war called for greater control and a generalized "intensification and ramification of power."[9]

The higher density of colonial power over such a short but intense period has left distinct traces in collective memories. When discussing colonialism, informants often pointed to the various impositions of the Second World War, especially to what they called the millet container famine (*gongon-nyo kungo*) caused by grain requisitions. Based on oral accounts, the case of Buguni is instructive as it provides a ground-level view of wartime mobilization of colonial subjects and resources and demonstrates the extent to which rural communities across the French empire-state felt the impact of the war on their own home fronts. Most archive-driven studies of the French empire under Vichy, with their foci on policy, national identity, and political culture, tend to lack this perspective. This is not to say that oral accounts necessarily provide a singular corrective. Indeed, informants rarely referred to Vichy by name or identified the Vichy years in any distinct way. Rather, elders tended to paper over differences between regimes, focusing their comments on the cruelty of individual chiefs or commandants. Yet even in their localist views, they emphasized continuities between Vichy and non-Vichy rule, which resonates with recent scholarship.[10] As Frederick Cooper has noted, although the Vichy government more overtly embraced forced labor and the corporatist ideal of rationally organized methods of production and labor discipline, there was considerable overlap with interwar development projects, personnel, and ideas. Even when the governor general switched sides, allowing Free French forces to take control of French West Africa in late 1942, forms of compulsory production continued, driven by the exigencies of war. In fact, forced labor became larger in scale and "probably more brutal," and "no-one was pretending it did not exist." Wartime hardships under both Vichy and the Free French weighed heavily on Africans. As a final authoritarian belt tightening, forced labor made the ensuing postwar reforms and social ruptures all the more dynamic.[11]

There were critical disjunctures in the history of labor migration, particularly as the state got involved in a kind of military recruitment of peanut farmers. As we have seen, there was a golden age of migrant peanut farming in the interwar years, when as many as 90,000 farmers per year migrated to Senegal and the Gambia. But as the war intensified, the peanut fields were abandoned. With the rapid deterioration of migrant purchasing power and the disappearance of consumer goods, many households elected to keep their young men at home, investing their labor in subsistence crops. In 1940 only 13,581 nawétaans migrated from the Sudan, the largest portion being drawn from Buguni, which, according to Philippe David, "remained at the head of supplying districts," with roughly 7,000 migrants. Then, to make matters worse, the rainy season came late in 1941, causing considerable administrative anxiety. In such wartime economic circumstances, with strict rationing of grain and fuel in full force, Vichy allowed the peanut trade to languish.[12]

The Free French administration made peanuts a priority, seeking to spur migration through propaganda and outright coercion. In the recruitment drive of 1943, which aimed at rounding up 10,000 workers from the French Sudan, the district of Buguni was singled out to provide 4,000. Officially, migrants were offered a bonus of six meters of cloth and given free passage and food en route. The result was that a staggering 24,023 men were enlisted, of whom roughly 5,033 came from Buguni. Many former migrants in Buguni were recruited in this manner. Siaka Diarra farmed peanuts during the war, just as his brother was sent to Europe as a soldier. He said, "We were taken by force by the French to grow peanuts in Senegal. We arrived in Kayes, and we found soldiers ready to go to the front. The train was stopped and the soldiers left on the train and after that we continued onward to Senegal. . . . Our brother Zumana was in the army by this time." Indeed, by 1944 the administration had embraced a more explicitly compulsory policy of forced peanut farming. Setting precedents for postwar labor recruitment, migrants were processed in a tightly regimented manner through transit camps like Tambakunda, where they were vaccinated and issued identity cards.[13]

While a handful of men went to Senegal, most inhabitants in Buguni contributed to the war effort by producing grain. Locally, the administration imposed draconian measures. District guards forced each village to cultivate fields of cotton, millet, peanuts, and rice for requisitions. At harvest time, villagers would bring all the products to Buguni. Under Vichy, the administration also created collective millet fields, each adult officially working "three days of prestations reserved for farming in the collective millet fields."[14] But informants remembered far more onerous demands. Adama Diallo of Niamala said, "When the war began with the Germans, the millet corvée became obligatory for everyone. They said that every inhabitant had to deliver millet to Buguni, which would be the food for the soldiers. We carried the millet on our heads to Buguni." Informants also spoke about the suffering caused by the millet container famine. In the words of Bakari Koné, "I personally lived through the millet container famine. Each person contributed one or two containers of millet. You could pay with rice, millet, and sorghum. Each person in the family paid. If there were thirty people in the family, you paid thirty containers. The village chief would send someone to measure the millet, and each person would carry their container to Buguni."[15]

The wartime demands weighed heavily on the Senufo canton of Niené, which was viewed as a regional granary. Under Vichy, the canton provided 2,562 forced laborers in 1942, roughly one quarter of the population. One elder in the village of Woblé recalled the difficulties: "The colonial administration sent its agents with a message, and they took away all the food of the family. We were left with nothing to eat. The people went into the forests searching for something to eat. We unearthed roots and plants and brought them home to prepare them for food to eat. Myself, I transported three containers of millet to Buguni. . . . It was a long journey. It was a difficult time. These years when we gave our food to the administration, some of the worst difficulties occurred here. The people were hardly capable of farming because of the famine." The sufferings were so great that the people beseeched the canton chief to do something to stop the requisitions. Finally, the canton chief called on a former student from the French school working in the administration to help them.[16]

Women often carried the burden of forced labor and grain requisitions. Across the district, officials reported on the lack of male labor. In 1943 one official observed, "We have been struck by the weak proportion of men. . . . Such a situation harms considerably the policy of intensification of crops asked from the district of Buguni." Many young men simply had abandoned their villages during the war years, which meant that women bore the brunt of colonial demands. One woman said, "When the young men fled from forced labor, the administration had recourse to the women. This forced labor was imposed on us women, and it was very difficult for us." Salimata Diallo of Tenemakana carried containers of millet on her head to Buguni every year through the war. She said, "Even if that was your only harvest of millet for the year, you carried it on your head all the way to Buguni."[17]

Many people died of starvation as a result of the millet requisitions. After the devastating famines of the Depression years, grain reserves were being depleted at a furious rate. Some informants suspected that the millet was not sent to France. They thought that officials and African chiefs took the grain for their own profit. Namakoro Bamba said, "The government imposed on us the payment in containers of millet. . . . The Commandant, the canton chiefs, and the village chiefs would even sell the grain and share the money. . . . And whether your harvest had been good or bad, whether you were rich or poor, you were forced to pay with these containers of millet. This had replaced taxes for the time. We saw such difficulties. We ate anything to survive."[18] Eventually, the war ended, but the hardships continued. In 1946, following the millet requisitions, there was widespread drought, combined with flooding, across the district. One official reported on the dearth in Wasulu: "The famine is such in Basidibé that even manioc is lacking. In the four cantons visited, Basidibé having been the hardest hit, not even having rice seeds." The famine also hit cantons in the southeastern quadrant of the district, where flooding destroyed all the crops grown near the river.[19]

These years of suffering, coupled with the repressive tactics of canton chiefs and household heads, resulted in a mass exodus in the postwar era.

Young people generally turned against the administration, particularly as the levers of control over junior males slipped from the hands of chiefs and elders. At the same time, the return of former tirailleurs from Europe politicized communities. In many rural villages veterans had been the first to hear Charles de Gaulle's "discourse in Brazzaville" in 1944 and took to heart his promise of reform, even as "each of them interpreted it in his own way." They joined the RDA and shared their political ideas with fellow young migrant workers. Furthermore, these processes in tandem with postwar reforms led to the weakening of canton chiefs and the break-up of old forms of "internal colonialism." In local understandings, the abolition of forced labor marked the end of slavery. Elders belonging to the generation of people born in the early 1930s idealized this period of their adolescence as one of equality, individualism, and freedom (hòrònya).[20]

PATTERNS AND PROCESSES OF CIRCULAR MIGRATION

The postwar era opened the floodgates to labor migration. Migrants continued to farm peanuts in Senegal and to work in commerce in Guinea. But the numbers of peanut farmers from the French Sudan dwindled after the war. In the place of Senegal, Ivory Coast emerged as the leading destination, as the end of forced labor and the coercive forms of contract work led to a general reorganization of labor recruitment. To maintain labor supplies from hinterland regions in the absence of coercion, planters and merchants resorted to new recruiting methods and offered higher salaries. For African employers, sharecropping arrangements were also expanded. In certain cases the colonial state offered free transportation. As a result of these incentives and opportunities, the number of migrants increased dramatically in the postwar era. Nevertheless, employers in rural Ivory Coast and elsewhere have left behind few written records from which historians might derive evidence. In contrast to cases in southern Africa, where workers were often employed in industrial or urban settings, sources for writing the history of labor migration in rural parts of West Africa are rather limited.[21]

As we have seen, labor migration had been widespread for decades and only grew in importance after the war. Tax burdens remained, but the higher salaries in Ivory Coast enabled young people to earn enough money to invest in their own lives. In time, Ivory Coast definitively overtook Senegal as the primary destination. Circular or seasonal migration slowly replaced the longer-term arrangements tied to rainy season peanut farming, and as household heads and chiefs lost control over labor, more young men migrated without the authorization of their elders. Migration became a sort of rite of passage, as young people left immediately after their circumcisions, around the age of fifteen, for adventure in Ivory Coast.[22] Once boys (*bilakòròw*) had become men (*cébakòròw*), they left their homes to prove themselves. By this phase in a young man's life, he would ordinarily belong to an age group (*filantòn*) and sought to conform to the interests and actions of his peers. Throughout his life the filantòn would be one of the most important social groups. Members of the filantòn worked together, migrated together, helped each other, and discussed together. But while there was much solidarity in the filantòn, there could also be competition and jealousy. Abou Sidibé explained as follows: "When young men from our filantòn came back from Senegal, Ivory Coast, or Guinea, we saw what they had and we knew that we had nothing. One man brought back a bicycle, he brought back money for his father, and already his father could search for a wife. He would be getting married. We were jealous of this. So we were obliged to leave. Now, we often had a girlfriend, and she would say that we had nothing and that our friend had gone to Ivory Coast and he had this and that. So everyone in the filantòn left the region on migration at this time."[23] Indeed, the decision to migrate was shaped by the experiences of migrants, whose social remittances, gift giving, and stories inspired others. As one official observed, "[Migrants] have been able to bring back some profits, which serve as gifts to family, women, and friends. . . . During their travels, they will have seen much . . . they will have something to recount, which flatters [the family]."[24]

Officially, at least, young men did not migrate until the lineage head had "given them the road." However, young men began leaving surreptitiously in small groups. Then, upon their return, when they remitted money with deference, their transgression was usually forgiven. Abou Sidibé continued his explanation: "Yes, of course, I hid this [leaving for migration], because the sotigi must not know. . . . The night before leaving, the young men in my filantòn came to play drums and the *ngoni* with me. I asked for benedictions for a safe migration and return. I went with my mother and did some sacrifices in hiding, not with my father. At four o'clock in the morning I left on foot, but I did not take the big road. I went through the bush to arrive at a village. . . . When I left he [household head] was not content, but when I brought the money back he was content." Young migrants traveled in groups, as traveling alone to Ivory Coast was considered far too dangerous. They continued going on foot primarily, although some people took advantage of the improved roads and wider diffusion of trucks. Once in Ivory Coast, most migrants found work in the cocoa, coffee, or kola nut trades, which were booming in the postwar period.[25]

Within the district of Buguni, not all cantons were uniformly sending regions. And contrary to certain assumptions, it was not necessarily the most destitute that sent migrants away. For example, Bambeledugu, one of the poorest cantons, "did not migrate" because, as an official noted, losing one or more family members would lead to starvation. Bambeledugu was the least salubrious of cantons: sleeping sickness, malaria, leprosy, elephantiasis, polio, and river blindness afflicted the population at alarming rates. Part of the vast no-man's land of the isolated northern parts of the district, Bambeledugu was far from migrant destinations and distant from local trade arteries. Many families depended on hunting to survive.[26] In most cantons, however, communities relied heavily on labor migration. The entire southeastern quadrant of the district was considered a sending region. In the case of Fulala, according to a census report, of the total population of 4,503, there were 400 absent young men away on migration in 1951. In Sibirila, young men were "flocking to Ivory Coast after the harvest to engage in work on the plantations of cocoa, coffee, and kola nuts." In Zana 12 percent of the total population was absent on migration in Ivory Coast in 1954, while in the large canton of Cémala roughly 1,667 men were away from home on migration, and in Siondugu 20 percent of the adult male population was away on migration in 1955. Almost all of the workers were in Ivory Coast. Like many other cantons, Siondugu was isolated and offered few opportunities to produce for the market. One report stated, "This life in a closed circuit provokes numerous migrations of young people, who have only this means at their disposal to procure resources." The region of Bilatuma, bordering Ivory Coast, saw many young men leave annually for work in Ivory Coast. The general state of the economy was summed up as follows: "There is important migration of labor to Ivory Coast. Only economic and agricultural development of the district will remedy this situation."[27]

The isolation of the Senufo canton of Niené along the border with Ivory Coast had forced its inhabitants to shift their economic lives toward Tengrela. During the rainy months, as the Kankelaba River rose, people could not travel to the north. Colonial officials lamented the fact that inadequate roads and bridges prevented one of the most productive regions from supplying grain to the north. The French Sudan had a granary in waiting but no way of accessing it: "The road is insufficient. . . . [It] does not permit connection with the capital except for eight of the twelve months, following the cutting off of the bridge over the Kankelaba. . . . Niené, with its hard-working population and rich soil and climate, must contribute to the prosperity of the district. But presently, its economic development is paralyzed by the lack of roads to Buguni; its commercial activity is oriented toward Tengrela in Ivory Coast." Jula traders from Niené had migrated annually to Ivory Coast, and there had been migrant peanut farmers recruited by the colonial state during the war, but voluntary labor migration on a mass level did not begin until the late 1940s.[28] Although there are no accurate districtwide statistics on labor migration, I estimate that overall about 20,000 to 30,000 workers were migrating annually to Ivory Coast and elsewhere.

Migration to Ivory Coast was seasonal and circular, rarely surpassing two or three months. Furthermore, migrants traveled widely, searching for the best opportunities: "People migrated to every part of Ivory Coast. . . . Each year, it would change. The migrants would decide where they would go to work. . . . After we earned some money, we would come back to the village because we had to farm with our family. Even to stay one year was too long. We would spend only two or three months and come back."[29] Often migrants were so-called target workers, preferring piecework for shorter duration, with specific goals, such as marriage or a bicycle, in mind. They usually found work on cocoa or coffee plantations or in felling trees for the lumber trade. One man said, "When we went to Ivory Coast, we were hired by the Ivoirians to clear the dense vegetation. . . . When you were hired to cut the trees, you had to negotiate the price of your work first. When you finished one area, they paid you a sum. When you earned enough money, you came back. We also harvested cocoa. After having harvested the cocoa, we transported the cocoa from the bush villages to the urban centers. They paid us for the work each time."[30]

Although most migrants were men, women also began migrating in the postwar era, usually accompanying their husbands or brothers. The picture of the household economy and of village life more generally being structured around absent men and stay-at-home women began to change. Recently, Teresa Barnes has drawn attention to the mobility of African women in southern Africa. She notes that while men dominated labor migration numerically, women were also highly mobile, playing important roles in the social reproduction of urban areas and other migrant destinations. It is crucial therefore to move beyond the image of the "passive rural widow," an image that marginalizes women in regional social history and reproduces certain gendered binary oppositions.[31] In the case of French Sudan, the archival record is relatively silent on the subject of female migrants, but oral accounts suggest that the mobility of women was not an isolated phenomenon.

Women migrants were present in most of the destinations the men were, including Guinea, Senegal, Ivory Coast, and the city of Bamako. Madji Konate, for example, worked in the gold mines, joining other women, working alongside their husbands, washing through the dirt for pieces of gold. According to one colonial official in 1947, this job was women's work and was done in streams or rivers with ordinary calabash bowls.[32] Madji elaborated on the roles of women in mine work: "We would take water and wash the dirt in a calabash. Eventually we would see a few crystals of gold at the bottom of the calabash and put them aside. Sometimes the gold pieces were small and sometimes big. The women would work by washing the dirt that was taken from the mines. They did not dig the mines; the men did that."[33] Even on migration women, far from being stay-at-home domestic workers, were integral to the labor process. Even so, most oral accounts do point to the ways in which women contributed to social reproduction. Young women often migrated with groups of men from their home village to provide domestic work. Such was the case in the story told by Bakari Koné: "I was in Ivory Coast with several people. Majan, she went with us. She prepared food for all of us, day and night. Everywhere that we went she cooked for us." The case of Fatumata Doumbia, from the village of Zimpiala, shows how women were early pioneers in rural-urban migration to Bamako after the war. She recalled the female workforce from Buguni: "There were other women from Buguni finding work in Bamako. We often went with our older brothers. We stayed with a jatigi and worked while our brothers went to find work with the French. . . . I worked in the homes of soldiers in the neighborhood of Madina-Kura, cleaning. . . . I prepared food for them. My brother found work doing construction."[34]

Although women usually migrated with their husbands or other family members, there were some unmarried women who went on migration, as one official reported: "We often see young women going alone to Ivory Coast before their marriage." It is unclear whether single women migrants traveled with the consent of the household or not. On rare occasions women went on migration to Senegal to work as cooks and domestic workers or as prostitutes. Such women were usually widows or runaways who followed migrants, finding work along the railway line or in trade towns. They usually remained unmarried and were viewed as spinsters. Although young men and women pushed the boundaries of their independence by leaving or threatening to leave, most of them did not seek a total rupture with their families and homelands. Compromise and negotiation were ongoing.[35]

INDIVIDUALISM AND INTERGENERATIONAL CONFLICT

While group solidarity was instrumental in migrant networks, the mobility of young men also generated divisions and intergenerational conflicts within communities. In discussing these household fissures, informants often spoke of the emergence of individualism (*tako*) and ownership (*tigiya*), which had previously been associated with greed, selfishness, and even sorcery. Individualism and ownership also connoted ideas of purposive action, choice, and property. But, as Charles Tilly has noted, individualism as a category of historical analysis raises red flags with its suggestions of individual rational decision making and of freedom from social constraints and responsibilities and its correspondences to Western notions of personhood. I use the term as a descriptive category employed by informants but falling well short of embracing "methodological individualism" as such.[36] In any case, a fairly typical testimony reveals how individualism was locally understood and historically situated: "At this time, young men started to have the money, but their father would have none. . . . There was individualism in the country and ownership. This all made difficulties. Everyone started to say, 'That is my property.' That had not existed before. But that is what brought difficulties between people."[37]

As this account suggests, individualism was linked to notions of property, producing "difficulties between people." And when young men and women pursued their own interests, they were forced to disavow the interests of household heads, which meant breaking with tradition.

While such processes of disintegration would not occur on a wide scale until after the Second World War, there is evidence from colonial documents that fissures in the household were already underway in the interwar years. In 1928, for example, one official noted the "progressive emancipation" of the young people, "who increasingly tend to break free of the guardianship of the head of the family and native command. Individualism is making great progress, and this new spirit does not facilitate our task, already clumsy and difficult."[38] Although individualism had been championed during the era of emancipation, now it was viewed as a symptom and cause of social breakdown and political disorder. Later, even the Antillian governor general of French Equatorial Africa, Félix Eboué, who embodied liberal colonialism, warned of "the evils of absurd individualism." The signs of "detribalization," a common colonial trope, were everywhere and appeared as the greatest threat to "native command," or chiefly authority.[39]

Notwithstanding the more reductive statements on detribalization, census officials in their visits to specific localities also remarked somewhat formulaically on the social processes behind the erosion of authority. In 1953 an official in Wasulu reported, "What the young men desire first of all is the ability to found their own household free of the multiple obligations of the larger traditional family; to have a patrimony for which they will be responsible and from which they draw the profit. It is certainly difficult to reconcile this point of view with that of the older generations." These sorts of descriptions resonate with the memories of informants, who emphasized the simple goal of establishing one's own household. Elsewhere, another census tour document reported that migration had its origins in the "gerontocracy that rules society." It went on to note that the only solution for young men seeking to marry was to migrate. Even so, migrants continued to support the household. The report stated, "[The migrant] participates in the life of the family by sending home funds, in particular at the moment when taxes are due."[40] As a case in point, one informant went to Ivory Coast after the war, against his father's wishes, and worked for four years growing cocoa. Eventually, he found a wife and lived abroad until his father died. He noted that he returned periodically to visit his family and sent gifts to appease elders and show respect for tradition. Indeed, there was considerable "cultural compliance" as migrants straddled two worlds, one foot in the localism of their home villages and the other in more cosmopolitan settings.[41]

There was also an independence of mind. Former migrants recalled how they returned home with stories, new ideas, and unusual experiences. One informant said that although he came back with very little money, he gained knowledge and ideas from his travels: "After my return, all I did was farm. I returned with not much money, but what I observed during my travels added to my experience of things. Even if I did not earn so much money, the things that I saw and the stories that I heard, this added to my personal experience. . . . My mind was opened."[42] The movement of people and ideas was also linked to broader political changes. In Ivory Coast and Guinea, migrants came in contact with local representatives of the RDA and got involved in politics. In fact, many young men got their first RDA cards while on migration. This does not mean that their thoughts and actions reflected elite discourse or the RDA party line verbatim. Migrants interpreted political messages according to local logics and personal interests. Still, many joined unions and learned about workers' rights and ideas of equality, lessons they put to good use in challenging elders and employers. Thus, the influence of politics should not be narrowly construed as engagement with the electoral process and party activism. Rather, one might also consider the ways in which new political ideas were deployed in local settings in interaction and conflict with elders, chiefs, and other authority figures. Moreover, these ideas were never strictly secular ones; they resonated with Muslim ideas of equality, solidarity, and social justice.[43]

The broadening of intellectual horizons, or changes in mentality in colonial parlance, also produced divisions within families. Young people became more impatient with the constraints and rigidities of tradition, as one official reported: "The inferiority complex vis-à-vis the elders is disappearing, above all following migration to Ivory Coast or Senegal."[44] Musa Diallo spent much of his adult life as a migrant worker. After the war, he first migrated to Guinea, where he got interested in politics and the RDA. Then, for several years, he traveled around working as a mason. One of the reasons for remaining "in exodus" for so long was that returning home would have meant relinquishing all the freedoms to which he had grown accustomed. But in addition he recalled how young men who returned to their home villages often felt superior to the elders and regarded their traditions as being backward. When asked how his own elders responded, he conveyed something of a generic account: "When we came back, we found our elders there and they would say, 'Ah, you have left on migration and you believe that you have done migration and you have learned some new ideas. And now you want to come change our ideas, you believe you are more intelligent now, you believe that we are inferior to you. It is true that you have done migration, but that does not mean that we are sheep. Your head is not clearer than ours. Migration, migration, what is that? Ha! You left here and you came back and paid the taxes, now you are coming back with some changes for our customary practices. You want to scoff at our customs.'" Indeed, what is clear from the oral record is that contestations over the old ways (*ko kòrò*) were inextricably linked to labor migration and the increasing politicization of young men and women.[45] There was no clean break. Rather, cultural contestation was a drawn-out process of negotiation, microadjustments, and small-scale war as each side sought to marshal its power at the other's expense. (I explore in later chapters what happens when the old ways no longer hold the same power over people's imaginations or when newer, perceptibly superior moral frameworks are available, structures which might allow young men to pry themselves loose from subordinate positions in the community or household.)

TRANSFORMATIONS IN MARRIAGE

With the end of forced labor and the indigénat, elders and authority figures lost considerable leverage over junior males. We have seen how village and canton chiefs counteracted the efforts of rebellious young men to win greater autonomy by sending them to forced labor as punishment. When these crucial tools of power were blunted, marriage became one of the last ways in which elders controlled junior males. As in many colonial African societies, control over marriage was often an expression of a lineage head's efforts to maintain "wealth in people" as power and resources slipped from his hands. But increasingly, as elders resisted authorization of marriage and withheld forms of social and economic capital, young men departed on migration. And in the absence of junior male labor, the value of women's labor increased, meaning contestations over marriage became even more acrimonious.[46]

Formerly, families mediated marriage through bride exchange practices (falen-ni-falen) or labor service (buranci), and marriages were arranged between families. Briefly, in falen-ni-falen two families agreed to exchange their daughters, whereas mediation via buranci entailed the husband performing farm labor for his future in-laws. One representative testimony sums up buranci: "When the family accepted the marriage, the young man would go and work for the in-laws. This work was called buranci. I did this for five years and had to walk for hours to the village and work the whole day and come back home at night."[47] In all cases, marriage was a long process that cemented alliances and expanded social networks. It included elaborate rituals and services, such as the bride traveling back and forth between villages. In short, marriage was one of the cornerstones of society. Therefore, disputes over the system represented direct affronts to the old ways and rights-in-people that elders were seeking to maintain.[48]

In certain localities that were tied directly into networks of commercial exchange, bridewealth systems had been in use during the early colonial period. According to colonial court records, bridewealth cases were occasionally brought before the Tribunal of Buguni from 1905 to 1912. However, most litigants came from trade towns or villages in eastern parts of the district that had seen a greater expansion of commercial transactions than other parts. Oral accounts and postwar colonial documents suggest that most families did not start mediating marriage via bridewealth until after the Second World War. But this transformation did not occur overnight. There were increments of change and overlapping practices which blended diverse elements en route to a more comprehensive system based solely on bridewealth.[49]

Aside from labor migration there were other agents of change, including the colonial state itself. Most important, under pressure from progressive groups, feminists, and religious missionaries, the state passed certain legal reforms aimed at transforming marriage practices. First, the Mandel Decree of 1939 fixed the minimum marriage age for girls at fourteen and for boys at sixteen, while also requiring mutual consent between the husband and wife. In other words, it sought to end forced or arranged marriage. Then, in 1951, the Jacquinot Decree took steps to end polygamy, allowed marriage without bridewealth, and empowered women seeking divorce. In most rural areas these decrees were unenforceable. Yet they did represent an important step in centralizing and regulating marriage laws, and this had an enduring influence on the development of marriage-related civil law.[50] While there was no formal declaration of policy in Buguni, the administration aimed locally to control and standardize marriage practices, partly to avoid the chaos of bridewealth inflation. At the same time, colonial officials held up changes in marriage practices as evidence of progress. According to one official, marriage by bridewealth "spurs growth to livestock rearing, favors marriage between the young, and provokes an augmentation in the figures of children," all of which were considered building blocks of modernization in rural areas.[51] Similarly, informants suggested that the administration advocated for bridewealth perhaps in the interest of generating more commercial activity or to demonstrate the alleged civilizing effects of French rule. The son of a former canton chief stated, "The French came to the canton chiefs and decided to transform our custom of bride exchange. They changed it into exchange based on cattle." Elsewhere, in the canton of Céndugu, a former migrant worker said, "Marriage by consent was something introduced here by the colonial administration, and this gave power to the women." In talking about bride exchange, the current village chief of Moro said, "When the French came here, they said that we must stop this type of marriage, saying that it was not good. When marriage by exchange stopped, the marriage by bride price and money began."[52] In this sample of oral testimonies, informants clearly problematized evolutionary narratives of bridewealth naturally replacing bride exchange as commercial transactions increased and migrant workers injected more cash into their communities. Still, it is unclear to what extent the administration enforced the Mandel and Jacquinot decrees and whether in advocating for changes in marriage mediation it was responding to initiatives already taken by young men, or vice versa.

In any case, oral accounts point to the emergence of hybrid systems of marriage mediation and to crucial transitional steps between bride exchange and bridewealth. These were not evolutionary stages but interstitial strategies and idioms deployed in particular cases. As informants noted, in the system of bride exchange not all men were guaranteed marriage in their lifetime. But to continue the lineage, the eldest son had to remarry and reproduce somehow, regardless of the gender composition of the household. Thus, flexibility grew out of the mutual sympathy that households had for one another. One of the most common solutions was a system of marrying girls on credit, referred to as *dendankana*. Essentially, when a family had no daughter to exchange, they would ask another family to give their daughter in exchange for a future (unborn) daughter. One elder explained: "There were some people who could give you their girl under the form of dendankana, which meant that I would give you my daughter even if you had nothing to exchange and this person would say, 'I know you have nothing today, but I give you my daughter. When Allah allows you to reproduce, you will give me one of your daughters in return.' "[53] Even when marriage was mediated via this credit system of dendankana, there was never a guarantee that the couple would have a daughter. In such cases, livestock could be substituted as payment for the daughter. Dendankana was a flexible, hybrid solution and a halfway point between bride exchange and bridewealth systems.[54]

As communities shifted in the direction of bridewealth practices, lineage heads struggled to hold onto their control over young men, who, in turn, were using labor migration to outflank the elders. As one official reported, "The young men have the habit of leaving the region to try to earn enough money for bride price; they do not achieve this in their homes, as the fruit of their labor is always at the disposition of the head of the family, who alone decides to give them a spouse of his choice. Many of these young men, seasonal workers in Ivory Coast and Senegal above all, and even in Bamako, end up settling there and marrying there or bringing their spouse back with them."[55] In some ways, searching for a woman became an act of rebellion. And men commonly fled on migration to accumulate bridewealth or negotiated marriages in neighboring cantons, where they could evade family controls. In Fulala, many young men went to find women in the canton of Céndugu and other surrounding cantons. As elsewhere in Africa, elders responded by increasing bridewealth rates as a way of countering the growing wealth of young men, while also profiting financially from an emerging institution which had yet to be stabilized. As a result, across the district the number of livestock rose as more people invested in cattle as a way of marrying. Nevertheless, bridewealth inflation was not inevitable. In Fulala, household heads even lowered bridewealth rates in order to keep young men from leaving the canton. Seeing the futility of preventing young men from marrying and watching as their neighbors accumulated greater wealth, elders decided to collectively stabilize bridewealth rates.[56]

According to Barbara Cooper, women's views and understandings of bridewealth have often been marginalized in the literature. Basing her study on rich oral testimonies, Cooper shows how women in the French colonial town of Maradi (Niger) were active participants in shaping idioms of gift exchange. Within the changing political economy, shifts in the material contents of wedding gifts affected the evaluation and worth of women. Women were active agents engaged in the process as a way of defining themselves.[57] Although the evidence is rather thin, I have also found that women in southern French Sudan actively contributed to contestations over marriage practices. It is unclear whether or not women contested the material contents of gifts. But they did challenge arranged marriages. In certain cases, women sought to escape the authority of their parents, as in the canton of Yorobadugu, where it was reported that "in the departure of young women . . . it appears that they are desirous of shaking off the traditional family constraints, notably concerning marriage." Fleeing one's village was undoubtedly a radical step, one with dire consequences, but young women started refusing the spouses selected by their families, leaving home, and marrying out of choice. Some young women simply ran away with their boyfriends and never returned.[58] At the same time, women were taking legal action to obtain divorces. According to Lamine Diakite, a former colonial interpreter, litigation over marriage was the most common cause of disputes in the village courts. Through the decisions of its indigenous tribunals, the administration occasionally supported the efforts of women, annulling marriages that lacked the consent of the women involved. Even outside the courts, marriage and divorce were burning topics.[59]

While changes in marriage practices were central issues in wide social contestations, the links between Islamization processes and shifts to bridewealth are still unclear. Much of what informants said was characterized by normative views and opinions on the proper place of women in the household. Nevertheless, there were linkages. To begin with, Muslims associated bride exchange with bamanaya. It was the old way of doing things, a way that had been replaced by a system more in keeping with Islam. And Muslims found support for forms of bridewealth or wedding gifts in Islamic law. In principle, as one imam noted, *mahr* was interpreted as a gift paid by the husband to the bride, even as it constituted a de facto payment to the bride's family.[60] In a census report from the canton of Kola, one official noted that "conversion to Islam" was bringing about "the regression of marriage by exchange."[61] Similarly, informants suggested that as Islam grew in strength within communities and more young men returned from migration with money to pay for bridewealth and prayer, bride exchange and labor service came to be viewed as *haramu*, or unlawful. In the view of the new generation Islam provided the moral language for critiquing a system that had served to keep them enslaved.[62] Hence young men embraced Islam partly as a way of breaking with the old ways. This was a multifarious process, one which included ongoing renegotiation of status hierarchies and the reordering of local gradients of privilege and power, particularly vis-à-vis caste boundaries and rules on intermarriage. In the canton of Fulala, one colonial official observed that "a certain flexibility" had emerged among people with respect to the "imperious rules of marriage that had separated the diverse castes." When a census official asked people why they had made these changes, the response was simply, "That is done now." The official speculated that the root of the changes could be found in Islam and the legacy of slavery: "Islam has something to do with [changes in marriage practices], but also, without doubt, the fact that a large part of the population was formerly slave, which has thus blurred the differences between the castes."[63] In assessing the transformations in marriage practices, contestations cannot be reduced to any single social logic. Various axes of power and status shaped the process, as competing and crosscutting groups pursued their discrete but overlapping interests. Indeed, in order to approach the question of religious change in a nonreductive way, one must cast the net as widely as possible to include certain dimensions of social life that at first glance seem to have had very little to do with religion.[64]

AGRARIAN INDIVIDUALISM: PLOWS, PRIVATE FIELDS, AND FRUIT TREES

Local ecologies were changing in the postwar era. As hunters enlarged their zones with more efficient use of firearms, much wild fauna, such as elephants and lions, disappeared from village landscapes. And as families invested in livestock to pay bridewealth and migrant remittances generated more commercial activity, domesticated animals became more common. Tied to these changes was the beginning of plow agriculture, which enabled farmers to till large swaths of land individually, without depending on collective labor. In short, the land was being domesticated. The use of the plow not only reinforced emergent notions of individualism and property but also reshaped the agricultural habitus. New body techniques were mastered, and new relationships with the land developed. Even the instrument of the plow itself represented a rupture. Not produced, as hoes were, by blacksmiths within the village, it came from abroad and was distributed by the colonial administration, usually via the Société de Prévoyance, the colonial government's local agricultural lending agency and mutual aid society in times of dearth. As we have seen, blacksmiths had been central to religious life, which was inextricably linked to farming and human fertility. As the role of blacksmiths was challenged by the import of plows, the reorganization of farming based on the plow meant a reordering of agrarian culture. The spread of the plow thereby had consequences that reached far beyond the strictly agricultural. Farming underwent a process of desacralization, as religious rites and rituals tied to collective work were eroded away.

These processes were linked to colonial projects of development and agricultural popularization (*vulgarisation agricole*). In the interwar era, the colonial state began pushing aggressively to expand cash crop production, while promoting the intensification of agriculture. It was also the era when labor migration became a regular fixture of village life. In 1923, when the first reports on migration circulated, officials observed that in the absence of young male laborers fields were being neglected. Then, assessing agriculture in Wasulu in 1928, administrators again suggested that the main reason for the lack of productivity was a local preference for migrant labor, rather than working the soil. One official stated, "The natives do not work as they should; they need to be stimulated; they produce very little millet and do not possess any reserves. . . . They also have a bad habit; as Fula-Bambaras, they have retained the nomadic habits of their ancestors; for no reason they travel around outside the district." It was easier for colonial officials to attribute labor migration to such characteristics as "nomadic habits" than to confront the burdens of taxation and forced labor. But the solution appeared simple: the people needed to be "stimulated" through the intensification of agricultural production.[65]

An article of colonial faith in such development endeavors was that the diffusion of the plow would enable peasants to produce more and, in any case, replace absent migrant workers. Ultimately, as Monica Van Beusekom has shown, it was hoped that Africans would settle into a mixed farming system of intensive agriculture and livestock rearing and leave shifting cultivation behind. This modern way of farming would encourage farmers to invest in permanent plots, private property, and nuclear family arrangements. Thus, from 1922, the administration began establishing farm schools and distributing plows across the French Sudan. A decade later, there were roughly 2,500 to 3,000 plows in the colony.[66] In Buguni, the first plows were distributed with the aim of increasing cotton production, and by 1930 there were 173 plows in use across the district. To assist in the diffusion of plows, the administration sent chiefs and other new colonial elites to agricultural research stations in Sikasso, Kutiala, and M'Pesoba and trained agricultural monitors who would serve as agents of agricultural modernization, a sort of peasant vanguard leading the way by creating "islands of prosperity" for others to emulate. Early focus was placed on pilot projects, experimental farms, and small "villages of colonization," where peasants worked by means of modern techniques.[67] Usually, the administration settled groups of farmers in key towns and villages rather than simply distributing plows to isolated farmers. These villages were often located near main roads, such as the "center of colonization" in the town of Zancébugu, along the main route from Buguni to Sikasso.[68]

Yet as French agricultural experts admitted, the popularization of the plow would take time, perhaps generations, as the new tool became habit. Repeating a common evolutionist view, one official noted, "In my opinion, there is a way to have the plow penetrate their habits. It is to allow the native to use it as he wishes and to help him while monitoring him. . . . We will obtain results only through patience and perseverance, while studying all the difficulties and remedying all the causes of lack of success. Plow agriculture will require several generations, and we will need to overcome great difficulties."[69] While colonial officials emphasized that the plow was popularized and not imposed, oral accounts suggest a different story. One man stated, "I learned how to use the plow from the agricultural monitors. At this time, Balan was the canton chief. . . . They called the people. They outfitted the oxen with yokes around their necks.

They drew the plow called *basaki*, which was a plow with two wheels; it was very heavy. . . . We had to remove all kinds of roots from the ground. They beat and hit the people to the point of killing them."[70] Although such training exercises targeted all people, the first families to farm with plows were large families with ample labor and livestock; often this meant the families of village chiefs. One elder said, "There were not many plows at this time. Our family did not have a plow. The village chief of Denso had a large family, and he was forced to take a plow. The village chief of Nenejana had a plow. He had a large family. . . . It was around 1935 or 1936 when the plow was first introduced here. . . . It was imposed by force. But nobody knew of the usefulness of the plow. . . . The agricultural agents would go from village to village to teach the peasants how to use the plow. . . . The people started to use the plow little by little. And finally they realized that it was useful. They could do more work, enlarge their fields under cultivation, and the yield was good."[71]

The plow continued to spread from the mid-1930s through the 1950s, as more people made requests for the new tool. But even as demands for plows grew across Buguni and more farmers began to see the advantages of plow agriculture, their utilization was limited by the lack of adequate oxen. The administration had distributed 333 plows by 1936, but the majority of them were Bajac Liancourtoise (Basaki) plows, which weighed seventy kilograms. The plows were simply too heavy for local oxen to pull, so peasants struggled to make use of them. During the war the administration pushed ahead with its development efforts, and by the end of the war there were 703 plows in the district. By 1951, one official reported that there were "about 1000 plows," after which the administration lost count. At this point there was an average of one plow for every village. M'Bemba Sidibé in Balanfina explained: "The plow spread just before independence. Eventually the people had begun to understand how to use the plow, and soon the French pushed to multiply the number of plows. Then everyone who could buy a plow would buy one. That was how it was spread here, and that was how the areas under cultivation enlarged and the production increased."[72]

Plows were also spreading through the initiative of locals, in particular migrant workers who used their incomes to invest in new farming technologies. As households and communities heard rumors of the benefits, people started using migrant remittances to buy plows.

By the early 1950s colonial officials reported that farmers in the region of Wasulu had two primary concerns: the migration of young men and the desire to acquire a plow. Oral accounts also reveal the importance of migrant investments in plows, as one elder explained: "When they sold the plows to people, they were sold on credit. People paid off their plows in different ways. People went to the gold mines to earn money to buy plows. In my case, I went on migration where I worked on contract on the construction of a road. I earned my salary, and I gave the money to my father, who used the money to buy a plow in Yanfolila."[73]

Agricultural production did intensify, but mostly in Wasulu. Using the plow, rice farmers responded to demand in nearby markets and produced for the mines of Kalana. By 1950 they were producing rice even for markets in Guinea. For the most part, the plow was put to use along the Sankarani River, where rice was farmed on the floodplains. And as farming along the Sankarani became more important to the local economy, villages relocated to settlements along the river. But although Wasulu was one of the most agriculturally modernized regions, the lack of all-weather rural roads was a serious impediment to the region's commercial integration with the rest of the colony. This explains why peasants usually marketed their crops in Kankan, Siguiri, Kalana, or Siekorole. Even the French post in Buguni was inaccessible in the rainy season.[74]

The plow followed a different trajectory in the southeastern quadrant of the district, which eventually became the Subdivision of Kolondieba, created by decree on June 7, 1955, and officially opened in April 1957. Before 1956 the Agricultural Service had spent little time in the region, so there were few plows in use. However, in contrast to localities in Wasulu, where the transition from hoe agriculture to plow agriculture was aided by lucrative markets for rice, farmers in the southeastern quadrant had few outlets for their products. There were also constraints on production owing to the shortage of draught animals. But in the canton of Niené a large colonial effort was made to encourage the use of plows in rice farming. At first, the region's inhabitants resisted.[75] Things began to change, however, particularly with the increase in migrant remittances. In some cases, peasants responded to the prodding and propaganda of the administration. Solo Sanogo summed it up as follows: "The biggest changes in agriculture during the French administration came when the plow was introduced here. The people started to work with the plow and this changed our methods. . . . But it was at this time that our father bought our first plow. . . . When he heard the publicity around it, that this was an efficient tool, he went and bought the plow. There was some news circulating about the plow, but we did not know anything about the plow. . . . I was performing forced labor near Buguni when I saw a plow for the first time. When we left here, we saw the plow at work in Buguni. They were using the plow to cultivate rice fields along the river." Shifting to plow agriculture could be a risky undertaking without proper training, as poor harvests meant famine. Oral accounts from the canton of Céndugu suggest that some of the first people to begin experimenting with plows later abandoned them. As Sekou Koné recalled, "After the first wave of plows, people abandoned them. . . . We ended up selling our plow. People just sold their plows to blacksmiths who broke them up to make hoes. . . . We had greater trust in our hoes than in the plows."[76] In the canton of Fulala, colonial officials reported "an enthusiasm for the purchase of plows and cattle." However, there were also clear impediments to agricultural intensification. An administrator noted, "The fact remains and is general that the distance of markets and the difficult access of villages are considerable obstacles to agricultural development of the cantons. . . . And this is regrettable in a district that should be more and more the millet granary of Bamako."[77]

While the district of Buguni was not living up to its billing as a regional granary, local settlement patterns and village social relations were being transformed. Most important was the gradual breakup of common fields and the wider proliferation of private plots. This transformation had far-reaching consequences, bringing with it a new ethos and practice of agrarian individualism. In many ways, it was the extension of processes begun at the end of slavery, when households moved away from village protective mud walls to create their own farming hamlets. Family-level communal fields (fòròbaw) had remained intact, with people farming collectively, as one elder recalled: "The elders, they would go measure the land and divide it, each person had their part to farm. So they would trace marks on the ground. . . . You could have twenty or thirty people in one field farming on one day, harvesting from field to field."[78] After the Second World War individuals began devoting more time to their own plots (jònfòròw), using plows and bringing larger swaths of land under cultivation. The jònfòrò fields were initially farmed in the afternoon or evening after work for the sotigi on the community fields had been done. And, as I have noted, this was the pattern of master–slave labor relations, in which the slave was permitted to work on his slave field (jònfòrò) in the evenings.[79] As young men began asserting more independence and founding their own separate households, they eventually shirked communal work entirely. Consequently, families started to atomize and subdivide as small groups moved away from their villages to form new hamlets. In 1950 one colonial official wrote, "Groups of huts dispersed across the fields. . . . It is that each family wants to live apart from the others."[80] In the village of Balanfina, M'Bemba Sidibé explained that as families started to splinter, individuals invested more in their personal plots: "Since the jònfòrò proliferated, the fòròba was no longer cultivated; it was abandoned. That was at the root of the disintegration of families. Everyone was looking for his own personal property. . . . Each person started covering his own head."[81] The plow played an important role in this process by enabling individuals to farm alone, independently of work groups. Across the district, the diffusion of the plow often correlated with local population shifts as more people searched for open land, particularly in the flood plains adjacent to local rivers.[82]

Not all changes in agricultural land use and settlement patterns were driven by technology. Even in zones with few plows individuals were reportedly spending more time on their jònfòròw, farming these plots two days a week and at night. In attempting to explain this process, Broulaye Doumbia noted that young people simply wanted to own the product of their labor. He suggested that the "stay-at-homes" resented migrants who returned with their money but refused to work in the fields. Thus, the stay-at-homes also became more selfish in their farming: "These lazy men disturbed the work. [Returning migrants] did not want to work in the fields. That was behind the division in the household as well. What happened in agriculture, it was the same thing for the migrants searching for money. Some people went to look for money on migration, while others stayed here to farm. Those who went on migration, they would not share their money with others. That did not conform to things, and this contributed to people working for themselves more and more."[83]

Individual interests found expression in the planting of fruit trees by migrant workers and soldiers. Just as in the early colonial period freed slaves and other mobile groups introduced certain fruit trees into their villages, migrant workers and soldiers brought mango, orange, and banana trees back to their homes. In the village of Tenetu, Gérard Brasseur, who conducted research there in 1955, recorded local accounts of how fruit trees were diffused. His informants attributed the introduction of mango trees into the village to returning tirailleurs, who, after the First World War, "having eaten mangoes that they brought from Bamako, threw the pits near the market," where they first grew. By 1960, there were 127 mango trees in the village. My informants in the cantons of Fulala and Céndugu emphasized the role of migrant workers in this process, as Sekou Koné recalled: "When the people went on migration, the most innovative of them would come back from their migration with mango pits. They would plant them in their village. The first pits in this area were planted near the home of Ba Tieman on the road to Siten." Elders in Wasulu also credited migrants with introducing mango and orange trees. One man said, "The idea to plant fruit trees came from Ivory Coast. It was an innovation brought from there. All the young men who came back from Ivory Coast began planting their mango trees and orange trees here."[84]

Because fruit trees were the property of those who planted them, migrant workers invested in mango trees as a way of building up their personal resources. Unlike other forms of wealth, the income migrants derived from their fruits trees did not have to be shared with the head of the household. But once introduced, fruit trees were diffused throughout the village and beyond through the agency of locals. As every household had mango trees planted near their homes, the market for selling mangoes evaporated. Sekou Koné recalled the changing value of mangoes: "The migrants planted the trees, and they became a source of revenue for them. But when the first mango trees bore fruits, the other people benefited by planting pits near their homes, and then the mango spread to every corner. These first mango trees, they became communal trees (fòròba yiri). Nobody was barred from collecting the fruits anymore. It was a source of food. . . . They would gather a few mangos and give them to you free. You did not pay anything. Then after this, the only fruit that was sold were oranges. The mango was not sold, only oranges."[85] Migrants were also responsible for introducing banana trees and orange trees from Ivory Coast. During a census tour of the canton of Fulala of 1951, one official noted that the region "owed its banana plantations" to young migrants.[86]

Finally, as more cash flowed into local economies, more people purchased firearms. Despite efforts during the Second World War to confiscate firearms, they were in wide circulation in the postwar period. While many people bought firearms for hunting, there is evidence that guns were status symbols for men; carrying a firearm became a statement of masculinity at a time when hunters' associations were being transformed into pseudopolitical organizations which had very little to do with hunting. One colonial official noted, "The number of guns in Gwanan has increased. . . . That represents not only a sign of richness, as in other cantons, but also the importance of hunting dress in this region." In the canton of Jallon-Fula, it was similarly observed that the increase in the number of firearms was owing to their symbolic value: "It is a sign of the enrichment of the country where the gun serves more in its public display than in hunting." Nevertheless, the wider availability of firearms led to more individual hunting, and such individualism often fueled rivalries and competition among hunters as resources in the region disappeared and hunters pushed further into the bush.[87]

In the end, plows, private fields, fruit trees, and other innovations were expressions of a new ethos of agrarian individualism, a development that would fundamentally reshape social relations. Moreover, there were subtle linkages between plow agriculture and the embrace of the new monotheistic faith. The plow not only undermined bamana forms of cooperative farm labor, characterized by shifting cultivation, polyculture, and intercropping, but also served to reorient farmers away from strict dependence on local earth spirits and to reframe farming practices within more individualized contexts. For some people, the embrace of the plow and prayer was part of larger trends of rationalization and individualization in farming and worship. In contrast to collective farming, among the bamana polytheist farmers, who mounded and hoed in a supposed disorderly manner and depended on innumerable power objects, Muslim informants emphasized how people could both pray and plow individually and in a more uniform, effective manner. In local understandings, such perceived rationalism found resonance in Islam, with its claims of omniscient and universally applicable laws and power. The political rationalism and techniques of the modern state, especially when mediated by Muslim functionaries and interpreters, could be seen as part of a larger package of modernity in local eyes, which conflated, rather than opposed, secular rationalism and monotheistic universalism. In short, a new agrocultural complex was slowly taking hold.[88]

Chapter 6

Migrants and the Dialectics of Conversion, 1930–1960

In the village of N'Golobala, Fula Musa Suntura has been remembered as the most charismatic Muslim holy man of his generation. Coming to prominence in the postwar period, he was the quintessential rural preacher: he cultivated the land and used his personal comportment to spread the faith. Around the time Fula Musa was emerging as an important leader, migrant workers were turning toward Islam. While on migration, they appropriated Muslim cultural styles and forms of material culture, which served as new markers of social distinction and religious belonging. When they returned home, pressures to convert among young people continued to grow, as the youth found religious reasons for challenging the authority of elders and chiefs. These pressures were accentuated by shifts in the political landscape.

When colonial rule was consolidated during the interwar years, Muslims entered the colonial bureaucracy, filling positions as interpreters, canton representatives, agricultural extension workers, teachers, midwives, nurses, district guards, and so forth, meaning that vectors of Islamization were now located within the colonial state's apparatus itself. Slowly, their religious influence would spread into rural areas within the context of routine government exercises, such as the colonial census. Still, this paltry number of Muslim civil servants would never have enough influence to impose religious conformity on the rural population. Rather, the local institutionalization of Muslim power would depend on more far-reaching social processes that facilitated the emergence of village holy men and Muslim canton chiefs.

Indeed, Fula Musa did not start out as a village holy man. In the interwar years, he, too, was a migrant worker, who embraced prayer while working in Siguiri, Guinea. Then, after his time in Guinea, he went to Ivory Coast, where he worked and started studying. His friend said, "People started going to Ivory Coast, and Fula Musa was the first person from our village to go to Ivory Coast. Musa would approach every good *mori* [holy man] he met in order to obtain further knowledge. It was in this way that, little by little, he came to acquire his knowledge."[1] Later, Musa would even be considered a saint, gaining a reputation for his humanity (*adamadenya*). Another elder recalled that "on the level of humanity, he did good things. Whether or not he knew someone, if he heard that there was conflict in the village somewhere, he would go there to help calm the conflict. He knew a lot of things, and he had a special manner of carrying himself. Some people have knowledge, but they have no comportment. He possessed this charisma, this way of carrying himself. If people were seated near him, he would say nothing about the person who just got up to leave, behind their backs. If he said something, he would say it in their presence. That was just how he was."[2] While most migrant workers did not become local Sufi saints, in village histories of Islam they were the unsung heroes of religious change, as many young men and women returned to their homes with prayer. Absent the social muscle they added to nascent Muslim communities, it would have been difficult for holy men to convert fellow villagers through preaching and prayer alone. The position of a Muslim chief or imam was rarely publicly accepted until a certain threshold of popular support had been achieved. The way in which returning slaves quietly introduced prayer into many villages before the First World War echoed in the way migrant workers deepened village-level processes of Islamization.

Most studies of labor migration emphasize how migrants consumed symbols of Western modernity. In other words, the focus has usually been on how migrants adopted secular elements of Western culture and converted to Christianity either by working for Europeans in urban and industrial settings or by attending mission schools. At the same time, studies of colonial labor in French West Africa have tended to emphasize more secular and economic dimensions, such as trade unionism, urbanization, forced labor, and such.[3] However, this represents only part of the picture. As we have seen, most migrants from Buguni found work with Muslims, and usually in rural settings. Migration may have enabled them to learn a bit of French and to buy Western commodities, but it also facilitated their appropriation of Muslim cultural styles. This chapter establishes linkages between migration, networks, and Islamization within the context of shifting power relations at local and regional levels. It examines changes in commodity consumption and cultural style and explores local social pressures to convert within communities. It also emphasizes the ways in which changing forms of colonial governmentality, such as the colonial census, served to recast the political and social bases of religious identification.

DISCURSIVE SHIFTS AND CONTINUITIES: COLONIAL FEARS AND THE MUSLIM FRONTIER

There were shifts and continuities in French Islamic policy. The primary concern of the administration continued to be monitoring Muslim notables and marabouts, reinforcing traditional authority structures, and containing the region from nefarious so-called international or Arab influences. There was also a commitment to the concept of Islam Noir, which posited a superficial, governable, and docile form of Islam. However, as scholars have noted, in the 1930s, after years of relative quiet in religious matters, fears of rebellion sporadically returned. Most markedly, with the spread of the Hamawiyya, a branch of the Tijaniyya led by Shaykh Hamallah, administrators reported anew on the dangers of Islamism.[4] Although Hamallah had no significant following in the district of Buguni, his return from a ten-year exile in prison was a cause for concern. Locally, officials were on the lookout for an abbreviated form of prayer, which might connote preparation for war. Officials also kept closer tabs on marabouts, whose insidious activities could serve larger political goals. In Buguni, as one official explained, "the propaganda of marabouts . . . tends more and more to regain activity and clarify itself in a sense, if not aggressive, at least unfavorable to our administration." These "travelers in subversive ideas" were being radicalized through the hajj, which was viewed as the "principal canal" through which seditious ideas spread to "the popular masses." It would be an oversimplification to suggest that the fears of the

French, and even their outright hostility toward Islam, ever really disappeared. Nevertheless, there were subtle official shifts as the colonial state sought to show greater respect for Islam. In Buguni, this meant recruiting prominent proadministration Muslims like Seydou Nourou Tall to travel around giving talks. Just as key marabouts had been co-opted elsewhere by the administration, officials hoped that good Muslims could help in the propaganda of empire by speaking to rural inhabitants on such issues as the payment of taxes, the importance of forced labor, hygiene, increasing agricultural production, fighting against locusts, paying bridewealth, and limiting rivalries over the position of chief.[5]

In any case, this mix of fantasy and intrigue reared up against the backdrop of a steadily expanding Muslim frontier. By the 1930s officials were forced to acknowledge that despite colonial efforts to thwart it, Islam was spreading. Census reports indicated that the Muslim population in French West Africa had increased by over two million in twelve years, from 3,875,000 in 1924 to 6,241,000 in 1936. And yet there was a prevailing sense that nothing could be done to slow it down.[6] In Buguni such concerns were initially dismissed. Officials continued to sum up the Muslim question in the phrase "Nothing to report." Statistics seemed to confirm this. Census reports registered only a very slight increase in the number of Muslims. In 1934, roughly 18,000 were described as being Islamized, compared to 169,250 animists. Officials described Muslims as superficial in their faith and "ignorant of the principles of prayer." Furthermore, viewing conversion processes through the lens of more visible Muslim institutions, such as Qur'anic schools and mosques, officials saw little reason to believe that Islamization was occurring. By 1931 there were only seven Qur'anic schools, an increase of two schools in twenty years, hardly an alarming rate. They also continued to invoke the notion of Islamic conquest, as one report in 1934 stated: "The Muslims of the district are for the most part converts of Samori." Thus, as long as the region was protected from holy warriors or other agents of the "conquering faith," then Islamization was unlikely.[7]

In the postwar era, legal reforms eased pressures on communities and created openings for African political participation. In such circumstances, one might have expected a more conciliatory attitude toward Islam. Yet geopolitical realignments and emergent Muslim reform movements forced the French administration further back on its heels. On the surface, most threats followed old discursive patterns, as received ideas and archival habits were passed down. But there was also new empirical truth. Improvements in communications and increased mobility were certainly fueling the internationalization of Islam. More Africans were making the pilgrimage to Mecca, and some were even studying at al-Azhar University in Cairo, one of the perceived crucibles of Islamic radicalism. Tracking such developments, the French took increasingly adversarial positions vis-à-vis Islam in the late 1940s and 1950s, pursuing a more rigorous policy of containment. As Jean-Louis Triaud has noted, there was a "three-zone theory" of Islamization structuring policies and patterns of intervention. In Islamized areas, the administration pushed a counterreform agenda, seeking to establish control over the curriculum of *madrasas*. In animist zones, such as the district of Buguni, the aim was to prevent the expansion of Arabic literacy. Now, after years of confidence in the strict localism of African Islam, officials were awakening to the reality that African Muslims, whether proficient in Arabic or not, were breaking out of their village enclaves. In the late 1940s colonial officials were reading "the signs of the internationalization of Islam" as well as census reports which documented a steady expansion of Islam in increasingly ominous terms.[8]

In 1952 Marcel Cardaire, a French military intelligence officer and ethnographer, arrived in Bamako as the new head of Muslim Affairs. Alongside Amadou Hampâté Bâ, Cardaire would become deeply involved in efforts to curb the influence of the Wahhabiyya. While the counter-reform movement is beyond the scope of this book, Cardaire's writings, in particular *L'Islam et le terroir africain*, published in 1954, provide insights into the French understanding of Islamization and the wider social dynamics of religious change. Revisiting certain ideas of Delafosse and Brévié, Cardaire argued that rapid Islamization in the postwar era stemmed from social breakdown in rural villages, resulting in a spiritual void in the lives of peasants. Basing his conceptualization on the French notion of *terroir*, Cardaire emphasized how African "social religions of the soil" were being uprooted and were withering away under the influence of expanding commercial networks, labor migration, and broader social changes. While in certain settings Africans could be encouraged to embrace forms of "neo-fetishism," those who had already drifted into the Muslim orbit could be reenclosed in localized forms of Islam Noir.[9]

Despite this embrace of Muslim traditionalism as a bulwark against the Wahhabiyya, colonial officials in Buguni continued to suspect Sufi marabouts of mischief and charlatanism. Recycling old motifs, one official reported, "Some individuals, without great prestige elsewhere, are playing on the ignorance of the masses and, making a profit from this current coming from the outside, call themselves 'marabouts.' Their understanding of the Qur'an is nothing, but they know how to pray; they are acquiring among the few naïve followers a certain renown that they exploit."[10]

By 1951 local officials reported that a student from al-Azhar had returned to the district of Buguni. This seemingly isolated case set off alarm bells. In the colonial imagination such individuals were harbingers. One official commented on the repercussions of the Muslim quest for deeper knowledge: "The attendance at reputable Qur'anic schools outside the district manifests an aspiration toward a more profound knowledge of Islam. . . . The Egyptian university of Al-Azhar counts one student from this district. This single case still constitutes a good example of what will be produced later on a larger scale. Starting in the Qur'anic school of his village, the young man is later drawn to education and perfects his knowledge . . . finally in Cairo. This inescapable movement will put the country more and more at spiritual dependence on the Arab world, where we no longer control the rallying slogans at the source." Colonial officials were still on the lookout for quick and massive conversion processes sweeping across the land. And in 1957 officials were stunned to discover that the number of Muslims (156,351) had surpassed that of fetishists (90,110) in the colonial census in Buguni. By this time, ground-level social processes such as labor migration had set in motion far-reaching cultural and social changes which contributed to the expansion of Islam.[11]

MEDIATING MIGRATION: FAMILIES AND SOCIAL NETWORKS

Moving away from narratives of individual conversion requires an appreciation of kinship and religious networks, as there were practical linkages between changes in the political economy and cultural styles. I have explained how young men and women sought to pry themselves loose from household constraints, and how individualism caused social fissures in communities and families. This picture demands a slight recalibration, as there was a constant dialectic of centripetal and centrifugal forces that shaped individual interests and strategies. Just as migrants sought to make money for themselves, they invested in social and kin networks through various remittances and gifts. Their rupture with their homelands was not permanent. They often sent money orders and, via literate scribes working at the colonial post offices, letters to their families, and they usually returned for long visits to attend ceremonies and to marry. Their goal was not to cut all ties with their homelands but to carve out greater autonomy, while making investments in their futures.[12]

Migrants based their decisions on the experiences of their predecessors; they followed well-worn paths and tapped into social networks to lower the costs and risks of migration. Along these lines, I have noted that deep historical webs of interconnection had preexisted colonialism. Many of these networks were in the hands of Muslim traders. However, pathways were constantly mutating as arteries of penetration and exploitation were being appropriated and turned to other purposes. State institutions were central to this process. As we have seen, the administration, despite its ambivalence toward African mobility, tried to engineer the movement of labor and capital. In a parasitic manner, it grafted a colonial layer onto the preexisting commercial infrastructure, deepening and expanding networks, while seeking to "canalize" workers from the hinterland to productive zones closer to the coast. Even as there was considerable overlap and reinforcement of networks, there was also the forging of new nodes and pathways.[13]

No individual operated outside of webs of affiliation or information movement. Some information and rumor networks were more amorphous and fleeting than others. For migrants who tapped into opportunities arising through rumor, the costs were much higher, as the information was far from reliable. In Buguni, such rumor networks were most notably linked to the gold trade, which prompted an exodus to the mines of Kekoro and Kalana after the war. As Namakoro Bamba recalled, "[After the war], I left and went to the gold mines of Kékoro. Men and women alike went there. I spent three months and came back. Everyone then learned that I had found gold, and I gained renown. The day I came back, the entire village emptied as people left for the mines after hearing about my gold. Everyone left. It was not easy to find people to put the roof on your hut."[14] Namakoro may have had an exaggerated sense of his role in spurring people to migrate to the gold mines, but census tour reports from Kékoro corroborate that a gold rush was motivating thousands of people to migrate, even as most people came up empty-handed.[15]

Migrants often tapped into kinship networks. The testimonies of former migrant workers are replete with references to family connections and assistance. I choose to highlight the itinerary of one man, Tenaiko Bamba, whose testimony adds complexity to the picture of postwar migration with its emphasis on Guinea rather than Ivory Coast. His story captures the role of family networks and the ways in which migrant strategies were socially embedded. Before migrating to Guinea, Tenaiko had tried his hand at gold mining in southern Wasulu and performed colonial military service. Then, in the 1950s, he set out for Kankan, where he had an uncle:

> We traveled on foot to Guinea. It took about five days to reach
> Kankan. But this was less than thirty days to Senegal to grow
> peanuts. When I left here, I walked straight across, and on the
> fourth day I slept at Kòba. The next day I crossed the river to
> arrive in Jangana. The wife of N'Tinemankòrò was Sumba. I met
> this elder woman in this village. She was very intelligent. She
> came out of her room and asked, "Where are you from?" I said I
> was from Kolondieba. She quickly said the name of my father and
> asked if I was from N'tinekala. I said yes, and she recognized my
> lineage. She was from N'tinekala also. After drinking something,
> she prepared rice for me and put a lot of fish in it. Jangana is not
> far from Kankan. Everything is connected by small villages. After
> eating the rice, I took my sack and I walked the long road that
> leads to Kankan. I arrived near the police station and saw a friend
> that I knew. He led me to his home, not far from the market of
> Kankan. That was how I first arrived in Kankan. I worked on the
> construction of a bridge and earned a lot of money.[16]

As we shall see, Kankan, the home of Shaykh Muhammad Sharif Fanta-Mady, was an important spiritual hub in regional Sufi networks. While much emphasis has been placed on the movement of marabouts out of Kankan, there were also mobile workers sojourning in Kankan, people who served to keep the links active, transmitting information and deepening connections. Perhaps more important than family ties, however, Islamic and ethnic networks expanded where kinship could not, reinforcing supranational bases of religious identification and creating openings for anyone belonging to the umma, or Muslim community.[17]

Young men who migrated to a particular locality for the first time or who had no apparent kinship ties to draw upon forged their own networks, which could later be used by kin. Oral accounts reveal that more nebulous webs of religious affiliation were crucial in this capacity. In particular, Muslim networks assisted migrants in finding employment and lodging. In this vein, many informants told of being aided through membership in the Muslim community. One of these informants, Yusuf Coulibaly, told of how on his first time to Ivory Coast he arrived in Bouaké after a long voyage on foot. The group of young men with whom he was traveling had run out of food and had no money, so they went to the local mosque to pray and make contacts. At the mosque, they found lodging with a Muslim holy man who was a friend of Yusuf's former Qur'anic teacher. Yusuf recalled the meeting as follows:

> We crossed a small watercourse heading west. There was a mori there, so we went to see him. Oh, Allah! He had pity! He was very instructed, and he had done the hajj and had come to settle in Bouaké. . . . When the mori greeted us, I said, "Salam," and that surprised him. He asked about us and we said that we were going to Ivory Coast. We said that we wanted to pass the night and continue the next day. He said there was no problem. . . . He then asked where I had studied. I responded that I studied with Lajji-Ba in Makanjana. The marabout stayed calm for a while. Then, he went to take two yams and gave them to his wife and said to cut them and put them on the fire for our conversation before sleeping. He had studied with the same mori as my master for three years.[18]

Yusuf and his friend stayed two weeks with the mori and then were sent to the trade town of Odienne, where their patron had another client. The two young men found work in the kola trade, and as the rainy season approached they stayed on to farm for their host. In subsequent migrations they would use the same networks, which expanded over time.

After such contacts had been made and networks established, families sent their sons to Ivory Coast in age sequence. Each son spent a few years working before giving way to the next in line. When possible, families would return to the same place, acquiring land for growing cocoa, coffee, or peanuts. Some peasants migrated to regions where they had family ties via slavery or trade. In the Danyoko family of Tenemakana, Tumani had been a slave and porter in Bouaké. Later, his son, Zumana Danyoko, spent dry seasons hunting in Ivory Coast. After the war, Zumana found land to grow cocoa, and by the 1950s he sent his nephew, Burama, to grow cocoa each year. All three of his nephews would do the same thing, the youngest working on the cocoa farm in the 1960s.[19] Commenting on this pattern among migrants, one colonial official in Ivory Coast wrote, "Foreigners immigrate each year into the district, either to engage in commerce or above all to create plantations [of cocoa]. . . . Once they have settled, their family members come and they found settlements, sometimes permanently; those who return to their districts of origin are generally replaced by fellow compatriots."[20] Scholars have referred to such migration processes mediated through kinship and friendship ties as "chain migration" or, more recently, "network-mediated migration." As the evidence suggests, migrant networks were constituted by interpersonal ties through kinship, friendship, and shared community of origin.[21]

"A QUESTION OF STYLE": MIGRANTS AND MATERIAL CULTURE

In 1953 a colonial report described Islam in the region as "a question of style" imported into the region "by the young men from the countries they visit as workers or as soldiers." There was no single style but instead polyvalent expressions of a more cosmopolitan way of being Muslim. Imported clothes served as stylistic markers of difference, which often corresponded to religious distinctions. The local lexicons in which distinctions were classified did not reflect strictly traditional versus Western cultural frameworks. In that much of the labor circulation was rural–rural and despite the fact that the French language was becoming an important lingua franca, the influence of Western civilization, as such, was more limited than in other parts of colonial Africa.[22] As a result, the ways in which local communities embraced new forms of material culture differed considerably in hinterland regions and in the coastal areas. In rural French Sudan the consumption of clothes, bicycles, hats, sunglasses, and so on was carried on in piecemeal fashion, the consumers often having no coherent Western cultural frames of reference in mind. And in the cultural imagination, Mecca was far more important than Paris. In short, given the lack of a consistent flow of such new things and other, parallel vectors of cultural transmission and consumption, such as radios, movies, music, and so on, the meanings tied to particular objects were fundamentally polysemous. The consumption of such objects was about adapting new and useful objects to familiar cultural settings and local classificatory lexicons.[23] The names given to new objects and tools were often neologisms based in indigenous languages. A bicycle was an iron horse (*négéso*), not a linguistic adaptation of *vélo*, and a plow was a cattle hoe (*misidaba*) rather than a *charrue*. The names of certain objects were linguistic derivations from French or Arabic, which also provided much religious vocabulary.[24]

Although there were many changes in material culture, the most commonly cited commodities purchased and brought back by migrant workers were clothes. In connection with the discussion of Islamization, I am not suggesting that religious practice was only clothing-deep. Wearing a *boubou* (a sort of long shirt) did not amount to conversion. But wearing certain clothes constituted a signifying practice. Depending on the context, clothes served as expressions of religious belonging. At the popular level, as more and more young people switched styles they internalized new sets of dispositions, practices, and performative competences. Corporeal techniques and bodily comportment were important dimensions of cultural style. The construction of the Muslim self had important external components, components which might be followed by a gradual internalization of beliefs and practices associated with Islamic material culture.

After the war, rural areas saw changes in styles of dress, as men and women began wearing imported cloth and clothing. Most informants told of buying boubous with their money. This meant that increasingly young men were dressing as Muslims even if they knew only the rudiments of prayer. Boubous were not new, having been part of elite dress and the cultural landscape for centuries. During most of the colonial period, young men dressed in loincloths or hand-woven bamana clothing. In fact, informants recalled wearing loincloths on migration and becoming "aware of their nudity" only when they arrived in trade towns.[25] In time, the wider diffusion of new clothing styles generated rivalries and competition and even drove young men to migrate. For example, one informant said, "When I was young, I had a friend named Mamadu. He went to the gold mines of Sirikila in Wasulu, and he came back with many clothes. The young men had rivalry and competed with each other over clothing. When the young men came back, they would mock all of us who did not migrate."[26]

Like other commodities, clothes had trajectories of meanings, and as the social field changed, the status tied to particular objects also changed. Once boubous became widely worn, even by bamana traditionalists, they no longer connoted being Muslim. In the same way that having a Muslim name was an expression of religious nominalism, wearing a boubou instead of a loincloth eventually lost its cachet. In addition to the ubiquitous influx of boubous and the growing number of young men taking on the external appearance of Muslims, some men developed a taste for Western clothing and shoes, partly to separate themselves from the emerging boubou-clad masses. Previously, there was a form of Western clothing that all the chiefs and new colonial elites wore that people called *falitulu*. Often the administration gave these clothes to colonial intermediaries as part of their salary. Falitulu clothing became a marker of their authority and prestige in that nobody else was allowed to wear it. As more young people began migrating and wearing Western clothing, however, the distinctions became difficult for chiefs and functionaries to maintain.[27]

Rural people were not passive consumers of cosmopolitan styles and imported cloth. They selectively chose patterns and created their own styles by mixing various materials together, and at a certain point new forms of material culture were being produced within villages and market towns. Tailors set up shop and figured out new ways of assembling traditional cotton garments. Pants made of traditional cotton bands, called *kulusi mugumba*, were stitched together. There were also longer garments to replace the loincloths, called *kòba*. One effect of these changes in styles of dress and the importation of cloth was the decline of locally produced cloth. Informants explained that with the arrival of imported cloth, the production of handicraft cotton cloth diminished. Sekou Diakite tied this change directly to migration: "When the men began to migrate, they found other cloth instead of the local cotton cloth. The men began to introduce many different styles of clothing in our region; they knew more variations of clothing than the women. . . . Many women stopped spinning cotton before independence; it was a few years before independence that all that stopped."[28]

There were symbolic implications to the wearing of imported clothing, even as it displayed exciting new patterns. Although not unchanging, locally produced clothing had incorporated patterns and motifs that corresponded to religious beliefs and myths. For example, the kapok tree was considered the sacred protective tree in most villages. As

the "ladder to the heavens," it was a link to the ancestors and other divini-
ties. Its representation and design were also used to symbolize the sacred
python in its movement of "expanding life." The zigzagging designs in
alternating squares in black, white, and red were inscribed on various
household objects and dwellings. This central motif representing fertility was also woven into women's clothing. Usually, after marriage, the
mother-in-law gave two skirt-wraps, or *pagnes*, to the bride. The pagnes
were white, with black lines and square designs, representing the branches
of the kapok tree, the mythic union of ancestral twins, and the sacred
python. This would ensure the fertility of the young woman being incorporated into the household.[29] The graphic representation of women's
reproductive powers and its cosmological importance were part of the local
religious landscape. Women commonly wore such cloth everyday without
necessarily being fully cognizant of the meanings. Yet it constituted one
strand of local cultural continuity in public visual culture that connected
the lives of villagers to divine forces. Eventually, women began opting for
imported cloth. And the webs of signification that people had, literally,
spun around them changed as coastal styles invaded the hinterland.

As we have seen, Tenaiko Bamba was working in Guinea in the
1950s, and eventually he got involved in the clothing trade with his uncle,
traveling to Conakry to buy cloth and then selling it in Kankan and in
the district of Buguni. He recalled how, at that time, there were specific
scarves, such as *jikòmajala*, worn by the women and different pagnes that
were growing in popularity and changed every year with the import of
new fabrics.[30] Elder women also recalled the styles of clothes they wore in
the 1950s. They talked about the skirts, scarves, and sashes they donned
to complement their pagnes. Salimata Diallo explained that women previously had worn one piece of traditional cloth woven from cotton strips that
they used to cover their bodies and to carry their babies. After the war, they
began wearing two pieces. In short, changes in women's style of dress
were certainly more loaded with cultural significance than simple seasonal fashion trends. Transformations in the religious habitus had important material dimensions, particularly as changes in bodily comportment
complemented the wearing of new clothes. The performative competence
of new cultural styles included a basic mastery over a whole ensemble
of new objects and minor props, including hats, sunglasses, umbrellas,
mirrors, watches, and so forth.[31]

Peasants adapted to more fundamental changes in material culture as households acquired new cooking utensils, condiments, and tools. In terms of housing, although most rural people continued to live in mud and thatched-roof huts, some veterans, functionaries, and traders had begun building *cases modernes* with cement walls and corrugated roofing.[32] Some forms of material culture stood alone in their transformative impact, and bicycles were one of them. During the interwar period bicycles had begun to spread, but cheap bicycles imported from Japan quickly earned the reputation of breaking down on the rugged dirt roads. Consumers stopped buying them. After the war, a wave of better-quality bicycles, primarily French and English, arrived. And by the early 1950s the demand was so great that the colonial Société de Prévoyance got involved, selling bicycles on credit. Peasants used them for personal transportation but also for carrying loads of wood, cloth, crops, and other goods long distances. Owing to the lack of tools for repairs and the frequency of flat tires, people often filled the tubes with straw.[33]

According to oral accounts, migrants were often the first in their villages to own bicycles. One elder in Wasulu explained: "The people would migrate together to work, and then we bought bicycles before coming back to our village. That was how the first bicycles were introduced here. With the arrival of the bicycle, the young people began to travel faster and further away from their village. That was how they began to learn about new things. The people really evolved because of the new ideas."[34] Although similar processes were underway on a much wider scale, few reliable statistics exist on the proliferation of bicycles. In the canton of Fulala, according to one census report, there were twenty-one bicycles in 1952, or roughly one bicycle per village. There were two bicycles in the village of Tenemakana.[35] Salimata Diallo recalled the first bicycle: "It was the first time we saw a bicycle [négéso] in the village. . . . The price of the bicycle was around the cost of a bull. The bicycle became an object of great curiosity."[36] In nearby Kolondieba, when Sekou Koné returned from migration with a bicycle there was much excitement. His wife recalled that "there were no bicycles at this time, so when this first bicycle arrived, crowds of people came to gather around it. The people were afraid to touch this négéso. They thought it would hurt them." Migrants were not the only ones who bought bicycles. Many people working for the colonial administration, including chiefs, soldiers, interpreters, and village representatives, also acquired bicycles, which made their work easier. One such man was Sidiki Diallo, who was the representative of the canton chief of Fulala in Buguni. His son recalled that his father was the first man to have a bicycle in the village of N'Golobala: "It was around the years of 1946, when he brought his bicycle back, and that was when the first bicycles came to this region. Bicycles started to appear little by little after 1946. Before, it took several days walking to arrive at Buguni. But with the bicycle they could go in the same day." The new individual transport technology allowed young men to travel more extensively than before. They could visit neighboring villages easily, ride to regional markets, and get news. They were often the first to know about new things and served to connect their villages to the outside world. The circulation of migrant workers played an important role in bringing new cultural styles, religious ideas, and practices to their villages.[37]

MIGRATION AND CONVERSION

In the village of Tienaga, Zumana Koné said, "When the people started to migrate, everyone began to pray, one after another." In this simple but representative statement the elder drew attention to an important linkage between labor migration and prayer.[38] The cultural contexts in which migrants learned to pray or began self-identifying as Muslim are of central importance. There was a strong correlation between high rates of return migration and the expansion of Islam in sending regions. Because of the sheer volume of migrant workers, widespread circular migration created a virtual transmission belt for cultural change. The psychological accounts of conversion, however, are not my interest here, as such narratives tend to ignore the mundane details of practice and social relations that structured conversion in the first place. I resist elevating the individual experience of conversion above underlying social processes.

An observation made by Marcel Cardaire explained that a key vector in the "Islamization of the countryside" was the "young detribalized black, poorly initiated into his cult," who had "left his village to work abroad." In drawing attention to the social bases of conversion, Cardaire emphasized the religious dimensions of migrants as they sojourned far from their homes. Of the "detribalized" young worker, he wrote, "He has endured a diversity of religions that he has encountered; he has endured the feelings of isolation. . . . He finds at each resting place a new cult from which he is excluded. It is therefore the unity of Islam that strikes him. Without any social, tribal, or geographic distinction, the believers pray at the same time, with the same words and the same gestures. . . . At each resting place, he is received not by the participants of the religion of the local terroir, a closed and secret milieu, but by the Muslim lodger, in a house where one is always welcome as long as one's name is Mamadu, Usman, or Umar. The communal strength of the Muslim milieu surprises and conquers him."[39] Although Cardaire oversimplified things, he drew attention to the crucial experiences of exile in the fashioning of religious identities. Indeed, leaving the local religious spheres of their homelands and being unable to gain admission into the religious associations of their hosts, many migrants were drawn to Islam for its universality. They began praying out of a sense of religious belonging and solidarity with fellow migrants. Oral testimonies also referred to these social contexts of conversion. Musa Diallo, a man who spent much of his adult life as a migrant worker, said, "When you went on migration, you were forced to enter into the host's customs, like religion. If at that time you did not pray, and you found yourself among people who prayed, you were forced to change and start praying. Otherwise, they would not even consider you for work." First, taking on a Muslim appearance meant adopting a Muslim name. If a young migrant worker, introducing himself to a potential employer or host, gave them a bamana name Muslims would often say, "You are not like us, we are not in the same religion," and the young worker would be turned away. Taking a common Muslim name such as Muhammad, Ibrahim, or Musa was the first test that workers had to pass. But name changing did not guarantee either employment or lodging, as further tests would quickly follow. Muslim employers and hosts would scrutinize young workers' knowledge of the basic protocols of Muslim prayer.[40] The following scenario, though presented in generic terms, was very common:

> You would arrive in a Muslim village to find work or a place to
> sleep. The woman would give you something to eat. But they
> would give you food separately at first. It was just to see if you
> were not Muslim. At the time of prayer, they would send you the
> water can for washing. The head of the family would sit near you
> and watch. There were rules. . . . So now, the head of the family
> would watch you to see how you were going to begin, how you

would end. He would watch you to see what you would do on the prayer mat. So if he saw that all that you did was normal, you passed the test. But if you did not pass the test, if you made a mistake, you failed. Sometimes they would not chase you away, but you would eat like a little dog, alone with your own bowl; you would never eat with them. Often they would not give you work.[41]

Many young men already knew how to pray. But neophytes learned to present at least the external manifestations of being Muslim. They took Muslim names, learned the rudimentary protocols of prayer, refrained from drinking alcohol, and peppered their language with Muslim expressions and benedictions. Still, in certain contexts Muslim prayer was a liability, and such religious identification could be a disadvantage. Therefore, migrant workers became adept at ascertaining the religious designations of villages before asking for employment, while learning to adapt themselves to the requirements of the setting. Muslim practices and cultural styles became part of a toolkit of migration survival skills that could be deployed or concealed depending on the context. Migrant workers effectively acquired two sets of religious dispositions and practices: a sort of Muslim habitus and bamana habitus.[42]

Once migrants had accepted the faith, they sought out other Muslims and even formed Muslim communities in exile. Some migrant workers, especially the sons of slave converts, had already been exposed to Islam. For them, migration served to deepen Muslim practices, as communal prayer became the basis of shared religious belonging. To be modern and accepted among one's peers required praying at the mosque together. At first, migrants created informal prayer groups, even in the absence of mosques. But with or without mosques, Muslim communities were composed of people from the broader region, suggesting the emergence of transnational forms of religious identification. Burama Dembele said, "We would group together in any place to pray when there was no mosque. In certain places, we would group together, all the Muslim inhabitants of the village. There was a man from Burkina Faso, a Mossi, who was leading us in prayer. Then, there was someone from Segu who led us in prayer. I would often go to pray with the people from Segu, when they were reciting the Qur'an."[43]

For migrant workers, converting to Islam was about trying on a new cultural style, a sort of temporary foray to be abandoned once back at home. After repeated travels, this conversion gained depth. Muslim cultural style became a new religious orientation. Indeed, colonial officials reported on what they considered a "deepening process" of Islamization, as young people moved beyond style to a "vague obedience to the new rules, prayer, and fasting."[44] For many, aside from the economic incentives, young men embraced Islam for what they deemed its moral correctness, ritual purity, aesthetic attractiveness, and superior power. As this deepening process continued, officials became increasingly aware of what they termed social Islam. In the neighboring district of Sikasso, one official stated, "[Islam] continues its penetration in the district, where it is carried by local traders and young people returning from Ivory Coast. . . . It is at base fundamentally social . . . in most cases, its acceptance represents for the newly converted only a certain number of conventional signs, the attachment to a certain social category, and, above all, the certainty that upon death the deceased is buried by his friends."[45]

Outside of the cantons of Fulala, Basidibé, and Céndugu, census tours recorded a steady expansion of Islam in the postwar era. Even on a wider level, across the French Sudan, similar processes were reported in other districts, such as Sikasso, Segu, Bamako, and Bandiagara. In Buguni, while on canton-level census tours officials observed the importance of labor circulation among migrant workers as well as other mobile social groups, such as colonial soldiers and rural holy men. For example, in the canton of Kola, one representative report stated, "The introduction of Islam has been according to the habitual processes of departure and return [of migrant workers]." In the Senufo canton of Niené, where Islam was spreading after the war, the main agents were migrant workers and soldiers.[46] Sirakoro Traoré explained these processes in Niené: "Many people went on migration and came back to the village converted to Islam, and they did not abandon Islam when they returned. They were very numerous. . . . It was these people who provoked conversions to Islam in the village. . . . These young men were obliged to pray. Otherwise they would not be able to get along with the Muslim population, who gave them employment."[47] Elsewhere, in the large central canton of Cémala the census showed that the rapid acceleration of religious change corresponded with high rates of migration. Similarly, in the canton of Siondugu, the influence of Islam was described as growing "under the pressure of young men" returning from Ivory Coast.[48]

Conversely, in cantons where migration was not an important factor, Muslims were far less numerous. In Kekoro, the number of migrant workers was minuscule, and, correspondingly, the canton was "in the vast majority fetishist." In Bambélédugu, migration was insignificant, and there was an overwhelming fetishist majority. The canton of Domba experienced very little migration, and most of the people were practitioners of bamanaya. Even colonial soldiers, who had missed initiation rituals and incorporation into such associations during their absence, were initiated upon demobilization. A report noted, "The soldiers themselves, who have not had the time to be initiated before their recruitment, are required to go through initiation on their return."[49]

The particular way in which a canton was incorporated into the regional economy also determined the course of its religious history. The canton of Dialakadugu was not isolated but "did not migrate" and was not Muslim. It sat astride a major trade artery, the intercolonial road connecting Bamako to Ivory Coast, with two important roadside market towns, Solo and Sido. Even though the canton was exposed to external influences, people's economic lives were lived out in their home villages, punctuated by periodic market days. Farmers produced enough for subsistence and often sold their surplus at the market without needing to migrate.[50] Although the canton was more incorporated into the wider economy, exposure to new ideas and trends was limited; people were never forced to assimilate for months or years at a time as migrant workers. As a result, despite the proximity of large markets, people did not convert to Islam. Villagers might throw on a boubou and utter *insh'allah* while visiting the market, but, short of in-depth cultural immersion or compelling reasons to convert, nonsending regions were the last to witness widespread Islamization. In those regions accustomed to migration, what sort of impact did migrants' new markers of Muslim identity have on their home villages? Upon their return, how and why did conversion proceed and according to what social and political factors?

TOWARD A TIPPING POINT? RELIGIOUS CONFORMITY AND PUBLIC PRESSURES

As most daily happenings in social life reproduced structures, subtle religious changes were often imperceptible to historical actors. This does not preclude the possibility of transformative events and conjunctural tipping points when communities rather suddenly became more aware of stark religious differences. The building of mosques and the appearance of public prayer signaled shifts in the religious habitus. Such historical events generated religious conflict (see chapter 7), but here I want to focus on the ways in which Islamization processes were quietly gaining momentum as migrant workers returned from abroad. In other words, before the public breakthrough there was an inchoate buildup behind the lines, as young men began praying together and pressuring family members to convert. This did not occur uniformly. Rates of Islamization differed from village to village, and many communities would remain bamana well into the postcolonial era. Nevertheless, given the transregional political and economic structures under colonial rule, common social processes were fundamentally reshaping village life.

We have seen how the first generation of Muslims hid their religious practices. And we have also seen how young people were losing faith and moral confidence in traditional religious authorities and village elders. Thus, in contrast to cases in which migrants went back to localist ways, the case of Buguni suggests that labor migration generated more enduring cultural changes in home villages. In this process, as religious fissures in communities and households formed, and the younger generation expressed new modalities of religious belonging, elders and lineage heads were increasingly marginalized. In 1956, one official reported, "Each new census leads one to register the ceaseless regression of animism. It is hardly more than an 'affair of the elders' and even if certain fetishes continue to be respected, one is obliged to declare oneself a Muslim."[51]

In such circumstances, there was a kind of inversion of tradition as people began disavowing the old ways. What was once valorized and respected now became the subject of ridicule and embarrassment. In recounting local religious history, Namakoro Bamba told how bamanaya became something shameful, as people gradually abandoned power objects and societies. He suggested a kind of threshold when the community tipped in the direction of a Muslim majority: "As for us here, we abandoned jòw due to shame. . . . We abandoned voluntarily our jòw, and left them in their huts along the pathways. Then these huts finally just collapsed on the jòw. . . . When the world tips in a certain direction, if you refuse to go to this side, the people will have no regard for you." As Muslims became more dominant, minority holdouts were tacitly coerced into abandoning their practices. Their views and rituals lost their influence over the community. As bamanaya connoted backwardness, remaining traditionalists were forced to take up their religious lives in the secrecy of nearby forests. In short, a powerful conformist bias had set in. People either embraced Islam or risked losing their place in society.[52]

Migrant workers were converting to Islam in an era when Muslims were emerging into public with their faith. Although he presented it as a somewhat inevitable and irreversible process, Cardaire nonetheless pointed to the ways in which change was being generated from below: "One has often noticed that such a worker returning to his little village does not dare to pray as long as he is the only 'believer.' . . . When two or three young people return from their temporary migration as converts, they unite with the others and all together they perform prayer on Friday. Once they have a dozen, they look to build a mosque."[53] Whereas former slaves and other early Muslims were forced to hide their practices, migrant workers were eventually able to show their new religious identities publicly. As the ranks swelled, social pressures mounted. In the canton of Céndugu, Musa Diallo explained, "When the migrant workers came back to their villages, they added themselves, and the village became Muslim. . . . Then you found that the village was divided in two parts. . . . [Then] there were ten people who came back and would try to convince the others in the village: 'You must recognize that there is Allah who created us; you must recognize that Allah is all-powerful.' After one or two years, there were thirty people, and then three or four years later, almost the whole village was praying." As momentum built and Muslims became dominant, they marginalized those who had not converted. This could mean exclusion from sharing meals or working with others in the household, as one elder recalled: "If you were not Muslim, you were looked down upon by society. If you did not pray, Muslims would say they could not put their hand in the same bowl with you. If you did not pray, they would not work with you in the village in different activities. There were many changes in favor of Muslims at this time." Even in such core bamana institutions as the youth farming association (tòn), once a Muslim majority had been reached the rest of the young people converted out of peer pressure.[54]

Although women have been rather invisible in village religious histories of Islam, informants indicated that as young women migrated and married Muslim men, they too began to convert. In addition, women living in trade towns found themselves learning prayer and joining Muslim communities in the marketplace. Some women suggested even that they deliberately converted because of their exclusion from the male-dominated power associations, which had also been used to reinforce patriarchy. For those who stayed at home in rural areas, the daughters of early Muslims were exchanged with the families of fellow Muslims and married into Muslim households. Although often uneducated, they exposed their children to the basic rules of the faith.[55]

As I have suggested, Islam provided an alternative moral framework through which young men critiqued their elders. In justifying their break with tradition, Islam provided the perfect wedge. In 1953 one colonial official reported, "When the young people come back, at the end of several years sometimes, their mentality is clearly modified. They have been in large part Islamized, superficially without doubt. It accentuates the rupture with the familial milieu."[56] Young men used religious difference to assert greater independence vis-à-vis their fathers. It gave them the confidence to challenge the authority and demands of elders on religious grounds. In Islam, young people found a place for the individual in communities controlled less by kinship ties and traditional obligations. These cultural changes tended to accentuate the emerging fissures within households. At a time when forced labor was ending and young men and women were enjoying more freedom, they found compelling and attractive arguments in Muslim messages of equality, social justice, solidarity, ritual purity, and moral correctness.[57]

Still, during the fraught transition, there was a period when village communities were divided religiously. These divisions led even to religious violence, as Namakoro Bamba recalled: "In certain places, Muslims attacked the bamana, and burned their jòw or threw them in the water right in front of their owners."[58] In most communities, given the history of overlapping and complementary religious practices, the shift was peaceful. The French ethnographers Viviana Pâques and Gérard Brasseur observed in the 1950s that rural villages in Buguni were characterized by considerable religious hybridity, as kòmò power associations and jò initiation societies and rituals, complete with their mask dances and music, often coexisted alongside Muslim prayer and community celebrations for Ramadan, Tabaski, and so forth.[59] This coexistence, however, did not necessarily mean things were harmonious or socially uncomplicated.

In situations of religious parity there was much social duress, as some people were effectively torn between subcommunities even as people belonged to both commingling groups. Each Muslim and bamana subcommunity had its ceremonies, rituals, and ideas of what constituted moral and social transgression. Furthermore, each community placed obligations on its members.[60] Adama Diallo said that in the village of Niamala, "Whether you were an infidel or a Muslim, you would be forced to go [to ceremonies] because of the fraternity. In the same way, if something came up with your Muslim brother, you would need to go because of Islam. So there were these different obligations that existed between people, making it difficult." One of the main reasons people, especially elders, eventually bent to the religious pressures was that they wanted people to attend their funeral. Diallo continued: "Many people converted then because, if someone remained an infidel, when he died few people would attend his burial. For the person who did not pray, few people would go to the ceremony."[61]

Aside from occasional ceremonies and life crisis rituals, public expressions of piety in the form of daily prayer became more common. Prayer continued to focus on the chanting of the kalima or shahada and of certain suras of the Qur'an, such as the Fatiha. In Fulala, Muslims would gather to pray and chant, as one elder recalled: "We would pass the night chanting the kalima together. The religion was not well planted yet. Education was just beginning. . . . When we heard [that people were] chanting the kalima in Tenemakana, then we would say, 'Eh! Someone is chanting the kalima, we will all go down there.' "[62] People did not usually understand the meanings of their prayer and chanting, and even Muslims who had some Qur'anic training learned to recite passages without understanding much of the Arabic grammar and vocabulary.

Qur'anic chanting served as an almost ritual musical experience characterized by mysterious incantations. In much the same way that song and dance were part of Mande religious practices, communal Qur'anic chanting brought people together and served as a vehicle for spiritual engagement with the invisible world. And certainly the music cultures and forms of expressive culture of southern Mali, especially Wasulu, were constantly innovating and drawing on new sources, whether Islamic or French.[63] In any case, Muslim holy men might explain the basic rules, rituals, and beliefs of Islam, but the first and second generations of

Muslims engaged in rather heterodox practices. In that individuals had no recourse to the Qur'an and few knowledgeable Qur'anic interpreters were present in most villages, there was a flexible definition of what it meant to be Muslim.[64] Furthermore, just as Mande religious practices had been fundamentally mutable in the absence of orthodoxies and fixed proscriptions tied to textual referents, so what passed as Muslim was in fact a set of eclectic practices that later reformists would deem pagan.

MAKING MUSLIMS: CONVERSION AND THE COLONIAL CENSUS

Normative local histories of Islam typically focus on the hagiography of local saints and religious events, such as the construction of mosques, the designation of village imams, the beginnings of public prayer, the conversion of the village or canton chief, and the abandonment of the kòmò. In local understandings, such symbolic actions have been interpreted as evidence of religious breakthroughs or the arrival of Islam. They were seemingly unambiguous moments when villagers knew that Islam had become the religion of the majority. However, an important, but often neglected, public event was the declaration of religious identity during the colonial census.[65]

The census sharpened the boundaries between religious categories and made people more conscious of where they were positioned in local social fields. Following Ian Hacking and his conceptualization of "dynamic nominalism," one might suggest that certain de facto religious categories came into being or were reinforced with their naming. In other words, once the census categories had been deployed, people officially sorted themselves out and, accordingly, even took on new ways of being. People based their identity assertions not only on who they were and what they had done, but also on who they might become, thus opening the door to future possibilities of personhood. In the colonial census, there was a kind of looping effect as social change produced categories, and the categories themselves subtly generated social change.[66]

Long before the use of nominative declarations, colonial governmentality had been built on indigenous forms of knowledge. Colonial discourses on religious differences were shaped by the local gaze of Muslim intermediaries, who inflected bureaucratic encounters with their own interests and values.[67] In the early colonial period, when most communities were still largely illegible to the colonial state, the administration relied heavily on the views of Muslim informants in assessing and assigning populations to religious categories. Muslim interpreters commonly made cursory observations and identity assignments of villages they visited, summing them as fetishists, with few qualifications.[68] Later, during the middle and late colonial periods, as census tours became more extensive and intensive, rural peoples began speaking for themselves in matters of religious identification. However, in this transformation of the census apparatus, which included a shift from identity assignment to identity assertion, rural people had only two categories to choose between. There was no intermediate category between Muslim and fetishist representing mixed or overlapping practices and social locations.[69]

Beyond the census takers and their categories, however, the social contexts in which the census was conducted influenced how people responded to questions related to religious identity. The census meant one thing to colonial officials and quite another to rural peoples. While it is true that the social categories of the census reflected certain epistemic habits and discursive formations created by and for the state, religious identities were not simply assigned to populations; they were also strategically asserted or deployed to various ends by people themselves. The census could be used as a preemptive way of securing a more accommodating or historically safer identity within changing political and social contexts. Typically, this meant declaring oneself to be a Muslim as opposed to a Fetishist (or Animist), the two categories available in the census. This assertion of religious identity at census time was frequently noted by colonial officials and also recalled by informants.

Commenting on the census, Cardaire hinted at its social role and the meaning of public declarations: "To have [census] figures approach reality, it would be necessary to microscopically study each small human grouping. . . . The response to a question such as: 'Are you Muslim?' corresponds to an infinite number of truths. The response will vary with the context, the social setting, and the standing of the individual interrogated. We admit that every affirmative response to this question reveals the position taking [*prise de position*], that is, itself, interesting. . . . Thus, the census figures appear to us, in the end, to be very meaningful."[70] In line with theorizations of Pierre Bourdieu on "position-taking," Cardaire drew attention to how the census provided the opportunity for people, as "social agents," to make choices and identify themselves relationally.[71] Certainly, there was a lot of feigning. But this is precisely the point. People were not asked questions on their religious identity in private, but in front of their fellow villagers. The crowd of people gathered at census time, when public declarations of faith were made, gave villagers a chance to glimpse the religious relations of force and the more objectified religious shifts in the village. Furthermore, the census brought about the emergence of religion as a discrete field of human activity. In Bamanankan, the word for religion, or *alasira*, literally meant the "path of Allah," so when people were asked if they were Muslim they were being asked whether or not they had a religion.[72]

While religious practices were rather eclectic, the census forced people to choose between two distinct categories. And such a stark decision was heightened by the census experience itself, which could be quite inquisitorial in nature. Lamine Diakité, a former colonial interpreter in Buguni in the postwar era, shared his recollections of how the census was conducted: "The census group would be sent to the village, to Solona, for example, and the population of the village was asked to meet in the courtyard of the village chief, or under the large tree, or wherever the village chief indicated. We called the heads of the families, one by one, who would come forward with their families standing behind them. Then, we would ask them the questions. Everything was recorded. . . . We took figures on their religion. All that went into the large book."[73] On the other side of the experience, peasants remembered the fear associated with the census. As an exercise of state power, it provoked anxiety among the people being assessed. Sekou Koné said, "Everyone was always traumatized by the fear of being beaten, tortured or imprisoned. During the census, when they asked you to give the name of your wife, you would forget her name because of the fear."[74] The census forced villagers to make public declarations of faith in situations of duress.

The social contexts in which the census was conducted influenced how people responded to questions related to religious identity. Often, the crowd itself played an important role in determining the outcome. As one official observed in the canton of Zana, "The designation 'Muslim' is more often than not a simple formality that they give on the occasion of the census to avoid the mockery and jeers of the audience. But when a notable fetishist declares himself Muslim, the reactions of the audience are just as significant."[75] Similarly, a census official in Gwancédugu noted that to avoid embarrassment people no longer "declared being a fetishist in front of the entire village."[76] As villagers saw how many people in the community were declaring themselves to be Muslims, they became ashamed to proclaim their bamana identities. Lamine Diakite, the former colonial interpreter, recalled that "they became aware of how much had changed, and they were ashamed that they did not pray. They were not Muslims, and the people knew. When they said they were Muslims, the young people would laugh at their fathers."[77] As a result, those who still practiced traditional religions, even elders, began identifying themselves publicly as Muslims, while concealing their bamana practices. In the district of Sikasso, officials reported on this bifurcated public–private religious quality. One official wrote, "It would be best to employ the term 'Islamized' instead of 'Muslim.' In effect, even though people 'do salam' and manifest publicly the current religious practices, few have actually broken completely with their ancestral beliefs and have maintained, just in case, their fetish in the corner of their home."[78]

In the end, the aversion to public criticism might have represented a general motivation on the behalf of rural peoples to declare what they thought was the safest identity vis-à-vis outsiders and the state. Most peasants did not have access to the synoptic views of the state and did not know how their answers would be used. And while the census was a rather infrequent event in everyday life and probably did not in itself produce on-the-spot conversions, it had the effect of making people more conscious of the religious changes occurring in their villages. Most communities had gradually drifted in the direction to Islam over many years. But now people were confronted with a stark choice at a time of rapid social and political change. The stakes were raised even further as key notables and chiefs began converting to Islam.

CHIEFS, ISLAM, AND THE POLITICAL ORDER

It would be misleading to narrowly conceptualize processes of Islamization as always beginning at the social bottom and proceeding vertically upward through the social order. In certain localities, conversion started at the top with chiefs or village notables, and in some cases Muslim canton chiefs even sought to impose the religion on their subjects. Such was the case of Kola, just north of Fulala. This canton had been the capital of the large precolonial kafo of Baninko. Its original founders, the Doumbia, had

fled Siguiri following internal wars and then later came under domination by the Togola clan, who had left Banan owing to "fear of a jò fetish."
As elsewhere, the wars of Samori led to its destruction, and under French
rule the kafo remained fragmented, divided into six much smaller cantons. But the Togola clan remained in power, and it was among the first
groups to embrace Islam. In 1947 the following information was reported:
"One notes numerous conversions to Islam in the Togola family, which
holds the majority of the chieftaincies in the canton. The conversion of the
current canton chief, Juracé Togola, dates from 1941." The chiefs were also
actively proselytizing in the villages and recruiting the sons of notables
for Qur'anic schools. A census official reported that one informant said,
"When the chief prays, then many are going to pray." These coercive
measures generated widespread "antagonisms between Muslims and
fetishists." After "stirring up difficulties for the chieftaincy" and to evade
forced conversion efforts, three villages, "all faithful to the fetishism of
the ancestors," emigrated from Kola in protest. The village of Kuruferela,
which opposed the canton chief for "leading his propaganda of Islamization," found safe haven under the canton chief of Falani, "a fetishist, who
was ready to welcome them." Two other villages also severed ties with
Kola and joined the canton of Debelendugu for the same reason. In short,
there were distinct limits to local forced conversions.[79] But, while the case
of Kola stands out anomalously, there were more general ways in which
hierarchies and gradients of privilege and status shaped religious change.
For example, in the district of Sikasso, one report noted that the "insidious
advance [of Islam] has been due to the example provided by the conversion of numerous influential people, chiefs and functionaries. The youth,
above all those who are detribalized after more or less abandoning the
traditional milieu, follow voluntarily this example."[80] In other words, even
when elites did not seek to impose Islam on rural communities, peasants
may have nevertheless been drawn to certain symbols of power.

Whether they sought to impose the religion on their subjects or not,
the presumed conversion of chiefs was an important local religious and
political event and a major local turning point. As noted earlier, in the precolonial era chiefs often converted and hosted marabouts in order to access
trade or to bring Muslim religious services, for example, rainmaking,
to their communities. Later, by the colonial period, the pressure to convert was being generated through religious change within communities

rather than through chiefly contacts with supralocal agencies and itinerant clerics. Many of the first Muslim chiefs had been introduced to prayer as slaves, soldiers, or migrant workers. They were the agents and products of grass-roots Islamization, simply bringing to fruition the institutionalization of local Muslim power. In this process, competition over the chieftaincy continued. But now it entailed wider struggles over symbolic power. Seeking to parlay cultural capital into political power, chiefs and their detractors continually sought to reinforce their own specific religious identity claims, while trying to define the identities of their competitors in disadvantageous terms. Such competitive claims making was marked as the chieftaincy waned after the Second World War as new forms of authority took over and new religious standards were used in weighing legitimacy.

Even before the chieftaincy was abolished, the political reforms of the postwar period effectively stripped chiefs of considerable power. First, as we have seen, forced labor and the indigénat were ended, eliminating the most coercive institutions associated with the chieftaincy. Then, following the elections to the Territorial Assembly in 1957 and the rise to power of the US-RDA, chiefs lost their judicial roles in the Customary Tribunals. Through a series of decrees in 1958, the remaining power of chiefs was whittled away. Finally, in 1959, the PSP was ousted from the Legislative Assembly, depriving chiefs of their last form of political organization. The ending of the chieftaincy was more of a process than a single event, one that was played out in local arenas. As such, in certain localities, in the north above all, chiefs would remain in place until independence and even well into the postcolonial period. But in southern French Sudan the chieftaincy had been abolished as a recognized institution of governance by 1959.[81]

In this era of rapid political change, it is unclear what role religious difference and in particular Muslim messages of equality played at a popular level leading up to independence. Certainly, as in Guinea, there were Islamic themes to the US-RDA campaigns and activism. And there were ties between the party and Muslim traders, marabouts, and reformists. This is not surprising, as Islam initially spread to urban centers and roadside villages before reaching the countryside. However, at the same time, the head of the PSP, Fily-Dabo Sissoko, despite his purported involvement in animist ritual, was considered a Muslim, and the executives and party leaders of the PSP were also overwhelmingly Muslim. Still, while scholars have been much more attuned to secular dimensions of decolonization, the linkages between religious change and the end of empire in French West Africa are understudied.[82]

In any case, more locally, as this-worldly power dissolved, chiefs looked to religion and spiritual bases of authority. In explaining this process and how Islam became central to the chieftaincy in the canton of Fulala, one official reported, "[As] the excess of centralization diminishes each day, these chieftaincies, who, having lost their former raison d'être, which was to maintain the peace and render justice, do not know where to hang their authority, fictive and pure tradition today."[83] Their temporal power waning, chiefs found themselves fulfilling largely empty ceremonial roles, so they invested in Muslim forms of authority. Islam became such a powerful referent in the refashioning of local moral discourses that Islamic practices and beliefs moved to the discursive center. Most of the chiefs who were already Muslim when they rose to power had come to Islam gradually—through slavery, migration, soldiering, or trade—and later carried their Muslim identities into the chieftaincy. As the colonial period extended, more chiefs entered service as new colonial elites, such as functionaries or former tirailleurs, who had converted while in military service or in the colonial bureaucracy.[84] However, in modernizing the chieftaincy, the colonial bureaucracy was also itself inadvertently turning out Muslim chiefs. Even former soldiers did their part, as in the canton of Siondugu, where former tirailleurs who had broken with tradition in a so-called *complot de l'armée* voted a fellow Muslim soldier, Tiemogo Sangaré, into power. Eight of the village chiefs as well as the canton chief were former soldiers and practicing Muslims. Again, to be a modern functionary meant subscribing to Islam.[85]

Not all Muslim chiefs had entered service as Muslims. As personnel records indicate, some converted while in power. Deciphering the motivations behind sitting canton chiefs who changed their religious designations is difficult. Cardaire provided a few clues: "How many of these chiefs have said: 'It is the new religion, it is necessary to adopt it.' The new chief, trying to impose himself on his neighbors, wants to establish his authority in an indisputable, therefore religious, manner. . . . [He] wants to free himself from the old obligations and render his command more acceptable. Therefore, he converts to Islam, which moreover seems to confer on its followers a particular prestige."[86] Often the religious authority of Muslim chiefs rested on their ties to powerful holy men. Of the many local examples of such ties, the most poignant one comes from the canton of Bolou, where the prestige of the district's most famous Sufi shaykh, Mamadu Touré, propped up the authority of the canton chief, Tumani Bagayoko, who was described as the "son of former slaves."[87]

In Fulala, Kojugu Suntura, a former slave-convert and prominent holy man, became the first Muslim canton chief in Fulala after the war. In 1952, a census official reported that his "religious prestige is great, and he has done much in the introduction of Islam in his canton."[88] But, as a Muslim, he never would have been accepted as the canton chief without the consent of the population. As in many cantons, in Fulala the religious landscape had changed so much that Kojugu was embraced because of his reputation as a tolerant Muslim notable who could bridge religious worlds.[89] Indeed, for a chief's authority to be indisputable and more acceptable, religious identity was carefully considered. Sometimes this meant mollifying and straddling two different religious communities. In her study of the jò power associations in Buguni in the 1950s, Pâques observed the religious syncretism of the political culture of chieftaincies. She wrote, "A canton chief cannot be elected as chief unless he has done [been initiated into] the jò, even when he has personally converted to Islam."[90] Generally, the emergence of Muslim chiefs rarely occurred without popular support. But, as I have suggested, chieftaincy politics were also being shaped by intergenerational conflicts. Cardaire stated, "At a given moment in his evolution, the chief senses that his authority, undisputed until then, [and] resting on a religious foundation, falters. He knows that 'only the fear of the elders still holds back the youth... .' And the elders are going to disappear."[91]

As elders passed on or were politically and religiously marginalized, chiefs looked increasingly to new social bases of legitimacy. In short, as the embattled chieftaincy began its march to extinction, chiefs sought to use their religious prestige to bolster their sagging authority. By this time, with the expansion of Qur'anic education, mosques, and Muslim networks of patronage, new forms of power and authority were being concentrated in the hands of holy men. In such contexts, imams and Muslim holy men provided guidance based on knowledge of the Qur'an and esoteric Sufi forms of knowledge and led prayer and life-crisis rituals. They also offered advice and mediated disputes. In communities looking for moral leadership, the growing authority and power of the mori dovetailed with the demise of the chieftaincy.

CHAPTER 7

Changes in the Religious Landscape

THE MAKING OF MUSLIM COMMUNITIES, C. 1930S–1950S

After returning to Tenemakana, Tumani Danyoko, the former slave who introduced prayer into the village, fathered a son and named him Mamadujan, after the Prophet Muhammad. At the time Mamadujan was born, the village was still dominated by traditionalists. Muslims had yet to begin praying publicly. But within the privacy of his compound, Tumani performed his prayers and raised his children in the Islamic faith. Eventually, he sent his son away to Qur'anic school in Masigi, where he spent a decade studying with a renowned holy man of the Haidara lineage. Then, in 1929, Mamadujan returned home and soon became the most important imam and *karamogo*, or Qur'anic teacher, in southern Fulala.[1]

"One could say that real prayer started with Mamadujan. He had studied the Qur'an in Masigi, and came back to the village. . . . He continued as imam for 30 years until his death," explained Yusuf Coulibaly, the current imam of Tenemakana, whose grandfather, Cemogo Coulibaly, had also returned from slavery as a practicing Muslim.[2] Cemogo's son, Sekou Moriba, would later serve as the village's prayer caller (*seliwelila* or *muezzin*) alongside Mamadujan. In the 1930s, Sekou Moriba sent his son, Yusuf, to Qur'anic school. Now in his eighties, Yusuf became the village imam after Mamadujan's death in 1959 and has held that position for nearly half a century. Outside of Tenemakana, similar stories are told across the canton of Fulala.

In the village of Niamala, informants told of N'Famusa Diallo, whose father had been a slave in Segu, where he embraced Islam. Later, in the 1930s, N'Famusa went away to study the Qur'an in Masigi with Mamadujan's former master.[3] As second-generation Muslims and the sons of slave converts, Mamadujan of Tenemakana, N'Famusa of Niamala, Kojugu of N'Golobala, and Lamine of Wakoro are remembered as the first great promoters of Islam in Fulala. But among them, Mamadujan emerged as the most respected and knowledgeable imam and karamogo. Beginning in the 1930s, he was drawing young Muslims from surrounding villages to hear his talks, study the Qur'an, and pray alongside him.[4]

As archival and oral sources indicate, unofficial Qur'anic schools had begun to spread across Wasulu and in the major trade towns, such as Garalo, Buguni, Tenetu, Madina, Koloni, Soloba, Yanfolila, and Siekorole, during the interwar years. In the postwar period, Qur'anic education took root elsewhere in the wider district. As more educated Muslims returned to their homes, they set up rudimentary rural schools and began influencing community-based rituals and the religious inculcation of children. Although migrant workers had contributed to the growing social depth of Muslim communities, there were distinct limits to their knowledge. The imam of N'Golobala explained: "Those who came from migration with prayer added themselves to the others. But they came to realize that the religion could not be developed without Qur'anic instruction."[5]

As many of the first educated Muslims and holy men had been part-time students, combining migrant work with their studies, their Qur'anic schooling was often sporadic and rudimentary. Furthermore, the first generation of imams had been adults when they attended Qur'anic schools, and, as a result, many of them never acquired advanced scholarly skills. Thus, despite the growing scriptural authority of the Qur'an in rural forms of religious expression and belonging, literacy remained rather restricted. Even one of the region's great Sufi holy men, Kelekele Sidiki, was remembered as someone "who had never studied the Qur'an" and who "could not even write his name in Arabic."[6] Nevertheless, the younger generation of Muslims would be trained from childhood and would deepen Islamic practices and knowledge in their villages. Colonial officials in the postwar period were attuned to this multigenerational process: "Islamization spreads rapidly and gains in depth. . . . The newly Islamized content themselves with a vague obedience to the new rules, prayer and fasting.

But their children go to the Qur'anic school, where their religion deepens. The phenomenon of conversion is not the form of absolute and personal adhesion to a body of moral doctrine as among the Christians. It produces itself rather at several moments in which each generation constitutes a new step."[7]

As a "new step" in this long-term process, Qur'anic education became central to the making of Muslim communities and the furthering of local religious transformations.[8] The seeds of Islam were finally bearing fruit as people became more open to the public piety and rituals of Muslim leaders and their constituencies. I want to examine the role of Qur'anic education and local Muslim holy men in further transforming the religious habitus. I also explore translocal Sufi currents and networks and the nascent reform movement as well as religious conflict and violence in the postwar era.

MOSQUES, QUR'ANIC SCHOOLS, AND THE RELIGIOUS HABITUS

Mosques, the paramount institution in Muslim societies, were visibly recognizable Islamic forms in the wider landscape. The building of a mosque represented a crucial turning point in local religious histories. With their universal characteristics, cultural references, and orientation, mosques afforded communities a public gathering place for prayer and a site for ritual excursions of the religious imagination. As symbols of solidarity and religious authority, they connected local practices to the wider umma. Whether a monumental edifice or a simple enclosure, the mosque served as a village's religious centerpiece, embodying unity both locally and globally.

Even in regions outside the so-called old Islamic lands of the Near East, from the earliest years of Islamic history the construction of mosques represented a crucial religious step, often linked to political patronage.[9] Richard Eaton has shown the ways in which the Mughal state in South Asia sought to expand its agrarian base in eastern Bengal by overseeing the construction of mosques and Sufi shrines. Eaton notes that whereas the endowed stone and brick mosques, patronized directly by the court, are the most visible reminders of the Mughal past, it was the small mosques sponsored by local gentry and built of bamboo and thatching that played "the more decisive role in the Islamization of the countryside."[10] These rural mosques, which have long since been worn away by time and replaced by more permanent ones, have their analog in parts of colonial Africa.

In the French Sudan, mosques and Qur'anic schools were sprouting up everywhere after the Second World War. Within the district of Buguni there had already been a small number of both institutions in major trade towns, but their construction in rural areas was new. Compared to the case of eastern Bengal, where the local gentry were the benefactors of the mosques, in rural French Sudan the financing of mosques was entirely the work of villagers. While the French state patronized Muslim institutions in other parts of the colonial world, in southern French Sudan it maintained a policy of curbing the expansion of mosques and Qur'anic schools, requiring authorizations and permissions and going so far as to demolish unauthorized mosques. Even its claimed secular neutrality could be politically motivated, aimed at thwarting local initiatives. For example, in 1956 the commandant sought to prohibit the main mosque in Buguni from using municipal tap water for ablutions. In a criticism of neutrality, he noted, "It has not been admissible to see the Administration using public funds to promote denominational constructions and to assume the subsequent maintenance . . . of mosques, that the temporal authority has found itself having many difficulties placating. . . . Neutrality cannot adorn itself with the qualifying 'benevolent' without lapsing into hypocritical paradox."[11] Fortunately, the politically interested neutrality of the administration has provided historians with a few indices of Islamization, in the form of canton-level census reports that chart the local diffusion of mosques and Qur'anic schools.

Although statistics on mosques were not recorded in districtwide annual reports, local census records offer snapshots of local religious complexions. In a way, they reveal the diversity of processes of religious change by showing varying stages of Islamization. These were not typical steps in a standard teleological arc of evolutionary religious change through which every locality passed. There was always considerable unevenness in processes of religious change. But, at the same time, on the long continuum of change such snapshots of stages help to identify some of the minor, incremental shifts that were occurring in communities.

Most cantons had three or four mosques, although statistics do not speak to the array of local political and religious conditions. Many bamana cantons had no mosques at all, and many Muslim cantons had a mosque in almost every village. And the absence of mosques did not mean the absence of Muslims, nor did the presence of a mosque mean the absence of bamanaya. Most of the mosques were small edifices that hardly looked like mosques to French officials, being made of mud walls and thatched roofing, not unlike bamana shrines, or fetish huts in colonial parlance. Sometimes the mosques were not even edifices, but open-air prayer areas demarcated by stones or fencing to keep animals from defiling the interior sites. Because colonial officials could not see them as mosques, they often did not count these prayer sites in their statistics. The mosque-hut varieties were also not considered genuine mosques.[12]

At one end of the spectrum were the cantons that had few, if any, mosques. As I have emphasized, however, even before mosques were built and more overt Islamic institutions were established there were informal gatherings of Muslims, and holy men were cultivating clients and providing services. In the small canton of Falani-Ouola, census records from 1955 indicate that there were 2,742 official fetishists and 2,433 Muslims. But only one mosque was noted and no official Qur'anic schools. Colonial officials catalogued numerous power objects and associations in the canton, perhaps in an optimistic effort to depict local resistance to Islam. There were vigorous jò societies, *nama* and *namakoro* (men's masking) societies, and, among others, there was a powerful *gwan* society whose reputation spread across the northern part of the district, prompting numerous people to make pilgrimages to see the *gwantigi* (head of gwan society) for assistance. In any case, while the colonial official noted that the practice of drinking dòlò was common and had put "serious brakes" on Islam's expansion, there were signs of Muslim communities in formation. A census official noted that Islam was "progressing . . . introduced by men returning from Senegal or Ivory Coast." There was evidence of large numbers of Muslims, particularly among young men, but few visible indicators of Islamic institutions: "In one single village there exists a mosque, still a simple thatched hut. In this village, I saw a man saying his rosary beads." The official also reported that despite there being no other mosques or official Qur'anic schools, there were several marabouts and many informal Qur'anic schools, teaching without authorization. Although the official dismissed the rural Qur'anic schools and their instructors for lacking serious Arabic, he ordered them to close until they had obtained administrative authorization.[13]

In the canton of Siondugu, despite the presence of a clear Muslim majority there were only four mosques, all of them the thatched-hut type, and no official Qur'anic schools were recorded in 1955. Even as Islam was expanding at the grass-roots level, and most people declared themselves Muslim, much of the canton was at a liminal stage at which Muslim leaders had not yet emerged. Few mosques or Qur'anic schools had been built, and yet many of the jòtigiw had already retreated from public view.[14] Similarly, in the canton of Debelendugu, far more people declared themselves as Muslims than as fetishists, yet only three mosques had been built, one of which, the main mosque in the village of Sunsunkoro, was crumbling owing to lack of maintenance.[15] After many years of misreading the religious landscape by correlating such institutions with the presence of Muslims, colonial officials in the postwar period had begun to see the more grass-roots formation of rural Muslim communities in the absence of such normal indices.

In many cantons, however, including Céndugu, Fulala, Gwancédugu, and Niené, rural thatched-roof mosques were sprouting up too fast for colonial officials to record their numbers. In such circumstances, officials made distinctions between mosque-huts and supposedly genuine mosques. In the canton of Fulala, a census official reported in 1951 that "mosque-huts [cases-mosquées] have been built in the majority of villages, but there is only one genuine mosque in Tenemakana." In places like Tiemala, Gwanan, Kurulamini, Basidibé, and Jallon-Fula, which had long-standing Muslim communities and important trade towns, mosques were built in most villages. In Basidibé, mosques had begun to spread into rural villages in the late 1920s, as a census report stated: "More or less rudimentary mosques are built in some villages." This process continued into the postwar period. In Tiemala, where Muslims had been confined to the trade town of Garalo, mosques spread into rural areas, as a census report in 1954 noted that "a bit everywhere mosques are being raised, some of which have a certain cachet."[16]

There were also efforts to build mosques made of stone and complete with the major features, such as the minaret, minbar (pulpit where the imam stood), prayer hall, and ablution pool. In the town of Buguni, French officials reported in a supposedly confidential report on the progress of what would become the district's largest community Friday mosque.[17] The mosque in Buguni was one of the few that appears to have received assistance from foreign Sufi shaykhs. So-called Kankan Musa, the younger brother of the renowned Shaykh Fanta Mady of Kankan, resided in Buguni for awhile and oversaw the construction of the mosque. His charisma played a role in drumming up support for the endeavor. Despite the lack of funding, masons and workers, many of whom had acquired skills as forced laborers, came to work on the project.[18] The imam of Tenemakana recalled the scene: "At that time, I had left to work for Sidiki [mori Sidiki Koné], and later the younger maternal brother of Kankan Sekuba, when he came to settle in Buguni. He built the stone mosque there in my presence, the stone mosque next to the market. . . . Musa was instructed in the Qur'an, and he had succeeded in traveling across the region, convincing the crowds of his cause. . . . You could come and find fifty people at his place at that time. You would ask yourself how he could feed and lodge all these people. . . . The people slept in the open air."[19]

In tandem with the building of mosques, Qur'anic schools were expanding within the district of Buguni. Qur'anic schools were usually loosely organized institutions with very little physical structure, and furthermore, as most rural schools were unauthorized and concealed from the state, statistics represent only the tip of the iceberg. In any case, in 1932 the census recorded just seven Qur'anic schools across the entire district. Twenty-five years later, in 1957, the number had grown to sixty-seven. Again, this does not include the large numbers of schools that were closed for improper authorization over this period. In 1953, for example, twenty-eight such schools were shut down for this reason.[20] Still, across much of the region, particularly in the eastern half of the district, Qur'anic schools did not begin to spread into the countryside until the postwar period. As we have seen, there had been Qur'anic schools in the canton of Gwanan and in the trade towns of Garalo and Tenetu since the Samorian era, and in the canton of Basidibé, Qur'anic schools had taken root by the 1920s. But colonial officials were dismissive of local Muslim practices. In 1928 one official observed, "[The inhabitants] remain dominated by fetishism and retain, despite their Muslim evolution, the habit of drinking alcoholic beverages and sometimes have more wives than stipulated in the Qur'an." In Basidibé only two of the rural marabouts could read and write Arabic; their knowledge was limited to the recitation of "just a few verses of the Qur'an that they learned by heart." Even the leading imam of Yanfolila, who had performed the pilgrimage to Mecca, was perceived to be illiterate. There was only one official Qur'anic school in the entire canton of Basidibé.[21]

Oral testimonies from Basidibé present a different picture. They suggest that children were learning the Qur'an in unauthorized neighborhood schools in the 1930s and completing their studies outside the region, mainly in Siguiri and Kankan. And as localities were drawn further into regional and translocal Sufi networks, itinerant holy men recruited Qur'anic students.[22] The imam of Jelifin, Sekou Sidibé, said, "In some villages, one person would send their son to the Qur'anic teacher. . . . These children were entrusted to masters who were usually not from this region. They came from all over. They were traveling marabouts and people would give them their children. Some of them brought the students all the way to Kankan." After their studies, these students returned to their home villages and set up schools of their own. Sekou Sidibé continued: "Soon there were some young people in the village who could educate the others, and families would send their children to the young teachers who just came back. When he came back he could find students for himself. When the children started to get instruction, they returned to their families and began to share the new ideas with the inhabitants of the village."[23]

Although most village Qur'anic schools were unauthorized and rather small, they were important in exposing people to elements of Islam and served to transform the religious habitus of a given community. People no longer needed to go on migration or visit the market towns to encounter Muslim practices. The Qur'anic presence was felt right at home, depending on social location. The focus of such schools was the memorization of parts of the Qur'an, such as the Fatiha, the opening verse of the Qur'an, written out on wooden slates. Students would spend most of the time simply reciting passages repeatedly. Over the years, this gave students the rudimentary ability to read Arabic and recite portions of the Qur'an but without understanding the meanings of classical Arabic words.[24] In a culture based on orality, the focus was not on acquiring literacy as such. But this practice of simple memorization and recitation without deeper understanding was not uncommon in Muslim societies. This was particularly the case in regions where Arabic was not a colloquial language, as Dale Eickelman has shown in the case of rural French Morocco.[25]

In many instances local Qur'anic schools were simply informal teaching sessions thrown together on an ad hoc, seasonal basis. They aimed at instructing students in the correct protocols of prayer (*salât*), ritual ablution (*wudû*), the basic formulations and recitations from the Qur'an, such as the shahada, and the sequences of bows and prostrations. Most children did not learn much beyond the Fatiha. These schools were often hosted in people's homes. As one woman, Hari Sidibé, recalled, "There was a butcher in our family. He was Muslim. My father gave us to him for instruction, and he taught us some Qur'an."[26] Such informal teaching sessions could also serve as foundations for the eventual establishment of mosques. The first imam of Yanfolila initially taught in an informal manner before a mosque could be constructed: "There was a large vestibule, and the imam asked to use the vestibule to teach children and adults how to pray. The adherents came to fill the house as people started to pray together. Finally, he built a small mosque."[27] Indeed, people prayed in improvised settings for years before mosques were built and received informal schooling in the absence of Qur'anic schools. Rather than viewing the emergence of Muslim communities and changes in the structures of everyday life as radiating out of mosques and Qur'anic schools, it might help to see such institutions as the historical products of changing practices, which in turn transformed the reproduction of ritual life. As embodiments of new ways of organizing religious practices, mosques and Qur'anic schools were both the medium and the outcome of multigenerational processes of religious change.

Outside of schools the roots of Islam were also being planted within households through private prayer and the incorporation of Islamic forms and norms into daily life. Sometimes a family member who had instruction in the Qur'an would take it upon himself to teach the children in the community. Children also watched their fathers and uncles praying together and began imitating their behavior. While children were not invited to pray until much later in age, things characteristically Islamic had begun to permeate the household. This does not mean children were capable of thinking in terms of Islam versus non-Islam. They were just observing and learning how things were done, picking up behavior and manners of speech that drew more openly on Arabic benedictions and forms of greeting. Even adults embraced religious practices in a pragmatic manner without necessarily being aware of any rigid boundaries between religions.[28]

Though not performing prayer, children were growing up in Islamic milieus, surrounded by symbolism in practice and discourse, styles of dress, behavioral interdictions, and dietary prohibitions, all of which served to familiarize young people with the world of Islam. A distinctly Muslim habitus was emerging. And once things began shifting, new institutions and forms of socialization evolved. Members of the family who had begun praying often took it upon themselves to teach others what they knew. Sometimes boys would learn by imitation, lining up behind the men, though prayer was viewed as an "affair of adults."[29] In certain contexts, once the head of the household had begun praying it meant all the children would be baptized and raised as Muslims. However, there was some discrepancy over normative rules and practices regarding children and prayer; theoretically at least, children had to choose to be Muslim, and whether or not they prayed was their decision to make once they had become adults. Some informants emphasized the freedom of each individual to self-assign his or her religious identity, while others claimed, "When the household head [sotigi] started to pray, then everyone had to pray."[30] One colonial official encountered this issue during a census tour in Diban: "In effect, the parents do not at all claim to impose on their children a given practice. If they are asked the question: what is the religion of such children, they respond regularly that they do not yet know, that the child is too young to have chosen."[31]

Children, because they had not sincerely uttered the shahada and learned the correct protocols of prayer, were not viewed as Muslims. They were kafirs, still in the age of jahiliyya, or pre-Islamic ignorance, until they had been incorporated into the Muslim community. They were untamed and unclean.[32] In time, in the same way that children were initiated into age groups and underwent circumcision rites, boys and girls learned the basics of prayer, sometimes at the age of seven or in adolescence. Moreover, with the first generation of children growing up Muslim, a further layer of community building was added in which the socialization of children shifted deeper into what would be recognizable as Muslim.[33] At the popular level, there was also growing curiosity about Islam, especially as people engaged more directly with Islamic healing practices or rain-making techniques. As part of expanding networks, social and cultural transformations were occurring which drew even the staunchest bamana traditionalists out to hear occasional itinerant preachers.[34]

"SUFFERING FOR KNOWLEDGE": FARM LABOR AND QUR'ANIC STUDIES

As we have seen, in the postemancipation societies of southern French Sudan, there was a deep sedimentation of slavery idioms in local understandings of involuntary and coerced labor. Having examined the cases of forced labor and pawning, I want to consider the agricultural labor of Qur'anic students, which was often described by former students as analogous to slavery. Even though slaves and the descendants of slaves in Buguni had broken completely with their former masters, the idea of slavery remained central as an explanatory metaphor for unequal social relations. While not exactly proud of having grandparents who were enslaved during the wars of Samori, informants did not seek to obscure their family histories. They even spoke quite proudly of the hardships and the slavery they had endured to acquire knowledge.

When a family gave their son to an itinerant or local master or teacher (karamogo), the son became the teacher's dependent, part of his wealth in people. Reflecting master–slave dynamics, the Qur'anic student was forced into submission and performed whatever labor the teacher demanded, accepting the disciplinary regime imposed upon him. Even the schooling was conducted through considerable violence. Students were routinely beaten and punished harshly for making mistakes during recitation, causing some students to flee after a few months. In addition, when the rainy season arrived many students who were of working age also left, either to go home or to go on migration to Ivory Coast. One colonial official observed that with the approach of the rainy seasons there was "an abandonment by the youth of the local schools, at the age of leaving for Ivory Coast, the students flee."[35] Usually, the students had been handed over willingly to the Qur'anic teacher as a kind of investment in future cultural and symbolic capital. And once living on the teacher's farm, students performed the kind of work that was virtually the same as that of domestic slaves or pawns. In fact, within the context of the Qur'anic master's household, students were viewed and treated as slaves.

The master–disciple relationship has been central to Sufi orders across Africa and beyond. And gift giving is quite common in such contexts. Sean Hanretta has drawn attention to the "gift of work" which his followers in Ivory Coast performed for the Sufi leader Yacouba Sylla. In his exploration of charitable gifts (sadaqa) and exchange gifts (hadâya), Hanretta shows how such devotional giving was central to this Sufi *zâwiya.*[36] In the case of Buguni, while most Muslims did not formally belong to the Sufi turuq, people gave gifts to holy men or sent their children to work on the farms of rural Sufi shaykhs. Thus, within the context of grass-roots and unaffiliated forms of rural Sufism, students' gift of work was based on the quid pro quo that their farm labor and suffering would yield Qur'anic education and perhaps a bit of divine blessing. In the wider French Sudan, Marcel Cardaire described, in less than flattering terms, the rural Qur'anic schools: "We know the usual ignorance of these masters, who decipher Arabic with difficulty, ignore the meaning of what they read [but benefit from] the gifts that the family provides and the work that their children owe them in their fields and with their herds."[37]

After learning the basics in local Qur'anic schools, a few students left the area to complete more advanced studies. Villages in northern Wasulu often sent one or two young men outside the village to attend Qur'anic schools in Guinea. In some villages, notables or chiefs asked families to send a child away as a sort of investment for the whole community.[38] In other cases, grown men sought knowledge on their own. For example, the elderly imam of Jelifin, El Hajj Sekou Sidibé, was born into a Muslim household in the 1920s and acquired rudimentary Qur'anic education with a local teacher. Then, when he was a teenager in the late 1930s, his father sent him to farm peanuts in Senegal, where he discovered a much larger Muslim community and began praying daily alongside other peasants. After a few seasons in Senegal, he migrated to Ivory Coast, where he worked in trade and pursued Qur'anic studies. After twelve years abroad he returned to Jelifin in 1952 and took up farming and teaching the Qur'an.[39]

In Fulala most students started out taking lessons from the many "small marabouts" in unauthorized village Qur'anic schools before going on to study in Tenemakana, itself a tiny village whose school was the only one authorized in the canton but considered to be "without great influence." Then, students usually attended the Qur'anic schools of "more rigorous masters" located in distant localities, most of which were affiliated with the main Sufi orders, the Tijaniyya and the Qadiriyya. Colonial officials estimated that roughly forty students from Fulala were migrating each year to study outside the district in the trade towns of northern Ivory Coast and along the Niger River.[40] Two of these students were Yusuf Coulibaly and Drissa Diallo, whose stories provide a more interior view of rural Qur'anic schools.

For poor families, sending children to Qur'anic school was somewhat like pawning. Indeed, previously the family of Yusuf Coulibaly had been forced to pawn a daughter during the Depression. Destitute, his father decided to relieve the household of an additional mouth to feed and made an investment in future trade connections by giving Yusuf to an itinerant marabout for instruction. What followed was a difficult period in his life. Yusuf remembered that "we stayed four years in the countryside there. The marabout put us to farming. We went into the bush, each with a cob of corn—that was our meal. We studied in conditions like that. We learned the Qur'an. We endured all sorts of suffering in the Qur'anic schools. There were so many people. The people from the canton who studied there were numerous, nineteen people. But those who accompanied the marabout to do the ceremony at the end of the Qur'an, there were only three of us. All the others fled because of the difficulties."[41]

During the dry season and the hungry seasons, schools provided the bare minimum for hungry children, who were sent around to beg for food. In their home villages, it would have brought shame to beg from neighbors. For Qur'anic students, such asking for alms was accepted and encouraged.[42] Not all Qur'anic students were from poor families. Drissa Diallo was the nephew of the canton chief and belonged to a prosperous family of farmers, but he, too, was sent to Qur'anic school in the late 1930s and would spend most of his adolescent years studying near the village of Domba. He worked in the fields, performed domestic chores, and ran errands to distant localities, while learning Arabic and the Qur'an. He recounted his experiences at Qur'anic school, which he described as slavery:

> The Qur'anic student was considered a slave. We farmed, went collecting wood in the bush, carried water, pounded millet, found grass for the horses and then studied the Qur'an. . . . Food was in short supply for everyone. Myself, I spent sixteen years total in my studies, and I endured every kind of suffering for my master. But we accepted the suffering in order to gain knowledge. We farmed, pounded millet for the women. At this time, agriculture was the base for the school. The master had very many Qur'anic students who worked for him. There was only one Qur'an that forty students shared for their lessons. We would pass entire days

without eating. There was nothing but water to drink. All of the students from this era, they experienced these hardships, from our fathers to us.[43]

As this testimony suggests, the position of Qur'anic students within the household of the master was analogous to that of slaves. In a way, sending boys to rural Qur'anic schools might be viewed as an expression of the pawning idiom, as families exchanged their sons' labor for financial relief or other sorts of social capital. At the same time, rural shaykhs could treat their students poorly and demand excess amounts of labor because they provided a service that was in short supply. Despite the rampant exploitation of *talib* labor in rural Qur'anic schools, oral accounts underscore the sentiment among former students that greater hardships meant deeper knowledge. When Qur'anic students returned, they often assumed positions of religious leadership in Muslim communities, serving as imams and local preachers. And as the religious practices of communities drifted more into the orbit of Islam, people turned away from bamanaya.[44]

ABANDONING THE KÒMÒ: QUIETISM AND RELIGIOUS VIOLENCE

Behind the village of Tenemakana there is a small stream known as *kòmò-ko*, so named because it is the place where Mamadujan Danyoko and the head of the kòmò society, Fa Dembélé, agreed to bury the kòmò mask in a collaborative ceremony. As Mamadujan's son recounted, "They went together, and took all the kòmò power objects and buried them there. From that day on, we started calling this part of the stream in Tenemakana kòmò-ko, because that is where the kòmò is buried." Long before, when Mamadujan was completing his studies, his teacher, Shaykh Haidara, had said to him, "When you return to your village, the kòmò will still be too powerful. You must not force yourself against the kòmò. Instead, go and dance with the kòmò; play the drums to the kòmò. You must take it with both hands. Allah will give you the power to eliminate the kòmò, but you must first celebrate alongside it." Mamadujan took his teacher's advice. But also, following the annual kòmò ceremonies, held at the beginning of the rainy season, he would visit Fa Dembele to talk about Islam. Finally, as the story goes, Fa Dembele said to Mamadujan, "I know that you are on a clean path. I see that the path that I have followed has been very dirty. Mamadu, since you came back, you have never once tried to force anything or try to stop us from doing our things. In your Muslim religion, you have gained respect among the people. Mamadu, today, I give you the kòmò. You must burn this kòmò. . . . But if I go to destroy it alone, you will say that I have kept it somewhere in my room. I ask that we destroy it together." Mamadujan consented to the elder's request, and the two men buried the kòmò together.[45]

Echoing testimonies which emphasize this sort of quietist approach of Muslim leaders, in the village of Niamala Adama Diallo recounted what he had learned about the history of Islam in Fulala: "The Muslims managed to convince the heads of the kòmò society to abandon the kòmò . . . little by little, until most of the people started to accept Islam. But for a long while when you said that you prayed you would be chased from the village."[46] In many settings this quietist path, which I do not mean to overdichotomize with a jihadist approach, was pursued tacitly through indirect social pressure and shame.[47] Furthermore, young educated Muslims started criticizing their fathers for not being good Muslims. And when the first generation of Qur'anic students returned, they sought to establish greater public piety. Although these social pressures and local conflicts have mostly faded from view over the years, some informants presented an alternate view of the prodigal sons returning with their new education. Musa Sumoaro argued that Qur'anic education created a sharp division in village life: "Qur'anic education transformed the elders into people who knew nothing in the eyes of their children. . . . But when [the student] finished and his teacher freed him, he would return to his home and build his own hut next to that of his elders. He would not even live in the same courtyard as them. He had disdain for them, and they became repugnant in his eyes. He became ashamed of them."[48] As the elders were increasingly marginalized and power objects were removed from known huts and hidden in the forest, preachers and village imams held public prayer meetings and sought to convince other villagers to convert. They explained the difference between believing in Allah and worshiping power objects, while striving to "unveil the secrets of bamanaya."[49]

Across Buguni rural holy men sought to win converts through preaching and challenging the authority of bamana priests. And as opportunities for alms collection grew, there were increasing numbers of foreign marabouts traveling across the region, "preaching to crowds of people in the villages." But, as Hari Sidibé emphasized, preaching always depended on the good will of locals and the consent of the village chief. She told of how the first imam gained a foothold by staying with the village chief: "When a foreign marabout came, the local people were more powerful, so if they did anything that did not please them, he could not stay. But Laji Kòròba stayed with the family of the village chief." Eventually, Laji Kòròba built a modest mosque and opened a Qur'anic school. His son is the current imam of the mosque.[50]

The abandonment of the kòmò occurred within different contexts, sometimes through door-to-door quietism and tacit social pressure and sometimes through violence and iconoclasm. When asked questions about the abandonment of the kòmò, informants often tied its decline to the growing power of Muslim leaders and converts but rarely suggested that people were forced to abandon the kòmò.[51] However, while the descendants of the first Muslims have a greater tendency to cite the role of their ancestors in defeating the kòmò, bamana religious specialists and kòmò initiates stressed how they voluntarily gave up their power objects and how nobody forced them to convert.[52] Still, as we have seen, people abandoned the kòmò and jò societies out of shame or concealed their practices deep in the forest. Namakoro Bamba said, "In a few places, Islam had been imposed. In other places, when they saw all Muslims around them, they were ashamed to remain bamana among them. This latter case is the most frequent."[53]

While the quietist approach was successful in many localities, there were also more strident preachers who resorted to violence. We have seen how Bakari Koné raided sacred bamana sites and burned power objects.[54] In the same way, the renowned preacher Dramane Konate in the canton of Gwancédugu fought "with force and fire against the fetishes," until he was arrested by colonial authorities. After a stint in the colonial prison of Buguni, where he was "sobered up," he returned to his village and contented himself with teaching a few students. In more urban settings, in fact, right under the colonial state's nose in the administrative center in Buguni, there were similar events. El Hajj Abdulaye Koné, among a growing number of returnees from Mecca and former al-Azhar students, desecrated kòmò society power objects publicly during his preaching. Colonial authorities were forced to step in to avoid violence, despite the large crowds of people who were drawn to hear his sermon outside the mosque.[55] The iconoclasm associated with such preachers could also occur more spontaneously, comprising a popular movement in which whole communities destroyed their sacred objects. In the remote, forested canton of Sibirila, located along the border with Ivory Coast, inhabitants who had previously been involved in the kòmò society collectively burned or abandoned their power objects. This movement was extended to the canton's sacred sites.[56]

The attacks on sacred sites by Muslim preachers generated fierce religious battles, resulting even in assassination and intercommunal violence. Yet such violence was just as often rooted in interlineage rivalry (fadenkélé), competition between supporters of the RDA and PSP, and contestations over the chieftaincy. Nevertheless, as informants and colonial documents attest, a postwar resurgence of anti-witchcraft campaigns swept across the region.[57] Faced with the weakening of the kòmò and direct challenges to the chieftaincy, village authorities often recruited sorcerers to kill or intimidate marabouts. Indeed, with the end of the indigénat and forced labor and the diminishing of chiefly power, village elders resorted to extreme measures to maintain control over junior male labor. Often this included murder, either through poisoning or outright assault.

In a different cultural context James Ferguson has demonstrated how sorcery was often linked to wider sanctions against returning migrant workers who, with their cosmopolitan styles, resisted "cultural compliance" with rural or localist ways. He argues that invocations of witchcraft went beyond beliefs and idioms; the popular obsession with sorcery was more than a "vague mystical fear." It referred to concrete concerns about being killed. Hence, Ferguson's suggestion that sorcery should be analyzed as a "form of violence" rather than just a belief system, finds resonance with cases from the district of Buguni in the postwar era.[58] But, while most incidences of sorcery were rooted in domestic jealousy and competition among kin, religious violence could also take on wider, intercommunal forms.

The heads of power associations used assassination by poisoning, or koroté, to combat the growing influence of their opponents, regardless of their religious identities. Even among traditional groups of hunters and blacksmiths, competition and jealousy resulted in koroté being "thrown" against coreligionists. One of my informants, who spoke on the condition of anonymity, worked as an assassin in the canton of Fulala. He noted that most assassins knew several kinds of magic and poisons based on knowledge of plants, roots, insects, and trees that were place-specific. While people generally thought of a koroté as a spell being cast or thrown, one which killed victims as they slept in dreamtime psychic incursions, in practical use it was a poison that was placed in someone's food or applied at the tip of a dart. Sometimes assassins enlisted children, who unwittingly carried out the acts clandestinely.[59]

In the canton of Kola a string of such killings followed the ascent of Muslims to positions of power. And conflicts erupted in Niamala, where the number of people killed by poisonings and witchcraft constituted an "epidemic." In Nafanandugu, the combustible mix of an assertive Muslim community, chieftaincy conflicts, and resistant bamana authorities also produced deadly disputes. In 1947, a special report noted, "Owing in large part to the poisonings by injection, whose actual epidemic has raged in the regions east and north of the district, the families of the victims, terrorized, do not come and complain ... fearful of reprisals, the heads of family prefer to continue paying the tax of the victims rather than denounce the crimes." Elsewhere, in the canton Kokoun, the severe decline in population was attributed to "the crimes of sorcerers and fetishists." Overall, nearly two thousand people were reportedly murdered through intercommunal poisonings across eight cantons during the late 1940s.[60]

In one fascinating case an assassin was caught in the act when he tried to murder a Muslim interpreter inside the colonial headquarters. The target for assassination, a blind Muslim interpreter named Massaman Sangaré, had recently lost his son to such poisonings and had since been leading the administration's investigation into the crimes. As a specialist in "Judicial Affairs," he was considered "the foil of the fetishists," as he "knew their secrets well." After the assassination attempt in the local administrative headquarters, Commandant Maurice Meker, who wrote about it in his memoirs, recommended that the accused be executed publicly.[61] A report stated, "A few days ago, a sorcerer tried in the office, and right in front of our eyes, to kill the blind interpreter, Massaman Sangare, using a poison-tipped arrow that he had hidden under his shirt. He was stopped and out of fear dropped the arrow under the chair of the interpreter.... Great publicity should be given to the sentences pronounced. It would even be excellent if the condemned could be executed in Buguni. A rapid and severe repression is the only means of putting an end to the agitations of these people whose only rule of life has been to impose themselves through terror."[62]

By this time, directly on the heels of the colonial reforms of 1946, which had whittled away the power of the chieftaincy, the religious and political tide had changed. Even as the administration fought hard to curb the influence of Muslim notables, particularly reformists linked to the anticolonial RDA, officials no longer automatically backed fetishist chiefs and their religious institutions. It is impossible to know the local religious and political repercussions of these widespread poisonings, but such acts likely alienated part of the population and maybe turned them more force-fully against chiefs and traditionalists. One thing is clear: Muslim preach-ers and canton chiefs stood to benefit from an administrative crackdown on the kòmò. And given that most colonial intermediaries were Muslim, some of the stories may have been exaggerated and even fabricated. Mus-lim functionaries and chiefs had the ear of the commandant and were keen to blame political turmoil on the local kòmòtigi.[63]

Although religious conflicts centered on the divide between Muslim and traditionalist authorities, combating sorcery was a major concern of all people. Reflecting the ubiquity of fear of sorcery, an innovative translo-cal religious movement, Allah Kura (new God), spread rapidly throughout southern French Sudan, Upper Volta, and northern Ivory Coast in the early 1950s. The Allah Kura fetish, which consisted of a ram's horn filled with various materials, was reportedly designed "to protect people from evil-doers and the deeds of sorcerers."[64] As Gregory Mann has shown, the movement originated in the district of San, the home of its founder, M'Pieni Dembélé, and addressed local concerns over farming, political authority, and gender relations at a time of rapid social change.[65] For colo-nial officials like Cardaire, the movement also represented the rebirth of a reconstituted fetishism that could serve as a bulwark against the further expansion of Islam.[66]

Within Buguni, Allah Kura was largely confined to the Senufo canton of Niené, where the movement also became known as Massa. The evidence suggests it was considered a sort of religious hybrid. As one colonial official reported, "This new religion arrives from the east and spreads little by little to the west, passing through the Senufo cantons of Ivory Coast and the only Senufo canton of Buguni. The inhabitants, under the guidance of the village chief, build a hut, though some call it a mosque. . . . It seems to be more of an association than a religion, more or less animism tending to blend intimately with Islam. . . . In certain localities Muslims and fetishists both embrace this Massa. It is an anti-witchcraft fetish."[67] One informant met many of the followers of Allah Kura and visited their worship sites. He indicated that Allah Kura appeared suddenly and gained popularity among both Muslims and bamana traditionalists, then disappeared. He remembered that most of its devotees in Buguni acquired the power object while on migration in Ivory Coast and used it in healing and fighting sorcery.[68] They also embraced it during a time of great religious and political turbulence, which saw the resurgence of other power associations, such as the gwan society, which addressed fertility issues. The popularity of these associations in the wake of wartime demands and famine was certainly linked to the elevated rates of infant mortality and widespread dearth. Indeed, the influence of such power associations ebbed and flowed and extended over numerous cantons. And just as bamanaya saw limited resurgence within wider translocal contexts in the postwar period, cultural change in Muslim communities also took on regional configurations.

RURAL SUFISM AND FORMS OF ISLAMIC KNOWLEDGE

Muslim communities forged connections and invested in social networks and patron–client relationships that reached outside the confines of the village. As a result, local Islamic forms of knowledge reflected the particular linkages that villages had with supralocal religious authorities. As we have seen, mobile social groups played important roles in this process, as migrants encountered and appropriated diverse practices. Concomitantly, transregional Sufi currents, carried by itinerant holy men, flowed into the region and intermingled with local religious practices and institutions. In the daily lives of most Muslims, rural holy men held sway. At first, they filled the roles of healers and magicians by providing religious services, such as rainmaking and amulet fabrication. Soon, however, they began performing prayer or bestowing blessings in exchange for gifts. Within this context, Muslim holy men moved rather freely and promiscuously between the established Sufi orders, and this flexibility facilitated the emergence of Muslim figures as powerful local political actors.

These particular social forms and sets of religious relationships are well established in the literature. However, recent scholarship has invited new ways of thinking about the political economy of religion. In particular, Benjamin Soares has developed a conceptual framework for exploring the "personalization" of religious authority in the Malian town of Nioro. According to Soares, a "prayer economy" linked to processes of commodification unfolded in the postcolonial period, an economy in which people gave gifts to religious leaders in exchange for their prayers and blessings. He argues that this prayer economy opened the way for shifts in religious authority, which came to center on individuals rather than on institutions.[69] The case of postcolonial Nioro is very different from that of colonial Buguni, yet one might conceive of a kind of prayer economy *avant la lettre*. Mapping this concept onto the case of Buguni requires a temporal shift and some recontextualization, as there were no radios or cassette tapes, that is, the "commodity form," in colonial Buguni. But as archival and oral sources suggest, the personalization of religious authority, with its focus on individuals instead of institutions, was occurring long before the postcolonial period. For quite different reasons and according to different social logics, Muslims in the district of Buguni embraced religious big men rather than the Sufi orders, which were still rather abstract and remote from people's lives. With its strong animist substratum and theodicy in times of dramatic social change, there was a popular devotionalism attached to renowned Sufi shaykhs living among decentralized societies.

As I have stated, Sufism in the district of Buguni was often unaffiliated or at most loosely affiliated with the Sufi brotherhoods. In contrast with most regional histories of Islam in West Africa, which have emphasized the importance of the Muridiyya, Tijaniyya, Qadiriyya, and Hamawiyya, the case of Buguni suggests that Sufism was much less institutionalized. While the majority of people preferred the Qadiriyya, there were no strict boundaries between brotherhoods. Along these lines, René Otayek and Robert Launay have provided something of a corrective to notions of Sufism being necessarily linked to such brotherhoods. While Otayek shows how models of typical Sufism do not apply to Burkina Faso, Launay goes one step further in positing what he terms "Sufism degree zero" among the Jula, revealing how people embraced Sufi practices but made few distinctions between the Qadiriyya and Tijaniyya.[70]

Resonating with these geographically adjacent cases, many self-styled Sufis in Buguni practiced rites and litanies linked to the Qadiriyya, but most Muslims belonged to what they considered one religion, or the path of Allah (alasira). Informants explained how diverse intellectual strands were interwoven, or "put in agreement"; practices, litanies, and beliefs drawn from the Qadiriyya and Tijaniyya were incorporated into a system of complementary religious practices. The imam of N'Golobala explained as follows: "When we came together after being abroad, we all got along, even though our studies had not been in the same place. Some people had studied towards the south. Others had done their studies in Bamako. My master was to the north. So everyone was coming with [religious knowledge] from different places. We grouped together all of the different ideas and put them in agreement. . . . But often we practiced the same wurudi [Sufi litany] of the Qadiriyya."[71]

The different forms of knowledge were blended in rural scholarly communities and slowly reinforced the scriptural authority of the book. But even as Qur'anic schools were spreading, literacy remained restricted, such that the Qur'an as a sacred scripture was used more in magical contexts. Beyond learning passages from the Qur'an, most Muslims sought to acquire baraka (divine blessing), baraji (divine recompense), and amulets (sébénw) from powerful holy men.[72] Verses of the Qur'an were viewed as symbolic power objects and sources of magic. Nonliterate Muslim healers made amulets out of scraps of Arabic writing, normally Qur'anic verses, which people used for healing and protection. Literacy was restricted even among those trained in Qur'anic schools. Holy men recited passages of the Qur'an from memory, and some could read, but most did not understand Arabic well enough to decipher the precise meanings of their recitations, oratory, or benedictions. Regardless of their abilities, holy men brought the authority of Allah's eternal and unchanging written word into local rituals. They often translated passages from the Qur'an and hadith into local dialects of Bamanankan, a process that was more than linguistic, as indigenous taxonomies and concepts provided the framework, or cultural grammar, for accommodating Islamic doctrines and Arabic terminology. Informants referred to this form of translated Islamic thought and practice as kankònòla, and it served as a linguistic and cultural interface between the Islamic world and local communities.[73]

As we have seen, Kojugu Suntura was one of the first people to possess a nominally Muslim form of esoteric knowledge and to master kankònòla. Though called a saint by some informants, one might question this status given Kojugu's close ties to colonial power. Yet since the precolonial period, political authorities have often been sanctified for great feats, such as founding villages or waging war. Canton chiefs, even as colonial government officials, could be elevated in religious status and remembered locally as saints owing to their actions and achievements, albeit underpinned by secular power. This was perhaps similar to the "sanctification of bureaucratic authority" on the Bengal frontier among Turkish soldiers who became remembered as saints because of their work in clearing jungles.[74]

Kojugu Suntura had converted to Islam while in slavery and later played a central role in bringing Islamic prayer to his village, while becoming the first Muslim canton chief of Fulala. He did not attend Qur'anic school, but he was known for his mastery of local forms of kankònòla as well as for his ability to perform miracles and fabricate powerful amulets. He was viewed as a magician and healer, and people made pilgrimages to ask for his assistance, as one informant recalled: "He had real 'magic' [jinémoriya]. All that he asked from Allah was done. Even if you were sick, and nobody knew the cause of this illness, he had the knowledge to heal you. When someone was fading, and everyone said that she was going to die, or that she was dead, when he worked and attached his amulet to the person's neck, you could go find their family and come back and find the person alive again."[75] Although Kojugu was nominally Muslim, his activities blurred the boundaries between religious systems. In community ritual life he performed Islamic ceremonies but also "celebrated among pagans." As expressions of kankònòla, with its eclectic integration of Islamic beliefs and practices, his practices found a wide audience.[76] In a way, these religious practices were characteristic of the long period of inclusion that Eaton has described, when Islamic "superhuman agencies" and practices slowly became accepted into local cosmologies and repertoires. In the case of Buguni, this process was much more rapid, inclusion quickly giving way to identification and eventually to displacement, in Eaton's conceptualization.[77]

Fula Musa Suntura from N'Golobala gained his knowledge as a migrant worker in Ivory Coast. In local traditions, the turning point was his consumption of a magic elixir (nasiji) filled with the words of the Qur'an. The purveyor of the nasiji was al-Hajj Yacouba, a Soninke holy man living in the port town of Bassam. A member of the Qadiriyya brotherhood, al-Hajj Yacouba had a following of twenty-five

Qur'an students, mostly the sons of merchants.[78] As the story goes, when Musa was working in Bassam he started attending the mosque where al-Hajj Yacouba led prayer and preached. Having passed the usual tests used to discern one's Muslim identity, he was accepted into the local umma: "We arrived in Bassam and were working in trade and we started going to the mosque. There was a mori named al-Hajj Yacouba. We told him we were from Buguni. He said to us, 'An inhabitant of Buguni praying to Allah, that would be the first time I've seen that here.' He gave the water can to Musa to see him do the ablutions. Fula Musa knew how to pray and the mori said, 'I see your comportment; you are Muslim then. If you want to come at the end of Ramadan for the feast, you can come here.' At the end of Ramadan, we went to the mosque. Then Lajji Yacouba gave Musa this Qur'anic potion. . . . Fula Musa decided to try a little bit. And right away he lost all reason."[79] After drinking the potion, he passed a month in an altered state of consciousness, "his mind completely gone" and "unable to recognize even his father, mother or brothers." Following the virtual possession, he returned and asked someone to bring him sand. He immediately started practicing a form of divination (*cénda*) which had come to him while in the trance. Although Musa could never read the Qur'an, he always advanced his studies with local moriw and became an expert in moriya.[80]

In the neighboring village of Niamala, N'Famusa Diallo, whose father had also been a slave and Muslim convert, had intellectual roots in Islam and the esoteric world of the numu (blacksmith). His father had been a blacksmith, and N'Famusa mastered certain forms of magic typical of the nyamakala, but he chose not to pursue blacksmithing and instead became a hunter in his youth, building up his knowledge of *donsoya* (hunting) alongside that of Islam. Therefore, as a sort of nyamakala Muslim hunter, he developed his own form of knowledge, one which blended Qur'anic benedictions and Muslim amulets with his knowledge of plants, magic, and hunters' rituals. Far from being an aberrant religious disposition, his intellectual itinerary and religious frames of reference represented the common experiences and practices of most rural people. For many, there were no strict boundaries between farming, hunting, and healing and their associated systems of knowledge.[81]

Alongside these practitioners of kankònòla characteristic of a kind of inclusion, more strictly Muslim intellectuals emerged in the postwar era and established their own lineages of healers and religious specialists. In this fissiparous religious landscape there was a continuum of modes of religious belonging: stages of inclusion, identification, and displacement often overlapped spatially and temporally, even within small communities. Nonetheless, at one end of the spectrum Mamadujan Danyoko of Tenemakana was regarded as the person who possessed the cleanest form of Islamic knowledge. He was also the first true village imam who followed a path that was free of magic. He brought the Qur'an into public rituals in more liturgical contexts by reciting passages at funerals, marriages, and naming ceremonies and during the Muslim communal celebrations.

Indeed, over time the central religious reference point became the Qur'an. Islam in rural areas, albeit mediated through processes of cultural translation, came to be seen as a separate religion. Through the elaboration of Islamic identities via Qur'anic schooling, the popular embrace of distinctly Muslim healers, and the objectification of religious categories within the context of the census, religious differences were being reinforced. And peasants began making distinctions between bamana healers and Muslim holy men. In Wasulu, the imam of Balanfina explained how the mori came to play an important role in people's lives: "All of the invocations of Allah that these moriw performed would lead to success for the population. They were useful because their invocations of Allah bore fruits. Each time that someone had a problem, if this person came to see them, in most cases the prayers made by these mori preachers were answered and the needs of the population were satisfied through the intervention of the moriw."[82] In the religious environment of Buguni, in which old status hierarchies had been leveled and reconfigured, moriya was very much open to anyone who had a hunger for knowledge and power. In time, authority began accruing to key lineages, transmitted between generations and structured through religious networks and hierarchies. In a way, there was a local and regional routinization of charismatic authority as forms of Islamic religious specialization and institutional positions, such as the village imam, stayed within families.[83]

SAINTS, SUFI SHAYKHS, AND BARAKA NETWORKS

As I have stated, the shape of local religious change depended on particular historical linkages that existed between communities and regional Muslim networks. I have highlighted local religious figures, particularly with respect to Fulala. In the broader religious context the postwar era saw the emergence of renowned Sufi shaykhs, whose reputations extended far beyond the village and canton levels. They left the most visible traces in the archival record, but there were hundreds of grass-roots rural holy men who never came to the attention of colonial officials. The fame of these healers and preachers was often short-lived, although some, such as Ousmane Cissé, Bakari Cissé, Bourama Konate, and Balla Sanogo, were known across the district. Today, oral traditions that treat these rural holy men lack specific biographical information. Instead, they refer to their mythic qualities and legendary miracles. One famous mori, Bereko Baba, was considered a powerful magician and a saint in Wasulu. His fame had spread from Wasulu across the district following a series of miracles and rainmaking ceremonies he performed in the 1930s, when rural communities were dealing with hardship and dearth. Although there is no archival trace of him, informants recalled the cleanliness of his white horse and white garments and recounted miraculous acts ranging from local rainmaking prayers and healing illnesses to casting spells on bamana priests. In one account, a prominent bamana priest confronted Baba in front of the mosque, drinking his dòlò and insulting the mori as a way of challenging his powers. Baba responded by tapping the pagan on the head and turning him into a donkey. In other accounts, informants told of how the prayers of Bereko Baba were "answered by God in the blink of an eye" and of how the "entire region depended on him for his prayers." In certain villages, he has been remembered as the last great saint of Wasulu.[84]

There were also Sufi shaykhs whose power transcended their villages and whose renown lasted for many years. The most important spiritual father of these religious figures, Shaykh Muhammad Fanta-Mady Sharif (1874–1955), resided outside the district, in Kankan. Having ancestors from Mauritania who claimed Sharifian descent, Muhammad Sharif's father, Abubakar Sidiki Sharif Haidara, had been considered a Sufi saint and had functioned as the head of the Qadiriyya in the town. Politically, Sidiki Sharif also served as a spiritual advisor of Samori Touré. Thus, ironically for followers in the district of Buguni, Muhammad Sharif grew up in the court of Samori in Bissandugu, where he received formal training in the Qur'an and religious sciences and eventually devoted himself to mysticism. He also witnessed the effects of the Samorian war machine, and this exposure to the brutalities and sufferings of war had the effect of reinforcing his peaceful temperament. Upon Samori's defeat and his father's death, Muhammad Sharif took up residence in Kankan and was initiated into the Qadiriyya. According to Lansine Kaba, he made an immediate impression on people for his "asceticism, generosity and compassion for the underprivileged." In time, aspirant holy men poured into Kankan to consult his voluminous library, study the Qur'an, and receive his blessings.[85]

Sharif's pedigree was further reinforced and legitimated through his ties to such spiritual leaders as Sidiyya Baba and the Mauritanian cleric Sa'ad Bu, whose Fadiliyya network stretched from the Adrar in Mauritania to the Gambia River and deep into the Upper Senegal River Valley. As early as 1908, Sa'ad Bu had sent symbolic gifts to Sharif, including a prayer rug, rosary, turban, and cane and had later initiated Sharif into the Tijaniyya. Muhammad Sharif eschewed all notions of exclusivity among the Sufi turuq and belonged openly to both the Qadiriyya and Tijaniyya, a tradition that his followers in Buguni would adopt. In spite of his mystical bent, though, he was viewed with suspicion by the colonial administration, that is, until he evinced support of the French during the Second World War.[86] Then, after the war, with the rise of the reform movement led by returning al-Azhar students and members of the new popular reformist association Shubban al-muslimin, or Society of Young Muslims, the French depended heavily on Muhammad Sharif in mediating conflicts between so-called Wahhabis and Sufis. Along with Cerno Bokar Salif Tal and Amadou Hampâté Ba, Sharif was considered one of the key figures in the "counter-reform" effort. According to Cardaire, the movement was "under the auspices of Sharif of Kankan," who "appeared to the leaders of the counter-reform as the most important individual in the region."[87]

For most Muslims the name Muhammad Sharif, or Kankan Sekuba, conjures up vague memories. However, for older imams and Muslim notables, Sharif is viewed as a real saint who had access to secrets of the Qur'an. In the postwar period, many Qur'anic students went to Kankan to receive religious instruction, blessings, and bits of these secrets. Louis Brenner has observed that there were hierarchical structures of knowledge and transmission belonging to what he calls an "esoteric episteme." Brenner notes that there were important distinctions between public and secret knowledge and that "all knowledge was not meant to be available to all persons." Access to such secrets was limited, as it could be acquired only "through personal transmission."[88] When educated Muslims spoke of their impressions of Sharif and of his having access to secrets, they were referring to forms of esoteric knowledge that were at the base of religious authority. An exemplary statement went as follows: "The people had recourse to Kankan Sekuba because he had studied a lot. He had learned the Qur'an to the point of fully mastering it. But the Qur'an also contained secrets, and Allah had rendered the secrets easy for Kankan Sekuba. . . . That is why you saw crowds of people going to see him. For Kankan Sekuba, the people considered him as a real saint. Everything that he uttered, truthfully, he knew how to implore Allah. Everything was answered."[89] In the postwar era, given the attractions of Sharif's knowledge, there were large numbers of foreign students in the Qur'anic schools of Kankan. Those who were able to pursue advanced studies with Sharif received secrets and were given white turbans as a distinctive sign of their new authority.[90]

In this way Kankan emerged as the most important extralocal pilgrimage site for Muslims in Buguni. However, in the opposite direction, there were also frequent visitors from Kankan, usually disciples of Muhammad Sharif, who traveled across Buguni collecting alms and gifts. One colonial official reported in 1953 that "an emissary of the Sharif of Kankan has visited most of the villages in the cantons of Basidibé and Bolou, spreading the instructions of the Sharif and collecting alms."[91] Echoing this report, informants in Wasulu recalled that Muhammad Sharif had a network of local holy men who sent out their own disciples to recruit students and collect alms and gifts. One man said, "These moriw sent their disciples to travel around the region. The disciples would go from village to village. Then at the end of the year, they would return to Kankan to give Sekuba all the money they had accumulated during their travels."[92] Holy men linked to Kankan traveled widely and functioned as preachers in their communities, even going door-to-door. A preacher named El Hajj Doumbia had just returned from Mecca to his home in Buguni after more than ten years of living and working in the Near East. An official reported that "[Doumbia] has been leading an ardent campaign of reviving the dormant Muslims, going from hut to hut inviting them to pray. . . . He travels frequently, above all in Guinea, where he has had certain interests near Kankan. His reputation is that of a sage, an intelligent

man, and a hardworking and inexhaustible preacher. He and his family
are the objects of greatest respect in the canton." Many other local but itinerant Sufis whose interests went beyond this-worldly ones also sought to
spread the faith.[93]

Within Buguni the two most prominent disciples of Muhammad
Sharif were Mamadu Touré and Sidiki Fodé Koné, who maintained their
connections with the saint of Kankan until his death. Having evaded
the colonial state's surveillance web for years, Mamadu Touré was first
mentioned in colonial correspondences in 1948, when processes of
Islamization were attributed to his preaching in the village of Koloni. An
official described the local scene as follows: "Under the influence of the
marabout Mamadu Touré of Koloni, the majority of the population is
Islamized. There remain nevertheless a number of fetishists, but they do
not want to recognize it. The case is typical for the village of Koloni, where
no inhabitant wants to declare himself as fetishist." If his political influence had been confined to Koloni, the administration probably would not
have expended much time on him. As his popularity grew beyond Koloni,
however, even spilling over into neighboring districts in Ivory Coast and
Guinea, Touré began sending out large contingents of disciples to collect
gifts in exchange for benedictions and baraji. At any given moment, hundreds of people were reportedly visiting him and returning to their homes
filled with stories of the shaykh's miracles. The French administration
reported on the constant buzz of activity around Koloni: "One must note
the stream created by the numerous visitors that the marabout Mamadu
Toure receives, arriving above all from Ivory Coast and Guinea as well
as many districts of the Sudan." Whereas colonial officials were primarily interested in monitoring potentially territory-wide movements, most
inhabitants sought divine assistance in the mundane concerns of everyday
life.[94] Accordingly, oral traditions emphasize how the shaykh traveled
throughout the region with his entourage, cultivating followers and
leaving miracles in his wake. The imam of Balanfina remembered one
incident when the holy man from Koloni played the role of rainmaker:

> Koloni Touré was one of the major moriw in this area. I met him
> and knew him. He worked with the spirits. Koloni Touré came
> one time here in Balanfina. . . . We had seeded our fields, but the
> rain refused to fall. That day, he stayed in the home of El Hajj

Barijan. He chanted the kalima. After the kalima, the elders of
the village gathered around him and he led prayers asking Allah
for rain. He chanted the kalima again. Toward the end of the
kalima, he said, 'Population of Balanfina, Allah will give you rain
in abundance.' He said this phrase three times: 'Allah has given
you rain.' After the kalima was performed again at night, we went
to sleep. Before the morning, rain was falling in the village! It
rained until places had been inundated.[95]

In many localities, after years of erratic rainfall and famine following
the millet requisitions of the war, people were receptive to the rainmaking
practices of such a powerful mori. Outside of Wasulu, the shaykh's disciples traveled around collecting alms and then eventually settled down to
build their own Qur'anic schools, leading to the development of a highly
ramified and hierarchical web of social networks ultimately centered on
Kankan. Although he attracted a large following, his critics contend that
his main goal was to accumulate material wealth, or "to benefit from
this world."[96] Informants also remembered the shaykh as someone who
carried himself like a king (fàama) and whose exercise of power could
be highly authoritarian. The imam of Tenemakana recalled, "When you
went to see Koloni Touré, you had to lower yourself when walking toward
him . . . or they would beat you. He was very authoritarian. It was because
of the baraka from Kankan Sekuba [but] he had transformed the baraka
into a form of divine power. . . . If you did anything that would bring the
least offense to Koloni Touré, they would beat you seriously."[97] It would
seem that as the power of the canton chiefs was eroded and village chiefs
lost much of their legitimacy and raison d'être, certain Sufi big men were
quick to fill the void, maximizing their social and intellectual capital for
economic gain.

Another Sufi shaykh, Sidiki Fodé Koné, surfaced as the preeminent
figure in the eastern half of the district of Buguni and developed close ties
to holy men in Fulala, including the imam of Tenemakana, Mamadujan
Danyoko. As in the case of Shaykh Touré, his religious celebrity was tied
to his affiliation and spiritual ties to Muhammad Sharif. Having his compound in the village of Kelekele, he founded a large Qur'anic school just
twenty kilometers from the canton of Fulala. Many of my informants had
studied with him. As oral accounts emphasize, after many years of total

obscurity Koné had returned from Kankan and immediately saw his fame skyrocket. Overnight his school near the trade town of Tousseguela was drawing students and disciples from across the southeastern quadrant. Yet he was not considered the one who started prayer in the canton. As in Fulala, there had been other, lesser holy men during the interwar years. For example, there was the blind old mori named Bakari Konaté, who never established a Qur'anic school but was regarded as a wise man and healer. He largely paved the way for later figures, such as Sidiki Koné, by building up a large client base and winning people over to Islamic forms of healing and divination. As in the case of Fula Musa Suntura, Sidiki Koné began his studies as a humble migrant worker in Guinea and eventually ended up in Kankan, studying at the school of Muhammad Sharif. Then, after Sharif "bestowed the white turban," he returned home and quickly rose through the ranks of holy men. By 1956 he had become something of a religious celebrity in Buguni, as one official noted: "A disciple of Sharif of Kankan, Sidiki Koné has grouped around him one hundred students and presently occupies the most important position among the religious personalities of the district of Buguni."[98] Most oral accounts similarly refer to Sidiki's great fame and large following. But informants also emphasized how the shaykh was not instructed and "could not even write his name in Arabic."[99] The imam of Tenemakana recalled the disappointing day when the gathered public witnessed the limits of the shaykh's knowledge:

The day that he returned from Kankan, the *kurana jigin* ceremony was held. They had a new Qur'an, which they took out and gave to Sidiki. Then when the moment came for him to read the *amana* part, Sidiki opened the Qur'an, he turned to the page, *suratu mariyana*, he stared at the page and repeated continually, 'Yes, yes. It is true. It is true,' until the *kurana jigin* ceremony was finished. After that, we said to him, 'You must read the *amana.*' He responded in a quiet voice, 'How do you expect one to finish reading such a long section in a public manner? I cannot do it.' He said that Adama could read it if he wanted, and that he could give commentary verbally. I said to him, 'But it should be the master who reads and comments at the same time in public.' He responded, 'Leave the affair as it is.' He was not able to read the

sura amana on that day of the *kurana jigin* ceremony. That was
how I realized that Sidiki could not even read his own name. Sidiki
had hired a young teacher who gave the courses to the students of
Sidiki, and each year he went around and collected money in this
region that he apparently gave to his master in Kankan.[100]

Indeed, in the postwar era educated Muslims were becoming more
critical of the older generation of supposed magicians, particularly as communities demanded more erudition from Muslim notables. Even in small
rural villages scriptural authority became more closely tied to liturgical
settings. And such public events and rituals required a more substantial
knowledge of the Qur'an. The era when Sufi saints built followings and
achieved local fame by performing miracles and magic was ending.

REFORM AND ANTI-SUFISM

Reformist ideas and their links to power have been present in West Africa
for centuries. One might cite Abdallah Ibn Yasin and the Almoravids in
the eleventh century, 'Abd al-Karim al-Maghili and Songhay in the fifteenth century, and the many reformists involved in the eighteenth- and
nineteenth-century jihads.[101] Islamic reform was not new in the twentieth
century. In the district of Buguni, however, there were few direct linkages
to such histories. And Arabic radio broadcasts and newspapers were a
nonfactor. Rather, Muslims primarily encountered the reform movement
through direct contact with pilgrims returning from Mecca and former
students at al-Azhar. Although Shubban al-muslimin had been founded
in Bamako in 1949 and opened a local chapter in Buguni, there were
few documented reformists in the district before independence. In most
communities, Wahhabis, as my informants called them, were "chased
away" and returned only in the 1970s and 1980s, when they built separate mosques and Qur'anic schools with Saudi backing.[102] Nevertheless,
the challenges posed by the reform movement were real and served to
reshape religious discourses and force confrontations with Sufi religious
authorities.[103]

At a time when the neo-Salafist movements were gaining ground in
French North Africa and the Muslim Brotherhood was becoming increasingly active in Egypt, a few forerunners of reform appeared on the scene in
the French Sudan. The first modern reformists were al-Hajj Abdullah ag

Muhammad and al-Hajj Tiekoro Kamagate, both of whom returned from the Near East during the 1930s and 1940s and began propagating the new ideas. In their preaching they emphasized the oneness of God (*tawhid*), the importance of reading and explaining the Qur'an (*tafsir*) as well as the right of every Muslim to strive to interpret the meanings of the Qur'an, commonly referred to as *ijtihad*.[104] Al-Hajj Tiekoro Kamagate, in particular, was credited with first carrying reformist ideas into southern French Sudan. Owing to the presence of Jula traders, former al-Azhar students, and Mecca pilgrims, the town of Bouaké, Ivory Coast, was one of the centers of the reform movement in the postwar era. In Bouaké, Tiekoro grew in popularity after returning from Mecca in 1944, although he was soon arrested by colonial authorities and confined to his home.[105] The current imam of N'Golobala was introduced to the reform movement while working in Bouaké, where he encountered Tiekoro preaching in a local mosque. At first he was repulsed by their new manner of prayer and their attitude of superiority vis-à-vis other Muslims. He noted that many of the converts to the new piety were young men who had jumped on the reform bandwagon for the prestige it represented, as it was associated with wealthy merchants and perceived Arab styles of dress, including a simple *chemise arabe*, white, brimless skullcap, and a beard. While he never defined himself as a Wahhabi, the imam admitted that people did adopt some of the principles:

> We followed the Wahhabi principles at that time, because we were young and we were curious about the newness of the ideas. . . . El Hajj Tiekoro had the gift of being able to convince people with his words. That was how he introduced Wahhabiyya in Ivory Coast from where it later spread to our region in Mali. But there was a fundamental difference between the principles of Wahhabiyya and that of the kind of Islam that existed before. . . . When El Hajj Tiekoro arrived from Mecca, he convinced the people that all they had learned formerly was false and the only truth was 'the oneness of God' [tawhid]. He taught also what one should do about the Sufi litanies [wurudi]. Because of the differences between him and the numerous moriw in the region, he was not able to emerge victorious, and he also did not live a long time.[106]

Many of the first reformists were inhabitants of trade towns like Garalo-Marka, which boasted fourteen Hajjis, or people who had made the pilgrimage to Mecca, including the Wahhabi El Hajj Musa Diallo, who had been a student at al-Azhar until his repatriation. Upon his return to Buguni, Musa Diallo had tried opening a Wahhabi-inspired mosque and Qur'anic school, but the colonial state stepped in and blocked his efforts. One report stated, "Of profound Wahhabi education, this latter has carefully hidden his game and has requested an authorization to teach. When he was notified of a negative response, the explosion of anger and words by him unveiled without equivocation his true religious position and his state of mind, entirely in keeping with Oriental Pan-Islamism." Given the colonial policy of containment and the perennial fears of Pan-Islamism, the crackdown on Musa Diallo was not unusual. Reformists were normally arrested and kept in their rural homes following their return from Cairo or Mecca.[107]

Despite the weak formal ties to the reform movement, many young Muslims took to heart the condemnation of the excesses of moriya, which the reformists considered *bid'a*, or unlawful innovation. Drawing on strands of Wahhabism imported from Mecca and Salafism from Cairo, reformers attacked Sufis for their reverence of saints, who had falsely served as intermediaries between people and God. They argued that there were no "friends of God" or need for intercessory prayers via holy men. Many reformers viewed Sufi shaykhs as colonial collaborators, as in French North Africa. Thus, there was a certain anticolonial message inherent in the reformist cause. With respect to ordinary people who followed rural holy men, their practices, including the wearing of amulets, were considered idolatry (*shirk*).

Most religious disputes centered on questions of Muslim prayer and ritual rather than of doctrine. In particular, young Muslims adopted the Wahhabi way of praying with arms crossed (*bolomina*). Like other reformists, they were seeking to model themselves on the Prophet Muhammad, who, they believed, had prayed in this manner. This way of praying was slow to gain in popularity in Buguni, as many of its practitioners were forced to leave their villages or revert to praying with their arms straight. Given the eclectic and pluralistic nature of religious practices in this region, it might be surprising that people were bothered by such a subtle difference in ritual. Yet informants indicated that while some people were initially open to the reformist ideas, once the Wahhabis showed their intolerance by criticizing holy men, defiling the tombs of saints, and generating conflict (fitna) between Muslims, they were rejected. They drew on the oft-quoted "No Compulsion" verse of the Qur'an, pointing out the hypocrisy of the proselytizing approach of the Wahhabis, who emphasized the oneness of God and yet sowed discord in Muslim communities.[108] The imam of Tenemakana said, "A person of the Qadiriyya or Tijaniyya sect could pray together without feeling that there was some division in the religion. But once a Wahhabi was at your side in the mosque, you realized that there was division in Islam."[109] In the end, few people declared themselves as Wahhabis during the 1950s. Nevertheless, many young migrants, veterans, and Muslim traders, such as the Kooroko, could not help being exposed to reformist ideas, which they used to pry Islam loose from the controls over knowledge and power that Sufi shaykhs had held. It represented a further elaboration of Muslim identities and a deepening of the scriptural authority of local notables.[110]

In 1959 the first imam of Tenemakana, Mamadujan Danyoko, was on his deathbed in the market town of Kolondieba when suddenly he started reciting the shahada. Shortly after completing his prayers, he passed away. The news spread, and soon the people of Tenemakana came to retrieve his body for burial at his home, where, as in the case of his father, Tumani, his tomb would become a sacred site. But when Mamadujan's family arrived, the people of Kolondieba reportedly argued that his death in their town would bring blessing to their land; his burial would ensure fertility and prosperity. They refused to relinquish the imam's body. Although the Danyoko family felt they had the right to reclaim the body, the town of Kolondieba had grown in strength to such a degree that the use of force was out of the question.[111]

Tenemakana, once an important place in southern Fulala by virtue of its autochthonous status, its powerful kòmò, and its first mosque and Qur'anic school, was now a small farming village of one hundred inhabitants.[112] By contrast, Kolondieba, the capital of the new subdivision, was becoming the regional center, with traders setting up shop and functionaries from Bamako assuming the role of new local rulers. However, beyond marking the end of the colonial period and of the shift of local authority to new nodes of economic and political power, the passing of Mamadujan also represented a sort of changing of the guard. Elsewhere, Muhammad Fanta Mady Sharif, the saint of Kankan, died in 1955. Soon after, Sidiki Koné and Mamadu Touré, the prominent disciples of Sharif and the leading Sufi shaykhs in Buguni, died just before independence. Their passing coincided with the spread of Muslim reform movements, as pilgrims and students returned from Mecca and Egypt with new ideas that would challenge the authority of Sufi holy men and the veneration of saints. An era had ended.

In this narrative of eighty or so years, I have explored the ways in which rural communities became Muslim in one corner of the French empire. Independence did not mark the beginning of an unambiguous Muslim society.[1] Nor did it preclude the possibility of countercurrents and little eddies in the opposite direction.[2] And as a process, the expansion of Islam was far from smooth, linear, or predictable. Thus, in telling this story I have framed Islamization within multiple local contexts, while emphasizing shifts in colonial power relationships and different social temporalities. But, my main contention in this book is that the spread of Islam into rural parts of French Sudan was a multigenerational process that owed much of its dynamism to the mobility of freed slaves, migrant workers, former soldiers, and local holy men.

POSTCOLONIAL ISLAMIC SPHERE, SITES OF MEMORY, AND THE PERSISTENCE OF TRADITION

Today, the former colonial district of Buguni is Muslim. Mosques are found in nearly every village. Ritual life and public holidays are structured around the Islamic calendar, and rites of passage like weddings, funerals, and naming ceremonies are all handled in more Islamic ways. However, these local shifts in the religious habitus have articulated with translocal and transnational currents. Across postcolonial Mali, the Islamic public

251

sphere, as it were, has expanded via electronic and print media, enabling urban and rural Muslims alike to imagine belonging to the larger community of the faithful. This wider diffusion of Muslim religious messages and styles through television, radio, and cassettes has proceeded apace in recent years. It has also benefited from other transformations in civil society, such as the growth of Islamic associations and educational institutions. At the same time, while the Malian government remains secular, the state apparatus has sought to promote public identification with Islam. The result has been the emergence of a more standardized way of being Muslim and supralocal consensus about proper religious conduct and public piety.[3] In rural southern Mali, the values, beliefs, and visible expressions of religious belonging have moved closer to the discursive center of Islam's normative traditions. And increasingly, through religious socialization and ritual, elements of Islamic religious culture have been encoded and embodied in new social norms and cultural styles. However, given the limited access to print media and televisions, the effects of unfolding transnational cultural processes in such rural areas have been very uneven and not nearly as totalizing as one might think.[4]

In the middle of N'Golobala, villagers make sacrifices and leave gifts at the former home and burial place of Fula Musa Suntura. As we have seen, long before becoming a holy man, Fula Musa had been a migrant worker in Ivory Coast. He was not unique in this regard but part of a generation of young men and women who, while performing migrant labor and striving for greater independence vis-à-vis their elders, embraced prayer. Yet Fula Musa had also followed in the footsteps of men like Kojugu Suntura and Tumani Danyoko, both former slaves, who, in the previous generation, had returned from slavery with prayer. Whether migrant workers, slaves, or veterans, many of these social actors became important religious figures in their communities. Trying to explain why a prominent rural Muslim would be buried in his hut rather than in a proper cemetery, an elder explained as follows: "When a person who has been blessed by Allah died, according to the elders, you buried him in his home. Then when some crisis comes to the village, the people would go and do prayers at the tomb."[5] Described in this way, such practices evoke forms of saint worship characteristic of North African societies, with their pilgrimages to visit the tombs of venerated holy men.[6] However, in rural southern French Sudan, there were no mawlids, or annual festivals in honor of Sufi shaykhs, and the worship of saints was limited in scope. These communities of farmers were only tenuously integrated into formal Sufi institutions and brotherhoods.

Instead, the posthumous reverence of local saints fits the mold of pre-colonial village and territorial cults of political ancestors. Often, renowned hunters, chiefs, village founders, and the heads of initiation societies were buried in tombs covered with stones or large trees.[7] In the village of Ten-emakana, behind the women's rice fields, one such burial site continues to draw villagers. Along the riverbed called kòmò-ko, where the kòmò mask and objects were buried, there is *tonjugu*, a large mound with a tree. It is a tomb, but in this case it marks the place where the founder of the village, Bazumana, is buried. In moments of personal crisis people secretively sacrifice a white rooster and ten kola nuts for tonjugu. Then, when the assistance from the ancestors proves successful, they follow up with the sacrifice of a sheep in gratitude. Elsewhere, Muslims have recourse to the old ways and sacred bamana sites hidden deep in the forests. There are deep cultural continuities and a certain persistence of tradition beneath the more visible shifts in the religious landscape.

COMPARATIVE PERSPECTIVES

In exploring the contingent nature of shifts in religious practice and iden-tification, I have situated local histories within regional contexts. I have tried to show how religious change at the village level stemmed from an accelerated pace of social transactions and exchanges, through which group differences and pressures led to conflicts and challenges to existing practices, beliefs, and norms. Depending on a multitude of factors, such as extralocal links via forms of mobility, communities became Muslim in various ways. In the canton of Fulala, most villages were left in ruins after the wars of Samori, and many people ended up in slavery. Although the region was far removed from main trade routes, slavery and emancipation resulted in the expansion of Islam among predominantly decentralized agrarian societies. These processes were reproduced in the neighboring cantons of Céndugu and Gwancédugu. Later, during the interwar years, as young people started migrating to find work in Ivory Coast, Senegal, and Guinea, aspiring Qur'anic students also left the area to study outside the canton. After the Second World War, as labor migration to Ivory Coast became a routine household survival strategy, numerous rural schools and

mosques spread across Fulala, opening the way for deeper religious transformations and the emergence of Muslim chiefs, holy men, and public
prayer. Things were very different in the Senufo canton of Niené. First of
all, parts of the region had been spared the worst warfare and depredation
in the late nineteenth century, partly owing to the region's remote location. As a result, far fewer people were initially enslaved, which meant that
emancipation did not translate into a sizeable influx of Muslim returnees,
at least not on the scale of Fulala, Céndugu, and Gwancédugu. At the
same time, the more insular Senufo communities were slower to embrace
labor migration, and when people did start migrating to Ivory Coast they
opted for short-term, circular migration. But even as young migrants
started bringing back prayer, Qur'anic education, Sufi holy men, and
mosques were few in number, even in the 1950s. In western parts of the
district, Islamization processes began earlier. The southwestern canton of
Gwanan and the trade towns of Garalo and Tenetu had been Muslim since
the late nineteenth century. However, they were anomalies. Still, in the
canton of Basidibé, because of its greater proximity to Guinea, itinerant
Sufi holy men and Muslim traders from Kankan played an important role
in introducing Islam into the region. And long before other regions northern Wasulu was sending migrants to the peanut zones of Senegal and
the Gambia. As rainy season migrants who often stayed a few years, they
assimilated into the local cultural ways of their hosts. Correspondingly,
with these early connections to Kankan and the peanut zone, Qur'anic
education and mosques began expanding in Basidibé in the interwar
years.

Although the aims of this book have been limited in geographical
scope, the processes examined transcended national borders and territorial frontiers.[8] In certain African settings Islamization in rural areas
was due to the activities of itinerant Sufi holy men, traders, and chiefs.
However, there is also evidence that across the continent more subaltern
social actors, such as slaves and migrant workers, played equally important roles. Among the Yoruba in British Nigeria, J. D. Y. Peel notes that of
"the two principal vectors of Islam," Muslim slaves were the more important in carrying Islam from Oyo further into the forest belt.[9] Deeper in
the hinterland, in French Upper Volta, slaves and migrants represented
an important population of early supposed converts to Islam among the
Mossi in the 1950s. As we have seen, these processes have also been

noted in other parts of French West Africa.[10] In East Africa, research on the Swahili coast has shown how the spread of Islam into upcountry regions followed paths similar to the sorts I have been exploring in rural French Sudan. At first, Islamization was linked to the caravan trade from the coast in the nineteenth century. As in West Africa, many of the new-comers to the faith were traders. But they were also slaves, porters, and migrants. Thus, increasingly, rural Islamization in East Africa resulted from the further expansion of commercial networks as well as inter-spersed settlement patterns. As Muslims established rural communities and local peoples began frequenting trade towns, the increased interac-tions between Muslims and non-Muslims opened the way for possible religious change.[11]

In examining the social dynamics of these changes in East Africa and the agency of slaves, Jonathon Glassman has shown how subaltern groups often converted in order to avoid being enslaved or to have access to trade. In time, their sense of Muslim identity deepened, despite the efforts of town-born Swahili patricians to marginalize them. For elites, Islam had served as a marker of social distinction separating them from their slaves and other allegedly uncivilized rural peoples. They saw auto-conversion of social subordinates as a form of theft of knowledge and status that properly belonged to them. But in the end slaves and other upcountry folk adopted new Muslim styles of dress and combined Islamic practices with their own rituals, which, in turn, contributed to the shaping of religious life and notions of Swahili citizenship in the towns.[12] Aside from slavery, the spread of Islam also followed forms of return migration. This pattern was common among the upper Pokomo in the Tana River region, from which young men began migrating in the late nineteenth century to find work. By the early twentieth century, after years of working alongside Muslims, they introduced Islamic religious practices into their homelands. Similarly, in southeastern Tanzania, migrants fetched the new religion from coastal towns and brought it back to their rural homes in the early twentieth century.[13]

Although the spread of Islam in Asia is far beyond the scope of this book, scholars have highlighted the role of ordinary people. For example, in explaining Islamization processes in the Malaysian archipelago, Mar-shall G. S. Hodgson observed, "Islam penetrated inland first among the lower classes, at least in the small towns . . . giving these humbler folk a more egalitarian equivalent to the proud Hinduism of the gentry."[14] Elsewhere in South Asia, scholars have similarly noted the importance of grass-roots processes of Islamization, and in particular the inconveniences of caste as a motivating factor behind conversion.[15] Still, one of the unique ways in which Africanists can contribute to studies of Muslim societies is through their access to case studies and histories of more recent Islamization processes in rural areas that have long been lost from view in the Arabic-speaking heartland of the Middle East and much of Asia. Such studies of Islam are crucial in the larger project to deprovincialize Islamic history while bringing more realistic accounts of religious change to light.[16] Much remains to be done to expand scholars' understanding of processes of Islamization. I hope my book will be an aid toward that end.

CONVERSION REVISITED

The story I have told is one of gradual religious drift. As such, conversion, as the movement across clear religious boundaries, is rather difficult to pinpoint. I have identified community-wide turning points and nominal shifts in religious identification. However, generally, I have moved away from the conversion concept. On an individual level, people were Muslim when they self-identified as such or prayed. But such subjective perspectives elide the deeper social dimensions of religious change that have been the subject of this book. Given the complexities of networks, layers of cultural translation, and small-group dynamics, how does one locate conversion socially and temporally? Does conversion mean subscribing to a more or less recognizable way of being Muslim? I have attempted to show how the embrace of Islam often proceeded in an ad hoc and incremental way. And among decentralized societies, with their fluid and polyvalent cultures of orality, even as Muslim ritual practices and techniques were adopted, converts did not necessarily internalize the core values, beliefs, cosmological orientations, and social rules commonly associated with Islam. Such processes were always characterized by a certain mutual assimilation: Islam was indigenized as much as rural communities were Islamized.[17]

Furthermore, grass-roots Islamization was embedded in larger social, agrarian, and political transformations. Within the context of forces and events such as war, colonialism, drought, and famine, religious changes reflected subtle shifts in local engagements with theodicy. Integrally linked to concerns over human and agricultural fertility, religious adjustments aimed at explaining suffering, misfortune, and the cruelties of humankind, while striving to increase community welfare and potential well-being. Peasants embraced prayer in an effort to secure more advantageous political identities and social affiliations in times of uncertainty.[18]

As we have seen, these profound religious changes overlapped with colonial rule. The relationship between French empire and religious difference was always ambiguous. Even as the French approached religious questions in a pragmatic way to maintain colonial order, there were crosscutting networks and connections within and across the empire. Relationships with Muslims ranged widely from friendship, accommodation, and tacit alliance to indifference, mistrust, and hostility. This also described rapport with other religions, including Christianity, as French officials dealt with problems of governance, legitimacy, lack of manpower, and concerns over potential rebellion.[19] Still, under French rule the expansion of Islam across rural Africa represented a major and unprecedented transformation. In the end, perhaps the most lasting legacy of colonialism was that it ushered in a new religious era by providing the circumstances in which Islam flourished. And in this process rural Africans played the leading roles.

All terms are in Bamanankan, unless indicated as French (Fr), Wolof (Wf), or
  Arabic (Ar).

aladeli—invocation of Allah

alasira—"religion" or "path of Allah"

baara-nyini—migrant worker

bamana—those who speak Bamanankan, often considered non-Muslim

baraji—divine recompense

baraka (Ar)—divine blessing or charisma among Muslim holy men

bid'a (Ar)—unlawful religious innovation

bilakoro—"uncircumcised boy," also low-level infantry in Samorian army

boli—power object or "fetish"

buranci—marriage via labor service

champ du commandant (Fr)—"field of the administrator," compulsory cotton field

commandant (Fr)—top French colonial official at the district (*cercle*) level

dalilu—esoteric knowledge

danbé—family honor or dignity

dasiri—village protective spirit site

dendankana—system of marriage

deuxième portion (Fr)—long-term forced labor

dhikr (Ar)—Sufi recitation or litany

dòlò—millet beer

doma—healer or religious specialist

donba—celebration of the Prophet Muhammad's birth

donso—hunter

dugukolotigi—"landowner," group claiming autochthonous status

dugutigi—village chief
fadenya—rivalry between people of the same paternal bloodline
falen-ni-falen—marriage by bride exchange practice
filantòn—age-set
fitna (Ar)—conflict or discord in Muslim community
fòn—bodily or facial scar
fòròba—common field
furuwari—bridewealth or bride price
gongon-nyo kòngò—famine caused by colonial millet requisitions
hadith (Ar)—traditions on the actions and sayings of the Prophet Muhammad
hadiya (Ar)—gift or offering
hajj (Ar)—pilgrimage to Mecca
hòròn—noble
imam (Ar)—Muslim prayer leader in mosque
indigénat (Fr)—system of colonial summary "native" justice and punishment
ijtihâd (Ar)—"systemic original thinking," or individual interpretation of
    religious texts
jamanatigi—canton chief
jamu—family or clan name
jatigi—host, usually in context of migration or resettlement
jeli—bard
jihad (Ar)—"struggle" or "effort," usually holy war
jiné—spirit
jò—initiation group, power association, or power object
jòn—slave
jònfòrò—individual field, or "slave field"
jònyàjuru—colonialism, meaning literally "the rope of slavery"
jula—trader
kabila—clan
kafir—non-Muslim, unbeliever, or pagan
kafo—small precolonial state
kalima—profession of faith
kankònòla—hybrid form of knowledge combining the Qur'an and bamanaya
karâmât (Ar)—miracles attributed to Sufis
karamògò—Qur'anic teacher
kékoro—"tradition" or "old ways"
kòmò—men's secret power association
kòmòtigi—head of the *kòmò* power association
koroté—evil spell, curse, or poison
laada (Ar)—custom or tradition
laptots (Wf)—sailors in the Senegal River trade
lasigiden—canton representative
mahr (Ar)—bride gifts
madrasa (Ar)—large Islamic school

marabout (Ar and Fr)—Muslim holy man
misidaba—plow
mori—Muslim holy man
muqaddam (Ar)—"deputy" of Sufi order authorized to initiate new members
muso-kòmò—women's power association
nawétaan (Wf)—migrant peanut farmer in Senegal, "he who passes the
     rainy season"
négéso—bicycle, "iron horse"
nisòngò—head tax, or "soul price"
numu—blacksmith
nyamakala—person of caste
prestations (Fr)—form of local and short-term forced labor
qadi (Ar)—Islamic judge
saraka—sacrifice or gift
sébén—powerful amulet
senankuya—"joking relationship"
sénékéla—cultivator
seyiba—Muslim saint
shari'a (Ar)—Islamic law
shaykh (Ar)—Sufi master
siya—regional or "ethnic" scar or marking
sofa—Samorian soldier
sotigi—household or lineage head
subagaya—sorcery
sun kalo—the month of fasting, Ramadan
sura (Ar)—verse of Qur'an
tabaski (Ar)—commemoration of Ibrahim's sacrifice of the ram
tako—"individualism"
tana—clan taboo
tariqa (Ar)—Sufi order or "way"
tata—mud wall fortification
tigiya—"ownership"
tirailleur (Fr)—African colonial soldier
tomo—village ruins
tòn—youth association
tònòmada—pawnship
'ulama (Ar)—class of Muslim scholars
umma (Ar)—worldwide Muslim community
wali (Ar)—Muslim saint
wird (Ar)—Sufi recitations
woloso—"house-born," or second-generation slave
zakat (Ar)—alms
zâwiya (Ar)—Sufi lodge or gathering place

INTRODUCTION

1. Although in 1911 there had been an itinerant holy man who married a local woman in Diaka and tried preaching. He was arrested and imprisoned by the colonial administration. *Archives Nationales du Mali* (ANM) *Fonds Anciens*, RP, August 1911, IE28.

2. This opening narrative is based on interviews with Bakari Koné's sister, nephew, and a non–family member from Diaka. Interviews are cited as follows: Name, Village, and Date: Mariame Koné, Tenemakana, 15 May 2002, and Yacouba Danyoko, 14 November 2002. People actually referred to the shahada as the *kalima* or *al-kalimat at-tayyiba* (the blessed word,) which comprises the profession of faith: *La-ilaha il-allah muhammadur rasul-allah* (There is no god but Allah, Muhammad is the messenger of Allah).

3. Mariame Koné, Tenemakana, 15 May 2002.

4. Marcel Cardaire, *L'Islam et le Terroir Africain* (Bamako, 1954), 57.

5. On habitus, see Pierre Bourdieu, *Outline of a Theory of Practice* (Cambridge, 1977), 72–95.

6. David Forgacs, ed., *An Antonio Gramsci Reader: Selected Writings, 1916–1935* (New York, 1988), 225–30, 430–31; and Stuart Hall, "Gramsci's Relevance for the Study of Race and Ethnicity," in D. Morley and K-H. Chen, eds., *Stuart Hall: Critical Dialogues in Cultural Studies* (London, 1996), 411–40.

7. On state-spaces, see James Scott, *The Art of Not Being Governed: An Anarchist History of Upland Southeast Asia* (New Haven, 2009).

8. Ian Hacking, *Historical Ontology* (Cambridge, 2002), 99–114; and I. Hacking, "The Looping Effect of Human Kinds," in D. Sperber et al., eds., *Causal Cognition: An Interdisciplinary Approach* (Oxford, 1996), 351–83.

9. J. D. Y. Peel, *Religious Encounter and the Making of the Yoruba* (Indiana, 2000), 1–26.

10. David Robinson, *Paths of Accommodation: Muslim Societies and French Authorities in Senegal and Mauritania, 1880–1920* (Athens, 2000). On empire-states, see Frederick Cooper, *Colonialism in Question: Theory, Knowledge, History* (Berkeley, 2005). On the Napoleonic expedition, see Jacques Fremeaux, *La France et l'Islam depuis 1789* (Paris, 1991); Henry Laurens, *L'expédition d'Egypte, 1798–1801* (Paris, 1997); and Edward Said, *Orientalism* (New York, 1978). On wider connections, see Jean-Loup Amselle, *Affirmative Exclusion: Cultural Pluralism and the Rule of Custom in France* (Ithaca, 2003).

11. See Christopher Harrison, *France and Islam in West Africa, 1860–1960* (Cambridge, 1988); and Louis Brenner, *Controlling Knowledge: Religion, Power, and Schooling in a West African Muslim Society* (Bloomington, 2001). On French empire in the Arab world, see Julia Clancy-Smith, *Rebel and Saint: Muslim Notables, Populist Protest, and Colonial Encounters in Algeria and Tunisia, 1800–1904* (Berkeley, 1994); Charles-Robert Ageron, *Histoire de l'Algérie Contemporaine, 1830–1964* (Paris, 1964), and *Les Algériens musulmanes et la France, 1871–1919* (Paris, 1968); Edmund Burke III, "The Image of the Moroccan State in French Ethnological Literature: A New Look at the Origins of Lyautey's Berber Policy," in E. Gellner and C. Micaud, eds., *Arabs and Berbers: From Tribe to Nation in North Africa* (London, 1972); Elizabeth Thompson, *Colonial Citizens: Republican Rights, Paternal Privilege, and Gender in French Syria and Lebanon* (Columbia, 2000); and Matthew Connelly, *A Diplomatic Revolution: Algeria's Fight for Independence and the Origins of the Post–Cold War Era* (New York, 2002). On cultural and racial difference in France, see Tyler Stovall and Sue Peabody, eds., *The Color of Liberty: Histories of Race in France* (Durham, 2003); and Herman Lebovics, *True France: The Wars over Cultural Identity, 1900–1945* (Ithaca, 1994).

12. A. Gouilly, *L'Islam dans l'Afrique Occidentale Française* (Paris, 1952), 247–75. On religion and rebellion, see also Mahir Saul and Patrick Royer, *West African Challenge to Empire: Culture and History in the Volta-Bani Anticolonial War* (Athens, 2001).

13. David Robinson and Jean-Louis Triaud, eds., *Le Temps des Marabouts: Itinéraires et stratégies islamiques en Afrique occidentale française* (Paris, 1997).

14. J. P. Daughton, *An Empire Divided: Religion, Republicanism, and the Making of French Colonialism, 1880–1914* (Oxford, 2006); and Joseph-Roger de Benoist, *Eglise et Pouvoir Colonial au Soudan Français* (Paris, 1987).

15. See Gary Wilder, *The French Imperial Nation-State: Negritude and Colonial Humanism between the Two World Wars* (Chicago, 2005); and Eugen Weber, *Peasants into Frenchmen: The Modernization of Rural France, 1870–1914* (Stanford, 1976). On the "civilizing mission" and its contradictions, see Alice Conklin, *A Mission to Civilize: The Republican Idea of Empire in France and West Africa, 1895–1930* (Stanford, 1997).

16. For an overview of Islamization processes in East Africa, see David Sperling, "The Coastal Hinterland and Interior of East Africa," in Nehemia Levtzion and

Randall Pouwels, eds., *The History of Islam in Africa* (Athens, 2000), 273–302; and Randall Pouwels, *Horn and Crescent: Cultural Change and Traditional Islam on the East African Coast, 800–1900* (Cambridge, 1987).

17. J. C. Froelich, "Essai sur les Causes et Méthodes de l'Islamisation de l'Afrique de l'Ouest du Xie au XIXe Siècle," in I. M. Lewis, ed., *Islam in Tropical Africa* (Oxford, 1966).

18. See Robinson, *Paths of Accommodation;* Charles Stewart, "Colonial Justice and the Spread of Islam in the Early Twentieth Century," in David Robinson and Jean-Louis Triaud, eds., *Le temps des marabouts;* Robert Launay and Benjamin Soares, "The Formation of an 'Islamic Sphere' in French Colonial West Africa," *Economy and Society* 28 (1999), 497–519; C. C. Stewart, "Popular Islam in Twentieth-Century Africa," *Africa: Journal of the International African Institute* 55, 4 (1985), 365.

19. This is not to say that scholars have been blind to the role of ordinary people in the expansion of Islam. For example, in southern Mali, Jean-Loup Amselle cites "migrants and former soldiers" in Islamization processes in the district of Buguni. *Mestizo Logics: Anthropology of Identity in Africa and Elsewhere* (Stanford, 1998), 125; and Amselle, *Les Négociants de la Savane: Histoire et organisation sociale des Kooroko* (Paris, 1977), 239–52. And Martin Klein comments that in the region of Wasulu "Islamization is recent, probably linked to migration." *Slavery and Colonial Rule in French West Africa* (Cambridge, 1998), 313–97. However, neither provides in-depth discussion of these processes. On labor migration and conversion in French West Africa, see also Richard Warms, "Merchants, Muslims, and Wahhabiyya: The Elaboration of Islamic Identity in Sikasso, Mali," *Canadian Journal of African Studies* 26, 3 (1992), 485–507; Danielle Jonckers, "Le temps de prier est venu: Islamisation et pluralité religieuse dans le sud du Mali," *Journal des Africanistes* 68, 1–2 (1998), 21–45; Peter Mark, "Urban Migration, Cash Cropping, and Calamity: The Spread of Islam among the Diola of Boulouf (Senegal), 1900–1940," *African Studies Review* 21, 2 (1978), 1–14. Most studies of conversion tend to emphasize the role of elites and states. Foundational works include Nehemia Levtzion, ed., *Conversion to Islam* (New York, 1979); and Richard Bulliet, *Conversion to Islam in the Medieval Period: An Essay in Quantitative History* (Harvard, 1979). More recently, see Marc David Baer, *Honored by the Glory of Islam: Conversion and Conquest in Ottoman Europe* (Oxford, 2008), which, despite its remarkable contributions to the literature, approaches the question of conversion from the viewpoint of the converters rather than the converted and thus tends to reinforce the top-down model.

20. Louis Brenner uses the notion of "Islamic religious culture" as a way of reframing religious histories in Africa with an eye to heterogeneity within Islam and histories of wider religious pluralism. See "Histories of Religion in Africa," *Journal of Religion in Africa*, 30, 2 (2000), 143–67.

21. Jonathon Glassman, *Feasts and Riot: Revelry, Rebellion, and Popular Consciousness on the Swahili Coast, 1856–1888* (Portsmouth, 1995), 134.

22. See J. D. Y. Peel, *Aladura: A Religious Movement among the Yoruba* (London, 1968), and "Conversion and Tradition in Two African Societies: Ijebu

and Buganda," *Past and Present* 77 (1977), 108–41; Jean Comaroff and
John Comaroff, *Of Revelation and Revolution: Christianity, Colonialism and
Consciousness in South Africa,* vol. 1 (Chicago, 1992); P. Landau, *The Realm of
the Word: Language, Gender and Christianity in a Southern African Kingdom*
(Portsmouth, 1995), and " 'Religion' and Christian Conversion in African
History: A New Model," *Journal of Religious History* 23, 1 (1999), 8–30; Lamin
Sanneh, *Translating the Message: The Missionary Impact on Culture* (Maryknoll,
1989); and Thomas O. Beidelman, *Colonial Evangelism: A Socio-Historical
Study of an East African Mission at the Grassroots* (Bloomington, 1982). See also
G. Viswanathan, *Outside the Fold: Conversion, Modernity and Belief* (Berkeley,
1998); and N. Dirks, *Castes of Mind: Colonialism and the Making of Modern India*
(Princeton, 2001).

23. Comaroff and Comaroff, *Of Revelation and Revolution,* 248–51. On questions of
choice in religious self-identification in Muslim communities in northern Ivory
Coast, see Robert Launay, *Beyond the Stream: Islam and Society in a West African
Town* (Berkeley, 1992), 22–35.

24. Peel, *Religious Encounter,* 216.

25. Horton, "African Conversion," *Africa* 41 (1971), 85-108; "On the Rationality
of Conversion: Part One," *Africa* 45 (1975), 219-35; and "On the Rationality of
Conversion: Part Two," *Africa* 45 (1975), 373-99.

26. See Humphrey Fisher in "Conversion Reconsidered: Some Historical Aspects
of Religious Conversion in Black Africa," *Africa* 43 (1973), 27-40, and "The
Juggernaut's Apologia: Conversion to Islam in Black Africa," *Africa* 55 (1985),
153-73; Robert Hefner, "Introduction: World Building and the Rationality
of Conversion," in R. Hefner, ed., *Conversion to Christianity: Historical and
Anthropological Perspectives on a Great Transformation* (Berkeley, 1993), 22–23.

27. Peel, *Religious Encounter,* 3.

28. James Searing, "Conversion to Islam: Military Recruitment and Generational
Conflict in a Sereer-Safèn Village (Bandia), 1920–38," *JAH* 44 (2003), 73–94.

29. On models, see Fisher, "Conversion Reconsidered"; Spencer Trimingham, *Islam
in West Africa* (Oxford, 1959), and *A History of Islam in West Africa* (Oxford,
1962); as well as Timothy Insoll, *The Archaeology of Islam in Sub-Saharan Africa*
(Cambridge, 2003), 27–32. On precolonial contexts, see D. Robinson, *The Holy
War of Umar Tal* (Oxford, 1985); M. Hiskett, *The Sword of Truth* (Oxford, 1973);
M. Klein, *Islam and Imperialism in Senegal* (Stanford, 1971); L. Sanneh, *The
Jakhanke: The History of an Islamic Clerical People of the Senegambia* (London,
1979); R. Roberts, *Warriors, Merchants, and Slaves* (Stanford, 1987); and Charles
Stewart, *Islam and Social Order in Mauritania* (Oxford, 1973). For more specific
focus on the spread of Islam, see J. R. Willis, *Studies in West African Islam,* Vol. 1:
The Cultivators of Islam (London, 1979); and Levtzion, ed., *Conversion to Islam.*

30. Launay and Soares, "The Formation of an 'Islamic Sphere,' " 497–519. See also,
R. Launay, *Traders without Trade: Responses to Change in Two Dyula Communities*
(Cambridge, 1982).

31. Scott, *The Art of Not Being Governed,* 166.

32. On roads and states, see Jeffrey Herbst, *States and Power in Africa: Comparative Lessons in Authority and Control* (Princeton, 2000); and on colonial states, Bruce Berman and John Lonsdale, *Unhappy Valley: Conflict in Kenya and Africa*, book 1: *State and Class*, and book 2: *Violence and Ethnicity* (London, 1992); Richard Roberts, *Two Worlds of Cotton: Colonialism and the Regional Economy in the French Soudan, 1800–1946* (Stanford, 1996); Mahmood Mamdani, *Citizen and Subject: Contemporary Africa and the Legacy of Late Colonialism* (Princeton, 1996); and Crawford Young, *The African Colonial State in Comparative Perspective* (New Haven, 1994).

33. On migrant labor in French West Africa, see François Manchuelle, *Willing Migrants: Soninke Labor Diasporas, 1848–1960* (Athens, 1997); and Dennis Cordell, Joel W. Gregory, and Victor Piché, *Hoe and Wage: A Social History of a Circular Migration System in West Africa* (Boulder, 1996). On the politics around African labor, see Frederick Cooper, *Decolonization and African Society: The Labor Question in French and British Africa* (Cambridge, 1996).

34. Babacar Fall, *Le Travail Forcé en Afrique occidentale française, 1900–1945* (Paris, 1993).

35. On the linkages between spiritual and temporal power, see Stephen Ellis and Gerrie Ter Haar, *Worlds of Power: Religious Thought and Political Practice in Africa* (Oxford, 2004).

36. See, for example, Donal Cruise O'Brien and Christian Coulon, eds., *Charisma and Brotherhood in African Islam* (Oxford, 1988); David Robinson and Jean-Louis Triaud, eds., *La Tijâniyya: Une confrérie musulmane à la conquête de l'Afrique* (Paris, 2000); Louis Brenner, *West Africa Sufi: The Religious Heritage and Spiritual Search of Cerno Bokar Taal* (Berkeley, 1984); and Alioune Traoré, *Islam et colonisation en Afrique: Cheikh Hamahoullah, homme de foi et résistant* (Paris, 1983).

37. The anthropologist Robert Launay emphasizes what he calls "Sufism Degree Zero" among the Dyula in northern Ivory Coast. See *Beyond the Stream;* and also A. Masquelier, *Prayer Has Spoiled Everything: Possession, Power, and Identity in an Islamic Town of Niger* (Durham, 2001).

38. N. Levtzion and H. Fisher, eds., *Rural and Urban Islam in West Africa* (Boulder, 1986).

39. Robinson, *Paths of Accommodation;* Robinson and Triaud, eds., *Le Temps des Marabouts;* Harrison, *France and Islam;* and Brenner, *Controlling Knowledge.*

40. On blind spots, see Steven Feierman, "Colonizers, Scholars, and the Creation of Invisible Histories," in V. Bonnell and L. Hunt, eds., *Beyond the Cultural Turn* (Berkeley, 1999), 189.

41. Cheikh Anta Babou, *Fighting the Greater Jihad: Amadou Bamba and the Founding of the Muridiyya of Senegal, 1853–1913* (Athens, 2007); and James Searing, *God Alone Is King: Islam and Emancipation in Senegal: The Wolof Kingdoms of Kajoor and Bawol, 1859–1914* (Portsmouth, 2002). The literature on the Muridiyya and Islam in Senegal is far too voluminous to cite here. However, see Donal B. Cruise O'Brien, *The Mourides of Senegal: The Political and Economic Organization*

of an Islamic Brotherhood in Senegal (Oxford, 1971); Jean Copans, *Les marabouts de l'arachide: la Confrérie mouride et les paysans du Sénégal* (Paris, 1980); Christian Coulon, *Le marabout et le prince: Islam et pouvoir au Sénégal* (Paris, 1981); and Leonardo Villalòn, *Islamic Society and State Power in Senegal: Disciples and Citizens in Fatick* (Cambridge, 1995).

42. On the French Sudan, see Brenner, *West Africa Sufi;* Benjamin Soares, *Islam and the Prayer Economy: History and Authority in a Malian Town* (Ann Arbor, 2005); Jonckers, "Le temps de prier est venu"; and Stephen Harmon, "The Expansion of Islam among the Bambara Under French Rule, 1890 to 1940," Ph.D. diss., University of California, Los Angeles, 1988. Sean Hanretta explores the entire colonial period, with important insights into postwar developments in Ivory Coast. See *Islam and Social Change in French West Africa: History of an Emancipatory Community* (Cambridge, 2009). On the Sahel, see also Barbara Cooper, *Evangelical Christians in the Muslim Sahel* (Indiana, 2006).

43. Stephen Humphreys, *Islamic History: A Framework for Inquiry* (Princeton, 1991), 274. Some more recent works show a renewed interest in conversion to Islam or questions of changing religious identities. See Jonathan Berkey, *The Formation of Islam: Religion and Society in the Near East, 600–1800* (Cambridge, 2003); Mercedes Garcia-Arenal, ed., *Conversions Islamiques: Identités religieuses en Islam méditerranéen* (Paris, 2001); and Selim Deringil, "There Is No Compulsion in Religion: On Conversion and Apostasy in the Late Ottoman Empire, 1839–1856," *CSSH* 42 (2000).

44. William Cummings notes that the study of conversion to Islam in Asia is still "in its infancy." See "Scripting Islamization: Arabic Texts in Early Makassar," *Ethnohistory* 48, 2001; and also Stephen Dale, "Trade, Conversion and the Growth of the Islamic Community of Kerala, South India," *Studia Islamica* 71 (1990).

45. Richard Eaton, *The Rise of Islam and the Bengal Frontier, 1204–1760* (Berkeley, 1993), and *Essays on Islam and Indian History* (Oxford, 2003).

46. See E. Ullmann-Margalit, "Big Decisions: Opting, Converting, Drifting," in Anthony O'Hear, ed., *Political Philosophy* (Cambridge, 2006); David N. Gellner, "The Emergence of Conversion in a Hindu–Buddhist Polytropy: The Kathmandu Valley, Nepal, c. 1600–1995," *CSSH* 47 (2005), 755–80.

47. David Schwartz, *Culture and Power: The Sociology of Pierre Bourdieu* (Chicago, 1997), 95–115.

48. P. Bourdieu, *The Logic of Practice* (Stanford, 1990), 53, and *Outline*, 83.

49. C. Calhoun, "Habitus, Field, and Capital: The Question of Historical Specificity," in C. Calhoun, E. LiPuma, and M. Postone, eds., *Bourdieu: Critical Perspectives* (Chicago, 1993), 61–88.

50. Bourdieu, *Outline*, 87.

51. William Sewell, *The Logic of History: Social Theory and Social Transformation* (Chicago, 2005), 141.

52. Clifford, *Routes: Travel and Translation in the Late Twentieth Century* (Harvard, 1997), 17–91. See also James Ferguson, *Expectations of Modernity: Myths and*

Meanings of Urban Life on the Zambian Copperbelt (Berkeley, 1999), which makes use of habitus in studying migrant worker subcultures.

53. Shaw, *Memories of the Slave Trade: Ritual and the Historical Imagination in Sierra Leone* (Chicago, 2002), 4–5.

54. See Insoll, *The Archaeology of Islam;* and Lamin Sanneh, "Translatability in Islam and in Christianity in Africa: A Thematic Approach," in T. Blakely, ed., *Religion in Africa: Experience and Expression* (Portsmouth, 1994).

55. Rapport Politique, 1957 Annual, ANM 1E10.

56. For a basic statement on this perspective, see Carlo Ginzburg, "Microhistory: Two or Three Things that I Know About It," *Critical Inquiry* 20 (1993); Edward Muir, "Introduction: Observing Trifles," in his edited volume *Microhistory and the Lost Peoples of Europe* (Baltimore, 1991); and Giovanni Levi, "On Microhistory," in Peter Burke, ed., *New Perspectives on Historical Writing* (Cambridge, 1991).

57. J. Revel, "Micro-analyse et construction du social," in J. Revel, ed., *Jeux d'échelles: la micro-analyse à l'experience* (Paris, 1996), 15–36. Quoted in Sewell, *The Logic of History*, 76–77.

58. See T.C. McKaskie, *Asante Identities: History and Identity in an African Village, 1850–1950* (London, 2000), 19–23.

59. The French colonial botanist A. Aubréville referred to this region as "Sudano-Guinean." See *Flore Forestière Soudano-Guinéenne, A.O.F.* (Paris, 1950). See G. Brasseur, *Étude de Géographie Régionale: Le Village de Tenentou (Mali)*, Bulletin I.F.A.N. (Dakar, 1961), 4–13. For an intriguing environmental-historical study of southern Guinea, see also James Fairhead and Melissa Leach, *Misreading the African Landscape: Society and Ecology in a Forest–Savanna Mosaic* (Cambridge, 1996).

60. Rapport Politique, 1894, ANM 1E27.

61. Typically, the dry season runs from November to May and the rainy season from June to October. Rainfall patterns are highly variable, in terms of both timing and spatial distribution, with somewhere between eight hundred and fourteen hundred millimeters per year. See also *Carte de l'Afrique de l'Ouest, République du Mali*, l'Institut Géographique National (Paris, 1955). For a more detailed look at contemporary southern Mali, see Pascal Schneider, *Sauvegarde et aménagement de la forêt classée de Farako, Région de Sikasso, Mali-Sud* (Zurich, 1996). For a useful model of environmental history among decentralized societies that examines ecocultural boundaries, see Robert Harms, *Games Against Nature: An Eco-Cultural History of the Nunu of Equatorial Africa* (Cambridge, 1987).

62. Brasseur, *Étude*, 12–13.

63. P. Marty, *Études sur l'Islam et les Tribus du Soudan*, 4 vols. (Paris, 1920).

64. Viviana Pâques, "Bouffons Sacrés du Cercle de Bougouni (Soudan Français)," *Journal de la Société des Africanistes* 24, 1 (1954), 81–87.

65. M. Méker, *Le Temps Colonial* (Dakar, 1980).

66. Ann Laura Stoler, *Along the Archival Grain: Epistemic Anxieties and Colonial Common Sense* (Princeton, 2009), 17–53.

67. See Marty, *Études sur l'Islam;* and Harrison, *France and Islam.*

68. L. White, *Comforts of Home: Prostitution in Colonial Nairobi* (Chicago, 1990), 21–28; and *Speaking with Vampires: Rumor and History in Colonial Africa* (Berkeley, 2000), 91.

69. Rapport du recensement, Foulala, 1951–52, ANM IE10.

70. Rapport de tournée, Foulala, 1912, ANM IE28.

71. Yusuf Coulibaly, Tenemakana, 16 May 2002.

72. On generation and oral history, see Jean Allman and Victoria Tashjian, *"I Will Not Eat Stone": A Women's History of Colonial Asante* (Portsmouth, 2000), xxxi–xxxiv.

73. Amadou Sidibe, Solona, 10 April 2002.

74. Namakoro Bamba, Kolondieba, 7 July 2002.

75. Hawa Diallo, Tenemakana, 13 May 2002.

76. Broulaye Doumbia, Tenemakana, 13 May 2002.

77. Jan Vansina, *Oral Tradition as History* (Madison, 1985), 17–32.

78. Mamadou Diawara, *La graine de la parole: dimension sociale et politique des traditions orales du royaume de Jaara (Mali) du XVème au milieu du XIXème siècle* (Stuttgart, 1990); M. Diawara, "Mande Oral Popular Culture Revisited by the Electronic Media," in K. Barber, ed., *Readings in African Popular Culture* (London, 1997), 40–48; Richard Roberts, *Litigants and Households: African Disputes and Colonial Courts in the French Soudan, 1895–1912* (Portsmouth, 2005), 20–23.

79. See Elizabeth Tonkin, *Narrating Our Pasts: The Social Construction of Oral History* (Cambridge, 1992), 11.

80. James Scott, *Weapons of the Weak: Everyday Forms of Peasant Resistance* (New Haven, 1985), 178.

81. C. Hamilton, "Ideology and Oral Traditions: Listening to the Voices 'From Below,'" *History in Africa* 14 (1987), 67–86.

82. J. Kotre, *White Gloves: How We Create Ourselves Through Memory* (New York, 1995), 6–7.

83. White, *Speaking with Vampires*, 30–53, 66–86.

84. See Luise White et al., eds., *African Words, Africans Voices: Critical Practices in Oral History* (Bloomington, 2001), 6–19; Allen and Barbara Isaacman, *Slavery and Beyond: The Making of Men and Chikunda Ethnic Identities in the Unstable World of South-Central Africa, 1750–1920* (Portsmouth, 2004), 26.

85. His collected oral traditions are mainly village foundation narratives, hunters' stories, and local legends. I have incorporated a few of these narratives but have yet to work systematically with them, as they are generally mythic in nature.

86. S. Camara, "The Epic of Sunjata: Structure, Preservation, and Transmission," in Ralph Austen, ed., *In Search of Sunjata: The Mande Oral Epic as History, Literature, and Performance* (Bloomington, 1999), 65.

87. See the essays in Jan Vansina and Carolyn Keyes Adenaike, eds., *In Pursuit of History: Fieldwork in Africa* (Portsmouth, 1996).

1. THE WARS OF SAMORI

1. Suleyman Sidibé, Solona, 10 April 2002.
2. L. Kesteloot and B. Dieng, *Les épopées d'Afrique noire* (Paris, 1997); J. W. Johnson, T. A. Hale and S. Belcher, eds., *Oral Epics from Africa: Vibrant Voices from the Vast Continent* (Bloomington, 1997), 68–79; and J. Jansen, "A Critical Note on the Epic of Samori Touré," *History in Africa* 29 (2002), 219–29. For the standard Guinean hagiography of Samori, see *L'Empereur Almamy Samori Touré: grand administrateur et grand stratège* (Conakry, 1971) by "Révolution démocratique africaine."
3. On Samori, see Yves Person, *Samori: Une Revolution Dyula*, vols. 1–3 (Paris, 1968–75); A. S. Kanya-Forstner, *The Conquest of the Western Sudan: A Study in French Military Imperialism* (Cambridge, 1969); M. Legassick, "Firearms, Horses and Samorian Army Administration, 1870–1898," *JAH* 7 (1966), 95–115; *Mande Studies* 3 (2001); and *Centenaire du souvenir: Almami Samori Touré, 1898–1998: Symposium international de Conakry du 29 September au 1 October 1998* (Conakry, 2000).
4. Person, *Samori*, 2:812–15.
5. See Jean Bazin, "A chacun son Bambara," in Jean-Loup Amselle and Elizabeth M'Bokolo, eds., *Au Coeur de l'ethnie* (Paris, 1985), 87–127; Jean-Loup Amselle, *Mestizo Logics: Anthropology of Identity in Africa and Elsewhere* (Stanford, 1998), 43–57; René Bravmann, *Islam and Tribal Art in West Africa* (Cambridge, 1974); R. Bravmann, "Islamic Ritual and Practice in Bamana Segou, the 19th Century 'Citadel of Paganism,'" and David Conrad, "Pilgrim *Fajigi* and *Basiw* from Mecca: Islam and Traditional Religion in the Former French Sudan," in Jean-Paul Colleyn, ed., *Bamana: The Art of Existence in Mali* (New York, 2001), 25–43. On the Segu Bambara state, see Richard Roberts, *Warriors, Merchants, and Slaves: The State and the Economy in the Middle Niger Valley, 1700–1914* (Stanford, 1986). For a statement on African religions, orality, and writing, see J. D. Y. Peel, "Syncretism and Religious Change," *Comparative Studies in Society and History* 10 (1967), 139–40; and Jack Goody, *The Logic of Writing and the Organization of Society* (Cambridge, 1986). On bricolage, see Claude Lévi-Strauss, *The Savage Mind* (Chicago, 1966), 16–22.
6. See George Brooks, *Landlords and Strangers: Ecology, Society and Trade in West Africa, 1000–1630* (Boulder, 1993); and David C. Conrad and Barbara E. Frank, eds., *Status and Identity in West Africa: Nyamakalaw of Mande* (Bloomington, 1995). On slavery, see Jean-Loup Amselle, *Les Négociants de la Savane: Histoire et organisation sociale des Kooroko* (Paris, 1977), 25–34; Martin Klein, *Slavery and Colonial Rule in French West Africa* (Cambridge, 1998), 1–18; Claude Meillassoux, *L'Esclavage en Afrique précoloniale* (Paris, 1971); Roberts, *Warriors, Merchants, and Slaves;* and Suzanne Miers and Igor Kopytoff, *Slavery in Africa: Historical and Anthropological Perspectives* (Madison, 1977).
7. Bangali Kone, Bunjoba, 19 June 2002; Adama Diallo, Niamala, 7 October 2002; Musa Sumoaro, Kolondieba, 20 November 2002.
8. Amselle, *Les Négociants*, 34, 37–48.

9. See Dominique Zahan, *Sociétés d'initiation Bambara* (Paris, 1963); Pâques, *Les Bambaras* (Paris, 1954); Germaine Dieterlen, *Essai sur la religion Bambara* (Paris, 1951); Patrick R. McNaughton, *The Mande Blacksmiths: Knowledge, Power, and Art in West Africa* (Bloomington, 1988); Charles Bird, "Heroic Songs of the Mande Hunters," in R. Dorson, ed., *African Folklore* (Garden City, 1972), 275–94.

10. Broulaye Doumbia, Tenemakana, 6 October 2002; and Yacouba Danyoko, Tenemakana, 21–23 June 2002. Much of this was also clarified during my discussions with Sekou Camara, Bamako, 2000–2003. On the "production of locality," see Arjun Appadurai, *Modernity at Large: Cultural Dimensions of Globalization* (Minneapolis, 1996).

11. Viviana Pâques, "Bouffons Sacrés du Cercle de Bougouni (Soudan Français)," *Journal de la Société des Africanistes* 24, 1 (1954), 63–110.

12. A useful overview is Hugh Kennedy, *The Great Arab Conquests: How the Spread of Islam Changed the World We Live In* (Philadelphia, 2007), 200–224.

13. On the archaeological evidence of Koumbi Saleh and the larger Sahelian context, see Timothy Insoll, *The Archaeology of Islam in Sub-Saharan Africa* (Cambridge, 2003), 207–62.

14. Abu 'Ubayd al-Bakri, "Kitâb al-masâlik," in N. Levtzion and J. F. P. Hopkins, eds., *Corpus of Early Arabic Sources for African History* (Princeton, 2000), 80.

15. Ibid., 82–83.

16. This location near Kangaba, or Ka-Ba, although unconfirmed, was just sixty kilometers from the heart of the district of Buguni and even closer to northern Wasulu. See Insoll, *Archaeology*, 314–43.

17. S. Hamdun and N. King, eds., *Ibn Battuta in Black Africa* (Princeton, 1975), 44–59.

18. Al-Bakri, "Kitâb al-masâlik," 62–87; N. Levtzion, " 'Abd Allah b. Yasin and the Almoravids," in J. R. Willis, ed., *Studies in West African Islam*, Vol. 1: *The Cultivators of Islam* (London, 1979), 78–111; J. O. Hunwick, *Shari'a in Songhay: The Replies of al-Maghili to the Questions of Askia al-Hajj Muhammad* (Oxford, 1985); and N. Levtzion and H. Fisher, eds., *Rural and Urban Islam in West Africa* (Boulder, 1986), 1–37.

19. M. G. S. Hodgson, *The Venture of Islam: The Expansion of Islam in the Middle Periods* (Chicago, 1961), 2:532–74.

20. Al-Bakri, "Kitâb al-masâlik," 82; Ivor Wilks, "The Transmission of Islamic Learning in the Western Sudan," in Jack Goody, ed., *Literacy in Traditional Societies* (Cambridge, 1968), 162–97; Robert Launay, *Beyond the Stream: Islam and Society in a West African Town* (Berkeley, 1992); and Lamin Sanneh, *The Jakhanke* (London, 1979).

21. For a general overview, see Hodgson, *The Venture of Islam*, 2:201–54; and Jonathan Berkey, *The Formation of Islam: Religion and Society in the Near East, 600–1800* (Cambridge, 2003), 152–59, 231–47.

22. Spencer Trimingham, *The Sufi Orders in Islam* (Oxford, 1971), 1–29, 40–43, 67–104; Vincent Cornell, *Realm of the Saint: Power and Authority in Moroccan*

Sufism (Austin, 1998); Fazlur Rahman, *Islam* (Chicago, 1979), 158–59. For comparative cases, see Nikki Keddie, ed., *Scholars, Saints, and Sufis* (Berkeley, 1972).

23. Mervyn Hiskett, *The Development of Islam in West Africa* (London, 1984), 44–51, 244–50; A. A. Batran, "The Kunta, Sidi al-Mukhtar al-Kunti, and the Office of Shaykh al-Tariqa'l-Qadiriyya," in Willis, *The Cultivators of Islam*, 113–46.

24. Alain Quella-Villéger, *René Caillié: Une Vie Pour Tombouctou* (Poitiers, 1999), 13–94; on France and the Atlantic slave trade, see Robert Harms, *The Diligent: A Voyage Through the Worlds of the Slave Trade* (New York, 2002).

25. René Caillié, *Voyage à Tombouctou*, vol. 1 (Paris, 1996); Philip Curtin, "The Jihads of West Africa: Early Relations and Linkages," *JAH* 2 (1971), 11–24; Walter Rodney, "Jihad and Social Revolution in Futa Jallon in the Eighteenth Century," *Journal of the Historical Society of Nigeria* 4 (1968), 269–84; and Tierno Diallo, *Les Institutions politiques du Fouta Dyalon au XIXe siècle* (Dakar, 1972).

26. Y. Person, "Samori and Islam," in Willis, *The Cultivators of Islam*, 268–69.

27. Caillié, *Voyage*, 1:307–9, 314–15, 325, 328. By the late eighteenth century Mungo Park had noted "Wassela" as an important source of slaves. See Park, *Travels into the Interior Districts of Africa* (London, 1816), 382. See also M. Klein, "Defensive Strategies: Wasulu, Masina, and the Slave Trade," in S. A. Diouf, ed., *Fighting the Slave Trade: West African Strategies* (Athens, 2003); and Martin Klein, "The Slave Trade and Decentralized Societies," *JAH* 42 (2001), 49–65.

28. Caillié, *Voyage*, 1:336–37, 2:77.

29. Ibid., 1:343–44, 366. See also David Robinson, *Muslim Societies in African History* (Cambridge, 2004), 124–38; and also Ivor Wilks, "The Juula and the Expansion of Islam into the Forest," in Nehemia Levtzion and Randall Pouwels, eds., *The History of Islam in Africa* (Athens 2000), 93–115.

30. Sirakoro Traore, Moro, 7 April 2002; Ngolo Sanogo, Woblé, 5 April 2002; see also Jean-Loup Amselle, "Un Etat contre l'etat: le Keleyadugu," *CEA* 28 (1988), 463–83; and Louis Brenner, "Histories of Religion in Africa," *JRA* 2000 (2), 143–67; Amselle, *Mestizo Logics*, 121.

31. Caillié, *Voyage*, 1:349, 2:85–86.

32. Ibid., 1:350.

33. On precolonial trade in Wasulu and the Kooroko merchants, see Amselle, *Les Négociants*, 37–112. See also Roberts, *Warrior, Merchants, and Slaves*, 21–134; Roberts, "Ideology, Slavery and Social Formation: The Evolution of Slavery in the Middle Niger Valley," in P. Lovejoy, ed., *Ideology of Slavery in Africa* (Beverly Hills, 1981); Klein, *Slavery and Colonial Rule*, 1–18, 37–58; and Sanneh, *The Jakhanke*. On broader religious questions, see Bernard Lewis, *Race and Slavery in the Middle East* (Oxford, 1990), 5–15, 21–27, 54–61; John Ralph Willis, ed., *Slaves and Slavery in Muslim Africa: Islam and the Ideology of Enslavement* (London, 1985); J. R. Willis, "Introduction: Reflections on the Diffusion of Islam in West Africa," in Willis, ed., *The Cultivators of Islam*, 1–39; and Humphrey Fisher, *Slavery in the History of Muslim Black Africa* (New York, 2001), 48.

34. Fisher, *Slavery*, 64–70.

35. Paul Marty, *Études sur l'Islam en Côte d'Ivoire* (Paris: 1922), 77–233, 89–101. Marty also reported slave conversions in the Sahel regions of the French Sudan. See *L'Islam et les Tribus du Soudan* (Paris, 1920), 2:180.

36. Marty, *Études*, 93.

37. Martin Klein, "Ethnic Pluralism and Homogeneity in the Western Sudan," *Mande Studies* 1 (1999).

38. Amselle, *Mestizo Logics*, 49, 122. On the wider literature, see Diouf, *Fighting the Slave Trade;* Klein, "Decentralized Societies"; Baum, *Shrines of the Slaves Trade: Diola Religion and Society in Precolonial Senegambia* (Oxford, 1999); and Walter Hawthorne, *Planting Rice and Harvesting Slaves: Transformations along the Guinea–Bissau Coast, 1400–1900* (Portsmouth, 2003).

39. James Scott, *The Art of Not Being Governed: An Anarchist History of Upland Southeast Asia* (New Haven, 2009), 7–32.

40. Caillié, *Voyage*, 1:347–49.

41. J. Gallieni, *Voyage au Soudan Français, Haut-Niger et Pays de Ségou, 1879–1881* (Paris, 1885), 597.

42. On important precursors in northern Nigeria, see Murray Last, *The Sokoto Caliphate* (London, 1967); and Mervyn Hiskett, *The Sword of Truth* (Oxford, 1973). For a brief overview of the Hamdullahi state, see David Robinson, "Revolutions in the Western Sudan," in Levtzion and Pouwels, *The History of Islam*, 139–40; and also Amadou Hampâté Ba and Serge Daget, *L'Empire Peul du Macina* (Dakar, 1955); and Bintou Sanankoua, *Un empire peul au XIXe siècle: La Diina du Massina* (Paris, 1990).

43. Nwaari Suntura, N'Golobala, 26 June 2002.

44. Drissa Diallo, N'Golobala, 18 May 2002.

45. Adama Diallo, Niamala, 10 October 2002.

46. Nouhou Diakite, Kologo, 4 October 2002.

47. Zumana Danyoko, Tenemakana, August 2000; Yacouba Danyoko, Tenemakana, 20–23 June 2002; Broulaye Doumbia, Tenemakana, 13 May 2002; Yusuf Coulibaly, Tenemakana, 6 October 2002.

48. Nwaari Suntura, N'Golobala, 26 June 2002.

49. Gallieni, *Voyage au Soudan Français*, 598.

50. Person, *Samori*, 1:489.

51. Tieba Traore was the king of Sikasso from 1877 to 1893. Upon his death, he was succeeded by his brother, Babemba, who, as the story goes, committed suicide rather than be taken by French troops after the siege on Sikasso in 1898. On the Kénédugu state, see L. Holmes, "Tieba Traore, Fama of Kenedougou: Two Decades of Political Development," Ph.D. diss., University of California, Berkeley, 1977; M. Collieaux, "Contribution à l'étude de l'histoire de l'ancien royaume de Kénédougou (1825–1898)," *Comité d'études historiques et scientifiques de l'Afrique Occidentale Française* 9 (1924), 128–81; and A. O. Konaré, *Sikasso Tata* (Bamako, 1983).

52. L.-G. Binger, *Du Niger au Golfe de Guinée par le pays du Kong et de Mossi, 1887–1889* (Paris, 1892), 1:220.

53. Person, *Samori*, 3:2039.

54. Bards (*jeliw*) sing praises to Samori while being fully aware of his destructive wars. Personal communications, Sekou Camara, Bamako, October 2002; and Mamadou Diabaté (*jeli*), New York, March 2007.

55. Person, *Samori*, 1:235–304.

56. Ibid., 315–410.

57. See Legassick, "Firearms," 95–115; see also Bruce Vandervort, *Wars of Imperial Conquest in Africa, 1830–1914* (Bloomington, 1998), 113–36; and Daniel Headrick, *The Tools of Empire: Technology and European Imperialism in the Nineteenth Century* (Oxford, 1981).

58. RP, May 1896, *Archives Nationales du Mali* (ANM) IE27; Lamine Diakité, Yanfolila, 14 April 2002; and Amadou Sidibé, Solona, 10 April 2002. Many of the early conquests in Wasulu were actually conducted by Samori's brother, Kémé-Brèma Touré. See Person, *Samori*, 1:391–96; and E. Péroz, *L'Empire de l'Almamy-Emir Samory ou empire du Ouassoulou* (Besançon, 1888).

59. Hari Sidibe, Yanfolila, 9 April 2002.

60. Person, *Samori*, 1:494–95; and Drissa Diallo, N'Golobala, 18–20 May 2002.

61. Doulaye Kone, Kolondieba, 19 November 2002; Broulaye Doumbia, Tenemakana, 13 May 2002.

62. Binger, *Du Niger*, 70–72.

63. Yusuf Coulibaly, Tenemakana, 15 May 2002; Broulaye Doumbia, Tenemakana, 13 May 2002.

64. Broulaye Kone, Kolondieba, 21 Nov. 2002.

65. Sirakoro Traore, Moro, 6 May 2002.

66. Solo Sanogo, Woblé, 4 May 2002.

67. Binger, *Du Niger*, 168–73.

68. Person, *Samori*, 1:503.

69. Ngolo Sanogo, Woblé, 5 May 2002.

70. Musa Sumoaro, Kolondieba, 20 November 2002.

71. Binger, *Du Niger*, 218–19.

72. Person, *Samori*, 2:810–17.

73. Binger, *Du Niger*, 52–59.

74. El Hajj Sekou Sidibé, Jelifin, 31 March 2002; Almami Sidibé, Balanfina, 2 April 2002. See Rapport Vuillemot, 1899, ANM 4E42.

75. Binger, *Du Niger*, 25–26.

76. Person, *Samori*, 1:503.

77. Binger, *Du Niger*, 150.

78. Musa Sumoaro, Kolondieba, 20 November 2002. On similar accounts in Guinea, see Emily Osborn, "Power, Authority, and Gender in Kankan-Baté," Ph.D. diss., Stanford University, 2000, 97; and Michael McGovern, "Unmasking the State: Developing Political Subjectivities in 20th-Century Guinea," Ph.D. diss., Emory University, 2004, 71–72.

79. Drissa Diallo, N'Golobala, 18 May 2002. For the background on French conquest, see Kanya-Forstner, *The Conquest of the Western Sudan*, 84–270.

80. Bakary Kone and Namakoro Bamba, Kolondieba, 1 June 2002.

81. Yusuf Coulibaly, Tenemakana, 21 May and 6 October 2002.

82. Karim Danyoko, Tenemakana, 11 and 12 October 2002; Yacouba Danyoko, Tenemakana, 20–23 June 2002; Musa Sumoaro, Kolondieba, 20 November 2002; Drissa Diallo, N'Golobala, 18 May 2002; Broulaye Kone, Kolondieba, 19 November 2002. See also Klein, "Defensive Strategies," 64–65. On the role of "women's power" in Mandé oral traditions, see David Conrad, "Mooning Armies and Mothering Heroes: Female Power in the Mande Epic Tradition," R. Austin, ed., *In Search of Sunjata: The Mande Oral Epic as History, Literature, and Performance* (Bloomington, 1999), 189–224.

83. Namakoro Bamba, Kolondieba, 7 July 2002.

84. On honor in comparative context in Africa, see J. Iliffe, *Honour in African History* (Cambridge, 2005).

85. Musa Sumoaro, Kolondieba, 20 November 2002.

86. Binger, *Du Niger*, 89–104, 109; Klein, *Slavery and Colonial Rule*, 109–10; A. O. Konaré, *Sikasso Tata* (Bamako, 1983). The uncle of one informant was enslaved as a boy and conscripted into Samori's army as a *bilakoro* (young infantryman) during the siege of Sikasso. He recalled the starvation that Samori's soldiers endured and how some people resorted to cannibalism. Drissa Diallo, N'Golobala, 18 May 2002.

87. Binger, *Du Niger*, 66–67.

88. Drissa Diallo, N'Golobala, 18 May 2002; Person, *Samori*, 2:1049–64.

89. Souleyman Sidibé and Amadou Sidibé, Solona, 10 April 2002; and Sekou Sidibé and Drissa Balla, Jelifin, 31 March 2002; Yusuf Sidibe, Koniba-Barila, 27 March 2002; Karim Sidibé, Jelifin, 7 April 2002; Musa Sumoaro, Kolondieba, 20 November 2002. See also Person, *Samori*, 2:1111n30.

90. Person, *Samori*, 2:817–19.

91. RP, 5 February 1894 and 11 January 1894, ANM 1E27. See Klein, *Slavery and Colonial Rule*, 109–11.

92. Drissa Diallo, N'Golobala, 18 May 2002.

93. Broulaye Doumbia, Tenemakana, 6 October 2002; Doulaye Kone, Kolondieba, 19 November 2002; Bangali Kone, Bunjoba, 19 June 2002; Nama Dembele, Kolondieba, 20 July 2002; Nouhou Diakite, Kologo, 5 October 2002; Souleyman Sidibe, Solona, 10 April 2002.

94. "No compulsion is there in religion. Rectitude has become clear from error" (2:256). See A. J. Arberry, trans., *The Koran Interpreted* (New York, 1955), 65; and El Hajj Sekou Sidibé, Jelifin, 31 March 2002, and Yusuf Coulibaly, Tenemakana, 21 May 2002.

95. Adama Diallo, Niamala, 10 October 2002.

96. Imam Sidibé, Balanfina, 2–3 April 2002; El Hajj Sekou Sidibé, Jelifin, 31 March 2002, and Yusuf Coulibaly, Tenemakana, 16–17 May 2002; Drissa Diallo, N'Golobala, 18 May 2002; Broulaye Doumbia, Tenemakana, 13 May 2002.

97. Doulaye Kone, Kolondieba, 19 November 2002.

98. Almamy Sidibé, Balanfina, 2 April 2002.

99. Jan-Jan Sidibé, Balanfina, 2–3 April 2002; Broulaye Doumbia, Tenemakana, 13 May 2002; see also Monograph, 1906, ANM 1D37.

100. See Robert Launay, "*La Trahison des Clercs?* The 'Collaboration' of a Suwarian 'Alim," in J. Hunwick and N. Lawler, eds., *The Cloth of Many Colored Silks* (Evanston, 1996), 297–318; Sanneh, *The Jakhanke;* and I. Wilks, *Wa and the Wala: Islam and Polity in Northwestern Ghana* (Cambridge, 1989).

101. John Hanson, *Migration, Jihad, and Muslim Authority in West Africa: The Futanke Colonies in Karta* (Bloomington, 1996), 39–47, 79–87.

2. RECONSTRUCTING A FRAGMENTED WORLD

1. Yusuf Sidibé, Koniba-Barila, 27 March 2002.

2. M'Bemba Sidibé, Balanfina, 3 April 2002; Hari Sidibé, Yanfolila, 9 April 2002; Lamine Diakité, Yanfolila, 14 April 2002; Zumana Koné, Bunjoba, 19 June 2002; Broulaye Doumbia, Tenemakana, 13–14 May 2002. On related environmental issues in other regions, see H. Kjekshus, *Ecology Control and Economic Development in East African History* (Portsmouth, 1977); E. Mandala, *Work and Control in a Peasant Economy: A History of the Lower Tchiri Valley, 1859–1960* (Madison, 1990). On postconquest reconstruction, with particular emphasis on refugee movements and efforts at environmental rehabilitation, see Emmanuel Kreike, *Re-Creating Eden: Land Use, Environment, and Society in Southern Angola and Northern Namibia* (Portsmouth, 2004).

3. L.-G. Binger, *Du Niger au Golfe de Guinée par le pays du Kong et de Mossi, 1887–1889* (Paris, 1892), 1:170.

4. RP, August 1900, *Archives Nationales du Mali* (ANM) *Fonds Anciens* IE27.

5. Jan-Jan Sidibé, Balanfina, 2 April 2002.

6. Doulaye Koné, Kolondieba, 21 November 2002.

7. Balla Kouyate and Sekou Diakite, Balanfina, 3 April 2002.

8. RP, May and July 1896, ANM IE27; Yusuf Coulibaly, Tenemakana, 15 May 2002; Hari Sidibé, Yanfolila, 9 April 2002; Lamine Diakité, Yanfolila, 14 April 2002; Sungalo Koné, Bunjoba, 20 June 2002; Yusuf Coulibaly, Tenemakana, 16–17 and 21 May 2002; Broulaye Doumbia, Tenemakana, 13–14 May 2002.

9. RP, May 1896; 1900 Annual; Tournée, 10 June 1899; RP, January 1899, ANM IE27. On the demographic impact of the Samorian wars in northern Ivory Coast, see T. Bassett, *The Peasant Cotton Revolution in West Africa: Côte d'Ivoire, 1880–1995* (Cambridge, 2001), 44–47.

10. RP, February 1894 and May 1896, ANM IE27.

11. RP, May 1896; February and March 1899; Census, March 1894, ANM IE27; Yves Person, *Samori: Une Revolution Dyula,* 3 vols. (Paris, 1968–75), 1:169–219, 2:1059.

12. RP, September 1897; 10 June 1899, ANM IE27; Broulaye Doumbia, Tenemakana, 10 October 2002.

13. A. S. Kanya-Forstner, *The Conquest of the Western Sudan: A Study in French Military Imperialism* (Cambridge, 1969), 216–21.

14. RP, March 1894; January 1895, ANM IE27; on refugees in France and French policies, see Gérard Noiriel, *Réfugiés et Sans-Papiers: la République face au droit d'XIXeme–XXeme siècle* (Paris, 1991). In other early colonial contexts, see Jan-Bart Gewald, *A Socio-Political History of the Herero of Namibia, 1890–1923* (Athens, 1999).

15. On legibility, see James Scott, *Seeing Like a State: How Certain Schemes to Improve the Human Condition Have Failed* (New Haven, 1998), esp. part 1, "State Projects of Legibility and Simplification."

16. RP, January 1895, ANM IE27.

17. RP, May 1894; January, April, May, June 1895; May, July, 1896; Annual and August 1897, ANM IE27; Solo Sanogo, Woblé, 4 May 2002.

18. Doulaye Koné, Kolondieba, 19 November 2002.

19. Yusuf Sidibé, Koniba-Barila, 27 March 2002; Martin Klein, *Slavery and Colonial Rule, in French West Africa* (Cambridge, 1998), 121.

20. RP, May 1898, ANM IE27; RP, Kita, August 1904, *Archives Nationales du Sénégal* (ANS) 2G4/16.

21. RP, March 1894, ANM IE27; Klein, *Slavery and Colonial Rule*, 111–13; Richard Roberts, "The End of Slavery in the French Soudan, 1905–1914," in S. Miers and R. Roberts, eds., *The End of Slavery in Africa* (Madison, 1988), 285–86; and Denis Bouche, *Les villages de liberté en Afrique noire française 1887–1910* (Paris, 1968).

22. Village de liberté, Bougouni, 1894–1909, ANM IE125; RP, November, August 1904, ANM IE27; Klein, *Slavery and Colonial Rule*, 165.

23. RP, Bamako, January 1904, CAOM, 2G4/16; RP, Côte d'Ivoire, 1902, 1904, Haut-Sénégal-Niger (HSN), *Archives Nationales de France, Centre des Archives d'Outre Mer* (CAOM), 2G4/16; and Timothy Weiskel, "Labor in the Emergent Periphery: From Slavery to Migrant Labor among the Baoulé Peoples, 1880–1925," in W. Goldfrank, ed., *The World-System of Capitalism: Past and Present* (Beverly Hills, 1979); and Timothy Weiskel, *French Colonial Rule and the Baoulé Peoples: Resistance and Collaboration, 1889–1911* (Oxford, 1980), 99–141.

24. RP, February 1894, ANM IE27.

25. Weiskel, *French Colonial Rule*, 87–90.

26. Broulaye Koné, Kolondieba, 21 Nov. 2002.

27. RP, May 1900, ANM IE27.

28. RP, January 1895, ANM IE27.

29. Broulaye Koné, Kolondieba, 21 November 2002.

30. Amadou Hampaté Bâ uses anagrams for historical place names and figures throughout the story. See Amadou Hampaté Bâ, *L'Étrange destin de Wangrin* (Paris, 1973). Translation from *The Fortunes of Wangrin* (Bloomington, 1999), trans. Aina Pavolini Taylor, 6.

31. Ibid.

32. RP, 5 July 1897; CdC to GG, 1894; Tournée, 10 June 1899, ANM IE27; and see my "History, Memory and the Legacy of Samori in Southern Mali, c. 1880–1898," *JAH* 49 (2008), 266–67.

33. Namakoro Bamba, Kolondieba, 7 July 2002.

34. Solo Sanogo, Woblé, 5 May 2002.

35. RP, June 1895; Letter 24 July 1895 CdC to GG; RP, December 1895, ANM IE27; and RP, 1934 1st trim, ANM IE10.

36. RP, August 1900, March 1902, ANM IE27. See General Duboc, *Samory le Sanglant* (Paris, 1947). On "moral memory," see Georg Simmel's seminal essay,

"Faithfulness and Gratitude," in K. Wolff, ed., *The Sociology of Georg Simmel* (Glencoe, 1950), 379–95.

37. Fiche de renseignements, Banimonotie and Kouroulamini, ANM 2E47.

38. Fiche de renseignements, Gouanan, ANM 2E47; see *Mestizo Logics: Anthropology of Identity in Africa and Elsewhere* (Stanford, 1998), 90–91.

39. Richard Roberts on "Landscapes of Power," in *Litigants and Households: African Disputes and Colonial Courts in the French Soudan, 1895–1912* (Portsmouth, 2005), 13–20, 99–123; see also R. Roberts, *Two Worlds of Cotton: Colonialism and the Regional Economy in the French Soudan, 1800–1946* (Stanford, 1996), 16.

40. Henri Brunschwig, *Noirs et Blancs dans l'Afrique Noire Française, ou comment le colonisé devient colonisateur, 1870–1914* (Paris, 1983); Heather Sharkey, *Living with Colonialism: Nationalism and Culture in the Anglo-Egyptian Sudan* (Berkeley, 2003); B. Lawrence, E. Osborn, and R. Robert, eds., *Intermediaries, Interpreters, and Clerks: African Employees in the Making of Colonial Africa* (Madison, 2006).

41. See Frederick Cooper, "States, Empires, and Political Imagination," in his *Colonialism in Question: Theory, Knowledge, History* (Berkeley, 2005), 153–203.

42. Fiche de renseignements, ANM 2E47.

43. Amselle, *Mestizo Logics*, 74–93, 111–19, 151–61, 74–93; Alice Conklin, *A Mission to Civilize: The Republican Idea of Empire in France and West Africa* (Stanford, 1997), 111–19.

44. On the shift from military to civilian rule in French Sudan, see Roberts, *Litigants and Households*, 35–123.

45. Fiche de renseignements, Foulala, ANM 2E47.

46. N'waari Suntura, N'Golobala, 26 June 2002.

47. Fiche de renseignements, Foulala, ANM 2E47.

48. Rapport sur le fonctionnement, 1894, ANM IE27.

49. Rapport sur Nonbougare Soumasurou, 1897; Rapport sur l'ex-tirailleur auxiliaire Moussa Traore, 2 August 1898; RP, May 1900, ANM IE27.

50. RP, April 1899; Tournée, 10 June 1899, ANM IE27.

51. Conklin, *Mission to Civilize*, 78–86.

52. RP, 24 July 1895; September 1903, ANM IE27.

53. RP, May, June, 1902; Annual 1903, ANM IE27.

54. James Scott, *The Art of Not Being Governed: An Anarchist History of Upland Southeast Asia* (New Haven, 2009), 127–77.

55. Frederick Cooper, *Decolonization and African Society: The Labor Question in French and British Africa* (Cambridge, 1996), 14–16.

56. Immanuel Wallerstein, *The Modern World System, III: The Second Era of Great Expansion of the Capitalist World-Economy, 1730s–1840s* (San Diego, 1989), 146–48, 164–69.

57. RP, May 1896; Annual 1903, ANM IE27.

58. Emily Lynn Osborn, "Rubber Fever, Long Distance Trade, and French Colonial Rule in Upper Guinée, 1890–1913," *JAH* 45 (2004), 451.

59. See Raymond Dument, *El Dorado in West Africa* (Athens, 1998); Jean Allman and Victoria Tashjian, *"I Will Not Eat Stone": A Women's History of Colonial Asante* (Portsmouth, 2000); and James Searing, *"God Alone is King": Islam and Emancipation in Senegal: The Wolof Kingdoms of Kajoor and Bawol, 1859–1914* (Portsmouth, 2002).

60. Osborn, "Rubber Fever," 445–65.

61. RP, February 1894; January 1899; August 1900, ANM IE27.

62. Rapport de Tournée, June 1899; RP, 1901, 1903, ANM IE27.

63. RP, January 1904, ANM IE27.

64. Regime Forestier, 1900, ANM 3R32.

65. RP, October and November 1903, ANM IE27.

66. Rapport Agricole, HSN, 1908, ANS 2G8/1; RP, January 1904, ANM IE27; and Robert Harms, "The End of Red Rubber: A Reassessment," *JAH* 16 (1975), 73–88; Adam Hochschild, *King Leopold's Ghost* (Boston, 1998); Richard Roberts, *Warriors, Merchants, and Slaves: The State and the Economy in the Middle Niger Valley, 1700–1914* (Stanford, 1987), 161–73.

67. RP, October 1903, 1904 Annual, ANM IE27; see also Jean-Luc Amselle, *Les Négociants de la Savane: Histoire et organisation sociale des Kooroko* (Paris, 1977), 131–50.

68. RP, December 1903; July 1904, ANM IE27.

69. RP, December 1905; July 1904, ANM IE27.

70. Rapport de tournée, 1914, ANM IE27.

71. See David Robinson, *Paths of Accommodation: Muslim Societies and French Authorities in Senegal and Mauritania, 1880–1920* (Athens, 2000); David Robinson and Jean-Louis Triaud, *Le Temps des Marabouts: Itinéraires et stratégies islamiques en Afrique occidentale française* (Paris, 1997); and Triaud, "Islam in Africa under French Colonial Rule," in N. Levtzion and R. L. Pouwels, eds., *The History of Islam in Africa* (Ohio, 2000), 169–87.

72. Maurice Delafosse, *Haut-Senegal Niger* (Paris, 1912), 3:186.

73. GG circular, 10 February 1906, ANS 19G1.

74. Amselle, *Mestizo Logics*, 124; Robinson, *Paths of Accommodation;* and David Robinson, "Review Article: Islam, Cash Crops, and Emancipation in Senegal," *JAH* 44 (2003), 141.

75. Lt adjoint CdC-Gov. Gen. 12 March 1894, ANM IE27. See also Louis-Gustave Binger, *Le Péril de l'Islam* (Paris, 1906); Alfred Le Chatelier, *L'Islam en Afrique occidentale* (Paris, 1899); and A. Le Chatelier, *Politique musulmane* (Tours, 1907). On the background, see Christopher Harrison, *France and Islam in West Africa, 1860–1960* (Cambridge, 1988), 29–56.

76. CdC to GG, 5 February 1894, RP May 1894, Rapport de Tournée, 1894, ANM IE27.

77. See Robert Launay, "Des infidèles d'un autre type: Les réponses au pouvoir colonial dans une communauté musulmane de Côte d'Ivoire," in Robinson and Triaud, *Le Temps des Marabouts*, 415–30.

78. RP, 1897, ANM IE27.

79. Rapports sur l'Islam et les confreries musulmanes, Bougouni, 1899 and 1905, Politique Musulmane, ANM 4E42; RP, August 1900; December 1903, ANM IE27. On Pan-Islam and rebellion in French North Africa, see Edmund Burke III, "Pan-Islam and Moroccan Resistance to French Colonial Penetration, 1900–1912," *JAH* 13 (1972); and J. Clancy-Smith, *Rebel and Saint: Muslim Notables, Populist Protest, Colonial Encounters* (Berkeley, 1994).

80. Rapport, 20 August 1905, Politique Musulmane, ANM 4E42; RP, September 1903, ANM IE27. On this broader thesis, see Richard Eaton, *The Rise of Islam and the Bengal Frontier, 1204–1760* (Berkeley, 1993), 113–34.

81. Rapports sur l'Islam, 1899, ANM 4E42. There are many examples of dòlò excess and in particular of the drunkenness of chiefs. See RP, August 1903; February 1904, ANM IE27. For concerns about the "plague of alcoholism," see also Delafosse, *Haut-Senegal Niger*, 3:214.

82. RP, August 1902, ANM IE27.

83. Rapports sur l'Islam, 1899, Politique Musulmane, ANM 4E42.

84. Rapport, August 1905, Politique Musulmane, ANM 4E42.

85. RP, September 1903, ANM IE27.

86. The interwar era was the heyday of French ethnographic research. On the Griaule "school," see James Clifford, "Power and Dialogue in Ethnography: Marcel Griaule's Initiation," in *The Predicament of Culture: Twentieth-Century Ethnography, Literature, and Art* (Cambridge, 1988), 55–91.

87. Doulaye Koné, Kolondieba, 19 November 2002; Martin Klein, "Ethnic Pluralism and Homogeneity in the Western Sudan: Saalum, Segou and Wasulu," *Mande Studies* 1 (1999).

88. Drissa Diallo, N'Golobala, 18 May 2002.

89. Hawa Diallo, Tenemakana, 13 May 2002.

90. Jan-Jan Sidibé, Balanfina, 2–3 April 2002.

91. Drissa Diallo, N'Golobala, 18 May 2002.

92. Broulaye Doumbia, Tenemakana, 13 May 2002.

93. Monographie de Bougouni, 1906, ANM ID37.

94. See Amselle, *Les Négociants de la Savane*, 119–20.

95. Broulaye Doumbia, Tenemakana, 6 October 2002; Bourama Dembele, Tenemakana, 13–14 June 2002.

96. Amselle, *Mestizo Logics*, 127–32; and on regional and translocal cultic networks among the Yoruba, see J. D. Y. Peel, *Religious Encounter and the Making of the Yoruba* (Indiana, 2000), 88–122.

97. Doulaye Koné, Kolondieba, 19 November 2002. On sacred sites and indigenous religions under colonialism, see Jean Allman and John Parker, *Tongnaab: The History of a West African God* (Bloomington, 2005); and Sandra E. Greene, *Sacred Sites and the Colonial Encounter: A History of Meaning and Memory in Ghana* (Bloomington, 2002).

98. Politique indigene, CAOM FM2188/5.

99. Souleyman Sidibé, Solona, 10 April 2002.

100. Musa Sumoaro, Kolondieba, 20 November 2002; Patrick McNaughton, "The Power Associations," in Jean-Paul Colleyn, ed., *Bamana: The Art of Existence in Mali* (New York, 2001), 167–81.

101. Amselle, *Mestizo Logics*, 132.

102. Broulaye Doumbia, Tenemakana, 6 October 2002; Adama Diallo, Niamala, 7 October 2002; Nouhou Diakite, Kologo, 4 October 2002; Drissa Diallo, N'Golobala, 18 May 2002.

103. Namakoro Bamba, Kolondieba, 7 July 2002; Sirakoro Traore, Moro, 7 April 2002; Ngolo Sanogo, Woblé, 5 April 2002; and Musa Sumoaro, Kolondieba, 20 November 2002.

104. Broulaye Koné, Kolondieba, 21 November 2002.

105. This narrative is a composite of various accounts recorded in Kolondieba, of which Broulaye Koné, Kolondieba, 21 November 2002, was the most historically specific.

106. Bakary Koné, Kolondieba, 1 June 2002.

107. Census, Zana, Malodina, and Fulala, 1912, ANM IE28.

108. Delafosse, *Haut-Senegal Niger*, 1:122–23. See the rich literature on the Maji Maji rebellion in German East Africa, for example, John Iliffe, "The Organisation of the Maji Maji Rebellion," *JAH* 8 (1967), 495–512; M. Wright, "Maji Maji: Prophecy and Historiography," in D. Anderson and D. Johnson, eds., *Revealing Prophets: Prophecy in East African History* (London, 1995), 124–42; and J. Monson, "Relocating Maji Maji: The Politics of Alliance and Authority in the Southern Highlands of Tanzania," *JAH* 39 (1998), 95–120. See also K. Fields, *Revival and Rebellion in Colonial Central Africa* (Princeton, 1985); and T. Ranger, "Religious Movements and Politics in Sub-Saharan Africa," *ASR* 29, 2 (1986), 1–69.

109. Peel, *Religious Encounter*, 112.

110. RP, April 1903, ANM IE27.

111. Ibid.

112. RP, Sikasso, February 1906, ANM IE73.

113. RP, Sikasso, May 1909, ANM IE73.

114. A. Aubert, *Coutumiers juridiques*, 2, Soudan, 1932, series A, no. 9.

3. SLAVE EMANCIPATION AND THE EXPANSION OF ISLAM

1. Yusuf Coulibaly, Tenemakana, 16 May 2002; Yacouba Danyoko, Tenemakana, 23 June 2002.

2. Zoumana Koné, Tienaga, 15 June 2002.

3. Census, Zana, Malodina, Foulala, April 1912, *Archives Nationales du Mali, Fonds Anciens*, IE28.

4. On theodicies, see Peter Berger, *The Sacred Canopy: Elements of a Sociological Theory of Religion* (New York, 1969), 53–80.

5. Rapport sur la situation de l'Islam, 1909, ANM 4E32.

6. Christopher Harrison, *France and Islam in West Africa, 1860–1960* (Cambridge, 1988), 49–56; see F. J. Clozel, *Les Coutumes Indigènes de la Côte d'Ivoire* (Paris, 1902).

7. On the emancipation processes in French West Africa, see M. Klein, *Slavery and Colonial Rule in French West Africa* (Cambridge, 1998), R. Roberts, "The End of Slavery in the French Soudan, 1905–1914," in S. Miers and R. Roberts, *The End of Slavery in Africa* (Madison, 1988), R. Roberts and M. Klein, "The Banamba Slave Exodus of 1905 and the Decline of Slavery in the Western Sudan," *JAH* 21 (1980), 375–94. On Senegal, see also J. Searing, *God Alone Is King: Islam and Emancipation in Senegal: The Wolof Kingdoms of Kajoor and Bawol, 1859–1914* (Portsmouth, 2002); and T. Getz, *Slavery and Reform in West Africa: Toward Emancipation in Nineteenth-Century Senegal and Gold Coast* (Athens, 2004).

8. Klein, *Slavery and Colonial Rule*, 170–73.

9. See Frederick Cooper, Thomas C. Holt, and Rebecca J. Scott, *Beyond Slavery: Explorations of Race, Labor, and Citizenship in Post-Emancipation Societies* (Chapel Hill, 2000); and Gregory Mann, *Native Sons: West African Veterans and France in the Twentieth Century* (Durham, 2006).

10. Orlando Patterson, *Slavery and Social Death: A Comparative Study* (Cambridge, 1982).

11. F. Cooper, *From Slaves to Squatters: Plantation Labor and Agriculture in Zanzibar and Coastal Kenya, 1890–1925* (New Haven, 1980); M. Klein, ed., *Breaking the Chains: Slavery, Bondage, and Emancipation in Modern Africa and Asia* (Madison, 1993); and P. E. Lovejoy and J. S. Hogendorn, *Slow Death for Slavery: The Course of Abolition in Northern Nigeria, 1897–1936* (Cambridge, 1993).

12. See Cooper et al., *Beyond Slavery*.

13. Klein, *Slavery and Colonial Rule*, 215.

14. See K. Mann, "Ending Slavery/Reforging Freedom: The Problem of Emancipation in Western Culture: A Review Essay," *CSSH* 45, 1 (2003), 29–40.

15. Klein's approximations are that two-thirds of slaves did not leave. *Slavery and Colonial Rule*, 197–98.

16. RP, April 1906, Haut-Sénégal-Niger, *Archives Nationales de France, Centre des Archives d'Outre Mer* (CAOM), 2G6/6.

17. Klein, *Slavery and Colonial Rule*, 203–05, 216–19.

18. RP, May 1906, CAOM, 2G6/6.

19. RP, 1905, ANM IE27.

20. RP, 1908 1st trim; 1909, CAOM 2G9/11, 2G8/1; RP, October 1906, ANM IE28.

21. Rapport, Inspection, 1910, ANM IE27; see also Klein, *Slavery and Colonial Rule*, 170–73.

22. RP, November 1906; Census, Zana, Malodina, Foulala (April 1912), ANM IE28.

23. RP, 1907 1st trim; 1908 2d trim; 1910 1st trim, CAOM, 2G7/3, 2G8/1, 2G10/17.

24. Klein, *Slavery and Colonial Rule*, 205–09, 219–28.

25. RP, 1908 3d and 4th trim, CAOM 2G8/1.

26. Klein, *Slavery and Colonial Rule*, 219–25; François Manchuelle, *Willing Migrants: Soninke Labor Diasporas, 1848–1960* (Ohio, 1997), 130–43.

27. RP, 1911, HSN; April 1903, Kankan; 1906, Guinea; 1908, HSN; October 1906, Ivory Coast, CAOM 2G11/9, 2G3/1, 2G/6, 2G8/1, and 2G6.

28. Salimata Diallo, Tenemakana, 15 May 2002; Mariame Koné, Tenemakana, 26 June 2002; Bakari Diarra, Kolondieba, 28 July 2002; Yusuf Coulibaly, Tenemakana, 16 May 2002.

29. Rapport Agricole, 1909, Senegal; 1908 1st trim, CAOM, 2G8/6 and 2G8/1; Monograph, 1906, ANM 1D37.

30. RP, February 1906; January 1907, ANM IE28.

31. RP, April 1907, ANM IE28.

32. Registres des affaires civiles et commerciales, Tribunal de Province, Bougouni, ANM 2M110; and R. Roberts, *Litigants and Households: African Disputes and Colonial Courts in the French Soudan, 1895–1912* (Portsmouth, 2005), 99–178.

33. Doulaye Koné, Kolondieba, 19 November 2002.

34. Broulaye Doumbia, Tenemakana, 8 October 2002.

35. Lamine Diakité, Yanfolila (Nénéjana), 14 April 2002.

36. Bulletin politique, February 1903, Kankan, Guinea, CAOM, 2G3/1.

37. Census, Guanan, November 1923, ANM IE28.

38. Bourama Dembele, Tenemakana, 14 June 2002.

39. Jan-Jan Sidibé, Balanfina, 2 April 2002.

40. Bulletin politique, February 1903, Kankan, Guinea, CAOM, 2G3/1.

41. Bakary Diarra, Kolondieba, 28 July 2000.

42. Doulaye Koné, Kolondieba, 19 November 2002.

43. Bourama Dembele, Tenemakana, 13–14 June 2002.

44. Jan-Jan Sidibé, Balanfina, 2 April 2002.

45. Doulaye Koné, Kolondieba, 19 November 2002.

46. Yacouba Danyoko, Tenemakana, 21–23 June 2002.

47. Adama Diallo, Niamala, 12 October 2002.

48. Census, Tiemala, July 1912, ANM IE28.

49. Drissa Diallo, N'Golobala, 10 July 2002.

50. Census, Sud-ouest du cercle, December 1910, ANM IE28.

51. Bangali Koné, Bunjoba, 24 June 2002; Salimata Diallo, Tenemakana, 15 May 2002; Mariame Koné, Tenemakana, 26 June 2002. See also R. Roberts, *Two Worlds of Cotton: Colonialism and the Regional Economy in the French Soudan, 1800–1946* (Stanford: 1996), 94–96.

52. Zumana Danyoko, Tenemakana, August 2000.

53. Broulaye Doumbia, Tenemakana, 8 October 2002.

54. Namakoro Bamba, Kolondieba, 7 July 2002.

55. Monographie, 1906, ANM 1D37.

56. Rapport sur l'état social des indigenes, Bougouni, 20 October 1910, ANM IE28.

57. RP, 1910 4th trim, CAOM, 2G10/17; Klein, *Slavery and Colonial Rule*, 219.

58. Souleyman Sidibé, Solona, 10 April 2002.

59. Dramane Doumbia, Tenemakana, 21 May 2002.

60. Monographie, 1906, ANM 1D37.

61. Census, Tiemala and Nienandougou, July 1912, ANM IE28.

62. Musa Sumoaro, Kolondieba, 20 November 2002; Yacouba Danyoko, Tenemakana, 20–23 June 2002; Monographie, 1906, ANM 1D37.

63. Klein, *Slavery and Colonial Rule*, 219.

64. RP, 1911, ANM IE28.

65. RP, October and November 1906, ANM IE28.

66. Jean-Loup Amselle, *Mestizo Logics: Anthropology of Identity in Africa and Elsewhere* (Stanford, 1998) 52–53.

67. James Scott, *Seeing Like a State: How Certain Schemes to Improve the Human Condition Have Failed* (New Haven: 1998), 64–71; and J. Scott, J. Tehranian, and J. Mathias, "The Production of Legal Identities Proper to States: The Case of the Permanent Family Surname," *CSSH* 44, 1 (2002), 4–44.

68. Bakary Diarra, Kolondieba, July 28, 2000.

69. RP, 1910, ANM IE28.

70. J. B. Foussagrives, Inspection, April 1910, ANM IE28.

71. RP, 1901, CAOM, 2G1/1; see also W. B. Cohen, *Rulers of Empire: The French Colonial Service in Africa* (Stanford, 1971).

72. Fiche de renseignements, Foulala, ANM 2E13; N'waari Suntura, N'Golobala, 24 June 2002; RP, January 1904, CAOM, 2G4/1. See K. Mann and R. Roberts, eds., *Law in Colonial Africa* (Portsmouth, 1991); M. Chanock, *Law, Custom, and Social Order* (Cambridge, 1985); and S. Berry, *Chiefs Know Their Boundaries: Essays on Property, Power, and the Past in Asante, 1896–1996* (Portsmouth, 2001).

73. Mahmoud Mamdani, *Citizen and Subject: Contemporary Africa and the Legacy of Late Colonialism* (Princeton, 1996).

74. Thomas Spear, "Neo-Traditionalism and the Limits of Invention in British Colonial Africa," *JAH* 41 (2000), 459–85.

75. RP, February 1904, CAOM, 2G4/1.

76. RP, 1907 3d trim, CAOM, 2G7/3.

77. Alice Conklin, *A Mission to Civilize: The Republican Idea of Empire in France and West Africa, 1895–1930* (Stanford, 1997), 107–18, 176–78; Harrison, *France and Islam*, 51.

78. RP, 1907 3d trim, CAOM, 2G7/3.

79. RP, 1910, ANM IE28.

80. Conklin, *A Mission to Civilize*, chaps. 5, 6.

81. RP, 1910, ANM IE28.

82. RP, July 1905, ANM IE28.

83. RP, 1905–14, ANM IE28.

84. Harrison, *France and Islam*, 15–23, 33–40; David Robinson, *Paths of Accommodation: Muslim Societies and French Authorities in Senegal and Mauritania, 1880–1920* (Athens, 2000), 64–69; Alfred Le Chatelier, *L'Islam en Afrique occidentale* (Paris, 1899); X. Coppolani and O. Depont, *Les Confréries religieuses musulmanes* (Algiers, 1897).

85. Harrison, *France and Islam*, 41–42.

86. RP, September and May 1903; April 1904, Sikasso, ANM IE73; August 1906; 1907, ANM IE28.

87. RP, January 1906; August 1907, November 1910, ANM IE73. On early colonial Sikasso, with particular attention to gender and the legal system, see Emily Burrill, "Meanings of Marriage in a Market Town: Gender, Conjugality, and Law in Sikasso, French Soudan, 1895–1960," Ph.D. diss., Stanford, 2007, 74–140.

88. RP, September and October 1907; March 1908, ANM IE73.

89. P. Marty, *Études sur l'Islam et les Tribus du Soudan*, 4 vols. (Paris, 1920); Marty, *Études sur l'Islam en Côte d'Ivoire* (Paris, 1922); David Robinson, "France as a 'Muslim Power' in West Africa," *Africa Today* 46, 3/4 (1999), 105–27; Harrison, *France and Islam*, 94–117; P. J. André, *L'Islam Noir* (Paris, 1924); L. Brenner, *Controlling Knowledge: Religion, Power, and Schooling in a West African Muslim Society* (Bloomington, 2001), 39–84.

90. RP, May 1914, ANM IE28.

91. RP, April 1912; August 1912; August 1911, ANM IE28.

92. On France as a Muslim power, see Robinson, *Paths of Accommodation*, 75–96.

93. RP, November 1911, ANM IE73.

94. RP, August 1912; May 1912; June 1912 and February 1913, ANM IE28; Harrison, *France and Islam*, 29–56; Brenner, *Controlling Knowledge*, 39–84.

95. RP, June 1912, ANM IE28.

96. RP, February 1913, ANM IE28.

97. RP, August 1913, ANM IE28.

98. RP, December 1914, ANM IE28.

99. Klein, *Slavery and Colonial Rule*, 229; Humphrey Fisher, *Slavery in the History of Muslim Black Africa* (London, 2001), 91; Searing, *God Alone Is King.* See also Jonathon Glassman, *Feasts and Riot: Revelry, Rebellion, and Popular Consciousness on the Swahili Coast, 1856–1888* (Portsmouth, 1995), 55–78, 117–45; and on slave-converts in British Nigeria, see J. D. Y. Peel, *Religious Encounter*, 191–93, 187–214; and Patrick Ryan, *Imale: Yoruba Participation in the Muslim Tradition* (Missoula, 1978), 99–131.

100. Rapport sur la situation de l'Islam, ANM 4E32.

101. Ibid.; and Maurice Delafosse, *Haut-Senegal Niger* (Paris, 1912), 1:86.

102. Richard Roberts, *Warriors, Merchants, and Slaves* (Stanford, 1987), 200–201; R. Launay and B. Soares, "The Formation of an 'Islamic Sphere' in French Colonial West Africa," *Economy and Society* 28 (1999), 504–05; and Benjamin Soares, *Islam and the Prayer Economy: History and Authority in a Malian Town* (Ann Arbor, 2005), 60–68.

103. Marty, *Études sur l'Islam et les Tribus du Soudan*, 4:178; Klein, *Slavery and Colonial Rule*, 4–5, 229; Roberts, *Warriors, Merchants, and Slaves*, 200–201.

104. On the "moment of conversion," see James Searing, "Conversion to Islam: Military Recruitment and Generational Conflict in a Sereer-Safèn Village (Bandia), 1920–38," *JAH* 44 (2003), 73–94.

105. Marty, *Études sur l'Islam en Côte d'Ivoire*, 93. Marty also reported on slave converts in the Sahel regions of the French Sudan: see *Études sur l'Islam et les Tribus du Soudan*, 2:180.

106. On individual versus communal conversions, see Nehemia Levtzion, "Toward a Comparative Study of Islamization," in N. Levtzion, ed, *Conversion to Islam* (New York, 1979), 19–20; Launay and Soares, "The Formation of an 'Islamic Sphere,'" 506.

107. Yusuf Coulibaly, Tenemakana, 16 May 2002.

108. Drissa Diallo, N'Golobala, 9 July 2002.

109. Delafosse, *Haut-Sénégal-Niger*, 1:165.

110. Drissa Diallo, N'Golobala, 18 May 2002.

111. Adama Diallo, Niamala, 7 October 2002; Nouhou Diakite, Kologo, 5 October 2002; Yusuf Coulibaly, Tenemakana, 16 May 2002.

112. Bakari Diarra, Kolondieba, 28 July 2002.

113. RP, February 1913, ANM IE28.

114. Zoumana Koné, Tienaga, 15 June 2002.

115. Drissa Diallo, N'Golobala, 9 July 2002.

116. Klein, *Slavery and Colonial Rule*, 197–251.

117. Fanta Koné v Mamadu Fofana, 11 July 1910; see also Mamadu Koné v Bakari Sidibé, Tribunal de Province de Bougouni, ANM 2M110. On women in the colonial courts in French Sudan, Roberts, *Litigants and Households*, 125–78.

118. Census, Tiemala and Nienandougou, July 1912, ANM IE28; Hawa Diallo, Tenemakana, 17 May 2002; Bakary Diarra, Kolondieba, July 28, 2000. Court documents from Tribunal de Province de Bougouni, ANM 2M110.

119. See James Scott, *Domination and the Arts of Resistance: Hidden Transcripts* (New Haven, 1990).

120. Yusuf Coulibaly, Tenemakana, 16 May 2002.

121. RP, November 1911, ANM IE73.

122. On social networks, see M. Emirbayer and J. Goodwin, "Network Analysis, Culture, and the Problem of Agency," *American Journal of Sociology* 99, 6 (1994), 1411–54.

123. Salimata Diallo, Tenemakana, 6 October 2002; Bakari Diarra, Kolondieba, 3 January 2002.

124. Drissa Diallo, N'Golobala, 9 July 2002.

125. Adama Diallo, Niamala, 7 October 2002.

126. Yusuf Coulibaly, Tenemakana, 16 May 2002.

127. Yacouba Danyoko, Tenemakana, 15 July 2002.

128. RP, November 1911, ANM IE73.

129. Yusuf Coulibaly, Tenemakana, 16 May 2002.

130. Broulaye Koné, 19 November 2002.

131. RP, November 1907, ANM IE28.

132. RP, November 1906, ANM IE28.

133. RP, September 1903, ANM IE27; see also Delafosse, *Haut-Sénégal-Niger*, 3:178.

134. Drissa Diallo, N'Golobala, 10 July 2002.

135. Almamy Sidibé, Balanfina, 2 April 2002. Similar forms of rainmaking existed throughout the region. See Hawa Diallo, Tenemakana, 17 May 2002; Dramane Doumbia, Tenemakana 17 May 2002; Delafosse, *Haut-Sénégal-Niger*, 3:175.

136. Drissa Diallo, N'Golobala, 10 July 2002.

137. Almamy Sidibé, Balanfina 2 April 2002.

138. Searing, *God Alone Is King*, 75–103, 195–262.

4. COPING WITH COLONIALISM

 1. Fiche de renseignements, canton de Foulala, *Archives Nationales du Mali* (ANM) *Fonds Récents* (FR) 2E13.

 2. N'waari Suntura, N'Golobala, 24 June 2002.

 3. Frederick Cooper, "Conditions Analogous to Slavery: Imperialism and Free Labor Ideology in Africa," *Beyond Slavery: Explorations of Race, Labor, and Citizenship in Post-Emancipation Societies* (Chapel Hill, 2000), 138–43.

 4. Alice Conklin, *A Mission to Civilize: The Republican Idea of Empire in France and West Africa, 1895–1930* (Stanford, 1997), 203–11.

 5. Michael Adas, *Machines as the Measure of Men: Science, Technology, and Ideologies of Western Dominance* (Ithaca, 1989).

 6. N'waari Suntura, N'Golobala, 24 June 2002; Adama Diallo, N'Golobala, 10 October 2002; Sidiki Diallo, N'Golobala, January 2000; CdC Gov.-Gen., 4 June 1929, ANM 2E13.

 7. RP, 1935 1st trim, ANM IE10. See also Gregory Mann, *Native Sons: West African Veterans and France in the Twentieth Century* (Durham, 2006).

 8. On the First World War see Marc Michel, *L'Appel à l'Afrique: Contributions et reactions à l'effort de guerre en A.O.F., 1914–1919* (Paris, 1982); Myron Echenberg, *Colonial Conscripts: The Tirailleurs Sénégalais in French West Africa, 1857–1960* (Portsmouth, 1991); and Joe Lunn, *Memoirs of the Maelstrom: A Senegalese Oral History of the First World War* (Portsmouth, 1999).

 9. Mann, *Native Sons*, 73.

10. Michel, *L'Appel à l'Afrique*, 54–56; Mahir Saul and Patrick Royer, *West African Challenge to Empire: Culture and History in the Volta-Bani Anticolonial War* (Athens, 2001); Finn Fugelstad, "Les révoltes du Touareg du Niger, 1916–1917," *Cahiers d'études africaines* 13, 1 (1973), 82–120.

11. Conklin, *A Mission to Civilize*, 148, 175–87.

12. David Robinson, *Paths of Accommodation: Muslim Societies and French Authorities in Senegal and Mauritania, 1880–1920* (Athens, 2000), chaps. 9–11.

13. Maurice Delafosse, *Haut-Senegal Niger* (Paris, 1912), 3:214–15; see also Jean-Loup-Amselle, "Maurice Delafosse: Un Africaniste ambigu," in J.-L. Amselle and E. Sibeud, eds., *Maurice Delafosse: Entre Orientalisme et Ethnographie: l'Itinéraire d'un Africaniste, 1870–1926* (Paris, 1998), 128; and, from the same volume, Jean-Louis Triaud, "*Haut-Sénégal et Niger*, un modèle 'positiviste'? De la coutume à l'histoire: Maurice Delafosse et l'invention de l'histoire africaine," 224.

14. Christopher Harrison, *France and Islam in West Africa, 1860–1960* (Cambridge, 1988), 144–82. On Brévié in Indochina and under Vichy, see Eric Jennings, *Vichy in the Tropics: Pétain's National Revolution in Madagascar, Guadeloupe, and Indochina, 1940–1944* (Stanford, 2001), 16–17, 130–98.

15. Brévié, *L'Islamisme contre Naturisme au Soudan Français: Essai de psychologie politique coloniale* (Paris, 1923).

16. See K. Brown, "The Impact of the *Dahir Berbère* in Salé," in E. Gellner and C. Micaud, eds., *Arabs and Berbers: From Tribe to Nation in North Africa* (London, 1972); and E. Burke III, "The Image of the Moroccan State in French Ethnological Literature: A New Look at the Origins of Lyautey's Berber Policy," in E. Gellner and C. Micaud, eds., *Arabs and Berbers*.

17. Lt.-Gov. to Gov.-Gen., March 1916, *Archives Nationales du Senegal*, (ANS), 4D71. See Gregory Mann, "The Tirailleur Elsewhere: Military Veterans in Colonial and Post-Colonial Mali, 1918–1968," PhD. diss., Northwestern University, 2000, 192–98; Mann, *Native Sons*, 153–71; James Searing, "Conversion to Islam: Military Recruitment and Generational Conflict in a Sereer-Safèn Village (Bandia), 1920–38," *JAH* 44 (2003), 73–94.

18. Marc Michel, "Pouvoirs Religieux et Pouvoirs d'Etat dans les Troupes Noires Pendant la Premiére Guerre Mondiale," *Economica* (1995), 295–308; Joe Lunn, "Kande Kamara Speaks: An Oral History of the West African Experience in France, 1914–1918," in Melvin Page, ed., *Africa and the First World War* (New York, 1987); Mann, "The Tirailleur Elsewhere," 192–98.

19. Louis Brenner, *West African Sufi: The Religious Heritage and Spiritual Search of Cerno Bokar Saalif Taal* (Berkeley, 1984), 37; see also Brenner, *Controlling Knowledge*, 90–91; Maurice Delafosse, "L'Animisme nègre et sa résistance à l'islamisation en Afrique occidentale," *Revue du Monde Musulman* 49 (1922), 121–63; Harrison, *France and Islam*, 128.

20. Affairs Politiques, Soudan, 1938–41, *Archives Nationales de France, Centre des Archives d'Outre Mer* (CAOM) FM603.

21. Mann, *Native Sons*, 86–93. As my informants noted, there were few *woloso* slaves in Buguni. But many of them did end up in the military. Tenaiko Bamba, Kolondieba, 12 October 2002; Bourama Dembele, Tenemakana, 16 June 2002.

22. RP, 1929 4th trim; Note sur le chef de canton de Bolou, 10 July 1928; RP, 1935 1st trim, ANM IE10.

23. RP, 1934, ANM IE10.

24. RP, 1935 1st trim, ANM IE10.

25. Jean-Loup Amselle, *Mestizo Logics: Anthropology of Identity in Africa and Elsewhere* (Stanford, 1998), 156; on uses of writing, see also Sean Hawkins, *Writing and Colonialism in Northern Ghana: The Encounter between the LoDagaa and "The World on Paper"* (Toronto, 2002); and Derek Peterson, *Creative Writing: Translation, Bookkeeping and the Work of Imagination in Colonial Kenya* (Portsmouth, 2004).

26. Letters, 6 June 1929, CdC to LG; 5 May 1929, Samba Diarra to M. Bancal; May 1929, Samba Diarra to Bureau Politique, ANM 2E13.

27. Letters, 4 June 1929, CdC; 6 June 1929, CdC to LG; Note, 23 May 1929, ANM 2E13.

28. RP, 1926 2d trim; 1935 2d trim; 1930 4th trim, ANM IE10. See also Frederick Cooper, "Africa and the World Economy," in F. Cooper et al., eds., *Confronting*

Historical Paradigms: Peasants, Labor, and the Capitalist World System in Africa and Latin America (Madison, 1993), 127.

29. RP, 1929 4th trim; 1931 3d trim, ANM IE10.

30. Letters, 4 June 1929, CdC to LG; J. Martin to LG, 25 July 1929; Confidential Telegram, 17 June and 6 July 1929, CdC to Koulouba; and Koulouba to CdC, ANM 2E13; RP, 1931 1st trim, ANM IE10.

31. RP, 1934 3d trim, ANM IE10.

32. N'waari Suntura, N'Golobala, 24 June 2002.

33. Sidiki Diallo, N'Golobala, January 2000; Adama Diallo, Niamala, 10 October 2002; Nouhou Diakite, Kologo, 5 October 2002. See also Stephen Ellis and Gerrie Ter Haar, *Worlds of Power: Religious Thought and Political Practice in Africa* (Oxford, 2004), esp. chaps. 4, 5.

34. N'waari Suntura, N'Golobala, 24 June 2002.

35. Procès-verbal, chefs de villages du Basidibé, 27 December 1937; Rapport, Basidibé, 1 January 1938; CdC to GG, 9 February 1938, ANM 2E12; RP, Note sur le chef de canton, Basidibé, 12 July 1928; Rapport 1936 1st trim, ANM IE10; Yusuf Sidibé, Koniba-Barila, 27 March 2002.

36. RP, 1934 4th trim, ANM IE10; Fiche de renseignements, Gouantiedougou, ANM 2E12.

37. CdC to LG, 16 February 1934; Fiche de renseignements, 1919–34 and 1934–50, ANM 2E14; RP, 1934 and 1935, ANM IE10; Namakoro Bamba, Kolondieba, 8 July 2002; Bakari Koné, Kolondieba, 7 June 2002; Bintu Koné, Kolondieba, 10 October 2002.

38. Cooper, "Conditions Analogous to Slavery," 107–49.

39. RP, 1934 4th trim, ANM IE10; Tenaiko Bamba, Kolondieba, 12 October 2002; Souleyman Sidibé, Solona, 10 April 2002; Babacar Fall, *Le Travail Forcé en Afrique occidentale française, 1900–1945* (Paris, 1993), chaps. 2, 3, 5, 6.

40. RE, 1933 4th trim, ANM IE10. See also Myron Echenberg and Jean Filipovich, "African Military Labor and the Building of the Office du Niger Installations, 1925–1950," *JAH* 27 (1986); Dennis Cordell and Joel Gregory, "Labor Reservoirs and Population: French Colonial Strategies in Koudougou, Upper Volta, 1914–1939," *JAH* 23 (1982); Frederick Cooper, *Decolonization and African Society: The Labor Question in French and British Africa* (Cambridge, 1996), 25–43; Monica Van Beusekom, *Negotiating Development: African Farmers and Colonial Experts at the Office du Niger, 1920–1960* (Portsmouth, 2002), 62–63.

41. RP, 1935, ANM IE10.

42. Bakari Koné, Kolondieba, 7 June 2002.

43. RE, 1933, ANM IE10; Bourama Dembele, Tenemakana, 14 June 2002; and Yusuf Coulibaly, Tenemakana, 26 May 2002.

44. Much of this was explained to me by Lamine Diakite, a former colonial interpreter in Buguni, and also Sidiki Suntura, a former *lasigiden*, or canton representative, and his son, Adama. Interviews, Lamine Diakite, Yanfolila, 14 April 2002; Sidiki Suntura, N'Golobala, August 2000; Adama Diallo, N'Golobala, 18 July 2002. On interpreters and intermediaries in the French

colonial West African context, see Henri Brunschwig, *Noirs et Blancs dans l'Afrique Noire Française, ou comment le colonisé devient colonisateur (1870–1914)* (Paris, 1983); Amadou Hampaté Bâ, *L'etrange destin de Wangrin* (Paris, 1973), which provides a unique insider's view; more recently Emily Lynn Osborn, " 'Circle of Iron' ": African Colonial Employees and the Interpretation of Colonial Rule in French West Africa," *JAH* 44 (2003), 29–50.

45. Sekou Koné, Kolondieba, 23 November 2002; and Sekou Diakite, Balanfina, 3 April 2002; Drissa Diallo, N'Golobala, 10 July 2002; Tenaiko Bamba, Kolondieba, 12 October 2002. For more on violence within colonial settings, see William Beinart, "Political and Collective Violence in Southern African Historiography," *Journal of Southern African Studies* 18, 3 (1992), 455–86.

46. Rapport de Tournée, Djallon-Foula, 6 July 1928; RP, 1934; 1930 1st trim, ANM IE10.

47. Rapport Agricole, 1924 4th trim; 1926, ANM IR111; Bakari Koné, Kolondieba, 7 June 2002. See Richard Roberts, *Two Worlds of Cotton: Colonialism and the Regional Economy in the French Soudan, 1800–1946* (Stanford, 1996); and Van Beusekom, *Negotiating Development*. On the broader picture, see also A. Isaacman and R. Roberts, eds., *Cotton, Colonialism and Social History in Sub-Saharan Africa* (Portsmouth, 1995); A. Isaacman, *Cotton Is the Mother of Poverty: Peasants, Work, and Rural Struggle in Colonial Mozambique, 1938–1961* (Portsmouth, 1996); E. Mandala, *Work and Control in a Peasant Economy: A History of the Lower Tchiri Valley, 1859–1960* (Madison, 1990); and T. Bassett, *The Peasant Cotton Revolution in West Africa: Côte d'Ivoire, 1880–1995* (Cambridge, 2001).

48. RE, 1935 2d trim, ANM 1Q332; RA, 1926 and 1928, ANM IR111; Lamine Diakite, Yanfolila, 10 April 2002; Souleyman Sidibé, Solona, 10 April 2002; M'Bemba Sidibé, Balanfina, 3 April 2002. On background, see Roberts, *Two Worlds of Cotton*, 174–75; and Isaacman, *Cotton Is the Mother of Poverty*.

49. Tenaiko Bamba, Kolondieba, 12 October 2002; Bourama Coulibaly, Tenemakana, July 2002; Sidiki Koné, Kolondieba, 9 October 2002; Bakari Koné, Kolondieba, 7 June 2002. On similar themes in African fiction, see Cheikh Hamidou Kane, *Ambiguous Adventure* (New York, 1963).

50. Drissa Diallo, N'Golobala, 17 July 2002; Brunschwig, *Noirs et Blancs dans L'Afrique Noire Française*, 105–47; Maurice Meker, *Le Temps Colonial* (Dakar, 1980), 117–84.

51. Robert Launay, *Beyond the Stream: Islam and Society in a West African Town* (Cambridge, 1992), 64–65.

52. Salimata Diallo, Tenemakana, 15 May 2002; Hawa Diallo, Tenemakana, 6 October 2002; Almamy Sidibé, Balanfina, 3 April 2002. On related processes in Senegal, see Peter Mark, "Urban Migration, Cash Cropping, and Calamity: The Spread of Islam among the Diola of Boulouf (Senegal), 1900–1940," *African Studies Review* 21, 2 (1978), 1–14.

53. RA, 1924 3d trim; 1925 4th trim; 1926 annual; 1928 4th trim; 1931 3d trim, ANM IR111; RE, 13 October 1926, ANM 1Q332; Souleyman Sidibé, Solona, 10 April 2002.

54. Salimata Diallo, Tenemakana, 15 May 2002; Sidiki Koné, Kolondieba, 9 October 2002, Hawa Diallo, Tenemakana, 19 May 2002.

55. RP, 1931 2d trim, ANM IE10; RE, 1932 and 1933, ANM 1Q332. On the wider context, see also Monique Lakroum, *Le travail inégal: Paysans et salariés sénégalais face à la crise des années trente* (Paris, 1982); and Catherine Coquery-Vidrovitch "Mutation de l'impérialisme français dans les années 30," *African Economic History* 4 (1977), 103–52, and "L'Afrique coloniale française et la crise de 1930: Crise structurelle et genése du sous-dévéloppement," *Revue Française d'histoire d'outre-mer* 63 (1976), 386–424.

56. James Ferguson, *Expectations of Modernity: Myths and Meanings of Urban Life on the Zambian Copperbelt* (Berkeley, 1999), 38–81; Jean-Loup Amselle, ed., *Les migrations africaines: réseau et processus migratoires* (Paris, 1976).

57. Sekou Koné, Kolondieba, 23 November 2002; Bourama Dembele, Tenemakana, 14 June 2002; Adama Diallo, Niamala, 10 October 2002. See Bourdieu, *Outline of a Theory of Practice* (Cambridge, 1977), 72–73; and on other methodological considerations, see Jane Guyer, "Household and Community in African Studies," *African Studies Review* 24, 2/3 (1981), 87–137.

58. RP, 1910, CAOM 2G10/17.

59. Philippe David, *Les Navétanes: Histoire des migrants saisonniers de l'arachide en Sénégambie des origins à nos jours* (Dakar, 1980), 31–33, 45–71, 113–20.

60. RP, 1910, CAOM 2G10/8; David, *Les Navétanes*, 122–28. On the early period, see David, *Les Navétanes*, chap. 1; K. Swindell, "Serawoolies, Tillibunkas and Strange Farmers: The Development of Migrant Groundnut Farming in the Gambia," *JAH* 21 (1980), 93–104; G. Brooks, "Peanuts and Colonialism: Consequences of the Commercialization of Peanuts in West Africa, 1830–1870," *JAH* 16 (1965), 29–54; J. Searing, *God Alone Is King: Islam and Emancipation in Senegal: The Wolof Kingdoms of Kajoor and Bawol, 1859–1914* (Portsmouth, 2002). The *laptots* have been studied most thoroughly by François Manchuelle in *Willing Migrants: Soninke Labor Diasporas, 1848–1960* (Ohio, 1997), 41–145. See also James Searing, *West African Slavery and Atlantic Commerce: The Senegal River Valley, 1700–1860* (Cambridge, 1993), 93–128.

61. RP, 1930 4th trim; 1937; Census, Guanan, 1923; Tournée, March 1928, ANM IE10; Rapport, 15 April 1923, ANM S126; and Yusuf Sidibé, Konimba-Barila, 27 March 2002; Moro Sidibé, Yanfolila, 10 March 2002.

62. Lamine Diakite, Yanfolila, 14 April 2002.

63. Moro Sidibé, Yanfolila, 10 March 2002; CdC Kita to Gov, 18 April 1923, ANM S126.

64. Yusuf Sidibé, Konimba-Barila, 27 March 2002; Moro Sidibé, Yanfolila, 10 March 2002; Jan-Jan Sidibé, Balanfina, 2 April 2002. On the railroad, see James Jones, *Industrial Labor in the Colonial World: Workers of the Chemin de Fer Dakar-Niger, 1881–1963* (Portsmouth, 2002).

65. David, *Les Navétanes*, 118–20, 163.

66. Ibid. 118–20, 163, 193–96; Abou Sidibé, Yanfolila, 14 March 2002; Zumana Koné, Tienaga, 15 June 2002; Adama Diallo, N'Golobala, 18 July 2002; Madou

Koné, Bunjoba, 19 June 2002. On religious conversion in Casamance, see Mark, "Urban Migration, Cash Cropping, and Calamity," 1–14; Peter Mark, *A Cultural, Economic, and Religious History of the Basse Casamance Since 1500* (Stuttgart, 1985); and Paul Nugent, "Cyclical History in the Gambia/Casamance Borderlands: Refuge, Settlement and Islam from c. 1880 to the Present," *JAH* 48 (2007), 221–43.

67. David, *Les Navétanes*, 193–96; Abou Sidibé, Yanfolila, 14 March 2002; Zumana Koné, Tienaga, 15 June 2002.

68. Rapport, 15 April 1923; CdC Kita to GG, 18 April 1923; ANM S126.

69. Jan-Jan Sidibé, Balanfina, 2 April 2002

70. Rapport, Bougouni, 15 April 1923; Rapport, Satadougou, 1923; Navétanes, 1932–41, ANM S126.

71. Searing, *God Alone Is King*, 212–13.

72. RP, 1934 4th trim, ANM 1E10; Rapport sur l'emigration volontaire des jeunes gens, Bougouni, Navétanes, 1932–41, ANM S126; Tenaiko Bamba, Kolondieba, 12 October 2002.

73. Bakari Koné, Kolondieba, 7 June 2002

74. In 1933, there were around two thousand gold miners in the region. By 1938 the number had grown to twenty thousand. See RE, 1934 and 1938, ANM 1Q332; École Coloniale Mémoire of Jean Réné Martin, *L'orpaillage indigene dans le cercle de Bougouni*, 8 April 1947, CAOM 3Ecol79/2; RP, 1935, ANM 1E10.

75. Tenaiko Bamba, Kolondieba, 12 October 2002.

76. RP, 1932, ANM 1E10; and Bourama Dembele, Tenemakana, 22 June 2002; Amadou Sidibé, Solona, 10 April 2002; Zumana Danyoko, Tenemakana, August 2000; Yacouba Danyoko, Tenemakana, 18 May 2002; Salimata Diallo, Tenemakana, 16 May 2002.

77. RP, 1926 4th trim; 1935 Annual; 1937 3d trim, ANM 1E10; Musa Diallo, Kolondieba, 17 June 2002; M'Bemba Sidibé, Balanfina, 3 April 2002; Jeneba Koné, Woblé, 6 May 2002; Madji Konate, Kolondieba, 23 November 2002; Salimata Diallo, Tenemakana, 15 May 2002; Solo Sanogo, Woblé, 5 May 2002; Madji Traore, Buguni, 9 August 2000; Bourama Dembele, Tenemakana, 22 June 2002; Broulaye Doumbia, Tenemakana, 13 May 2002.

78. Nancy Rose Hunt, *A Colonial Lexicon: Of Birth Ritual, Medicalization, and Mobility in the Congo* (Durham, 1999), 323. See also a useful critique of modernity in Frederick Cooper, *Colonialism in Question: Theory, Knowledge, History* (Berkeley, 2005), 113–49.

79. James Clifford, "Indigenous Articulations," *The Contemporary Pacific* 13, 2 (2001), 470; see also Murray Chapman, "On the Cross-Cultural Study of Circulation," *International Migration Review* 12 (1978), 559–69.

80. Sekou Koné, Kolondieba, 23 November 2002.

81. Martin Klein and Richard Roberts, "The Resurgence of Pawning in French West Africa during the Depression of the 1930s," in Paul E. Lovejoy and Toyin Falola, eds., *Pawnship, Slavery and Colonialism in Africa* (Trenton, 2003), 409–26.

82. Suzanne Miers and Igor Kopytoff, eds., *Slavery in Africa: Historical and Anthropological Perspectives* (Madison, 1977), 10.

83. RP, 4th trim 1932, ANM IE10. On pawning in neighboring Sikasso, see Emily Burrill, "Meanings of Marriage in a Market Town: Gender, Conjugality, and Law in Sikasso, French Soudan, 1895–1960," Ph.D. diss., Stanford, 2007, 161–72.

84. Tenaiko Bamba, Kolondieba, 12 October 2002.

85. Madji Konate, Binka, 23 November 2002; see also Sekou Diakite, Balanfina, 2 April 2002; Siaka Diarra, Woblé, 5 May 2002; Diahara Coulibaly and Kapicòri Coulibaly, Woblé, 4 May 2002.

86. Klein and Roberts, "The Resurgence of Pawning," 409–11, 426.

87. Cooper, "Conditions Analogous," 107–49.

88. Sekou Koné, Kolondieba, 23 November 2002; Adama Diallo, N'Golobala, 18 July 2002; Madji Konate, Kolondieba, 23 November 2002; Namakoro Bamba, Kolondieba, 7 July 2002; Jahara Coulibaly and Jeneba Koné, Woblé, 5 May 2002; Hawa Diallo, Tenemakana, 14 and 19 May 2002; Bintu Koné, Kolondieba, 10 October 2002.

89. Kapicòri Coulibaly, Woblé, 5 May 2002. On Senufo peasant women, see Chantal Rondeau, *Les paysannes du Mali: especes de liberté et changements* (Paris, 1994); and Burrill, "Meanings of Marriage," 141–60.

90. RP, 1930 4th trim, ANM IE10; RE, 1933, ANM 1Q332.

91. Bintu Koné, Kolondieba, 10 October 2002; Kani Sidibé, Yanfolila, 11 March 2002.

92. Kani Sidibé, Yanfolila, 11 March 2002; Salimata Diallo, Tenemakana, 15 May 2002; Kadia Diarra, Woblé, 6 May 2002; Hawa Diallo, Tenemakana, 13 May 2002. See also M. P. Moor, "Cooperative Labor in Peasant Agriculture," *Journal of Peasant Studies* (1975), 270–91.

93. M'Bemba Sidibé, Balanfina, 3 April 2002; and Dramane Doumbia, Tenemakana, 16 May 2002.

94. Madji Konate, Kolondieba, 23 November 2002; Namakoro Bamba, Kolondieba, 7 July 2002; Sekou Koné, Kolondieba, 23 November 2002.

5. TRANSFORMING THE VILLAGE

1. Rapport de tournée, Canton de Foulala, 1941, *Archives Nationales du Mali* (ANM) *Fonds Récents* (FR) IE10; Broulaye Doumbia, Tenemakana, 8 October 2002.

2. On tirailleurs in the Second World War, see Myron Echenberg, *Colonial Conscripts: Tirailleurs Sénégalais in French West Africa, 1857–1960* (Portsmouth, 1991); Bakari Kamian, *Des tranchées de Verdun à l'église Saint-Bernard* (Paris, 2001); Gregory Mann, *Native Sons: West African Veterans and France in the Twentieth Century* (Durham, 2006); and Nancy Lawler, *Soldiers of Misfortune: Ivoirien Tirailleurs of World War Two* (Athens, 1992).

3. Jean-Loup Amselle, *Mestizo Logics: Anthropology of Identity in Africa and Elsewhere* (Stanford, 1998), 157.

4. On election results in Buguni, see Rapports Politiques, Annual 1956 and 1957, ANM IE10; Kani Sidibé, Yanfolila, 11 March 2002; Musa Diallo, Kolondieba, 17 June 2002; Salimata Diallo, Tenemakana, 17 May 2002.

5. Ruth Morgenthau, *Political Parties in French-Speaking West Africa* (Oxford, 1964), 276–84; W. J. Foltz, *From French West Africa to the Mali Federation* (New Haven, 1965), 119–65, 144; see also my "History, Memory and the Legacy of Samori in Southern Mali, c. 1880–1898," *JAH* 49 (2008), 266–67.

6. Tony Chafer, *The End of Empire in French West Africa: France's Successful Decolonization* (Oxford, 2002), 163–92; Frederick Cooper, *Decolonization and African Society: The Labor Question in French and British Africa* (Cambridge, 1996), 424–30; and Frederick Cooper, *Africa since 1940: The Past of the Present* (Cambridge, 2002), 76–84.

7. Broulaye Doumbia, Tenemakana, 13 May 2002.

8. Frederick Cooper, "Africa and the World Economy," in F. Cooper et al., eds., *Confronting Historical Paradigms: Peasants, Labor, and the Capitalist World System in Africa and Latin America* (Madison, 1993), 127; F. Cooper, *On the African Waterfront: Urban Disorder and the Transformation of Work in Colonial Mombassa* (New Haven: 1987), 10; Maurice Méker, *Le Temps Colonial* (Dakar, 1980), 122–84.

9. Census, Gouanan, 1942; RP, 1940 and 1941, ANM IE10. See also M. Foucault, *Discipline and Punish: The Birth of the Prison* (New York, 1979), 195–228; Méker, *Le Temps,* 122–24.

10. See Ruth Ginio, *French Colonialism Unmasked: The Vichy Years in French West Africa* (Lincoln, 2008); Martin Thomas, *The French Empire at War, 1940–1945* (Manchester, 2007); Eric Jennings, *Vichy in the Tropics: Pétain's National Revolution in Madagascar, Guadeloupe, and Indonesia, 1940–44* (Stanford, 2001).

11. Cooper, *Decolonization,* 141–56, 161.

12. Philippe David, *Les Navétanes: Histoire des migrants saisonniers de l'arachide en Sénégambie des origins à nos jours* (Dakar, 1980), 218–42, 298–312.

13. Ibid., 298–312; Census, Falani-Ouola, 1943, ANM IE10; Siaka Diarra, Woblé, 5 May 2002; M'Bemba Sidibé, Balanfina, 3 April 2002; Bakari Koné, Kolondieba, 7 June 2002.

14. RP, 1940, ANM IE10.

15. Bakari Koné, Kolondieba, 7 June 2002; Adama Diallo, Niamala, 12 October 2002; Nouhou Diakite, Koloko, 4–7 October 2002; Mameri Konate, Koloni, 25 July 2002; Fatumata Doumbia, Zimpiala, 8 October 2002; and Sekou Koné, Kolondieba, 23 November 2002.

16. Census, Gouantiedougou and Niené, 1942, ANM IE10; Doulaye Diarra, Woblé, 5 May 2002; Solo Sanogo, Woblé, 5 May 2002.

17. RP, 1943, ANM IE10; Jeneba Koné, Woblé, 6 May 2002; Salimata Diallo, Tenemakana, 15 May 2002.

18. Namakoro Bamba, Kolondieba, 7 July 2002.

19. Tournée, Ouassoulou-Balé, 1946, ANM IE10.

20. Sekou Koné, Kolondieba, 23 November 2002; Méker, *Le Temps,* 123; on veterans and politics after the war, see also Mann, *Native Sons,* 108–45.

21. David, *Les Navétanes,* 297–323; Dennis Cordell, Joel W. Gregory, and Victor Piché, *Hoe and Wage: A Social History of a Circular Migration System in*

West Africa (Boulder, 1996); Thomas J. Bassett, *The Peasant Cotton Revolution in West Africa, Côte d'Ivoire, 1880–1995* (Cambridge, 2001), 51–106; and Samir Amin, *Le développement du capitalisme en Côte d'Ivoire* (Paris, 1967), 30–45. On labor migration in South Africa, see Patrick Harries, *Work, Culture and Identity: Migrant Workers in Mozambique and South Africa, 1860–1910* (Portsmouth, 1994); Charles Van Onselen, *Chibaro: African Mine Labor in Southern Rhodesia, 1900–1933* (London, 1976); T. Dunbar Moodie, *Going for Gold: Men, Mines and Migration* (Berkeley, 1994); and Collin Murray, *Families Divided: The Impact of Migrant Labour in Lesotho* (Cambridge, 1981).

22. Census, Gouanan (March–December 1950), ANM IE10. For an evocative exploration of migrant subcultures, see the film by Jean Rouch, *Jaguar* (1954), as well as his ethnography "Migrations au Ghana," *Journal de la Société des Africanistes* 26 (1956), 33–196.

23. Abou Sidibé, Yanfolila, 14 March 2002.

24. RP, 1953, Subdivision de Yanfolila, ANM IE10.

25. Abou Sidibé, Yanfolila, 14 March 2002; Sirakoro Traore, Moro, 7 May 2002; Sekou Diakite, Balanfina, 2 April 2002; Broulaye Doumbia, Tenemakana, 8 October 2002.

26. Census, Bambeledougou, 1955, ANM IE10.

27. Census, Foulala 1951; Sibirila 1950; Zana 1954; Tiemala 1954 and 1955; Siondougou 1949 and 1955; Bilatouma 1954, ANM IE10.

28. Monograph, Niené, 1952; Tournée, Niené 1953, ANM IE10.

29. N'Golo Sangare, Woble, 6 May 2002.

30. Doulaye Diarra, Woble, 6 May 2002.

31. T. Barnes, "Virgin Territory? Travel and Migration by African Women in Twentieth-Century Southern Africa," in S. Geiger, J. Allman, and N. Musisi, eds., *Women in African Colonial Histories* (Bloomington, 2002), 165–90; see also Luise White, *Comforts of Home: Prostitution in Colonial Nairobi* (Chicago, 1990). On women migrants from French Sudan, particularly the region around Kayes and Kita, see Marie Rodet, *Les Migrantes Ignorées du Haut-Sénégal, 1900–1946* (Paris, 2007).

32. RP, 1957, ANM IE10; and École Coloniale Memoire of Jean Rene Martin, L'orpaillage indigene dans le cercle de Bougouni, 8 April 1947, Archives Nationales de France, Centre des Archives d'Outre Mer (CAOM) 3Ecol79/2.

33. Madji Konate, Kolondieba, 23 November 2002.

34. Bakari Koné, Kolondieba, 7 June 2002; Fatumata Doumbia, Zimpiala, 8 October 2002. On migration to Bamako, see Claude Meillassoux, *Urbanization of an African Community: Voluntary Associations in Bamako* (London, 1968); on Wasulunké immigrants in Bamako, see Jean-Loup Amselle, *Les Négociants de la Savane: Histoire et organisation sociale des Kooroko* (Paris, 1977), 151–268.

35. RP, 1957, ANM IE10; Yusuf Sidibé, Koniba-Barila, 27 March 2002. See also Sara Berry, *No Condition is Permanent: The Social Dynamics of Agrarian Change in Sub-Saharan Africa* (Madison, 1993); S. Berry, *Fathers Work for Their Sons: Accumulation, Mobility, and Class Formation in an Extended Yoruba Community* (Berkeley, 1984).

36. See Charles Tilly, *Durable Inequality* (Berkeley, 1999), 16–25. For useful studies of intergenerational politics tied to gender, see Benedict Carton, *Blood from Your Children: The Colonial Origins of Generational Conflict in South Africa* (Charlottesville, 2000); and Meredith McKittrick, *To Dwell Secure: Generation, Christianity, and Colonialism in Ovamboland* (Portsmouth, 2002).

37. Jan-Jan Sidibé, Balanfina, 2 April 2002.

38. RP, 1928 4th trim, ANM IE10.

39. Cooper, *Decolonization*, 156–57.

40. RP, 1953, 3d trim, Subdivision de Yanfolila; Census, Niené, 1953, ANM IE10.

41. Nouhou Diakite, Kologo, 4 and 7 October 2002. On localism and cosmopolitanism, see James Ferguson, *Expectations of Modernity: Myths and Meanings of Urban Life on the Zambian Copperbelt* (Berkeley, 1999), 82–165.

42. Jan-Jan Sidibé, Balanfina, 2 April 2002.

43. Ali Diallo, N'Golobala, 12 June 2002; Nouhou Diakite, Koloko, 7 October 2002; Broulaye Doumbia, Tenemakana, 8 October 2002; Bakari Koné, Kolondieba, 7 June 2002; Abou Sidibé, Yanfolila, 14 March 2002; Sirakoro Traore, Moro, 7 May 2002; Sekou Diakite, Balanfina, 2 April 2002.

44. RP, 1953 3d trim, Subdivision de Yanfolila, ANM IE10.

45. Musa Diallo, Kolondieba, 17 June 2002; Namakoro Bamba, Kolondieba, 7 July 2002; Tenaiko Bamba, Kolondieba, 12 October 2002.

46. See Jane Guyer and Samuel Eno Belinga, "Wealth in People as Wealth in Knowledge: Accumulation and Composition in Equatorial Africa," *JAH* 36 (1995), 91–120.

47. Nufòn Koné, Woblé, 4 May 2002.

48. Bintu Fané, 19 May 2002; Drissa Diallo, N'Golobala, 19 May 2002; M'Bemba Sidibé, Balanfina, 3 April 2002; Broulaye Doumbia, Tenemakana, 10 October 2002; Hawa Diallo, Tenemakana, 13 May 2002; Madji Konate, Kolondieba, 23 November 2002.

49. Although there was one dispute over bridewealth in the canton of Fulala, the case concerned litigants in the trade town of Massala. Still, it shows that bridewealth was not unknown in the southeastern quadrant. Ba Sangaré v N'Tene Sangaré, 25 August 1910, Tribunal de Province de Bougouni, ANM 2M110. See also R. Roberts, *Litigants and Households: African Disputes and Colonial Courts in the French Soudan, 1895–1912* (Portsmouth, 2005), chaps. 5, 6.

50. Catherine Coquery-Vidrovitch, *African Women: A Modern History* (Boulder, 1997), 214–15; and Jeanne Maddox Toungara, "Changing the Meaning of Marriage: Women and Family Law in Côte d'Ivoire," in Gwendolyn Mikell, ed., *African Feminism: The Politics of Survival in Sub-Saharan Africa* (Philadelphia, 1997), 53–76.

51. Census, Gouantiedugu and Niené, 1942; Danou 1948; Kola, 1947, ANM IE10.

52. Doulaye Koné, Woblé, 4 May 2002; Drissa Diallo, N'Golobala, 18 May 2002; Tenaiko Bamba, Kolondieba, 12 October 2002; Sirakoro Traoré, Moro, 7 May 2002.

53. Tenaiko Bamba, Kolondieba, 12 October 2002; Sekou Koné, Kolondieba, 23 November 2002; Doulaye Koné, Woblé, 4 May 2002.

54. Sekou Koné, Kolondieba, 23 November 2002.
55. RP, 1957 Annual, ANM IE10; Census, Sibirila, 1950, and Foulala, 1951, ANM IE10.
56. Yusuf Coulibaly, Tenemakana, 17 May 2002.
57. B. Cooper, *Marriage in Maradi: Gender and Culture in a Hausa Society in Niger, 1900–1989* (Portsmouth, 1997), 90–109.
58. Census, Foulala, 1951; Census, Yorobadougou, 1957–58, ANM IE10; Salimata Diallo, Tenemakana, 16 May 2002; Kapicori Coulibaly, Woblé, 6 May 2002; Kadia Diarra, Woblé, 5 May 2002; Sanata Sangare, Woblé, 6 May 2002; Nouhou Diakite, Kologo, 4 October 2002.
59. Lamine Diakite, Yanfolila, 14 April 2002; RP, 1953 3d trim, Subdivision de Yanfolila, ANM IE10. For an account of litigation over marriage and domestic abuse in the colonial courts in the neighboring district of Sikasso, see Emily Burrill, "Meanings of Marriage in a Market Town: Gender, Conjugality, and Law in Sikasso, French Soudan, 1895–1960," Ph.D. diss., Stanford, 2007, 141–233.
60. Yusuf Coulibaly, Tenemakana, 15 May 2002.
61. Census, Kola, 1947, ANM IE10.
62. Broulaye Koné, Kolondieba, 19 November 2002.
63. Census, Foulala, 1951, ANM IE10.
64. Cooper, *Marriage in Maradi*, 91.
65. Census, Guanan, 1923; Rapport de tournée, 21 March 1928, ANM IE10.
66. See Monica Van Beusekom, *Negotiating Development: African Farmers and Colonial Experts at the Office du Niger, 1920–1960* (Portsmouth, 2002), 33–56.
67. RP, 1930 4th, ANM IE10; Rapport Agricole, 1928 2d, ANM IR111; RE, 1931 1st; Rapport, Vulgarisation Agricole, 25 January 1931, ANM IQ332; and Lamine Diakite, Yanfolila, 14 April 2002.
68. RE, 1938 2d trim, ANM IQ332; Souleyman Sidibé and Amadou Sidibé, Solona, 10 April 2002.
69. RE, 1931, ANM IQ332; see also Van Beusekom, *Negotiating Development*, 37–38.
70. Yusuf Sidibé, Koniba-Barila, 27 March 2002.
71. Lamine Diakite, Yanfolila, 14 April 2002.
72. RE, 1934, 1936, 1937, 1945, ANM IQ332; Note sur l'outillage de vulgarisation agricole, 8 October 1928, ANM IR95; Census, Djallon-Foula, 1950, ANM IE10; M'Bemba Sidibé, Balanfina, 3 April 2002.
73. RP, Census, Gouanan, 1950; 1955 Annual; Subdivision de Yanfolila, 1953, ANM IE10; El-Hajj Sekou Sidibé, Jelifin, 31 March 2002.
74. Census, Djallon-Foula, 1950, ANM IE10.
75. Census reports, Foulala, 1951; Zana, 1954; Siondougou, 1955; Bilatouma, 1954; Niené, 1953, ANM IE10.
76. Solo Sanogo, Woblé, 5 May 2002; Sirakoro Traore, Moro, 7 May 2002; Siaka Traore, Moro, 7 May 2002; Sekou Koné, Kolondieba, 23 November 2002.
77. Note de tournée, Foulala, 9 January 1958; Census, Zana, 1954, ANM IE10.
78. Adama Diallo, N'Golobala, 18 July 2002.

79. Amselle, *Les Négociants de la Savane*, 32.
80. Census, Djallon-Foula, 1950, ANM IE10.
81. M'Bemba Sidibé, Balanfina, 3 April 2002.
82. Census, Gouanan, March–December 1950, ANM IE10; Souleyman Sidibé and Amadou Sidibé, Solona, 10 April 2002.
83. Broulaye Doumbia, Tenemakana, 15 May 2002.
84. Adama Diallo, N'Golobala, 18 July 2002; Broulaye Doumbia, Tenemakana, 13 May 2002; Yusuf Coulibaly, Tenemakana, 17 May 2002; and Nouhou Diakite, Kologo, 8 October 2002; Sekou Koné, Kolondieba, 23 November 2002; Jan-Jan Sidibé, Balanfina, 3 April 2002. See also G. Brasseur, *Étude de Géographie Régionale: Le Village de Tenentou (Mali)*, Bulletin I.F.A.N. (Dakar, 1961), 48.
85. Yacouba Danyoko, Tenemakana, 10 October 2002; Sekou Koné, Kolondieba, 23 November 2002.
86. Census, Foulala, 1951, ANM IE10.
87. Census, Gouanan, March–December 1950; Siondougou, 1949; Djallon-Foula, December 1950, ANM IE10; Bisil Diakite, Buguni, August 2000; Salimata Diallo, Tenemakana, 16 May 2002.
88. Broulaye Doumbia, Tenemakana, 13 May 2002; Yusuf Coulibaly, Tenemakana, 17 May 2002; Adama Diallo, N'Golobala, 18 July 2002; and Nouhou Diakite, Kologo, 8 October 2002.

6. MIGRANTS AND THE DIALECTICS OF CONVERSION

1. Drissa Diallo, N'Golobala 17 July 2002.
2. Adama Diallo, N'Golobala, 18 July 2002.
3. See Babacar Fall, *Le Travail Forcé en Afrique occidentale française, 1900–1945* (Paris, 1993); Dennis Cordell et al., *Hoe and Wage: A Social History of a Circular Migration System in West Africa* (Boulder, 1996); Monique Lakroum, *Le travail inégal: Paysans et salariés sénégalais face à la crise des années trente* (Paris, 1982); and Frederick Cooper, *Decolonization and African Society: The Labor Question in French and British Africa* (Cambridge, 1996). See also Patrick Harries, *Work, Culture and Identity: Migrant Workers in Mozambique and South Africa, 1860–1910* (Portsmouth, 1994); and James Ferguson, *Expectations of Modernity: Myths and Meanings of Urban Life on the Zambian Copperbelt* (California, 1999).
4. See B. Soares, *Islam and the Prayer Economy: History and Authority in a Malian Town* (Ann Arbor, 2005), 69–105; A. Traore, *Islam et Colonisation en Afrique; Cheick Hamahoullah, Homme de foi et resistant* (Paris, 1983). An important offshoot of the Hamawiyya was the reform movement of Yacouba Sylla, covered in Sean Hanretta, *Islam and Social Change in French West Africa: History of an Emancipatory Community* (Cambridge, 2009).
5. RP, 1933 2d; 1936 2d; 1937, *Archives Nationales du Mali* (ANM) *Fonds Récents* IE10; see also Sylvianne Garcia, "Al-Hajj Seydou Nourou Tall, 'Grand Marabout' Tijani: l'Histoire d'une carrière, v. 1880–1980," in David Robinson and J. L. Triaud, eds., *Le Temps des Marabouts: Itinéraires et stratégies islamiques en Afrique*

occidentale française (Paris, 1997), 247–75; and, more broadly, Christopher Harrison, *France and Islam in West Africa, 1860–1960* (Cambridge, 1988), 144–93.

6. Louis Brenner, *Controlling Knowledge: Religion, Power, and Schooling in a West African Muslim Society* (Bloomington, 2001), 88–89.

7. RP, 1934; 1931 4th trim; 1936 2d trim; ANM IE10.

8. Jean-Louis Triaud, "Le crépuscule des 'Affaires musulmanes' en AOF, 1950–1956," in D. Robinson and J. L. Triaud, eds., *Le temps des marabouts*, 493–519; Brenner, *Controlling Knowledge*, 102–05.

9. Marcel Cardaire, *L'Islam et le Terroir Africain* (Bamako, 1954), 11–29.

10. Census, Niené, 1953, ANM IE10.

11. RP, 1951 4th trim; RP, 1957 Annual, ANM IE10.

12. G. Brasseur, *Étude de Géographie Régionale: Le Village de Tenentou (Mali)*, Bulletin I.F.A.N. (Dakar, 1961), 56.

13. See Robert Launay, *Traders without Trade: Responses to Change in Two Dyula Communities* (Cambridge, 1982); Richard Roberts, *Warriors, Merchants, and Slaves: The State and the Economy in the Middle Niger Valley, 1700–1914* (Stanford, 1987), 135–73; M. Emirbayer and J. Goodwin, "Network Analysis, Culture, and the Problem of Agency," *American Journal of Sociology* 99, 6 (1994), 1411–54; and Frederick Cooper, "What Is the Concept of Globalization Good For? An African Historian's Perspective," *African Affairs* 100 (2001), 189–213.

14. Namakoro Bamba, Kolondieba, 7 July 2002.

15. Census, Keikoro, 1955, ANM IE10; Balla Kouyate, Balanfina, 2 April 2002.

16. Tenaiko Bamba, Kolondieba, 12 October 2002.

17. L. Kaba, "Sheikh Mouhammad Chérif de Kankan: Le Devoir d'obéissance et la colonisation (1923–1955)," in D. Robinson and J. Triaud, eds., *Le Temps des Marabouts*, 277–97; and Soares, *Islam and the Prayer Economy*, 153–80. On trade and ethnic and Islamic networks, see A. Cohen, *Custom and Politics in Urban Africa: A Study of Migrants in Yoruba Towns* (Berkeley, 1969).

18. Yusuf Coulibaly, Tenemakana, 18 May 2002; Burama Coulibaly, Tenemakana, 18 June 2002.

19. Sidiki Koné, Kolondieba, 9 October 2002; Nouhou Diakite, Kologo, 5 and 7 October 2002; Karim Danyoko, Tenemakana, 11 October 2002; Zumana Danyoko, Tenemakana, August 2000; Yacouba Danyoko, Tenemakana, 22 June 2002.

20. RP, Côte d'Ivoire, 1946, *Archives Nationales de France, Centre des Archives d'Outre Mer* (CAOM) 2G46/28.

21. Tamar Diana Wilson, "What Determines Where Transnational Labor Migrants Go? Modifications in Migration Theories," *Human Organization* 53, 3 (1994); Douglas Massey et al., "Theories of International Migration: A Review and Appraisal," *Population and Development Review* 19 (1993), 431–66.

22. Census, Niené, 1953, ANM IE10; Ferguson, *Expectations of Modernity*, 82–122.

23. Nancy Rose Hunt, *A Colonial Lexicon: Of Birth Ritual, Medicalization, and Mobility in the Congo* (Durham, 1999).

24. Alphonse Gouilly, *L'Islam dans l'Afrique Occidentale Française* (Paris, 1952), 207–20.

25. Ali Diallo, N'Golobala, 12 June 2002; Yusuf Coulibaly, Tenemakana, 18 May 2002; Nouhou Diakite, Koloko, 7 October 2002; Broulaye Doumbia, Tenemakana, 8 October 2002; Bakari Koné, Kolondieba, 7 June 2002; Sirakoro Traore, Moro, 7 May 2002; Sekou Diakite, Balanfina, 2 April 2002.

26. Salimata Diallo, Tenemakana, 15 May 2002; Sidiki Koné, Kolondieba, 9 October 2002; Namakoro Bamba, Kolondieba, 7 July 2002.

27. Drissa Diallo, N'Golobala, 19 May 2002; Namakoro Bamba, Kolondieba, 7 July 2002; Tenaiko Bamba, Kolondieba, 12 October 2002. See also Arjun Appadurai, ed., *Social Life of Things: Commodities in Cultural Perspective* (Cambridge, 1986).

28. Yusuf Sidibé, Koniba-Barila, 27 March 2002; Sekou Diakite, Balanfina, 3 April 2002.

29. Viviana Pâques, "Bouffons Sacrés du Cercle de Bougouni (Soudan Français)," *Journal de la Société des Africanistes* 24, 1 (1954), 68–71.

30. Tenaiko Bamba, Kolondieba, 12 October 2002.

31. Salimata Diallo, Tenemakana, 15 May 2002; Bakari Koné, Kolondieba, 7 June 2002; Adama Diallo, Niamala, 12 October 2002; Fatumata Doumbia, Zimpiala, 8 October 2002; and Sekou Koné, Kolondieba, 23 November 2002.

32. Maurice Méker, *Le Temps Colonial* (Dakar, 1980), 121–22. For a useful collection of essays on material culture, see M. J. Arnoldi, C. M. Geary, and K. L. Hardin, *African Material Culture* (Bloomington, 1996).

33. Brasseur, *Étude*, 56–58; Méker, *Le Temps*, 160; on commodity consumption in Africa and an interesting local interpretation of bicycles, see Timothy Burke, *Lifebuoy Men, Lux Women: Commodification, Consumption, and Cleanliness in Modern Zimbabwe* (Durham, 1996).

34. Jan-Jan Sidibé, Balanfina, 2 April 2002.

35. Census, Foulala, 1951, ANM IE10.

36. Salimata Diallo, Tenemakana, 15 May 2002.

37. Madji Konate, Kolondieba, 23 November 2002; Sidiki Diallo, N'Golobala, January 2000; Adama Diallo, N'Golobala, 18 July 2002.

38. Zoumana Koné, Tienaga, 15 June 2002.

39. Cardaire, *L'Islam et le Terroir*, 49–53.

40. Abou Sidibé, Yanfolila, 14 March 2002; Drissa Balla, Jelifin, 31 March 2002; Yusuf Sidibé, Konima-Barila, 27 March 2002; Balla Kouyate, Balanfina, 2 April 2002; Musa Diallo, Kolondieba, 17 June 2002; Yusuf Coulibaly, 17–19 May 2002. See also Danielle Jonckers, "Le temps de prier est venu: Islamisation et pluralité religieuse dans le sud du Mali," *Journal des Africanistes* 68, 1–2 (1998); Richard Warms, "Merchants, Muslims, and Wahhabiyya: The Elaboration of Islamic Identity in Sikasso, Mali," *Canadian Journal of African Studies* 26, 3 (1992), 485–507; E. Skinner, "Islam in Mossi Society," in I. M. Lewis, ed., *Islam in Tropical Africa* (Oxford, 1966), 362; and Marie Miran, *Islam, histoire et modernité en Côte d'Ivoire* (Paris, 2006), 37–84.

41. Yacouba Danyoko, Tenemakana, 23 July 2002.

42. Musa Diallo, Kolondieba, 17 June 2002.

43. Bourama Dembele, Tenemakana, 13 June 2002.

44. RP, 1951 4th trim, ANM IE10.

45. RP, Sikasso, Annual 1956, ANM IE41.

46. Census, Kola, 1954; Niené, 1953, ANM IE10.

47. Sirakoro Traore, Moro, 6 May 2002.

48. Census, Tiemala, 1954; Siondougou, 1955, ANM IE10.

49. Census, Keikoro, 1955; Bambeledougou, 1955; Domba, 1947, ANM IE10.

50. Census, Dialakadougou, 1948, ANM IE10.

51. RP, Annual 1956, ANM IE10; Ferguson, *Expectations of Modernity*, 82–122.

52. Namakoro Bamba, Kolondieba, 1 June 2002; Musa Sumoaro, Kolondieba, 20 November 2002. See Nicholas Thomas, "The Inversion of Tradition," *American Ethnologist* 19, 2 (1992), 213–32.

53. Cardaire, *L'Islam et le Terroir*, 51.

54. Musa Diallo, Kolondieba, 17 June 2002; Sirakoro Traore, Moro, 6 May 2002; M'Bemba Sidibé, Balanfina, 3 April 2002.

55. Madja Traore, Buguni, 9 August 2000; Fatumata Doumbia, Zimpiala, 8 October 2002; Mariame Koné, Tenemakana, 5 October 2002; Hawa Diallo, Tenemakana, 14 May 2002; Bintu Koné, Kolondieba, 10 October 2002; Madji Konate, Kolondieba, 23 November 2002; Salimata Diallo, Tenemakana, 15 May 2002. Few studies have dealt with the question of conversion among African women. However, see Barbara Cooper, *Marriage in Maradi: Gender and Culture in a Hausa Society in Niger, 1900–1989* (Portsmouth, 1997); Margaret Strobel, *Muslim Women in Mombasa, 1890–1975* (New Haven, 1979); and Roberta Ann Dunbar, "Muslim Women in African History," in Nehemia Levtzion and Randall Pouwels, eds., *The History of Islam in Africa* (Athens, 2000), 397–417.

56. CdC to GG, April 1953, ANM IE10.

57. Musa Sumoaro, Kolondieba, 20 November 2002.

58. Namakoro Bamba, Kolondieba, 1 June 2002.

59. Pâques, "Bouffons Sacrés"; and Brasseur, *Étude de Géographie*.

60. Yusuf Coulibaly, 17–19 May 2002; Drissa Diallo, N'Golobala, 18 May and 9 July 2002; El Hajj Sekou Sidibé, Jelifin, 31 March 2002; Almamy Sidibé, Balanfina, 3 April 2002; Imam Bakari Koné, Kolondieba, 7 June 2002.

61. Adama Diallo, Niamala, 12 October 2002.

62. Drissa Diallo, N'Golobala, 9 July 2002.

63. See Eric Charry, *Mande Music: Traditional and Modern Music of the Maninka and Mandinka of Western Africa* (Chicago, 2000); E. Charry, "Music and Islam in Sub-Saharan Africa," in Nehemia Levtzion and Randall Pouwels, eds., *The History of Islam in Africa* (Athens, 2000), 545–63; and Lucy Duran, "Birds of Wasulu: Freedom of Expression and Expressions of Freedom in the Popular Music of Southern Mali," *British Journal of Ethnomusicology* 4 (1995), 101–34.

64. Adama Diallo, Niamala, 12 October 2002; Musa Diallo, Kolondieba, 17 June 2002; Bourama Dembele, Tenemakana, 13 June 2002; Yusuf Coulibaly, Tenemakana, 17 May 2002.

65. See Bernard Cohn, "The Census, Social Structure and Objectification in South Asia," in *An Anthropologist among the Historians and Other Essays* (Chicago, 1987); Arjun Appadurai's chapter, "Number in the Colonial Imagination," in his *Modernity at Large: Cultural Dimensions of Globalization* (Minneapolis, 1998); James Scott, *Seeing Like a State: How Certain Schemes to Improve the Human Condition Have Failed* (New Haven, 1998), esp. part 1, "State Projects of Legibility and Simplification."

66. Ian Hacking, *Historical Ontology* (Cambridge, 2002), 99–114; and I. Hacking, "The Looping Effect of Human Kinds," in D. Sperber et al., eds., *Causal Cognition: An Interdisciplinary Approach* (Oxford, 1996), 351–83.

67. Affairs Politiques, Soudan, 1938–1941, CAOM FM/603; see also Norbert Peabody, "Cents, Sense, Census: Human Inventories in Late Precolonial and Early Colonial India," *CSSH* 43, 4 (2001), 819–50.

68. Maurice Delafosse, *Haut-Sénégal-Niger* (Paris, 1912), 3:162. Officials experimented with the nominative census before the First World War but found it too arduous.

69. For a useful theoretical comment, see Frederick Cooper and Rogers Brubaker, "Beyond Identity," *Theory and Society* 29 (2000), 1–47.

70. Cardaire, *L'Islam et le Terroir*, 53n1.

71. See P. Bourdieu, *Distinction: A Social Critique of the Judgment of Taste* (Cambridge, 1984).

72. On related concerns, see J. D. Y. Peel, *Religious Encounter and the Making of the Yoruba* (Bloomington, 2000), 88–90; and also Paul Landau, " 'Religion' and Christian Conversion in African History," *Journal of Religious History* 23 (1999), 8–30.

73. Lamine Diakité, Yanfolila (Nénéjana), 14 April 2002.

74. Sekou Koné, Kolondieba, 23 November 2002.

75. Census, Zana, 1954, ANM IE10.

76. Census, Gouantiedougou, 1956, ANM IE10.

77. Lamine Diakité, Yanfolila, 14 April 2002.

78. RP, Sikasso, 1955 Annual, ANM IE41.

79. Census, Kola, 1947 and 1954; Falani-Ouola, 1955; Debelendugu, 1955, ANM IE10.

80. RP, Sikasso, 1955 Annual, ANM IE41.

81. Klaus Ernst, *Tradition and Progress in the African Village: Non-Capitalist Transformation of Rural Communities in Mali* (New York, 1976), 91–100; Jean-Loup Amselle, *Mestizo Logics: Anthropology of Identity in Africa and Elsewhere* (Stanford, 1998), 92–93.

82. Ruth Morgenthau, *Political Parties in French-Speaking West Africa* (Oxford, 1964), 234–38, 276–84; Elizabeth Schmidt, *Mobilizing the Masses: Gender, Ethnicity, and Class in the Nationalist Movement in Guinea, 1939–1958* (Portsmouth, 2005), chaps. 5, 6; Jean Suret-Canale, "La fin de la Chefferie en Guinée," *JAH* 7, 3 (1966), 459–93; Lansiné Kaba, *The Wahhabiyya: Islamic Reform and Politics in French West Africa* (Evanston, 1974), 169–252.

83. Census, Foulala, 1952, ANM IE10.

84. Census, Falani-Ouola, 1955, ANM IE10.

85. Census, Siondougou 1949 and 1955, ANM IE10.
86. Cardaire, *L'Islam et le Terroir*, 53–54.
87. Note, 10 July 1928; Census, Bolou, 1947; Revue politique, 1953 1st trim, Subdivision de Yanfolila, ANM IE10.
88. Census, Foulala, 1955, ANM IE10.
89. Drissa Diallo, N'Golobala, 17 July 2002; Yusuf Coulibaly, Tenemakana, 17 May 2002; Adama Diallo, Niamala, 12 October 2002; Toma Diallo, N'Golobala, 25 July 2002.
90. Pâques, "Bouffons Sacrés," 87.
91. Cardaire, *L'Islam et le Terroir*, 53.

7. CHANGES IN THE RELIGIOUS LANDSCAPE

1. Yacouba Danyoko, Tenemakana, 23 June 2002; and Mariame Koné, Tenemakana, 15 May 2002. On Qur'anic education in the French Sudan, see L. Brenner, *Controlling Knowledge: Religion, Power and Schooling in a West African Muslim Society* (Bloomington, 2001).
2. Yusuf Coulibaly, Tenemakana, 17–19 May 2002.
3. Adama Diallo, Niamala, 12 October 2002.
4. Drissa Diallo, N'Golobala, 9 July 2002.
5. Marcel Cardaire, *L'Islam et le Terroir Africain* (Bamako, 1954), 57.
6. Yusuf Coulibaly, Tenemakana, 19 May 2002.
7. RP, 1951 4th trim, *Archives Nationales du Mali* (ANM) *Fonds Récents* IE10.
8. Musa Sumoaro, Kolondieba, 20 November 2002.
9. See Marshall G. S. Hodgson, *The Venture of Islam: The Classical Age of Islam* (Chicago, 1961), 1:209; Ira Lapidus, *A History of Islamic Societies* (Cambridge, 2002), 200.
10. Richard Eaton, *The Rise of Islam and the Bengal Frontier, 1205–1760* (Berkeley, 1993), 231.
11. RP, 1956, ANM IE10.
12. Census, Foulala, 1951, 1958, ANM IE10; Drissa Diallo, N'Golobala, 9 July 2002; Zumana Koné, Tienaga, 15 June 2002; M'Bemba Sidibé, Balanfina, 3 April 2002.
13. Census, Falani Ouola, 1955, ANM IE10.
14. Census, Siondougou, 1955, ANM IE10.
15. Census, Debelendougou, 1955, ANM IE10.
16. Census, Foulala 1951, 1958; Basidibé 1928; Tiemala 1954, ANM IE10.
17. RP, 1953 2d trim, ANM IE10.
18. Musa Diallo, Kolondieba, 17 June 2002.
19. Yusuf Coulibaly, Tenemakana, 19 May 2002.
20. RP, 1932 2d trim; RP, 1953, ANM IE10.
21. Census, Basidibé, 1928, ANM IE10.
22. Souleyman Sidibé, Solona, 10 April 2002; and Amadou Sidibé, Solona, 10 April 2002. For Qur'an schooling in one part of Wasulu, see Etienne Gérard, *La tentation du savoir en Afrique: Politiques, mythes et stratégies d'éducation au Mali* (Paris, 1997).

23. Sekou Sidibé, Jelifin, 31 March 2002.

24. Drissa Diallo, N'Golobala, 9 July 2002; on early Qur'anic education in West Africa, see also Lamin Sanneh, *The Crown and the Turban: Muslims and West African Pluralism* (Boulder, 1997), esp. chap. 7.

25. D. Eickelman, *Knowledge and Power in Morocco: The Education of a Twentieth-Century Notable* (Princeton, 1985), 57–71.

26. RP, 1953 3d trim, ANM IE10; Hari Sidibé, Yanfolila, 28 March 2002.

27. Drissa Balla, Jelifin, 31 March 2002.

28. El Hajj Sekou Sidibé, Jelifin, 31 March 2002; Bintu Koné, Kolondieba, 10 October 2002.

29. Yacouba Danyoko, Tenemakana, 23 June 2002.

30. Sekou Diakite, Balanfina, 3 April 2002; Hari Sidibé, Yanfolila, 28 March 2002; on similar ideas in northern Burkina Faso, see also Paul Riesman, *Freedom in Fulani Social Life* (Chicago, 1977), 95–115.

31. Census, Diban, 1955, ANM IE10.

32. Yusuf Sidibé, Koniba-Barila, 27 March 2002; Sekou Diakite, Balanfina, 3 April 2002; Hari Sidibé, Yanfolila, 28 March 2002.

33. Mariame Koné, Tenemakana, 15 May 2002.

34. El Hajj Sekou Sidibé, Jelifin, 31 March 2002.

35. Bulletin politique, 1953 3d trim, Yanfolila, ANM E10.

36. Sean Hanretta, *Islam and Social Change in French West Africa: History of an Emancipatory Community* (Cambridge, 2009), 227–52.

37. Maurice Cardaire, *L'Islam et le Terroir Africain* (Bamako, 1954), 57.

38. Almamy Sidibé, Balanfina, 3 April 2002.

39. El Hajj Sekou Sidibé, Jelifin, 31 March 2002; and Drissa Balla, Jelifin, 31 March 2002.

40. Census, Foulala, 1951, 1958; Siondougou, 1955, ANM IE10.

41. Yusuf Coulibaly, Tenemakana, 17 May 2002. On discipline and techniques in traditional Qur'an schooling, see Sanneh, *The Crown and the Turban;* and the depictions in Cheikh Hamidou Kane's novel, *Ambiguous Adventure* (New York, 1963).

42. Adama Diallo, Niamala, 12 October 2002.

43. Drissa Diallo, N'Golobala, 18 May 2002.

44. Burama Dembele, Tenemakana, 13 June 2002; Adama Diallo, Niamala, 12 October 2002.

45. Yacouba Danyoko, Tenemakana, 2 May, 21–23 June 2002; Burama Dembele, Tenemakana, 2 May 2002.

46. Adama Diallo, Niamala, 12 October 2002. On the quietist approach of clerics, see Lamin Sanneh, *The Jakhanke: The History of an Islamic Clerical People of the Senegambia* (London, 1979).

47. Robert Launay, "*La Trahison des Clercs?* The 'Collaboration' of a Suwarian 'Alim," in J. Hunwick and N. Lawler, eds., *The Cloth of Many Colored Silks* (Evanston, 1996), 315.

48. Musa Sumoaro, Kolondieba, 20 November 2002.

49. Drissa Diallo, N'Golobala, 18 May 2002.

50. Amadou Sidibé, Solona, 10 April 2002; Yusuf Sidibé, Konimba-Barila, 27 March 2002; Hari Sidibé, Yanfolila, 28 March 2002; El Hajj Sekou Sidibé, Jelifin, 31 March 2002.

51. Yusuf Coulibaly, 17 May 2002; Drissa Balla, Jelifin, 31 March 2002; and Bakari Koné, Kolondieba, 7 June 2002.

52. Chaka Bamba, Kolondieba, 12 October 2002; Sirakoro Traore, Moro, 7 May 2002; Ngolo Sanogo, Woblé, 5 May 2002.

53. Namakoro Bamba, Kolondieba, 1 June 2002.

54. Mariame Koné, Tenemakana, 15 May 2002.

55. RP, August 1957; Census, Gouantiedougou, 1956, ANM IE10.

56. Census, Sibirila, 1949, ANM IE10.

57. Broulaye Koné, 19 November 2002; Drissa Diallo, N'Golobala, 18 May and 9 July 2002; and Adama Diallo, Niamala, 12 October 2002.

58. James Ferguson, *Expectations of Modernity: Myths and Meanings of Urban Life on the Zambian Copperbelt* (Berkeley, 1999), 117–120.

59. Musa Diarra, Massala, 22 May 2002.

60. Census, Kola, 1947; CdC to GG, 19 June 1947; Tournée, Nafanandougou, 1947; Kokoun, 1948, ANM IE10.

61. Maurice Méker, *Le Temps Colonial* (Dakar, 1980), 144–45.

62. Rapport sur sorcellerie, Kokoun, 1948, ANM IE10. See also Méker, *Le Temps Colonial*, which provides insights into the lives of postwar colonial administrators and also into development projects in Buguni but otherwise contains little useful information on the social lives of Africans.

63. Drissa Diallo, N'Golobala, 17 July 2002.

64. Census, Niené, 1953 ANM IE10.

65. G. Mann, "Fetishizing Religion: Allah Koura and French 'Islamic Policy' in Late Colonial French Soudan (Mali)," *JAH* 44 (2003), 263–82.

66. See Cardaire, *L'Islam et le Terroir Africain*, 30–46.

67. RP, May–August, 1954, ANM IE10.

68. Musa Diarra, Massala, 22 May 2002.

69. Benjamin F. Soares, *Islam and the Prayer Economy: History and Authority in a Malian Town* (Ann Arbor, 2005), 153–80.

70. See Robert Launay, *Beyond the Stream: Islam and Society in a West African Town* (Berkeley, 1992), 179–95; and René Otayek, "Muslim Charisma in Burkina Faso," in Donal Cruise O'Brien and Christian Coulon, eds., *Charisma and Brotherhood in African Islam* (Oxford, 1988), 90–112; A. Masquelier, *Prayer Has Spoiled Everything: Possession, Power, and Identity in an Islamic Town of Niger* (Durham, 2001).

71. Drissa Diallo, N'Golobala, 9 July 2002.

72. Adama Diallo, Niamala, 12 October 2002.

73. Yusuf Coulibaly, Tenemakana, 21 May 2002; Nouhou Diakite, Kologo, 4 and 5 October 2002; Drissa Diallo, N'Golobala, 17 July 2002.

74. Eaton, *Rise of Islam*, 257.

75. Nwaari Suntura, N'Golobala, 24 July 2002.

76. Yacouba Diallo, N'Golobala, 10 July 2002.
77. Eaton, *Rise of Islam*, 269.
78. Paul Marty, *Études sur l'Islam en Côte d'Ivoire* (Paris, 1922), 28–29.
79. Drissa Diallo, N'Golobala, 17 July 2002.
80. Yusuf Coulibaly, Tenemakana, 15 May 2002.
81. Adama Diallo, Niamala, 12 October 2002; Yacouba Diallo, N'Golobala, 10 July 2002; Kissa Domba, Niamala, 10 October 2002.
82. Almamy Sidibé, Balanfina, 3 April 2002.
83. Max Weber, *Economy and Society*, 2 vols. (Berkeley, 1978), 1:246–54.
84. Amadou Sidibé, Solona, 10 April 2002; El Hajj Sekou Sidibé, Jelifin, 31 March 2002; Yusuf Sidibé, Konimba-Barila, 27 March 2002; M'Bemba Sidibé, Balanfina, 3 April 2002; Drissa Diallo, N'Golobala, 11 July 2002; Almamy Sidibé, Balanfina, 3 April 2002.
85. Lansine Kaba, "Sheikh Mouhammad Chérif de Kankan: Le Devoir d'obéissance et la colonisation (1923–1955)," in Robinson and Triaud, eds., *Le temps des marabouts*, 277–97; El Hajj Sekou Sidibé, Jelifin, 31 March 2002.
86. David Robinson, *Paths of Accommodation: Muslim Societies and French Authorities in Senegal and Mauritania, 1880–1920* (Athens, 2000), 161–77; Kaba, "Sheikh Mouhammad Chérif," 286–97.
87. Cardaire, *L'Islam et le Terroir Africain*, 154–60, 145–68; Brenner, *Controlling Knowledge*, chaps. 2, 3.
88. Brenner, *Controlling Knowledge*, 6–11.
89. Yusuf Coulibaly, Tenemakana, 19 may 2002.
90. Drissa Diallo, N'Golobala, 17 July 2002.
91. Revue Politique, 1953, Yanfolila, ANM IE10.
92. Amadou Sidibé, Solona, 10 April 2002.
93. Census, Debelendougou, 1955, ANM IE10.
94. Census, Bolou, 13 February 1948, ANM IE10.
95. Madou Sidibé, Balanfina, 3 April 2002; and M'Bemba Sidibé, Balanfina, 3 April 2002; Almamy Sidibé, Balanfina, 3 April 2002.
96. Amadou Sidibé, Solona, 10 April 2002.
97. Yusuf Coulibaly, Tenemakana, 17 May 2002.
98. Census, Gouantiedougou, 1956, ANM IE10; Mameri Konate, Tousseguela, 7 October 2002; Drissa Diallo, N'Golobala, 17 May 2002.
99. Zumana Koné, Tienaga, 15 June 2002; Fanta Bamba, Tienaga, 25 June 2002; Mameri Konate, Tousseguela, 7 October and 15 November 2002.
100. Yusuf Coulibaly, Tenemakana, 19 May 2002.
101. See J. O. Hunwick, *Shari'a in Songhay: The Replies of al-Maghili to the Questions of Askia al-Hajj Muhammad* (Oxford, 1985); D. Robinson, *The Holy War of Umar Tal: The Western Sudan in the Mid-Nineteenth Century* (Oxford, 1985); and M. Hiskett, *The Sword of Truth: The Life and Times of the Shehu Usuman dan Fodio* (Oxford, 1973).
102. Yusuf Coulibaly, Tenemakana, 19 May 2002. The best source on this history is Lansiné Kaba, *The Wahhabiyya: Islamic Reform and Politics in French West Africa*

(Evanston, 1974); on the connections between Shubban al-muslimin and the madrasa movement, see also Brenner, *Controlling Knowledge,* chaps. 2, 3.

103. On the reform movement in contemporary Mali, see L. Brenner, "Constructing Muslim Identities in Mali," in Louis Brenner, ed., *Muslim Identity and Social Change in Sub-Saharan Africa* (Bloomington, 1993), 59–78; and also Soares, *Islam and the Prayer Economy,* 181–209.

104. See Kaba, *The Wahhabiyya,* 21–45; J.-L. Amselle, "Le Wahabisme à Bamako (1945–1985)," *Canadian Journal of African Studies,* 19, 2 (1985), 345–57; see also the case of Wahhabiyya in rural northern Mali, R. Niezen, "The 'Community of the Helpers of the Sunna': Islamic Reform among the Songhay of Gao (Mali)," *Africa* 60, 3 (1990), 399–424; and also Eickelman, *Knowledge and Power in Morocco;* R. Mitchell, *The Society of the Muslim Brothers* (Oxford, 1993).

105. Kaba, *The Wahhabiyya,* 32–39, 197–202; R. Warms, "Merchants, Muslims, and Wahhabiyya: The Elaboration of Islamic Identity in Sikasso, Mali," *Canadian Journal of African Studies* 26, 3 (1992), 485–507; R. Launay, *Beyond the Stream: Islam and Society in a West African Town* (Berkeley, 1992); and Sinali Traore, Sikasso, 6 August 2000; Abdulaye Traore, Sikasso, 5 August 2000.

106. Drissa Diallo, N'Golobala, 14 July 2002.

107. RP, 1955; 1956, ANM IE10.

108. Amadou Sidibé, Solona, 10 April 2002; El Hajj Sekou Sidibé, Jelifin, 31 March 2002; M'Bemba Sidibé, Balanfina, 3 April 2002; Bakari Diarra, Kolondieba, 3 August 2000.

109. Yusuf Coulibaly, Tenemakana, 17 May 2002.

110. Jean-Loup Amselle, *Les Négociants de la Savane: Histoire et organisation sociale des Kooroko* (Paris, 1977), 239–60; Brenner, "Constructing Muslim Identities."

111. Yacouba Danyoko, Tenemakana, 15 July 2002.

112. Census, Foulala, 1951; RP 1957, ANM IE10.

CONCLUSION

1. E. Gellner, *Muslim Society* (Cambridge, 1981); and M. Gilsenan, *Recognizing Islam: Religion and Society in the Modern Arab World* (New York, 1982).

2. James Clifford, "Indigenous Articulations," *The Contemporary Pacific* 13, 2 (2001), 467–90.

3. B. Soares, *Islam and the Prayer Economy: History and Authority in a Malian Town* (Ann Arbor, 2005), 210–43, 244–56; D. Schulz, "Charisma and Brotherhood Revisited: Mass-Mediated Forms of Spirituality in Urban Mali," *Journal of Religion in Africa,* 33, 2 (2003), 146-71; Robert Launay and Benjamin Soares, "The Formation of an 'Islamic Sphere' in French Colonial West Africa," *Economy and Society* 28 (1999), 497–519.

4. See A. Masquelier, *Prayer Has Spoiled Everything: Possession, Power, and Identity in an Islamic Town of Niger* (Durham, 2001).

5. Nwaari Suntura, N'Golobala, 24 July 2002.

6. E. Gellner, *Saints of the Atlas* (London, 1969).

7. V. Pâques, "Bouffons Sacrés du Cercle de Bougouni (Soudan Français)," *Journal de la Société des Africanistes* 24, 1 (1954), 81–87.

8. For an excellent study of transnational Atlantic religious links, see J. Lorand Matory, *Black Atlantic Religion: Tradition, Transnationalism, and Matriarchy in the Afro-Brazilian Candomblé* (Princeton, 2005).

9. J. D. Y. Peel, *Religious Encounter and the Making of the Yoruba* (Indiana, 2000), 191–93, 187–214; see also Patrick Ryan, *Imale: Yoruba Participation in the Muslim Tradition* (Missoula, 1978), 99–131.

10. E. Skinner, "Islam in Mossi Society," in I. M. Lewis, ed., *Islam in Tropical Africa* (Oxford, 1966), 362. See also Marie Miran, *Islam, histoire et modernité en Côte d'Ivoire* (Paris, 2006), 37–84; Danielle Jonckers, "Le temps de prier est venu: Islamisation et pluralité religieuse dans le sud du Mali," *Journal des Africanistes* 68, 1–2 (1998), 21–45; Richard Warms, "Merchants, Muslims, and Wahhabiyya: The Elaboration of Islamic Identity in Sikasso, Mali," *Canadian Journal of African Studies* 26, 3 (1992), 485–507; and Peter Mark, "Urban Migration, Cash Cropping, and Calamity: The Spread of Islam among the Diola of Boulouf (Senegal), 1900–1940," *African Studies Review* 21, 2 (1978), 1–14.

11. S. Feierman, *Peasant Intellectuals: Anthropology and History in Tanzania* (Madison, 1990), 120–53.

12. Jonathon Glassman, *Feasts and Riot: Revelry, Rebellion, and Popular Consciousness on the Swahili Coast, 1856–1888* (Portsmouth, 1995), 55–78, 117–45; and Frederick Cooper, *Plantation Slavery on the East Coast of Africa* (New Haven, 1977), 215–17.

13. D. Sperling, "The Coastal Hinterland and Interior of East Africa," in Nehemia Levtzion and Randall Pouwels, eds., *The History of Islam in Africa* (Athens, 2000), 273–302. See also R. Bunger, *Islamization among the Upper Pokomo* (Syracuse, 1973); Felicitas Becker, *Becoming Muslim in Mainland Tanzania* (Oxford, 2008), 53–113.

14. M. G. S. Hodgson, *The Venture of Islam: Conscience and History in a World Civilization*. Volume 2: *The Expansion of Islam in the Middle Periods* (Chicago, 1961) 548–49. On "ordinary people" in Muslim societies, see Edmund Burke III, and David Yaghoubian, "Middle Eastern Societies and Ordinary People's Lives," in E. Burke and D. Yaghoubian, eds., *Struggle and Survival in the Modern Middle East* (Berkeley, 2006); and Michael Peletz, *Islamic Modern: Religious Courts and Cultural Politics in Malaysia* (Princeton, 2002), and " 'Ordinary Muslims' and Muslim Resurgents in Contemporary Malaysia," in R. Hefner and P. Hovatich, eds., *Islam in an Era of Nation-States: Politics and Religious Renewal in Muslim Southeast Asia* (Honolulu, 1997).

15. Richard Eaton, *The Rise of Islam and the Bengal Frontier, 1204–1760* (Berkeley, 1993); and Stephen Dale, "Trade, Conversion and the Growth of the Islamic Community of Kerala, South India," *Studia Islamica* 71 (1990).

16. See R. Bulliet, *Islam: The View from the Edge* (New York, 1994), which seeks to revise the historical development of Islamic societies by bringing non-Arab peripheries, as it were, into the analysis. For one of the pioneering works on

the comparative study of Islam, see Clifford Geertz, *Islam Observed: Religious Development in Morocco and Indonesia* (Chicago, 1968).

17. Peel, *Religious Encounter*, 248–77; on conversion as translation, see Lamin Sanneh, "Translatability in Islam and in Christianity in Africa: A Thematic Approach," in T. Blakely, ed., *Religion in Africa: Experience and Expression* (Portsmouth, 1994).

18. On theodicy, see Peter Berger, *The Sacred Canopy: Elements of a Sociological Theory of Religion* (New York, 1967), 53–80.

19. On crosscutting networks, see Frederick Cooper, *Colonialism in Question: Theory, Knowledge, History* (Berkeley, 2005), 198. On France and Islam, see Jacques Fremeaux, *La France et l'Islam depuis 1789* (Paris, 1991); and David Robinson, *Paths of Accommodation: Muslim Societies and French Authorities in Senegal and Mauritania, 1880–1920* (Athens, 2000). On missionaries and the colonial state, see Joseph-Roger de Benoist, *Eglise et Pouvoir Colonial au Soudan Français* (Paris, 1987); and J. P. Daughton, *An Empire Divided: Religion, Republicanism, and the Making of French Colonialism, 1880–1914* (Oxford, 2006). For a useful study of religion, rebellion, and French suppression, see Mahir Saul and Patrick Royer, *West African Challenge to Empire: Culture and History in the Volta-Bani Anticolonial War* (Athens, 2001).